HAMPSHIRE

&

THE ISLE OF WIGHT

THE COUNTY BOOK SERIES

PLEASE WRITE TO THE PUBLISHERS
FOR FULL DESCRIPTIVE PROSPECTUS

HAMPSHIRE

&

The Isle of Wight

by

BRIAN
VESEY-FITZGERALD

Illustrated and with a Map

London
Robert Hale Limited
18 Bedford Square W.C. 1

First published 1949

MADE AND PRINTED IN GREAT BRITAIN
BY EBENEZER BAYLIS AND SON, LTD., THE
TRINITY PRESS, WORCESTER, AND LONDON

DEDICATED
with
awe and affection
to
C. B. FRY

FOREWORD

HAMPSHIRE inevitably occupied a position of great strategic importance during the Second Great War. But in this book I have for the most part ignored the war, severe though its impact on the county was at the time. Much of it was taken over by the military, much of it was out of bounds to the general public, its two largest cities suffered very heavy bombing and were largely laid waste, huge aerodromes were constructed, farming experienced a revolution, many miles of new railway line were laid. (At Dunbridge, for example, some fifteen miles of sidings were built and covered sheds stretching for more than three miles were put up to deal with the traffic for D-day.) Little or no mention of all this will be found in the following pages. War leaves its scars. A great deal of the damage done in Southampton and Portsmouth can never be made good. But the towns will be rebuilt. In the same way a great deal of the building made necessary by the demands of war will have no use in peace, and will either be taken down or will fall into decay through disuse. Dunbridge, before the war, was a little village hidden in the Test Valley, with a station lit by oil lamps and with one tap supplied by the neighbouring pub. I think it very unlikely that Dunbridge will ever be anything more than a little village hidden in the Test Valley.

Many people have at different times and in different ways helped me during the years this book was in the making. In particular my grateful thanks are due to Lady Ursula Abbey, H. S. Altham, Sir Charles Arden-Close, Arthur Arnold, Brig.-Gen. C. F. Aspinall-Oglander, W. Hugh Curtis, Lord Dorchester, Rev. Purefoy FitzGerald, Canon A. W. Goodman, Colonel W. L. Julyan, Sir Francis Lindley, Sir Eustace Missenden, Lord Mottistone, Lord Northbrook, F. W. C. Pepper, W. R. Ponting, Major Maurice Portal, Monica Stratton, Lord Templemore, Frank M. Walker, Sylvia Wallis, Frank Warren, S. E. Winbolt, David Young and Sheila Young.

B. V-F.

CONTENTS

CONTENTS

ILLUSTRATIONS

ILLUSTRATIONS

ACKNOWLEDGMENTS

The illustration above numbered 41 is reproduced from a photograph by *The Times*. The remaining 48 are reproduced from photographs supplied by Miss Kathleen Winn of Warash, Hampshire.

HAMPSHIRE
long time been in the habit of bringing their camp followers
with them.
Aldershot is, of course, the centre of all this district.
Aldershot is not a part.... Indeed, I do not know
that it deserves the name of town at all. It is rather a large
.... and ....
find even a mention of Aldershot in most of the books about

CHAPTER I

THE NORTH-EASTERN BORDER

MOST people come into Hampshire from the north-east: either by rail from Waterloo through Farnborough on the main steam line, or through Aldershot on the electric line to Alton, or by car on the main roads through Staines or Guildford and Farnham. It is not a very exciting way of entering the county, and if you get off the trains as soon as you are within the boundaries or stop your car as soon as you have left Berkshire or Surrey, you find yourself almost certainly in a very dull country. This is the area of the London basin, and it seems to have caught a good deal of infection from the Great Wen. It is land that once was sandy heaths, open and pleasant. There is not much left that is open; there is practically nothing left that is pleasant; but there is still a great deal of sand. I have heard it suggested that there is a great deal too much sand. And, of course, there are buildings. If you are quite a way from a town or village, you will never be very far from a building. This is a squatters' area. It looks it and it very often smells it.

But, though all this comes within the county boundary, it has long since ceased to be Hampshire. It is international. The towns might be anywhere in England. For that matter they might be anywhere in the middle west of the United States, say a hundred years ago. The accents of the people tell you that you are in Britain, but the buildings and the almost total lack of amenity (I do not include the cinema among the amenities) are strongly reminiscent of the small back-end towns of the middle west in the 'sixties, if the films do not lie. And the fault is not Hampshire's. It is the Army's. The Army does not improve the districts that it takes over, as most people in Britain realized during the war. Well, the Army has been in charge here and hereabouts for a very long time. And they have for a very long time been in the habit of bringing their camp followers with them.

Aldershot is, of course, the centre of all this district. Aldershot is not a pretty town. Indeed, I do not know that it deserves the name of town at all. It is rather a large and hideous conglomeration of buildings. You will not find even a mention of Aldershot in most of the books about Hampshire. The *Highways and Byways* dismisses it in one sentence right at the very end: the story of Aldershot, it says, is one "of continual change, shift—and make-shift." And that is about as much as anyone should have time to say about Aldershot. However, I have plenty of time, and anyway I hope that this book is going to be different from all the many others that have been written on the county, and so I shall break new ground and spend a little time in Aldershot.

In 1850 Aldershot was a small village, with a church, a couple of large houses, a few cottages and a green. It was right off the beaten track. If people went anywhere they went to Farnham on the one side or to Basingstoke on the other. No traveller ever came to Aldershot, and soldiers were unheard of. If you wanted to join the Army, you went to Guildford or to Winchester. It was easier to go to Guildford, and so most of the Hampshire men of the district joined the Surrey regiments. The Manor in those days belonged to the Tichborne family—or perhaps it was a little earlier than that that this famous Hampshire family owned property in the neighbourhood—and there are Tichborne monuments in the church. They are seventeenth-century monuments and they are very much better in every way than any of the other monuments in the building. Aldershot is a healthy place, and in 1854 the Government, with a regard for the welfare of their soldiers that it has not always displayed, bought a large amount of land there and proceeded to build a camp. This land is crossed by the Basingstoke Canal. South Camp with the huge statue of the Duke of Wellington (which used to be over the arch at Hyde Park Corner) lies on the one side of the canal, and is in Aldershot proper. North Camp lies on the other side of the canal, and is actually not in Aldershot at all, but in the parish of Farnborough. Farnborough is a separate town, but it is virtually a part of Aldershot. It, too, until the advent of the military, was a lonely village, but it has its place in English history for (and this will show how remote it was) it was here that great prize-fights took place. Here, in fact, the last of the great prize-fights took place, that between the American-Irishman Henan and the English Gypsy Sayers. The reason for the popularity of Farnborough for this sort of amusement was that it is right on the border of Surrey and it was a simple matter to slip over the Blackwater river, which forms the boundary here, into Surrey and so avoid the police. Dick Turpin is supposed to have had something to do with the place as well. There is an inn called the Dick Inn, and I suppose that this has given rise to the legend. Turpin, at any rate, is connected with almost as many places as Good Queen Bess. Once there was a lovely church at Farnborough. There are still twelfth-century paintings on the north wall, and the fifteenth-century porch is still there. But the church has been greatly enlarged, and the restoration has been done in anything but the best of taste. And there is another church in Farnborough, the Benedictine church, which was built by the Empress Eugenie, when she lived at Farnborough Hill. It is built over the mausoleum of Napoleon and her son, the Prince Imperial, who was killed in the Zulu War. It is said to be modelled on the tomb of Napoleon in Les Invalides. There is some resemblance.

And that is about all the history you can dig up about the two towns. Until they became the headquarters of the British Army, of course, and then I suppose you could dig up a great deal of history—of the doings of this famous general as a subaltern and so on—if you had a mind to do so. But it would not be the history of Aldershot. In fact Aldershot has no other history. Even the doings of its football team, which is composed of professionals mostly from other parts of the country and which plays in League Three (South) without undue distinction, will not make history. No, Aldershot has endless streets of small houses —just the same as any other garrison town, only rather more of them—and some very large and ugly barracks, and many pubs and a few cinemas and a theatre. The shops are not impressive to look at, but one or two of them are very good indeed. There is not a good bookshop in the place, which is about the best commentary that one can make on a place of the size. You need permanency for a good bookshop. There is absolutely nothing about Aldershot that gives any idea of permanency. Even the rows and rows of little houses look as though they might be packed up and removed at a moment's notice by a fatigue squad.

There is, too, curiously little life about the place. Occasionally, some more than usually bored soldier breaks a window, and every now and then the "glasshouse," which is the name of the military prison, provides a little light amusement for the populace, when some of the inmates set it on fire or try to do so. That, however, does not happen often enough to prevent the town as a whole looking as if it did not want to be there. I suppose you cannot really expect much of a purely military camp, but I cannot help wondering if it is really necessary for it to be quite so horrible. And if you think that my opinion of Aldershot is exaggerated, read Mrs. Ewing on how the place was built. She says:

Take a Highwayman's Heath. Destroy every vestige of life with fire and axe, from the pine that has longest been a landmark to the smallest beetle smothered in smoking moss. Burn acres of purple and pink heather, and pare away the young bracken that springs verdant from its ashes. Let flame consume the perfumed gorse in all its glory and not spare the broom, whose more exquisite yellow atones for its lack of fragrance. In this common ruin be every lesser flower involved: blue beds of speedwell by the wayfarer's path, the daintier milkwort and rougher red rattle, down to the very dodder that clasps the heather; let them perish and the face of Dame Nature be utterly blackened! Then shave the heath as bare as the back of your hand, and if you have felled every tree, and left not so much as a tussock of grass or a scarlet toadstool to break the

4

The porch of Breamore Church

force of the winds, then shall the winds come, from the east and from the west, from the north and from the south, and shall raise on your shaven heath clouds of sand that would not disgrace a desert in the heart of Africa. By some such recipe the ground was prepared for that Camp of Instruction.

Mrs. Ewing wrote stories for children, and perhaps you may discredit her on that account. But she lived in the neighbourhood and knew the old Aldershot well, and she was there when it had happened. I do not think that she exaggerated, for the town looks just as if something of the sort had happened. It is not derelict. It never had enough life to be that. But it is dejected and hopeless, and a place to be avoided at all costs by those who have no business there.

But there is one good thing about Aldershot, and I must in fairness not forget to mention that one thing. It is the bus service. Aldershot is the headquarters of the Aldershot and District Traction Company, and this, I am sure, must be the most efficient bus company outside London, and the most polite and helpful anywhere in the country. I suppose the reason is that so many people in Aldershot want to get out of the place as quickly as possible. But whatever the reason, the fact is there. I have travelled miles and miles by this company's buses—you can go pretty well anywhere by bus from Aldershot—and I have never found, even on the most out-of-the-way country routes, anything but helpful and polite and efficient service. No, this is not a *quid pro quo*. I paid my due fares, and no member of the Company ever had the slightest idea that I was going to write a book about Hampshire or mention their concern in it when I did.

However, as the buses are there, let us get on one and out of Aldershot as quickly as may be. Let us go to Fleet. Fleet is not a place that one would choose to go to just for fun, but it is a great deal better than staying in Aldershot. And it has got a pond. Fleet itself is just prosperous villadom: red brick villas set among the pines, and a few rows of little houses that look as if they had escaped from

5   B

The Bullington River near Sutton Scotney

Aldershot and were rather pleased about it. Fleet is in fact a typical product of the district. It is not Army; but it is retired Army. The pond was once a great place of resort for all sorts of wild life, and there was a time when I spent a good deal of time on its banks. Here one never-to-be-forgotten Monday I disturbed a bittern, and here I have spent many happy hours watching the duck. But during the war they drained the pond, and it has not recovered from that operation yet. They drained it, I understand, in order that the shining water should not help to guide the German aircraft on their way to London or wherever it may have been. Maybe it was a good idea. But the main railway from the coast to London cuts the pond in two, and, of course, the shining metals were left. I think that the pond might just as well have been left also. Frensham Ponds were drained, too. But the great reservoirs were left to guide all who flew by night.

The road runs on from Fleet through the remains of woodland to Hartley Row, which has a few pleasant Georgian houses and a lot of traffic. Here you turn up a lane to Hazely Heath, and so to Bramshill, and one of the great sights of Britain.

Bramshill, standing high on its hill, dominates the country-side. It is, in point of time, a Stuart building, but it is, with its dignified brick elevations, much closer to the middle Tudor period than to the Stuarts. There was a manor here in Saxon times (when it was called Bromselle) and this was one of the manors that was given to the great Hugh de Port. Later it passed into the hands of the Foxley family, and they built a manor house and a chapel. They also enclosed a park of nearly 6,000 acres, and this caused a little trouble with the peasants of the neighbourhood, who even in those days objected to enclosure where no enclosure had been before, and who then as later were quite powerless to prevent the powerful from doing as they pleased. The Foxleys departed in due course, and then began a period of many changes. Finally, in 1602, the estate came into the possession of Edward, Lord Zouche. He commenced building the great house in 1605, and he employed to do the work the man who designed Hatfield

6

and Holland House. The story is that he intended to give it to Prince Henry, the eldest son of James I. It may well be so, for the house is royally designed and is royally beautiful, but Henry died and Charles was not so honoured by the owner. Seven years in the building was Bramshill House, but much of this time must have been taken up with the ornamenting of the interior and the building of the great terraces outside. Interiorly, there are secret doors and sliding panels, and the ceiling of the great drawing-room is most beautifully moulded. But the place is just as beautiful outside and the grounds make a fitting background for the wonderful rose-pink of the dwelling itself. In the park there is some magnificent timber. James I was here in 1612, and is said to have planted some of the Scots firs, the first to be planted in the south of England. Kingsley maintained that Bramshill was the only place in England where you could really see Scots firs growing as they should grow. That would certainly not be true to-day, but there can be no doubt that Bramshill is supremely beautiful. The lines of William Browne in his *Shepherd's Pipe*,

> Be pleased, great Lord, when underneath the shades
> Of your delightful Bramshill, when the Spring
> Her flowers for gentle blasts with zephyrs trades,
> Once more to hear a silly shepherd sing.

are not inaccurate to-day. Spring at Bramshill is something to be remembered lovingly for ever by all those who have experienced it.

The house is haunted, of course. It is, in fact, one of the three Hampshire houses said to have been the scene of the Mistletoe Bough tragedy. A ghost in bridal dress is said to visit the "Flower-de-luce" room, but the chest has disappeared. You may, or you may not, believe in ghosts, but I think that even if there is a ghost in Bramshill—and personally I should be surprised if there was not—she can have nothing to do with the Mistletoe Bough tragedy. That belongs properly to Marwell, and another part of this book. But there was a tragedy at Bramshill. It occurred in the park, and soon after the house was built. George Abbott, then Archbishop of Canterbury, was staying with Lord Zouche, and they went out shooting and the prelate shot a keeper. That no doubt had happened before, and it has certainly happened often enough since, but not so far as I am aware to Archbishops. The incident caused a good deal of comment, so much so, in fact, that the Archbishop had to resign his office. James I, a broad-minded man, said that no one but a fool would think the worse of a man for an accident, but the general opinion seems to have been that Archbishops should not go out shooting anyway, and that if they did they should be more careful, and Abbott retired into private life. Abbott was a kinsman of Charles Kingsley, and there is reference to the tragedy in one of Kingsley's letters:

I went the other day to Bramshill Park, the home of the lord of the manor here, Sir John Cope. And there I saw the very tree where an ancestor of mine, Archbishop Abbott, in James the First's time, shot the keeper by accident!

I sat under the tree, and it all seemed to me like a present reality. I could fancy the noble old man, very different then from his picture as it hangs in our dining-room at Chelsea. I could fancy the deer sweeping by, and the rattle of the cross-bow, and the white splinters sparkling off the fated tree as the bolt glanced and turned—and then the death shriek. He never smiled again! And that solemn form always spoke to me, though I did not then know what it meant.

It is strange that that is almost the only portrait saved in the wreck of our family. As I sat under the tree there seemed to be a solemn and remorseful moan in the long branches, mixed with the airy whisper of the lighter leaves that told of present as well as past!

Charles Kingsley was ordained to the curacy of Eversley in 1842. And two years later, after a brief absence, he returned there as Rector. Eversley is the village beyond Bramshill. It is a long village, straggling rather untidily

8

down the road, and it is right on the Berkshire border. The Blackwater, which takes its name from the peat through which it flows, marks the boundary. There is a modern suburb here, which is rather suggestive of Reading, but the river all the way to its junction with the Loddon beyond Bramshill, cannot have altered very much since the days when Kingsley used to throw a fly over it. And, perhaps, the country-side has not altered quite so much as a casual glance would suggest. There is less peat, there are now gravelled roads through the heather, there are a great many more houses everywhere—and one or two really horrible little villas standing as a memento to the greed of the jerry-builder—but it is still a quiet country-side away from the great roads and the rush of traffic. You can still smell the flowers by the lane-sides and not only petrol fumes. And you may still see gipsy wagons here, and smell the smoke of wood fires, and—if you are not bound tight by the conventions and the fear of your neighbours—you may still eat exciting meals that have come from the fresh country-side and listen to the tales by the camp-fire.

When Kingsley came to Eversley it was a rough parish. It was not quite so rough as it used to be, for this part of Hampshire had a very unenviable reputation in the old days. Not far away is Darley Green, and that village has got its name because of its parson, who lived and preached at Eversley, but made up his income by somewhat unorthodox means. At night he was a highwayman, and most of the villagers around helped him in one way or another, and presumably got a "rake-off." In the end he was betrayed—by one of the girls of the village, it is said, for the reverend gentleman was fond of the ladies—and was duly hanged from a tree by the side of what is now known as Darley Green. The highwaymen had gone for good by the time that Kingsley took on the living, but there were still plenty of poachers. They were poachers by descent, and the women were about as skilful as the men. It was to this parish that Kingsley came as curate. There was then a broken kitchen chair by the altar, and a cracked settle did duty at the font. Kingsley spent a great deal of time in the village school. It was a small room, only ten

9

feet by nine, and the heat and the smell was almost more than he could bear, but day after day for hours at a time he taught in that little room. Then he left, and shortly afterwards the Rector died. The parishioners petitioned Sir John Cope, in whose gift the living lay, for the return of the curate as rector, and Cope gave the living to Kingsley. He remained as rector for the rest of his life. If the parish had liked their curate, they soon learned to love their rector, for he understood and loved them and he worked for them as few parsons have ever worked for their parishioners anywhere. It was because of their poaching tendencies that he refused to carry a gun or to become a magistrate. "The clod of these parts is a thoroughly good fellow nevertheless. Civil, contented, industrious, and often very handsome; a far shrewder fellow, too—owing to his dash of wild forest blood, gipsy, highwayman and what-not —than his bullet-headed and flaxen-polled cousin, the pure South Saxon of the chalk downs." Yes, he understood them and worked for them and he helped them too. The Rector, whom he succeeded, was a lazy man. He never visited the school, and he never held a Communion service save on Christmas Day and Easter Day. He would make the collections himself in a rough wooden bowl, and he had a habit of cancelling services at the last moment or even when actually in the church, if he did not think that the congregation was large enough. When Kingsley came to Eversley there was not a grown-up man or woman, excluding the one family of gentry, who could write his or her name, and not one who could read. Kingsley also taught the grown-ups. He visited them all regularly and he was better than any doctor or nurse when they were ill. He held his services regularly, and he provided his own communion wine. He worked in the fields, too, turning a swathe with the best of the mowers and using a flail as well as any man in the parish. And he loved sport, and was a fisherman as good as many far better known than himself.

As befits such a man, his grave is as simple as a man's grave could be, and, save for the beautiful sculptured figure of Dame Marianne Cope on her tomb in the chancel, the best and most restful thing about a singularly ugly church.

The grave is placed between the church and the rectory, both of which he loved dearly, and the simple white cross with the passion flowers bears three Latin words, which sum up the whole of Kingsley's life and are the perfect expression of his faith, *We Love, We Loved, We Will Love.* Charles Kingsley died in 1875. And this rector of a small and isolated Hampshire village was given a funeral which can never have been accorded to a small country parson before and has certainly never been repeated since. He was carried to his grave on a bleak January 28th by six of his villagers, and three of them wore the Victoria Cross. But let the great Max Muller tell of the scene in his own words:

> There was the representative of the Prince of Wales and the gipsies of Eversley Common. There was the squire of his village and the labourers young and old. There were governors of colonies, officers and sailors, the Bishop of his diocese and the Dean of his abbey. There were leading Nonconformists and his devoted curates, peers and members of the House of Commons, authors and publishers, and huntsmen in pink.
>
> All that he had loved and all that loved him were there, and few eyes were dry when he was laid in his own gravel bed, the old trees he had planted and cared for waving their branches to him for the last time, and the gray sky looking down with calm pity on the deserted rectory.

Yes, Charles Kingsley was an astonishing character. He was a poet, a sportsman, a keen and very expert angler, a romanticist, and a militant exponent of Protestantism. He loved walking and preaching, he loved walking and talking, he loved walking and fishing. He had a lively and most curious mind. He was never afraid himself of inquiring (what a change from modern parsons!) and he would never shut out those whose curiosity led them to inquire, even when the paths of inquiry led through dangerous ground. For himself his inquiries soon produced in him conviction, and he fought fiercely for those things which he believed to be right. The causes for which he fought are now largely forgotten. In his lifetime they made him the centre of many storms. How many people remember that it was Charles Kingsley who produced Newman's *Apologia pro Vita sua*? His passion for straight dealing, his passionate humanity, brought him much hatred, much opposition and much detraction. He conquered them all and died widely loved and widely lamented. Yet how many people think of Charles Kingsley now, even in his own county of Hampshire? Hampshire has produced many literary giants—we shall be considering many more in the pages that follow—but none more earnestly and wholeheartedly Hampshire than Charles Kingsley. Hampshire appears again and again in his writings, prose and poetry alike. He loved the Hampshire downs and heaths, and he loved the Hampshire streams, and especially did he love the Itchen. There are many places in the county that used to boast a connexion with him in the days when he was fashionable. To-day you will find his name in no guide-books—just the bare note that he is buried in Eversley churchyard—but one place might remember him again with some profit. And that is Itchen Abbas. It was at Itchen Abbas that he wrote (with the exception of the first chapter "written off without a check" in half an hour at Eversley) the whole of *Water Babies*. And this book still sells a great many copies every year, largely due to an American genius, Walt Disney, who has rediscovered the fact that we are all children at heart and has made a fortune out of that discovery. The story should never have been allowed to fall as low as it did in the public favour, for it is one of the very best children's stories that has ever been written, but we must be grateful to an American for having the faith in Kingsley that his own countrymen had lost.

And what of his other writings? Almost all the fiction is obtainable in cheap editions. I wonder how many are read? Yet once he was a best seller. And even to-day his books will hold their own—and surpass—any of their type. *Yeast* has many charming descriptions of the chalk hills, the woods and the fields and the streams of Hampshire, and remains a fine country book even in this age of country books. But his gems were *Westward Ho!*, *Hypatia*, *Hereward the Wake*, and *Water Babies*. And a book that is now little read, for some unknown reason, *Chalk Stream Studies*, which was originally published as *Prose Idylls* by Macmillan. Of all the many fishing books that I have in my library, of all the many fishing books that I read, I come back most often to this book by Charles Kingsley. It is one of the very best fishing books ever written in any language, as fresh to-day as when it was published in 1873, as full of sound sense as any modern book, and putting forward the philosophy of the true angler as it has never been put forward before or since. I read *Chalk Stream Studies* frequently, but then at the risk of being considered old-fashioned I will admit that I read Charles Kingsley frequently. *Westward Ho!*, *Hypatia* and *Hereward the Wake* are magnificent tales of adventure, and I regret that they are not more widely read to-day. They sank to the level of "boys' books" about twenty years ago, and now, I suppose, no boy would read them unless forced to do so. (I understand that *Hypatia* is now used in some schools at any rate as a text-book. I had no idea that our educational authorities were so intelligent.) They never deserved such a fate. Kingsley wrote more than good historical adventure stories. He wrote beautiful English prose.

And *Water Babies*? That remains one of my favourite books. It is a child's book, true. But it is a child's book for children of all ages in all ages.

A little further west along this Berkshire border of Hampshire you come to another of the great homes of England. This is Stratfieldsaye, which was presented to the Duke of Wellington by a grateful nation after Waterloo. But the house is very much older than that. The place gets its name from the Roman road that runs from London to Bath through Silchester and here forms the boundary between Berkshire and Hampshire, and originally it was called Stratfield-Stotevil from the name of the family that owned it. It became Stratfieldsaye when Sir William de Saye bought it, and thus it passed in the reign of Richard II to the D'Abridgecourts, for the de Saye family was reduced to one girl and she married John D'Abrichcourt. In the fourteenth century the D'Abrichcourt married Queen Philippa's niece Elizabeth, the daughter of William, Duke of Juliers. This lady had already been married to John Plantagenet, Earl of Kent, and when he died she had felt his loss so grievously that she donned the veil. But, like a good many widows before and since, she found that the memory of her adored husband soon faded, and the cloisters did not provide a suitable substitute. She left and married again. She chose a rich man, and she took her own not-inconsiderable fortune with her. It was no light thing in those days to marry a nun, but to marry a nun and her fortune was almost more than the Church could bear. Probably if Sir Eustace D'Abrichcourt had not been so powerful a lord, and the lady so powerfully connected, there would have been trouble. As it was a penance was imposed on the lord and his lady. History says that the man found the penance trying in the extreme, but faithfully carried it out to the end, but that the lady adopted the sensible attitude of "in for a penny, in for a pound." ignored it completely and lived a very happy life. Three hundred years later the fortunes of the D'Abridgecourts suffered a decline, and Stratfieldsaye was bought by Sir William Pitt. It was this William Pitt's grandson who became the first Lord Rivers, and it was he who built the extraordinarily ugly church. Fortunately, he left the very interesting monuments to the old D'Abridgecourt family, and so one must not think of him too hardly when the eyes turn shuddering away from his church. It was the second Lord Rivers who sold Stratfieldsaye to the nation to be given to the Iron Duke after Waterloo. It is held, like Blenheim, by the payment of a tenure flag to be sent to Windsor Castle on the anniversary of Waterloo.

The gift was of little use to the Duke. It cost over a quarter of a million, which was no small sum of money in those days, but the Duke always declared that it was a thoroughly bad investment, which would have ruined almost any man. And, anyhow, the house is most unimpressive. A low, ugly creation of yellow brick, mostly Queen Anne, but not good Queen Anne. The park, however, is magnificent, with a fine elm avenue and some really great trees, and the Loddon has been widened to form several lakes. In a corner of the park is buried Copenhagen, the Irish charger that carried the Duke for sixteen hours at Waterloo.

So far we have been journeying along the Berkshire border. The London basin stretches some little way into the county hereabouts, pretty enough country, gently undulating and watered by the Loddon. Right on the border of this country and the rising ground that forms the backbone of Hampshire, right on the border of the arable and the chalk, are the Sherbornes—Monk Sherborne and Sherborne St. John. Of Monk Sherborne there is little that is important save the porch of the church, a solid timber porch that must be nearly six hundred years old. The church of Sherborne St. John is also very interesting and very old. The walls are of flint and plaster, and the porch is a lovely rosy pink. This porch was built in 1533 by Jamys Spyre, a farmer, and there is a stone inside the porch begging us to pray for the souls of the worthy Jamys and his wife Jane. But the whole building is chock full of history. The oldest of the old bells has been there five hundred years, the font is Norman (though the covering is probably Jacobean), there is a reading desk with three volumes of *Foxe's Book of Martyrs* printed in 1641 chained to it, and there is a lovely pulpit and canopy "Mad by Henri Sly 1634." By the chancel is a chapel founded by Bernard Brocas, a friend of the Black Prince and of William of Wykeham. He died in 1395 and was buried with great pomp and ceremony in Westminster Abbey. This chapel is a veritable museum of beauty and history, full of brasses of the Brocas family, all wonderfully engraved. The earliest are those of Raulin Brocas (who seems to have had enormous ears) and his sister Margaret. These must, from the costumes, date from the early fourteenth century. Then there is John Brocas who died about 1415. He has two portraits of himself, for he is shown with each of his two wives and their children. Bernard Brocas is shown with a skeleton for company, and there is William Brocas kneeling with his helmet and gauntlets beside him holding what appears to be a heart. All these Brocas men

15

are in full armour. And in the chapel hang two of their iron helmets.

The Brocas family lived in the manor of Beaurepaire, which is about two miles from the village. Moated and ancient it stands there still and still bears the lovely old name. Brocas was a great name in Hampshire once—and you may still come across it occasionally—but they did not hold lands from the time of the Conqueror as Miss Mitford maintains that they did. The founder of the family was John Brocas, whose father, it is believed, was killed at the battle of Bannockburn. John was one of three brothers who were brought up at the court of Edward II and his successor. One brother became the rector of Guildford and another Master of the Horse to Prince John, while John, the eldest, became Master of the Horse to Edward III. That was a most important post in those days, for the King knew a good horse when he saw one, and he expected his horses always to be in the pink of condition. Furthermore, he was accustomed to pay high prices for his horses. We are accustomed to high prices for thoroughbreds nowadays, and perhaps a little inclined to think that they are inflated prices. It is salutary to find Edward III paying more than £2,500 for a horse bred in Ireland (and the best weight-carriers still come from that island) and on several occasions paying sums in excess of £1,000. John Brocas was in charge of this buying as he was of all the king's horses.

The first grant of lands in Hampshire seems to have been in 1337, by which time John Brocas had been knighted. But the bright particular star of the family was not the founder, but the founder's third son, Bernard. This was the man who was buried in Westminster Abbey. This Bernard was a very considerable person in more ways than one, a romantic adventurer of more than usual stature. He became, indeed, a legendary figure, but there is no need to go into legend here, for that has already been done by Addison. Fact is thrilling enough. Bernard married Agnes, the daughter of Sir Mauger Vavasour. She was the heiress of manors in Yorkshire and Northamptonshire, and Bernard acquired these in due course. But of the marriage we have no details. Six years afterwards there was a divorce (strange enough in those days) and there was a young Bernard who seems to have been the result of waywardness on the part of Agnes. Agnes married again very shortly, but Bernard hung on to the manors, though after a while he did give back the most valuable. It might have been thought that once bitten, but Bernard was not that sort of a man. He had taken risks all his life, and he was prepared to risk matrimony again. Furthermore, he believed in playing for high stakes. He paid suit to none other than the Fair Maid of Kent herself. He was not successful, wasted no time on grief, and married a rich widow, who brought with her several rich manors and the Mastership of the Royal Buckhounds, which remained in the Brocas family for the next two hundred and sixty-seven years. The widow died, and Bernard built chantries to her memory. But he married another widow, and a rich one, almost immediately. The later years of his life seem to have been spent quietly at Beaurepaire in the management of his estates there and elsewhere and in hunting with the Buckhounds. In his sixty years of life he had married thrice, served much in foreign wars, been Master of the Royal Buckhounds, Constable of Acquitaine, Constable of Corfe Castle, Warden of the Episcopal Parks, Chamberlain to Queen Anne, Captain of Sandgate Castle, Controller of Calais, Commissioner for the Defence of Hampshire and a Knight of the Shire. I think that he deserved his burial in Westminster Abbey.

He was succeeded by his son Bernard (a son by his second wife) and it is this son that appears in Shakespeare's *Richard II*. His story is the story of the "dark conspiracy" of 1399–1400, the story of its failure, and of the forfeiture of the Beaurepaire estates. But Shakespeare is not correct in making Fitzwater tell Bolingbroke that he had

> . . . from Oxford sent to London
> The heads of Brocas and Sir Bennet Seely,
> Two of the dangerous consorted traitors.

for, actually, this Sir Bernard Brocas was tried in London

17

in February 1400 and beheaded upon Tyburn Hill. In the words of Captain Montagu Burrows in his book, *The Family of Brocas of Beaurepaire and Roche Court*: "Thus set upon a bloody horizon along with the sun of Plantagenet, the star of Brocas." The glory had indeed departed, but the forfeiture was not complete, and the family did not depart from Beaurepaire. Indeed four more generations succeeded to the old manor, before the direct male line ended in that daughter of William Brocas, who lies by the side of her husband, Ralph Pexsall in the church of Sherborne St. John. It was in their day that Henry VIII paid a visit to "Baraper." Their son, Sir Richard Pexsall, did not live at Beaurepaire, but in the new manor house at Steventon, and the house was, I think, unoccupied for some years. But Sir Richard's daughter married her cousin, another Bernard Brocas, and they and the name returned to Beaurepaire, for she was an only child. There is a story that this marriage was not a love-match but a compromise for a law-suit between Sir Richard Brocas and the Buckinghamshire branch of the family over the Mastership of the Royal Buckhounds. I do not know if that is so or not, but there is plenty of evidence that it was a happy marriage, family quarrels or not. It was a quiet marriage spent on the estate, but if fame had departed from the family long since, notoriety had not, for the scamp of the family had yet to come. This was Sir Pexsall Brocas. In 1603 he was charged with riot and forgery, and you may find him in Stowe's *History of England*:

> On Sunday, October 23, 1613, Sir Pecsall Brocas did open penance at St. Paul's Cross: he stood in a white sheete, and held a stick in his hand, having been formerly convicted before the High Commissioners for secret and notorious adulteries with divers women.

But it took more than that to put down a Brocas. For, having done his penance, he went with "thirty men in scarlet that waited upon him to the Lord Mayor . . . to de, and a dinner after doing penance." I have some admiration for Sir Pexsall Brocas.

The history of the manor and the family does not end there. Both played their part in the Civil War. One of the heirs was found dead in a ditch outside Oxford, and the reason for that murder—for murder it seems to have been —has never been ascertained. He was, it appears, a youth of strong Roundhead sympathies. And there was certainly division in the family, as there was in so many families, at the time. One uncle of the murdered man, and that was Thomas Brocas who rose high in Cromwell's favour for a while, joined the Roundheads, but the manor of Beaurepaire itself was held for the Royalists. With its moat and strongly built walls, it made a good outpost for two Royalist troops of horse and sixty musketeers. These managed to make the country very uncomfortable as far north as Reading, but they were not strong enough to stand a siege, and on the approach of the main Roundhead forces they retired to Basing, "a welcome business" as a Roundhead writer of the time puts it. The fact that Cromwell won the Civil War did not, owing to the foresight of Thomas, lose Beaurepaire to the family. But there was a good deal of family bargaining at this time, for the sole heir-at-law was a girl, Jane, and she married Sir William Gardiner. It was thought in the family that a Brocas and not a Gardiner should live at Beaurepaire, and to this view Jane seems to have agreed. Sir William Gardiner seems to have held the opposite view, but the family prevailed. Jane went to live at Roche Court, another of the family properties, in Buckinghamshire, and Thomas Brocas, son of the Roundhead Thomas, moved in to Beaurepaire. And there the family remained, rebuilding the house about 1746, until 1873 when financial difficulties compelled them to sell and caused the suicide through grief of yet another Bernard Brocas. But the name still lingers in the neighbourhood—and Fortune is notorious for her waywardness.

Not far away, for it is also in the parish of Sherborne St. John, is another famous Hampshire house: The Vyne. Quite apart from its historical interest this is one of the most attractive houses in Hampshire, or, for that matter, in England. And nowadays you can get to it. It used to be said (and not much more than a hundred years ago) that "The Vyne was the last place upon the earth, and Beaurepaire was beyond it." Horace Walpole had quite a lot to say about it also. He did not like its dampness; "I don't believe that the Vine is within the verge of the rainbow." He did not like the roads; "In October, you will find it a little difficult to persuade me to accompany you there on stilts," he wrote to Montagu. And to another friend: "No post but a dove can come from thence." It is different now. And if Walpole could find little to say in its favour, it must be remembered that he went there often enough, and it was he that gave to his friend John Chute the eagles that still flank the entrance.

The house is of a mellow Tudor red brick, long and low. It stands about a hundred yards back from the road from Sherborne St. John to Bramley, set in the midst of an ample park, of lawns and gardens, in a simple gently pretty, undulating valley. It is clearly visible from the road, and you cannot miss it, yet I know no other house in all the county that is so absolutely part of its surroundings, has so absolutely the air of having grown out of the soil rather than of having been built, that clearly visible though it is I am always surprised at my first sight of it, surprised to find that it is in fact a house. Before the present manor, there was a manor house here occupied by a branch of the Brocas family. The last of this branch was a Bernard Brocas who died in 1488 without issue, and the manor passed to Sir William Sandys, who died of a seizure in 1496 and was succeeded by his son William. This Sir William Sandys enjoyed the favour of Henry VIII, who made him Lord Chamberlain and created him Lord Sandys of The Vyne in 1523. It was this Lord Sandys, who, in the early years of the sixteenth century, built the present house and chapel of The Vyne. Shakespeare describes him as "mad, exceeding mad." If he was mad, then madness should be regarded as an essential qualification in a good architect. There were some alterations and extensions by Inigo Jones or a pupil of his, but in the main the present house is the house in which Henry VIII and Queen Elizabeth were entertained. It was from The Vyne that Elizabeth wrote

"The last place upon the earth"—
The Vyne, near Sherborne St. John

to the Earl of Huntingdon her orders for the safe keeping of her cousin, poor Mary Queen of Scots.

The third Lord Sandys died without issue, and the estate passed to Colonel Henry Sandys. He was mortally wounded at Cheriton Field, and his son, William, sold it nine years later (in 1653) to Chaloner Chute, one of the most celebrated lawyers of the day. Chaloner Chute was unanimously chosen Speaker of the House of Commons upon the assembling of Parliament under Richard Cromwell in 1659. "He would never," wrote Clarendon, "have subjected himself to that place if he had not entertained some hope of being able to serve the King." He did not, however, live to see the Restoration, but in his six years of ownership he had made considerable improvements to the estate. And each of his descendants has in some measure carried on his work. The wonderful staircase, and the memorial to the Speaker, are the work of John Chute, the friend of Walpole, who managed to resist all the wild suggestions for improvements that the latter made to him. The pack of foxhounds was founded by William John Chute in 1790 and was maintained by him at his own expense until his death in 1824. He believed in small hounds, and put up *"Multum in parvo"* over the kennels, and for the country he hunted there can be no doubt that he was right. When he died he was succeeded by his brother, Thomas, who died unmarried in 1827. The estate then passed by will to William Lyde Wiggett, who was the second son of one James Wiggett, the rector of Crudwell in Wiltshire. This William Lyde Wiggett assumed the name and the arms of Chute, and so the name remains at The Vyne to this day. William Wiggett, who was a distant cousin of the original Chutes, made enormous improvements to the estate by enclosing the common fields and making new roads, and was indeed regarded as something of a pioneer in these matters, for his work is described at some length in the Journal of the Royal Agricultural Society of England. He died in 1879, and was succeeded by his son Chaloner (the old name comes back again) who died in 1892, to be succeeded by the present owner, Mr. Charles Leonard Chute.

A few miles to the south-east lies Basing, where once

River Loddon near Old Basing

stood one of the greatest houses in all England. This was the house of the Paulets, and to know something of them we must go into the church which still stands, though the house is a ruin. The church was taken by both sides in the Civil War and suffered accordingly, but it was restored at the Restoration. The top of the tower was made new, but the lower part remains Norman with the original arches. Under the arches between the chapels and the chancel are the tombs of the Paulets, one of a fifteenth-century Sir John, two of sixteenth-century Sir Johns, and one of the truly remarkable sixteenth-century Sir William, who built the great house. Carlyle called him a magnificent kind of man "whose best bed excited the wonder of the world."

This William Paulet, who was born in 1485, was one of the most extraordinary men of his age, and it was an age of extraordinary men. He was the eldest son of Sir John Paulet, who commanded the force against the Cornish rebels in 1497. In 1512, at the age of twenty-seven, he was Sheriff of Hampshire. In 1532 Henry created him Controller of the Household. That was the year before the divorce from Catherine, and it was William Paulet who had to tell the Queen that her husband intended to get rid of her. After the death of Henry VIII he shared power with Northumberland after the fall of the Protector Somerset, taking office as Lord Treasurer, an office he held until the end of his life twenty-two years later. He was created the Marquess of Winchester, and when the boy king died he wished for the observance of the Act of Succession. But Northumberland was at the moment too powerful, and proclaimed Lady Jane Grey as Queen. It was the Marquess of Winchester who placed the Crown Jewels in her hands on July 12th, but he was at the same time carefully watching Northumberland and plotting against him, and within the week he had triumphed over the powerful duke. He persuaded him to lead the forces that were being gathered to fight Mary, who had raised her standard at Framlingham, and Northumberland did so. But he had his suspicions of Winchester's good faith, and before he left he made arrangements for him and the rest of the Council to be kept in the

Tower under the watchful eye of Suffolk, Lady Jane's father. On July 19th Winchester and the other members of the Council made an excuse to visit Baynard's Castle to levy more troops to fight Mary, and there they declared for her. Winchester rode through London to proclaim her accession. Mary made him Lord Privy Seal, and when she married Philip of Spain in Winchester Cathedral she took her husband five days after the wedding to Basing House and they feasted there, royally entertained by Winchester. When Mary died, Winchester, now an old man, rode once again through the streets of London to proclaim Elizabeth as Queen, and Elizabeth confirmed him in his high office. She did more; she visited him at Basing House. And she was so delighted with him and the wonderful house that he owned that she declared: "By my troth, if my Lord Treasurer were but a young man I could find it in my heart to have him for a husband before any man in England." Proud William Paulet, Marquess of Winchester, died at Basing House in 1572. Of him Fuller wrote: "He *got, spent*, and *left*, more than any Subject since the Conquest." Of himself he wrote in his old age:

> Late supping I forbear
> Wine and women I forswear;
> My neck and feet I keep from cold.
> No marvel then, though I be old,
> I am a willow, not an oak:
> I chide, but never hurt a stroke.

A willow, indeed: for he married twice and lived to see 103 descendants. But more remarkable even than that is the fact that he lived through the reigns of four Tudor sovereigns and died in a fifth. That for a man who held the highest offices in the land was a truly miraculous performance in an age when the heads of the mighty fell from their shoulders on the slightest excuse. Even more remarkable, perhaps, was his feat of being Lord Privy Seal to the most ardent Catholic of all our monarchs, and yet to be confirmed in that high office by the most ardent Protestant of them all. And this he did without changing his religion. He remained a Catholic and a good one. There have been few men as remarkable in our history; none more remarkable.

But we must return to Basing House. The place is in ruins; there is not much to see, and it will cost you sixpence to see that little. But it is well worth a visit, for Basing House was the scene of a three-year siege during the Civil War, and the story is one to thrill the hearts of all who revere great courage.

At the very commencement of the struggle—indeed even before hostilities broke out—John Paulet, the "Loyal" Marquis, declared for the King and set about fortifying the house. He was a Roman Catholic, a man of letters and a patron of the arts. He said that "if the King had no more ground in England than Basing House, he would maintain it to the uttermost." His wife was the daughter of the Earl of St. Albans, and the sister of Lord Essex, the Roundhead general. She might well have used this connexion to escape what followed. She did not even try to do so. Instead she shared all the dangers of the siege, saw her maid killed by a shell, which she herself narrowly escaped, and with the other ladies of the garrison she cast into bullets the lead stripped from the roofs and turrets. Moreover, she successfully organized the relieving expedition of Colonel Gage.

The Marquis began by collecting arms for fifteen hundred men, but these he was obliged to sell by order of the House of Commons. Left with only six men and six muskets he was attacked by the Parliamentarians. The small party beat off that attack and another. And, the gloves being now off, the Marquis set about strengthening his position again. He also offered sanctuary to a number of people who must have been an encumbrance when the heavy fighting began, but Winchester was not the man to desert his friends. Old Thomas Fuller was one, and Inigo Jones, distraught and trembling, was another. But he also collected a garrison. At the end of July he was heavily attacked by Colonel Harvey, "a decayed silk man," who had recently won somewhat doubtful glory by dispersing a crowd of women in London who were shouting for peace, and Colonel Norton, of Southwick Park and the Old Manor House at Alresford, the "Idle Dick Norton" of Cromwell. The attack was staved off, but no more, and help came in the nick of time from Oxford. It was brought by Lieutenant-Colonel Peake, a London print-seller, who had with him one hundred musketeers, and two famous craftsmen, well-known even then but famous indeed now: William Faithorne, the father of English engraving, and Wenceslaus Hollar, the artist. Another member of the band was Thomas Johnston, who was the first man to write a book about all our English plants. He enlarged Gerard's *Herbal* and did 2,766 illustrations for it. A man of great courage, he was shot during the siege and killed.

Peake's arrival meant the withdrawal of Harvey and Norton. But a few days later the siege began in earnest, for the London Trained Bands, the ancestors of the Royal Marines and The Buffs, were ordered to Basing to deal with the garrison, which was said to consist of some five hundred men, "all in a manner Papists." However, much work had by now been done, and in all about fourteen and a half acres were now protected by strong but rough fortifications. Peake, Faithorne, and Hollar all took commissions in the King's service—there is, by the way, a curious etching of Basing Siege done by Hollar during a lull—but the Governor was Sir Marmaduke Rawdon, a London merchant, whom the Parliament had "decayed" with Peake as his deputy. Peake had a long white beard and was styled "a seller of picture babies." The garrison was armed with muskets and had mounted eleven guns of various calibre at points of vantage. The London Trained Bands reported that the house was as large as the Tower of London and was "built upright, so that no man can command the roof." But five hundred men with muskets and eleven guns did not seem much to the Roundheads with all their force. General Waller—Sir William Waller—advanced from Farnham with seven thousand men, deployed outside the grounds, and offered free passage to all the women and children. It was refused, and nine days of hard fighting and blockade began. Then Waller tried to storm the place, and after three days of savage fighting he was obliged to

25

retire to Farnham, "having dishonoured and bruised his army, whereof abundance were lost, without the death of more than two in the garrison, and some little damage to the house by battery," because Lord Hopton, the Royalist general in Hampshire, was on the march to relieve the house.

On 18 August 1643 Parliament declared the Marquis of Winchester guilty of high treason, and confiscated his large estates, but that cannot have worried Winchester very much after all that had passed. Basing House, together with Donnington Castle near Newbury, effectually commanded the road to the west, and Winchester was determined that they should continue to do so for as long as possible. Lord Hopton, a Cornishman, was holding Winchester in force for the King, though he had a good deal of trouble with his Cornish levies who suffered much from home-sickness, and he did much to help Basing, for he, too, realized the value of the position. Basing, too, did more than just stay besieged. Many a raiding party went out from the house, and many a heavily-laden waggon bound for London was intercepted and its goods taken into the garrison. There were spies, of course, on both sides, and when caught they received short shrift. We have record only of one, Tobias Beasley, who made bullets at Basing, and who, we are told, "showed great relauctance to go off the ladder."

In December 1643 certain Royal cooks came to Basing with a detachment of Prince Rupert's Horse, and this led to the rumour that the King had removed much plate and treasure from the fortress himself. It was an unfounded rumour, but it caused a good deal of excitement at the time. In March 1644 came Cheriton Fight which "broke all the measures and altered the whole scheme of the King's counsels." Hopton made good his retreat in the night to Basing, and thence fell back on Reading and Oxford, but only Winchester and Basing in all Hampshire were now left to the King. The garrison, who were known as "foxes and wolves" by their enemies and lasted well through the winter and had shown in many a daring foray that they had teeth and were not afraid to use them, must have

thought the outlook pretty black after Waller's victory at
Cheriton. And a few of them lost heart. The Marquis's
brother, Lord Edward Paulet, turned traitor and opened
negotiations with Waller. He was "as unsuspected as a
brother ought to be" and the plot was only discovered
through the quite unexpected desertion of Sir Richard
Granville from the Roundhead forces. All the conspirators,
with the exception of Lord Edward, were executed. Lord
Edward was spared . . . to hang them. The garrison had a
pretty sense of humour!

All through 1644 the garrison held out in the face of
heavy assaults. They were hard pressed by shot and by
hunger, for the blockade of the house was now very well
maintained, and it was only a very gallant relieving expedition led by Colonel Sir Henry Gage that enabled the
garrison to last through the winter. Gage made a forced
march from Oxford, and then with wearied troops fought a
hard action against overwhelming numbers on Chinham
Down, won it in a thick fog, and got through to the house.
"That lovers met that day, and blushed and kissed; and
old grey-bearded friends embraced each other, too; that
good Catholic comrades exchanged prayers at Basing altar;
that brave fathers kissed the wives and children they had
left shut up in brave old 'Loyalty,' needs no telling. But
not alone in kissing and quaffing did Gage and his troops
spend those two merry days." Indeed, no. They chased
the Roundheads out of Basingstoke, and all the Roundhead stores, so laboriously collected, were captured and
carried off to Basing House. Then Gage retired by night to
Oxford. It was a gallant effort, but the relief it brought was
short lived. The Roundheads were soon back again and
pressing hard. But all through the winter, despite famine
and disease, the little garrison held out, and all demands
for surrender were refused. In London it was said that
"Basing garrison had neither shoes nor stockings, drank
water, and looked all as if they had been rather the
prisoners of the grave than the keepers of a castle."

And then religious strife broke out among the garrison.
On May Day 1645 all those members of the garrison who
were not Catholics marched out. There were about five

hundred of them, and they went over to Donnington Castle, still held for the King and still unbesieged, where they were very properly refused admission by gallant Sir John Boys, himself a Protestant. There was now left but a small body of Catholics and their wives and children and a few elderly women. But further demands to surrender were refused and the siege went on throughout the summer, with attack after attack being repulsed. Then on October 8th Cromwell himself arrived with a brigade of the New Model Army, fresh from the capture of Winchester. The end was in sight. But the garrison were determined to go down fighting, and on the 13th they made a last sortie and captured prisoners, among them Colonel Robert Hammond, who was afterwards the King's gaoler at Carisbrooke Castle. On the 14th, the Ironsides launched the final attack very early in the morning. The garrison was worn out, and could not have stopped these fresh soldiers—fanatics all of them—but it is said that they were surprised playing cards. The story is most unlikely, but it has caught on and "Clubs are trumps, as when Basing House was taken" is a well-known Hampshire saying. The final assault did not last long. Three thousand men were employed in the attack, and a further four thousand ringed the house about. There was no escape. Yet men fought to the death at the sword's point and at the end there were only two hundred prisoners, including all the women and children.

At the end of the fighting came the looting. All the women, and most of the men, were stripped of their clothes. Most of the men were then hanged—that was certainly the fate of the four Catholic priests—but only one of the women was killed, though several were shamefully used, and that was the daughter of Dr. Griffith, "a gallant gentlewoman whom the enemy shamefully left naked."

In all about a quarter of a million pounds' worth of loot was taken out of Basingstoke, which Cromwell called "a good encouragement," and then the house was set on fire. Some seventy-four of the garrison were burnt in the flames, and this, remember, was long after the fighting was over. It is often said that this fire was accidental. But I do not think that there can be any doubt about it. The looting was over. Cromwell had had his "good encouragement." It must have been the result of his deliberate order. And that would be in keeping with the character of the man (he was as fanatical as Hitler and as ruthless as Himmler) and in keeping with the general attitude of the Roundheads to things which did not belong to them. At any rate Basing House disappeared for ever. You pay sixpence to see what Cromwell and the centuries have left.

Of the famous in the house when the end came, Inigo Jones was carried out in a blanket, having lost all his clothes; Peake, now Sir Robert Peake, for he was knighted by Charles during the siege, was exiled for refusing to take the oath to Cromwell; Faithorne also refused to have anything to do with Cromwell and he, too, was exiled, going to live in Paris, but returning to London some ten years later; Wenceslaus Hollar was luckier than all the others, for after the final assault he managed to escape; the Marquis of Winchester was taken prisoner and confined first in the Bell Inn at Basingstoke and later in the Tower. But Cromwell spared his life, and allowed him to retire to France. One of the best actions that that bloodstained man ever did.

Throughout the siege a diary was kept. It closes with these noble words:

> Let no man, therefore, think himself an instrument, only in giving thanks that God had made him so, for here was evidently seen "He chose the weak to confound the strong." *Non nobis Domine.* "Not unto us, not unto us, O Lord, but to Thine own Name be all glory for ever. Amen."

The grass grows green to-day over the ruins of Basing House. But as long as Englishmen retain any of the feelings of chivalry, as long as Loyalty has any hold on Englishmen, so long will the story of Basing House remain as green as the grass on her ruins.

Basingstoke, just to the south, is modern. It has one or two old corners: there are the ruins of the thirteenth-century Holy Ghost Chapel, standing in an ancient burial ground just to the north of the station; St. Michael's Church has some interesting glass and the chantry chapel is worth more than a moment. But Basingstoke has nothing to do with these things. Basingstoke is modern, and proud of it. Indeed the people of Basingstoke are immensely proud of their town. The population of about fourteen and a half thousand is engaged almost entirely in manufacture. There are big motor works and engineering shops and metal foundries; good clothing and raincoat factories; good leather works; big brick and tile yards. (Basingstoke was a very busy and important place during the late war.) Now, usually when you find all these things in a town you also find a cosmopolitan population and a cosmopolitan outlook. Basingstoke has a cosmopolitan population all right, but it does not appear, so far as I have been able to judge (and I have spent a good deal of time in Basingstoke during the last fifteen years) to have a cosmopolitan outlook at all. I do not know how many Hampshire men and women still live and work in the town. Quite a number I have no doubt. But you do not seem to meet them. You meet—at least this has been my experience—Scots and men from Lancashire and Yorkshire and Cheshire, Cockneys and men from the Midlands. I suppose this is because of the engineering works: wherever there are engineering works you will find men from Scotland and the North and the Midlands.

Market Day in Basingstoke is particularly interesting. The market is just like any other market in any other country town in essentials. There are cheapjacks and there is quite frequently an itinerant preacher breathing fire and thunder, coupling Christian goodwill with the most awful threats of eternal damnation. The mixture always goes down very well, and he holds his audience as the man in the pulpit rarely does nowadays. He is always particularly hot on the perils of strong liquor. His audience usually leave him for the pubs. And a little later you may be sure to find him in a pub sampling with every sign of pleasure the road to eternal damnation. There are country men and women with deep, slow, country voices, pleasant, jolly people with weather-beaten faces and friendly smiles that altogether belie their capacity for driving a hard bargain. All that is usual. But here too are the soft burr of the Scottish lowlands, and broad accents of Bolton and Wigan, the hard voices of Leicester and Stafford. They may be few in number—I do not think that they are—but you certainly notice them.

That is all cosmopolitan. But the outlook of them all— whether they come from Hampshire or Scotland or Lancashire or Durham or Leicester—is most definitely Basingstoke. If you meet a Lancashire man in London he will talk of Lancashire as home, even though he last saw the county twenty years ago. He has lost neither his accent nor his local patriotism. A Yorkshireman is a Yorkshireman wherever he may be. And so is a Scot. Successful Lancashiremen do not retire to Lancashire; they choose Surrey or Hampshire or Sussex. But they remain Lancashire, and they lose no opportunity of impressing the fact—already obvious enough—upon you. It is a characteristic that I honour; though I do not admire a local patriotism that dictates the "soft" south once money has been made. Yes, but you do not find that sort of thing in Basingstoke.

The Lancashireman I talked to came from Nelson. His talk was broadly Nelsonian. He was tremendously proud of Basingstoke, and he thought the downland just as good as the moors, better if I saw what he meant. I met a Scot from Motherwell. He preferred Basingstoke. And a Yorkshireman from Castleton. The only grumble he had about Hampshire (and he had none about Basingstoke) was the quality of their cricket. I gathered that they would never win a county championship because they treated cricket as a game. And he had another bitter and brooded deeply on the matter. I met a man from Dorset even, and he said he would not go back. Basingstoke was good enough for him. They were one and all pleased with Basingstoke and proud of Basingstoke.

I am not a Basingstoke man, and I do not know that I share their feelings. But I have no doubt that I would if I lived in Basingstoke. There is, evidently, something about the town. And I know at least a little what it is. Basingstoke is a manufacturing town without any of the horrors that one usually associates with manufacturing towns. The houses are cleaner than you would expect to find in an industrial area, and there is very little smoke. And the gardens, very small gardens, most of them, are wonderfully and carefully tended. And the streets are clean and the traffic orderly. Basingstoke is an important road centre, and though the by-pass now carries the body of through traffic away from the town, is always remarkably busy. The police are both courteous and efficient. Basingstoke is also an important railway centre. The less said about Basingstoke railway station, the better.

And around Basingstoke there is some lovely country. The Basingstoke canal, which is very little known, is well worth exploring. In places it is really beautiful. And it is much favoured by kingfishers.

CHAPTER II

SILCHESTER AND ROMAN HAMPSHIRE

BEFORE we leave this low land of the London basin in the north-east corner of the county—and it is low-lying land, for scarcely any of it is over three hundred feet, and most of it is between one hundred and two hundred feet, above sea-level—we must return to the Berkshire border. For here on the Berkshire border is Silchester. Of course, you can get to Silchester from any of the places we visited in the previous chapter—it is but a short distance from Stratfieldsaye—and the most pleasant of those ways is by the little lanes from Beaurepaire. But I think that Silchester should always be approached from over the Berkshire border, from Mortimer, for thus you can see, away to the south and the south-west, the blue line of the downs, and you get suddenly an impression of distance and height and loneliness, and somehow, too, from that blue line, even on the stillest day (though much more so on a day of storms), an overwhelming sense of power away there on the distant heights. You get, I think, a little of the feeling that the original inhabitants of the place must have had.

There are quite a number of remarkable things about Silchester—not the least of which is the fact that it is so little visited—and the most remarkable is that we know so little about it. We know that there was a great earthwork camp here before the Romans came; and we know that the Romans came. That is about the sum total of our knowledge. We can guess a great deal more. But that is really all we know absolutely for certain. We do not even know for certain that Silchester is the place that we think it is.

In the great itinerary of the Roman Empire, which is supposed to have been compiled about the year A.D. 320, and is called the *Antoninus Augustus*, there is a place called *Calleva Atrebatum* mentioned five times. It is named in

33

Route No. 7, the route which ran from *Regnum* (Chichester) to London through *Clausentum* (Bitterne near Southampton): in Route 12, a very circuitous route (supposing that the names have been correctly identified) from *Venta Belgarum* (Winchester) through *Vindomis* (which may be Whitchurch), *Muridunum* (which may be Honiton) to *Viriconium* (Wroxeter): in Route 13, which ran from *Isca Silurum* (Caerleon) through *Glevum* (Gloucester) and *Durocornovium* (Cirencester), to Calleva: in Route 14, which was another route from Caerleon through Caerwent and *Aquae Sulis* (Bath) to Calleva: and in Route 15, which ran from Calleva to *Isca Damnoriorum* (Exeter) through *Venta Belgarum* and *Muridunum*. It is quite clear that a place through which so many routes passed must have been a place of great importance, and it is rather astonishing that, when so much is known about the Roman Empire and the Roman occupation of Britain, so important a place should have been completely lost for so long. Indeed there was a great deal of guesswork about it, and some truly astonishing suggestions, until Horsely by careful measurements identified it with Silchester. That identification has been so generally accepted that there is no need for me to go into the reasons on which it is based. It may well be the correct identification, though there are points about Silchester itself that do not altogether fit in with it.

One of the chief troubles, of course, is that the place is quite unknown to history. Besides the mentions in the *Antoninus*, there is one in the *Ravenna Geographer* (where it is spelt *Caleba Atrebatium*) and the only other mention of it is in Ptolemy's great geographical work, and even there it is by no means clear. We have, in fact, no direct proof that Silchester is Calleva. But the distances on the *Itinerary* provide very strong circumstantial evidence in favour; so strong indeed that one can only wonder how any other place could possibly fit the facts. And, in addition to the mileages given in the *Itinerary*, there is very strong circumstantial evidence in favour of the identification in the name.

The addition of the name of the tribe to that of the town shows that it was the capital, as is the case with similar names like *Venta Belgarum* and *Isurium Brigantum* (Ald-

34

borough) in Yorkshire. In all cases like these there is a very strong reason to believe that the place was an important tribal centre before the Romans came. And in the case of Silchester this may be taken as a certainty. You can still see the earthwork, which formed the protection of the centre before the Romans came. The place is built on a little hill, and in a most commanding position, for originally it must have been situated between Pamber Forest and the end of the great forest that stretched through Kent and Sussex, the Andraedswald. The name Calleva means "the town in the wood," and Silchester, in pre-Roman and Roman times, was certainly surrounded by thick woods. You may remember a remark of Cæsar in *De Bello Gallico*: "The Britons call a place a town when they have fortified a thick wood with a rampart and a ditch, and to such places they are wont to retreat when they want to avoid an inroad of the enemy." Indeed, the word Calleva has survived to this day in a corrupt form. Silva would be what the Romans called Calleva, and the town would have been Silva Castra. But the contraction Silchester is not wholly Roman. There is an allied Welsh word, "cell-i," which means a wood or a copse, and this has a contracted form "cell." In the *Domesday Book* the name of the place is given as Cilcestre, which is an obvious union between the Celtic and the Roman and means "the fort in the wood."

The *Domesday Book* is, in fact, the first mention we have of the place since Roman times. We learn there that it was held by Ralf de Mortemer. The next allusions to it come in some of the medieval chronicles, and all of them provide puzzles. In Geoffrey of Monmouth, who wrote about 1154 we find:

in VI, 5	After this the Britons, before dispersed, flocked together from all parts, and in a council held at Silchester made Constantine King, and placed the crown of the kingdom upon his head.
in IX, 1	Uther Pendragon being dead, the nobles from several provinces assembled together at Silchester, and proposed to Dubricius,

Archbishop of Caerleon, that he should consecrate Arthur, Uther's son, to be King. Dubricius, therefore, in conjunction with the other bishops, set the crown upon Arthur's head.

in IX, 15   The Bishopric of Silchester was conferred upon Mauganius, that of Winchester upon Diwanius, and that of Alclud upon Eledanius.

In Henry of Huntingdon, who wrote about 1155, we find:

in I, 3   Kair Segent, which was situated upon the Thames not far from Redinge, and is now called Silcestre.

And in the *Eulogium Historiarum*, 1366, we find:

in IV, 170   Caer Segent, situated not far from Redinge, now called Silcestre, and almost destroyed.

in V, 58   The Bishopric of Silcestre was given to Mauganus, that of Winchester to Dumanus.

Geoffrey of Monmouth, of course, was a liar. We must start by remembering that. He was not just a compiler of legends; he was a liar, and a deliberate one. He falsified history. He wrote a Romance—and a pretty good one at that—but he passed it off as genuine history culled from authoritative sources. He probably did have access to genuine documents that have since disappeared—there can be no doubt that there is a genuine historical background to some of his tales—but it has become almost impossible to know when he is speaking the truth, so often does he do the reverse. In the story of the crowning of Constantine, for example, we have from Geoffrey of Monmouth a perversion of genuine history. You can make what you like of the story of Arthur. You can believe, if you wish, that it was at Silchester that he was crowned by Merlin. It is generally admitted now that Arthur was a historical per-

Godshill in the centre of the Isle of Wight

sonage, and it is quite probable that he had some connexion with Silchester at some time in his life, but it would be foolish to go beyond that. So far as the bishops are concerned you must please yourself. The only one that is certainly historical is Dubricius. But all the same it is difficult to see why Geoffrey should connect all these things with such a completely unknown place as Silchester without some authority for doing so. Why, for example, crown such a man as Constantine at such a place? A better story could have been made of it had the place been somewhere well known. And the same thing applies to Arthur. There must, I think, have been some authority extant in the days when Geoffrey wrote on which he based these assertions.

But the other chroniclers set us a greater puzzle than does Geoffrey. And that puzzle is the name Kair Segent, which they introduce. Kair is, of course, the same as Caer. And the facts appear to be as follows.

The name appears in a curious passage of Nennius:

> The fifth (that is the fifth Roman Emperor that visited Britain) was Constantine, the son of Constantine the Great, and he died there, and his sepulchre is shown near the city, which is called Cair Segeint, as the letters which are upon the stone of the tomb show. And he sowed there three seeds—that is, of Gold, of Silver, and of Copper, in the pavement of the aforesaid city, so that no poor man might dwell in it for ever; and it is called by another name, Minmanton.

The name appears in both the lists of towns given in Mommsen's edition of Nennius, and in both it appears in the form of Cair Segeint. In one list it is followed by Cair Legeion Guar Usic, which is Caerleon-upon-Usk; in the other it is preceded by Cair Guoranegon, which is probably Worcester. Now among the Roman towns of Wales there is Segontium, and the walls of this town are still visible at Caer Seiont, near Carnarvon. The similarity between Cair Segeint and Caer Seiont is obvious, and the position of Cair Segeint next to Caerleon-upon-Usk in the one list and next to Worcester in the other seems to identify the place with

The old church at Bonchurch

Segontium rather than with Calleva. But I do not think that that is the answer.

If you read Cæsar I think that you will agree that in his day the Segontiaci lived in the neighbourhood of the Thames. I am inclined to think that they were driven westwards by the Atrebates, when these people came over the channel seeking refuge from the Romans. We know that the Atrebates were also found in Gaul, and we have the evidence of Cæsar that they crossed to Britain. Before Silchester became the capital of the Atrebates, before it was called Calleva Atrebatum, it was the capital of the Segontes and was called Cair Segeint. And, later, when the Romans had gone, the Segontes came back and again the place became Cair Segeint. It may seem a long while for a name to stick, especially when the Roman occupation changed so many names in Britain, but we do know from internal evidence in the ruins of Silchester that there was something of a Celtic revival, and it is a fact that the Welsh language shows practically no traces of Latin influence save for the few that can be accounted for by ecclesiastical influences.

And there we must leave the mystery of Silchester, and come to the place itself. For, if it is a place without history, it is at the same time the most remarkable of all the Roman remains of Hampshire. It is a place without history and yet it is the best known of all the Romano-British towns, better known, perhaps, than any other provincial town in the whole Roman Empire outside the metropolitan area. You would never guess that because all you can see is a wall. The wall is at its highest by the farm. Here it touches twenty feet (the average height being a bit above twelve feet, and the lowest being a little under ten feet) and I think that here by the farm you see the wall at its magnificent best, free of vegetation, massive, enduring. But you may only look. Once you could go up and touch: once you might walk all around the queer irregular octagon of walls and note the four gates set at the points of the compass in Roman fashion and the two additional gates (the shape so foreign to the geometrical tidiness of the Roman mind was due to the great British earthwork within which the Roman town was built): once you might walk in at the gap that was the south gate and stand in the middle of Silchester, which was just about the best place from which to gain a proper impression of the might that once was Rome's. Now you cannot go near. Silchester is fenced off. Some twenty-five yards from the walls there is an unclimbable fence running right round the town. They are working (at least they were working up to the outbreak of total war) on Silchester, restoring it, so I have been told, so that one day, many, many years hence, it may be one of the show places of the country, a perfect Roman town. Well, I liked it as a ruin. As a ruin it had atmosphere, which I am quite sure it will never have when it has been restored. For all that, I do not really grumble at that fence. I know that the trees and the holly and the bramble and the ivy and the thorns would one day have destroyed the great walls of Silchester—and that I should not have regretted greatly, for the death would have been a natural death—but I should not have liked them after all these years destroyed by trippers. And the danger was great.

Outside the walls is the amphitheatre. Amphitheatres have not been found in connexion with many Roman towns in Britain. Indeed, in addition to this one, there are amphitheatres only at Richborough, Colchester, Cirencester, Caerleon-upon-Usk, Dorchester, and Wroxeter. The Dorchester one is the largest, being 218 feet in length and 163 feet in width. This amphitheatre at Silchester is 150 feet in length and 120 feet in width, which is about the size of the one at Cirencester. In 1760 it is said that there were five rows of seats distinctly visible. All traces of them have now disappeared. The walls of the city had a circuit of 2,670 yards, enclosing an area of 102 acres, which is about the same size as Cirencester and Wroxeter. It is very probable that these walls were built at a much later date than the city itself. During the occupation inland towns were not exposed to danger and there was no need for the expensive building and upkeep of walls. It is probable that they were built towards the end of the occupation when conditions were distinctly unsettled. Moreover, the mass of the walls consists of flint rubble. Most Roman walls have bonding courses of tiles, but no tiles were used at Silchester where the bonding courses consist of single rows of large flat stones. The walls are faced with dressed flints and supported by internal buttresses, but there are no towers. There is evidence that the building, though very well done, was done in something of a hurry.

The ground plan of the old town is like a chess-board. All the streets are straight and all are at right-angles. And in the centre, where the four main roads which enter by the four main gates meet, there is a large square some two acres in extent. This is the Forum. There were colonnades round it on three sides, the other—the west—being formed by the eastern wall of the Basilica. Behind these colonnades there were wide walks and behind them were the shops. But the shape of the chambers on the south side seems to indicate that here there was a series of public offices. The lay-out is very similar to that of any Italian Forum, but the Basilica is unusually large, while the public offices are on the whole rather small and the arrangements are all very simple. Other public buildings in the town include three small temples, the wholly remarkable little Christian church, and a large building with baths attached, which may have been the public guest-house.

The Basilica occupied the whole breadth of the Forum from north to south. The excavators formed the opinion that the original building had been destroyed by fire, and then rebuilt in a very debased style. The original building, they thought, consisted of a great hall, 240 feet long and 58 feet wide, divided into a central nave with narrow aisles by colonnades, and with a semi-circular apse at each end with a raised floor, which formed the tribune of the Court of Justice. In the centre of the hall was a still larger apse raised three steps above the floor of the hall, and this was probably the council chamber of the town's governing body. They thought that the original building had a height of about 60 feet. Generally in a Roman town you find that the Basilica and the public baths are very close together, and here again Silchester differs from the usual run, for the building containing the baths is a considerable way away.

The three temples were not important—they were, in fact, rather poor specimens of their type—but the little

Christian church is quite another matter. The remains were found in 1892 just outside the south-eastern corner of the Forum. This tiny little church—it was not more than 42 feet long—is the only example of a Christian church of Roman date that has been found in this country. The only entrance was at the east end; the apse with the seats for the clergy was at the west end, and there also stood the altar, which was based on a platform of rich mosaics. The character and workmanship of these mosaics show that the church must have been built not long after Constantine's edict of toleration in A.D. 313. This is very interesting, for the remains of Christianity in Roman Britain are very few and scanty. Furthermore, legend has been pretty busy with what records there are and in inventing its own, with the result that there have been those that denied that there was any Christianity in Roman Britain at all. This we know to be wrong, but it is certain that the stories of a sudden and widespread conversion to Christianity—"conversion by explosion" as one French historian has put it—are quite untrue. Christianity in England was received in a very lukewarm fashion. There was no enthusiasm. No enthusiasm among the natives, at any rate, though it is not unlikely that among the Roman officials it may have spread fairly rapidly at first. You do not come across Christian inscriptions in Britain much before the middle of the fifth century, and even then they are much more frequent in Wales than anywhere else. So it may be taken that this church was not so much an English church as a church for the Christian members of the Roman community, and judging by the size of the building there were not so many of them.

It was possible from the remains that were found to say with reasonable accuracy what were the various trades in the town. Among the shops there were, for example, a butcher, a poultry-monger, an ironmonger, a money-changer, and so on. In the butcher's shop there were found flesh-hooks and the remains of the steelyards. In the poultry-monger's there were the bones and skulls of birds, and also the spurs of game-cocks, in some cases supplemented by the steel spurs. In the money-changer's there was a small bar of silver and a few coins. In another place there was found a great quantity of oyster-shells, and this has been taken to indicate a taste for the luxurious on the part of the inhabitants and thus to indicate a very prosperous community. But they were, of course, used for pounding into lime. The chief industry of the place seems to have been dying.

The houses were of two types—the corridor and the courtyard—the normal types found in Roman Britain. The corridor house had a row of rooms lined on one or both sides by corridors serving for communication; in the other type there was a similar series of rooms and corridors, but they were arranged around three or four sides of a courtyard. These types of houses are quite different from the town houses of Rome and other big towns in Italy, but they are very similar to the houses found in Gaul, and it is quite likely that they are really Celtic houses adapted by the Romans, in the same way as we adopt foreign styles of architecture when we colonize. But the interior fittings are absolutely Roman. The hypocausts, the frescoes, the mosaics might well be found in any house in Rome, and show no signs of any outside influence.

Silchester was laid out by a Roman engineer. The straight streets crossing each other at right-angles, and the central Forum, were the work of a Roman surveyor. And it seems evident that he did his work at an early date, for none of the streets cross the remains of earlier Roman buildings. There may have been a few Roman buildings in the place before the town was planned, for one or two of the houses which front the streets are not absolutely flush with the street line, but there were certainly not many. Moreover, the design of the buildings, the ornamentation of the private houses, the domestic utensils, even the words scratched by workmen on pottery and bricks, are Roman, entirely Roman. Latin was the language written and spoken in Silchester. Yet despite all the trouble that was taken in laying out the town, despite the size of the Basilica, the remains do not point to a large town and certainly not to a heavily populated one. Nor is there anything to suggest that it was a particularly prosperous one. None of the

mosaics are of especial elegance, and none of the houses
were of great wealth or splendour. It is commonly stated in
all the guide books that Silchester was a large and important Roman city. In fact, it is very doubtful if it ever contained more than seventy or eighty houses of any size.
Furthermore, there were large spaces within the walls that
were never built over at all. It is difficult to know what to
make of this. It seems likely that the Romans intended to
make the place a city of size and importance, but that they
dropped the idea for some reason which we shall now never
know. But having dropped it, it is evident that Silchester
never had more than an artificial existence. It was a place
that was not wanted. Probably it had throughout its
Roman life a population solely composed of officials with
the sort of foreign following that occupation officials gather
about them. When the Roman occupation ended, these
officials departed and their followers went with them. The
place died.

The place died. Cair Segeint was overwhelmed by no
disaster. It was not stormed and sacked. It was not burnt.
It just died, decayed. Unfortunately we know absolutely
nothing for certain about the downfall of the Roman power
in Britain. We know less about it than about the same
disaster in other parts of the Empire. There is no authority
contemporary with the event. The original authority most
nearly contemporary is Gildas (though parts of the so-called
Nennius may be about the same time as Gildas) and Gildas
gives us very little history, and that little, whenever we
have the opportunity of checking the facts, is found to be
inaccurate. Gildas, too, for some reason, which no doubt
was a good one from his own point of view, was most
violently prejudiced. But we do know a little of what went
on before the invasions of the Saxons. There were some inroads by the Picts, that mysterious people, for example.
These have been grossly exaggerated by the books. You
would think, from some of the books, that these people just
swarmed over the wall and ravaged all over the place and
that no one could do anything about it. That there were
attacks from the north is beyond doubt, but there seems to
be no doubt that the Britons were well able to deal with

them. There is absolutely no evidence that the Picts or any other Caledonians were ever able to effect any settlement south of the Clyde or the Forth. Gildas altogether exaggerates the effect of the Pictish raids. Whether there was some invasion from Ireland or not is a more difficult question. But there can be no doubt that there was civil war in Britain. And it was war between two well-defined classes— the Britons proper and those Britons who had become Romanized by marriage or just by the passage of time. The unconquered came back. We know that a large number of people left these islands, and though it is almost certainly an exaggeration to say, as we might say if we believed all that Gildas tells us, that by A.D. 446 there was scarcely a Roman family left in Britain, it is probably true that by that date most of them had left and that within a few more years they had all gone and taken their followers with them. They went to France, to that part of France which is now called Brittany. In their place came the real owners of the country, back from the highlands of the West where they had remained throughout the occupation unconquered. They came back to Silchester and they brought with them the old name, Cair Segeint. They would have come back to the place and probably occupied it for a while because of its importance as a road junction. But they did not make it a town, because there was not, as the Romans had found, need for a town there. And when they left in the face of the Saxon invasions there was nothing for them to leave; as they had found when the Romans left, so the Saxons found when the Britons left—nothing worth the taking. The place was again deserted.

From Silchester Roman roads radiate in all directions. There is the road in from London, the road north to Dorchester, the road to Speen and Cirencester, the road to Winchester, and the road—the Port Way—to Salisbury. These are true Roman roads; that is to say, they are roads that were built and formed part of an elaborate system. There was nothing haphazard about them. They were *built*. More often than not they consisted of a raised causeway of earth and stones, and the material used in their construction was almost invariably obtained in the immediate neighbourhood. In certain places the pits that were thus formed can still be seen alongside the roads. For metalling the surface, local stone was used, and as a general rule the surface was made of small stones or gravel very much in the same way as our modern macadamized roads (so far have we progressed!) but occasionally a pavement of slabs was made. And so well were these roads made that they can still to-day be traced all over the country. They are, indeed, the best-known feature of the Roman occupation. They have names, and almost everyone knows a Roman road when he sees one because it is so straight! Straight they are, for they were laid out from hill-top to hill-top in straight sections by the surveyor. Except in very hilly country they are seldom deflected by natural features. The Romans had no need to worry about small details like natural features; they had plenty of forced labour at their command. But all straight roads are not Roman roads. And the names! The *Via Porta*, the *Via Julia*, the *Via Devana*, and so on. Well, we do not know by what names the Romans called their roads nor even if they were in the habit of giving names to their roads. A great many were in use for years after their departure, and these were named by the Saxons—among them are Akeman Street, Ermine Street, the Fosse Way, and Watling Street. But the Latin names were given to the roads long after the Romans and the Saxons had gone as entities by imaginative antiquarians. And some of the roads are much older than the Romans, very much older. The Icknield Way, the White Way, the Peddars Way, the Ridge Way, the Harrow Way —that greatest of British prehistoric roads, which passes a few miles south of Silchester, on its astonishing journey from Marazion in Cornwall to Dover—yes, even the Port Way (which was taken over by the Romans) and, yes, even the Pilgrim's Way, all these are very much older than the Romans. They are not Roman roads though—except the Port Way and the Fosse Way which were built up by the Romans—though no doubt they were all used to some extent by the Romans. They are native roads, and they provide evidence of a considerable civilization before the Romans came. And that is something that we should not forget, for there is a good deal of misconception about the Romans in Britain and especially about Julius Cæsar. It is generally thought, for example, that the Roman occupation of Britain began with the invasion of Julius Cæsar.

It is still too generally believed that Julius Cæsar came to the island of Britain in the year 55 B.C., and found it inhabited by a lot of naked savages who painted themselves a bright blue with woad, that he conquered them, and that he made a lot of roads that were remarkable for their straightness. The only fact in all that is that Julius Cæsar landed in Britain in the year 55 B.C. Britain, so far from being a land of naked painted savages when Julius Cæsar landed, was a land highly civilized, a land, indeed, that slipped back a little in the way of civilization because of the recent inroads of refugees from the Roman conquest of Western Europe. Julius Cæsar was a propagandist. He wrote for his own purposes and for his own aggrandisement. Time has made him even more successful than he could ever have imagined, for now his propaganda is used in our schools as text-books, and from a very early age we get a swollen idea of him, which is just what he wanted his own people to get. Cæsar's naked savages were in reality more highly civilized than any people on the continent (with the exception of the Romans) and were but little behind the Irish. They had an excellent system of tribal government. They were exceptional craftsmen in metal. They were excellent farmers. They had a good system of roads. They had their own token currency, and a gold coin for trade with the Continent. They had a close trading connexion with the Continent which was some hundreds of years old when the great Cæsar came. They wore good decorative clothing. And they were too much for Julius Cæsar.

Julius Cæsar did not conquer Britain. On the contrary, the Britons administered two severe defeats to Julius Cæsar, the second so severe that it was nearly a hundred years before the mighty Roman Empire dared try again. Julius Cæsar made no roads in Britain. His first invasion in 55 B.C. lasted no more than three weeks, and he penetrated no more than a few miles from the coast. His second in 54 B.C. was only made after the most careful preparations.

But it was little more successful. It is possible that he managed to reach the Thames—some historians maintain that he reached Wallingford—but it is more likely that he never left Kent. His own account of the invasion and the subsequent operations is necessarily vague. We had plenty of experience of the vagueness of communiqués from both sides when things were not going too well for them in the last war. Cæsar in this respect differed not one whit from twentieth-century generals. He did not like to admit defeat. It would not have done him any good had he done so. But if you read his *Commentaries* you will find, I think, nothing to suggest that he ever succeeded in penetrating further inland than the Medway.

His *Commentaries* are revealing, however, in another direction. He lays great stress on the chariots employed by the Britons. Neither he nor the legions liked the chariots. They were unaccustomed to being attacked by them and they did not relish the experience at all. And the Britons had a great number of chariots. One chief alone, says Cæsar, produced four thousand of them. Some allowance must be made for exaggeration (Julius Cæsar was probably no different in this respect from certain other war leaders more recent in time), but even when all allowance has been made for exaggeration, his assertion effectually disposes of his other assertion that his enemies were untamed savages. Chariots could not travel over unsuitable ground, for they would easily get bogged. Obviously they needed roads: not just one good road, but a whole network of good roads (and roads are among the surest signs of civilization) to enable them to get from one place to another. At any rate the chariots of the Britons manœuvred to some purpose. Julius Cæsar went back to Gaul. Despite the innumerable "Cæsar's Camps" in Hampshire, Cæsar was never in Hampshire. And the same applies to every one of his legionaries. Hampshire did not know the might of Rome until A.D. 43 at the earliest, and probably not for some time later.

After Cæsar's defeat Rome left Britain alone for almost a hundred years. But those hundred years saw a rapid decline in power, and in the organization and determination of the Britons. More and more refugees sought shelter in

Britain from the yoke of Rome. They brought troubles with them, and inevitably they brought with them some of the ideas and some of the ways of Imperial Rome. I think, too, that for many of those hundred years Roman propaganda was rife in southern England and in certain districts—notably in Essex—it was thoroughly successful. There were Quislings in Europe long before a certain citizen of Norway gave his name to the breed. Thus, while some of the tribes continued to help their cousins over the water, others traded directly with Rome. What finally decided the Roman Emperor to attempt conquest again is uncertain, but probably it was Britain's rumoured wealth in metals. At any rate, in A.D. 43 the third Roman invasion of Britain was launched.

The invasion was under the direction of Aulus Plautus. It is generally accepted that the landing—or rather the three landings—were made in Kent, and probably in the neighbourhoods of Dover, Lympne and Richborough. That there were three landings is beyond question, but personally I am not convinced that they were all made in Kent, or if they were then I think that there was at least one other landing after. Dio Cassius is the historian upon whom we depend for the details of the invasion, and his account is not very clear nor is his text impeccable. But it is clear enough from his account that Aulus Plautus had under him Vespasian (the future Emperor) and Flavius Sabinus, and that the expedition was divided into three separate forces. It is clear, too, that their landings were unopposed, and were made at places that were not expected (the latter, by the way, is just the sort of point that would be remembered). It is also quite clear that soon after their landing they encountered a people called the Boduni, "whom they that are called the Catuvellauni had under their dominion," and that soon after this they came to a river that was so wide and deep that the natives thought that the Romans could not cross it without a bridge. All that is clear enough from the account of Dio Cassius. But the Boduni are not known as one of the tribes of Britain, and it has been suggested that the Dobuni are meant. This was the tribe that lived immediately to the west of the Atrebates, and their chief town was Cirencester. And, personally, I think that this is a correct identification, because of the river. The Thames cannot be intended from the description. The only river that will fit it is the Severn. This account implies a landing somewhere in the neighbourhood of Southampton Water. The obvious place to land would be the coast of Kent. The Britons with their connexion with the Continent would have known that an expedition was being prepared, and they would have been prepared to receive it in the obvious place. But Dio Cassius goes out of his way to tell us that the landing was made in a place where it was not expected. There is another point, too. The Romans would have known all about the impenetrable forest of Anderida. That forest stretched from the open chalk downs of Kent to the open chalk downs of Hampshire and would have been quite impassable for an army. It was impassable even in the eleventh century, for William the Conqueror, when he wanted to go from Hastings to London, had to go round by way of Dover. The Romans would have been likely to do all they could to avoid such an obstacle. I think it probable that there were landings at unexpected places on the coast of Kent, but against all the weight of modern opinion I remain convinced that the main landing of the expedition was made on the coast of Hampshire and was under the direct command of Vespasian. And there is one other point in favour of this view: the tides. We know that Cæsar had trouble with the tides on the Kent coast. They might have been very troublesome indeed for a big expedition as this one was. There would have been no trouble of that sort in a landing on the Hampshire coast. And Suetonius records that Vespasian conquered the two most powerful tribes in Britain, took more than twenty towns, and captured the Isle of Wight. It seems obvious that he was in command of the most powerful force, and there is every indication by implication that his was a separate expedition.

Vespasian established garrisons at Portchester (Portus Magnus) and Bitterne (Clausentum) and penetrated the interior by means of galleys and the waterways. He sailed up the Itchen, and towards the head of the valley he found a stockaded village or town in the marsh and an earthwork fort upon the summit of the neighbouring hill. This was Caer Gwent (the modern Winchester) and it commanded the open country to the north with its promise of easy and rapid advance. The town, perhaps, fell easily enough, but there must have been heavy fighting before the hill-fort fell and there must have been heavy casualties among the legionaries before all opposition ceased. There is no record that the great battle that saw the overthrow of the Belgae took place at or near Caer Gwent, but I think that it must have been here. All the geographical features point to it. The Itchen is the great natural opening in the chalk hills. Beyond Caer Gwent is fairly open country for some twenty-two miles across the downs to the forests of the Thames Valley, and junction with the legions, if there was a landing in Kent, that had come up that valley. If there was resistance still in the thick woods there it would be taken in the rear by Vespasian's advance. Everything points to the neighbourhood of Caer Gwent as the site of the great battle in which the strength of the two most powerful tribes in Britain was destroyed. Once that battle was won progress became easy. In less than four years the Romans had reached the line Lincoln-Leicester-Cirencester-Axminster, which is the line of the old Fosse Way. The area behind this line was thoroughly conquered, and especially was this true of Hampshire where the might of the tribes was destroyed, so thoroughly conquered that it never had to be done again. Hampshire became the most Romanized area in the whole country. That is why this part of the country has no Roman history. You hear of other parts of the country simply because they were never thoroughly conquered. Britain was never wholly conquered by the Romans. It took Cæsar no more than eight years to conquer the whole of Gaul, and he used only four legions and their auxiliaries. It took the Romans thirty-six years to conquer Britain with the same number of legions (and they the best Rome could produce) and even then the conquest beyond the Fosse Way was only partial. Beyond the Fosse Way there was a military occupation upheld by means of forts and military roads. South of the Fosse Way there was a Roman province. Almost all the towns and villas have been found to the south of that road. Beyond the country remained British; isolated points only were Roman. And Hampshire was so thoroughly Romanized that there was not even need for a large garrison town. It was so thoroughly Romanized that it was absolutely safe. It was so thoroughly Romanized that it was dull. So dull that it has no Roman history at all.

The main artery of communication in this southern province ran from London to Southampton. It started north of the Thames, which it probably crossed at Staines, and ran due west, passing a little to the north of Sandhurst. After crossing the Blackwater it enters Hampshire and passes by Stanford, Cold Harbour Wood and Stratfieldsaye to the east gate of Silchester. For part of this way (all of which I have walked) it forms the county boundary, and for part of the way it coincides with a modern road, which is known as the Devil's Highway. Near Silchester it crosses fields, but its course can still be traced without difficulty. From Silchester four roads branch. That going north to Dorchester can no longer be followed, and some authorities are doubtful if it ever existed. That going westwards to Speen cannot be followed either, but there can be no doubt that it existed. It appears in the *Itinerary*, and though that road-book is not always accurate, owing to the mistakes of later scribes, it is never deliberately misleading nor does it invent roads that never existed. The road going south-west to Old Sarum can still be followed for mile upon mile, though it is not quite so clear as the maps would suggest. You can buy maps with the Port Way clearly marked all the way from Silchester to the Wiltshire border, sometimes as a footpath, sometimes as a road. Well, for some miles from Silchester you can see nothing at all of the Port Way. Indeed, at one time—and quite recently—the road was thought to run from the South Gate whereas it actually runs through the West Gate. It is said to be visible between two woods about a mile and a half from Silchester, but I have not been able to find it, though just a little further on there is a ridge in a field that is obviously part of it. The best way to pick it up is to go to Kingsclere and to take the road which runs pretty well due south. You climb up over White

Hill and see the downs for miles ahead of you, and on them (actually in a dip) is a long line of larch and lime crossing the road diagonally. The line of trees—it is not deep enough to call a wood—is Cæsar's Bench, and here the Port Way shows up clearly, a raised causeway about fifteen feet wide. Beyond the road is lost, but it can be picked up again past St. Mary Bourne where it runs through a hazel copse. Then it disappears until beyond Andover at Hundred Acre Corner. It runs, having disappeared in the meanwhile, just to the south of Quarley Hill, and if you climb to the top of the hill you can look back and see the ridge beyond Cæsar's Bench. From Quarley Hill the old road is easily followed as a raised causeway—sometimes nearly three feet high—all the way to Old Sarum. But in Hampshire for the most part the Port Way just is not. I know because I have walked every inch of the way.

But let us go back to Silchester and take the road southwards, the most important of the roads, and never, so far as I am aware, accorded the dignity of a name. This also has disappeared in the immediate vicinity of Silchester. But from Sherborne St. John to Winchester it is almost continuously traceable and a very great deal of it is still in constant use. I have walked the whole length of it from Sherborne St. John. It passes by Waltham, Popham, and Stratton, but from King's Worthy the old road passes through the fields by Hyde Abbey to the old North Gate of Winchester. It is clearly visible here. From the South Gate it runs on to Otterbourne. This, too, is the modern road, and it carries a tremendous amount of traffic. After Otterbourne the old road is not clearly traceable any of the way to Bitterne.

From Winchester also there was a considerable branching of roads in the Roman times. In addition to the southward one to Bitterne, there was the road to Cirencester, which seems to have left the town by the North Gate. The actual exit from the town is no longer traceable, but almost immediately afterwards the road is clear enough, and it can be followed almost without a break all the way to Marlborough, which the Romans knew as Cunetio. A good deal of the way is followed by the modern road over the chalk

52

Droxford Church, where Isaak Walton worshipped before fishing

hills, but even where there is no modern road and the old road is no more than a track (as is the case in Harewood Forest) there can be no doubt about its course. It cuts the Port Way and passes into Wiltshire at Conholt Park, and again I have walked the whole of its length. The road that leaves the West Gate is the old road to Old Sarum, and this can be traced for the whole of its length, and I have walked the whole of it on several occasions. From the West Gate, climbing up the hill, it runs between Crab Wood and Pitt Down, and here it is still in use. Then as a track rather than a road, but a track that is difficult to follow only near King's Somborne and Horsebridge, it runs to Broughton crossing the Test at Horsebridge, and from Broughton to Old Sarum it is still in use. A very interesting point about this road is that a pig of lead was found at Bossington, close to the point where the track crosses the Test, and this suggests that some at least of the trade of the lead mines on Mendip came this way to the coast and so to the Continent. Two other roads sprang from Winchester. One ran south-east to Portchester, starting apparently from the East Gate. It can still be traced to Morestead and Owlesbury, but beyond that village it is completely lost. The other is more doubtful. It was supposed to run north-east to Alton and Farnham, starting also from the East Gate. This road, which is used to-day, is as straight as an arrow over Magdalen Hill and as far as Avington Lodge, and may well be Roman in origin. But beyond Avington Lodge there is no sign at all that can be called Roman. And there is no evidence that the Romans ever had a station at Farnham or, indeed, that they were ever there in any capacity. This, of course, does not necessarily mean that the road as far as Avington Lodge is not Roman, but if it is it can only mean that the Romans gave up the building shortly after they had started. Perhaps it was commenced towards the end of the occupation.

There are other Roman roads in the county, of course. One obviously ran from Clausentum to Regnum, which is the modern Chichester, and so to the Stane Street and on to London. The modern road through Havant probably follows the old fairly closely. And, of course, there are plenty

Warnford, the Norman
church of the de Ports

of roads that have acquired the name Roman on totally insufficient evidence. Two of these are in the New Forest. One of these is not worth a moment's consideration. The other is supposed to have run from Bitterne through Nursling to Lepe near Exbury. This has received a great deal of consideration from the experts, and little support. But the Romans were certainly at Lepe, and presumably they must have had a road of some sort there.

Only two of these roads were in my opinion designed by the Romans; the road that was never finished and the road from Winchester to Portchester. And I would not care to be dogmatic about the latter. The early British trackway ran, I think, to Morestead, but then I think that it went on to the Downs behind Beacon Hill and, crossing the Meon above Warnford, ran up Old Winchester Hill and so over the tops to Butser and War Down and on to Harting and Cocking and even further. There is at any rate a magnificent walk along these hills and you can follow an ancient trackway almost all the way. I have walked the whole distance from Winchester to Beachy Head, and though there is not a track all the way, there are plenty of signs that there was once a track all the way. The other Roman roads in Hampshire were, I feel sure, well-used and well-defined trackways long before the Romans came. They were adapted and modernized in the same way as was the Fosse Way. No doubt they, as the Fosse Way, had fallen into some disrepair during the troublesome times that followed Julius Cæsar's abortive excursions. Probably they were at their best during the peaceful times of the later Bronze Age. But, judging by what can still be seen of their courses after two thousand years of indifference and neglect (the Ridgeway is a good example), they must have been plainly visible, and inviting, to the Romans. The Romans were a horribly sensible people, and they would have used all those they wanted in order to save themselves trouble. There would have been little need for surveying except where occasional gaps needed to be bridged with new sections. All that would have been necessary in taking over the old trackways would have been the repair of the surfaces to Roman military standards—and there was plenty of forced labour available for that purpose. That does not detract from the work of the Roman engineers in the least. Their repair work and the roads they built from scratch lasted for centuries in spite of neglect, and when in the end it did collapse it did so more often than not from causes other than wear and tear. But for all that we grossly exaggerate the works of the Romans in Britain. They had all the resources they needed, and they had magnificent skill, but they did remarkably little to develop the undeveloped areas of Britain. They found an upland civilization linked by upland roads and hemmed in by almost impenetrable forest. They made little or no attempt to cultivate the rich but heavier soils. Except where military necessity made it imperative, they left the face of the country very much as they had found it. Theirs was a surface occupation. Britain was a conquered country; or at least, south of the Fosse Way it was a conquered country. The Romans did not come to Britain out of the kindness of their hearts. They did not come for Britain's good. They were in Britain for what they could get out of it. They put in as little as possible. Empires are not forged from altruistic motives.

The Roman occupation of Britain falls into well-defined periods. The first triumphant conquest up to the line of the Fosse Way; the long and severe task of subduing the hill tribes of the north and Wales, a task which took thirty years and in Wales was never completed, was indeed never successful at all; the advance into Scotland, which was begun about forty years after the invasion proper and which forty years later resulted in the building of the wall from Wallsend to Carlisle. (The invasion of Scotland was not a success any more than the invasion of Wales had been. The wall thereafter was the boundary of the Roman province of Britain, though there were frequently garrisons north of it just as there were garrisons always in Wales.) And finally the period of the Saxon raids.

During the first stage part of the conquered territory was annexed and part was left in the hands of "protected" chieftains. One of these men was named Cogidubnos, and he seems to have had control of at least a part of Hampshire. During the second stage these subordinate chieftains were gradually absorbed into the full Roman administration, and the garrisons were gradually reduced in strength. Probably at the end of the first fifty years of the occupation there was not a true fort in the south of England and very few garrisons. But that was never the case in the north. The Roman province of Britain fell naturally into two divisions (though this was never admitted by the Imperial Government): the south, which was peaceful and settled, and the highlands of the north and Wales and Scotland, which was a purely military area with forts and fortresses and roads, but with no settled civilian life. This area was garrisoned by an army of forty thousand men, one of the most important of the provincial armies, and it was certainly the most important element in Roman Britain. So far as the south of the country was concerned with the Army at all, it was concerned as a leave area, a place to which men weary with the strain of constant watch, men nervy and tired with the strain of constant guerrilla warfare, could be sent for relaxation. It is for this reason that we find so few traces of Roman military occupation in Hampshire. There was no need for the military. If they were here they were here to enjoy themselves.

There are two points that must be stressed when writing or thinking of Roman Hampshire. Firstly, that Britain was merely an outlying province of the Roman Empire. There is some history of the province as a whole, but there is very little history of the units that made up the province. The Roman Empire was too big for such little details to assume importance. Secondly, that there was no such unit as Roman Hampshire. The boundaries of the British tribes did not correspond to our present county boundaries and nor did the Roman administrative areas. Roman Hampshire is a convenient but quite meaningless term. It is not possible to write a history of Roman Hampshire. All that one can do is to study the Roman remains found in the county in relation to the whole of the province of Roman Britain, or to study them as individual units.

Southern Britain did become Romanized. I have said that we greatly exaggerate the works of the Romans in Britain. That is perfectly true. They were in occupation for nearly four hundred years, and they left behind them practically nothing; a few roads, a few walls, a pavement or two, no more. But it would be idle to pretend that they did not have an enormous effect on the settled portions of the country for most of the occupation. They did. There was an almost complete capitulation to Roman influence, how complete can be judged by the almost total disappearance of the British culture. Before the invasion of Aulus Plautus there had been a British art of considerable merit. The British were well known for their work in metals, and their pottery was by no means ordinary with its use of plant and animal forms, its enamelling, and its use of the returning spiral. And with this art went a definite culture. Both art and culture vanished before the art and culture of the Romans. It lingered on in just a few places, as for example the New Forest, but probably it survived only as a curiosity, something for the tourists, for the sightseers, for soldiers on leave from the inhospitable frontiers. The art that was common in the Roman areas was Roman entirely. The pottery was mainly imported: where it was not, it was copied from a Roman original. Samian ware shows no signs of British influence. And the culture was exclusively Roman also. The mosaics, the painted stuccos, the bath-rooms, the hypocausts, all were Roman. Nor was all this confined to the wealthy. The pottery found in the houses of the poor was Samian and not British. But although the Romans brought these additions to life (and they were taken up by the British with some eagerness) they did not change the essential way of life.

The Romans relied on the towns for their power. It was by the towns and through the towns that the country was Romanized. Most of the Roman towns in Britain were built late in the first or early in the second century. A few— London is the best example—were of economic importance: a few may have been no more than colonies for soldiers whose period of service was over: but most of them were undoubtedly built for political reasons. The towns were the centres from which the Romanized chiefs governed their districts. Big cities were not common in Roman Britain. The highest form of town life known to the Romans, the *coloniae* and the *municipia*, were rare in Britain. Neither occurred in Hampshire, and there were only five in the whole country—Colchester, Gloucester, Lincoln and York were *coloniae*, and Verulam was a *municipium*. But if Hampshire had no town of high legal status, it had two towns that must have occupied a considerable place in the Roman political system. These towns are Silchester (at least during the latter part of the occupation) and Winchester (probably throughout the occupation) and they correspond to a number of smaller centres that grew up under the general plan of the conquerors. Canterbury, Cirencester, Dorchester, Exeter, Leicester, and Rochester are other examples. All may have been, and Silchester and Winchester certainly were, tribal centres before the invasion, but under the Romans they became towns built on the Roman plan.

Outside these towns the country was divided into estates. These estates (they are called villas) were large. We do not know if they were in being before the Romans came, but the Romans certainly encouraged them. Nor do we know when the villas began to play a really important part in the life of the country, because most of our information about them comes from the end of the occupation when they were playing a very important part indeed. But it seems certain that these villas must have had some importance early in the occupation, though their great importance came only with the decay of the towns, a decay with which, incidentally, they had a great deal to do.

The building of the towns was unpopular. We know from Tacitus that it met with considerable resistance. The Britons were compelled to build the towns. The population of Britain was a rural population, and the labour had to come from the country-side. Moreover, since there is absolutely no evidence that there was any increase in the population under the Romans, the people to live in the towns had to come from the country-side. This is a most uneconomic process, as we have found in this twentieth century. It can only have meant that instead of the country becoming richer because of the towns, it became poorer. The towns could only have flourished if the country had

greatly increased in productivity. We know that it did not.
Pre-Roman Britain was agricultural, and its agriculture was
perfectly adequate for its needs. Roman Britain was also
agricultural, but now it had not only to support itself but
also the towns, and it had to export a proportion of its
produce as well. The Romans super-imposed an urban
civilization upon a rural one, but they did nothing to
strengthen the rural one which should have been the foundation of the urban. So in the end the urban superstructure
collapsed (looking back it is little short of miraculous that
it lasted so long) and there was left the rural civilization of
Britain in essentials not very different from what it had
been before the invasion. Then the wheel turned full circle,
and there began what Haverfield called "The Celtic Revival." This spread out from the villas. By the middle of
the fourth century, so far as one can judge, all the power
rested in the hands of the large landowners. As the towns
decayed the landowners prospered; and as the landowners
prospered, so the peasants fell into serfdom. It was in this
state that Britain had to meet the raids of the Saxon bands.
The great Saxon invasion came in A.D. 367, and it over-
ran almost all the country. Had the towns been strong they
might have repelled the raiders and saved their wealth. But
they were decayed. Had the civilization been a purely
rural one, a peasant civilization, it would certainly not have
suffered too much, for its wealth would have been for the
most part in the soil. But Britain was now a civilization of
great country houses, unfortified country houses. There
could not have been anything easier for the Saxon raiders.
And it was fatal for the Roman civilization of Britain.
Almost all the villas of Britain were destroyed in or about
A.D. 367, and certainly all the Hampshire ones disappeared
about that time. Theodosius arrived in time to save a few
in the south of Kent, and he arrived in time to give the
Romans a few more years in Britain; but he did not arrive
in time to save Roman Britain. That died in the Saxon
invasion of 367. From then on it was the British rural
civilization, the civilization that survived more or less untouched in the peasants of the villas, that mattered. The
destruction of the power of the big landowner and the

destruction of the villa system did more than release a few serfs from bondage.

There are traces of many villas in Hampshire, and there must be many more still to be found. The landowner of the villa lived in the big house, and the land immediately around it was cultivated by his slaves. The rest of the land was let to half-freed slaves, who were called *coloni*. We do not know how large these villas grew to in Britain, but in Gaul they were sometimes as large as ten thousand acres. Having regard to the type of land in Hampshire it seems probable that some of them were very large. The owners were probably members of the British upper class, thoroughly Romanized and so considered a good safe influence on the lower classes of natives. The houses in which these great landowners lived, though they showed many Roman influences, were not, perhaps surprisingly, like the houses in Italy of similar class. They are of two types, both definitely Celtic, for they occur only in Britain and northern Gaul. These two types occur also in the towns, but in the country both corridor and courtyard types had barns and out-houses as well. In the country, generally speaking, the courtyard type is the larger, and some of the courtyard houses in Hampshire were really surprisingly large. The slaves who worked the land lived in huts, mainly daub and wattle huts, and even occasionally in pit-dwellings. There was a vast contrast between the house of the landowner and the houses of his slaves, but towards the end of the occupation the condition of the slaves improved a good deal.

The industry of Roman Hampshire was agriculture. Chiefly the county produced wool and wheat. To begin with this industry was centred round the towns of Silchester and Winchester, but it must soon have centred round the big villas. The villas in Hampshire are pretty evenly distributed over the county, except in the extreme north and the south-west. The south-west of the county, the area between Southampton and the Dorset border, was then, as it is now, sandy heath and forest, not very suitable for agriculture. It was untouched by the Romans, and it remained a refuge for the traditional British way of life. The extreme north of the county, the rather high barren land which stretches from Inkpen Beacon towards Kingsclere, cannot have attracted settlers. Elsewhere in the county, however, there is ample evidence of a flourishing agriculture in the form of villas and other buildings connected with farming. The Isle of Wight provides similar evidence. And comparatively few of these sites have been fully excavated. Our picture is incomplete; we have no more than a hint of what must once have existed.

It is no part of the purpose of this book to give a full list of the Roman remains in Hampshire—if you wish to make a tour of all the villa sites that have been excavated you will find a full list in the *Victoria County History* (though if you want to view the finds that come from Silchester, you will, for some reason that no one has ever explained, have to go to Reading for they are stored in the museum there, when they should be in a Hampshire museum; there are however some excellent exhibits of Roman interest in the little Winchester museum)—but I think that the villa at Brading in the Isle of Wight should be described briefly here, for it is one of the most famous villas in Britain.

The owner's house of this island estate was made up of three isolated buildings situated on the north, west and south sides of a courtyard that measures about 185 feet each way. The dwelling-house was on the west side, was oblong in shape and measured 55 by 90 feet. It had twelve rooms. The front of the building was formed by a corridor 50 feet long, at each end of which was a room which projected slightly and so formed two wings. Opening on to the corridor were three central rooms, and the others were grouped round these three and had their windows on the outside. This dwelling-house was furnished in the most elaborate style with mosaics. The front corridor, which we should call the front hall, had in the middle of its rather plain paving a decorated panel of Orpheus with his lute charming the animals—two birds, a fox, and a monkey. This is, of course, a subject that occurs on many mosaics. In the room at the south end of the hall is a damaged mosaic of a most unusual and intricate design. In the centre is a head, and on each of the three remaining sides a curious scene—a man with a cock's head facing two winged leopards and a house with steps leading up to it; a pair of gladiators, one with a dagger and a trident, the other defaced; a fox under a tree creeping up to a building (presumably a farmyard). The man with the cock's head is the most interesting of these designs, and he has given rise to a good deal of argument among the experts. Probably he represents Abraxas, a mythical figure connected with a strange and obscure form of religion that flourished in the later Roman Empire, and which is thought by some authorities to have some connexion with Gnosticism. The room at the other end of the hall, which formed with an adjoining room one large apartment, not unlike a Victorian drawing-room or one of the double rooms with sliding doors that are now popular in the small houses of the London suburbs, was most elaborately ornamented with figured mosaics. The front part of this room, the part nearest to the hall, has a square panel with Medusa's head in the centre and round it in triangles four heads of hornblowers, the four winds, and in squares four pairs of figures—a fountain nymph with her urn and a shepherd, Ceres offering the fruits of the earth to Triptolemus, a Satyr chasing a Maenad, and Lycurgus persecuting a Maenad. Between the two rooms, marking the division between them, is a panel showing a man with a sundial, a globe, a column, and a cup, the instruments which are generally used to indicate a scientist or a philosopher. The other room has a mosaic, 14 by 14 feet, which is much defaced, but originally contained a circular piece in the centre, four oblong scenes and four heads in the four corners. The only oblong scene left depicts an incident from classical mythology—Perseus and Andromeda sitting together after her rescue and looking at the reflection of the Gorgon's head in a pool of water. The four heads seem to be those of the four seasons.

In artistic achievement these mosaics are not quite up to the highest standard of some that have been found in Britain, but they are elaborate and they were executed by a craftsman of considerable spirit and artistic ability. There are definite signs of an individual touch about them that is missing from some that have a greater artistic merit. Some of the stucco in the big apartment is painted with birds and flowers, and is rather unusual, but none of the other objects found in the dwelling-house are unusual in any way. They consist of Samian, New Forest and other pottery, some ordinary roofing slates, some glass, and the ordinary run of domestic utensils of average standard. The coins cover the whole period from Domitian to Honorius, but few are earlier than A.D. 250, and it seems probable that the villa was occupied during the third and fourth centuries.

The northern block was an oblong, 55 by 140 feet, and one half of it at any rate was inhabited. Most of the rooms have concrete floors, and one of them has a hypocaust, and plenty of roof slates, window glass, and painted wall-plaster was found here. At the eastern end there were two large rooms, and these are crossed by parallel rows of rough column bases. The southern block is also an oblong, 30 by 160 feet, and is divided into four rooms, one of which takes up more than half the whole building. There were no signs of pavements or of wall-plaster here, and the walls are roughly built. This building was in all probability used as storerooms and sheds. A little to the east of it, but quite distinct from it, stood another building, which contained a hypocaust and a bath and coloured wall-plaster.

This villa was not the property of a man of great wealth, but it was the property of people of the upper class. It does not seem that the owner was himself a farmer, but he probably owned some of the land around. And it must be remembered that the fact that no objects of luxury were found on the site does not mean that the owners of the place did not possess any. They may, and probably would have done so, have carried them away with them when they abandoned the place. And if they had left much behind them it would have been looted by the natives or by the raiders who, shortly after the departure of the Romans, burnt the place.

One other feature of rural life in Hampshire during the Roman occupation must be mentioned: the potteries. There were the purely British potteries of the New Forest and there were also Romano-British potteries at various places in the Petersfield area. Very large remains of this Romano-British industry were found in Alice Holt during the recent war. The New Forest potteries were situated in the north-west corner between Fordingbridge and Bramshaw, a district that was not touched by the Romans. The sites are in Pit's Inclosure, Oakley Inclosure, Anderwood, the Isle of Thorns, Ashley, Crockle and Eyeworth. The pottery made in the New Forest kilns was of two varieties. One is a thin, hard, dark slate-coloured ware upon which patterns, sometimes representing flowers or grasses, were laid in white. Examples of this ware are usually small jars and vases between four and eight inches in height. The other sort of ware was thicker with a dull white or yellowish ground on which the patterns were painted in red or brown. Examples of this ware are usually dishes. Specimens of this New Forest pottery are found on most of the Roman sites in the county and even as far away as Oxford. Found in the Forest with the remains of the pottery are a few iron tools, some bits of Samian ware, some beads of Kimmeridge clay, and some Roman coins. It must have been a flourishing industry for the greater part of the occupation.

Naturally the Roman remains of Hampshire do not occur only at such sites as villas or military fortifications or in towns. I have not the space nor is this the place to give a detailed list of the Roman remains of the county. Actually Roman remains are continually being dug up in all sorts of places, in back gardens and the like, and these isolated finds do not alter the general picture of Roman Hampshire in the least. But one find of an isolated nature does deserve special mention. The find near Blackmoor House, which is in the parish of Selborne, is altogether remarkable.

Gilbert White records in his *Natural History of Selborne* that in 1741 Woolmer Pond dried up, and several hundred coins of copper and some medallions were found lying together as though they had been in a sack. White saw some of them and found that they were coins of Marcus and his wife Faustina. In 1774 more coins were found (the type of metal is not stated) and these represented all the Emperors from Claudius to Commodus, that is, all the Emperors from A.D. 43 to 192. In 1867, when the then Lord Selborne was rebuilding Blackmoor House, more finds were made. There was a sepulchral urn, which contained some bones, a bronze enamelled cup, a bronze patera, a coin of Lucius Verus; there was also some Samian ware and other pottery, some iron axe-heads, and many tiles, which may indicate that there was a building there at some time. A little later, about a mile to the north of Blackmoor House, there were found some bronze sword-blades and spear-heads, and nearby in an urn about a hundred coins of Gallienius, the Tetrici and Victorinus, and a mile to the west of this find some pottery was discovered. Then in 1873 a positively enormous hoard of coins was dug up about half-way between Blackmoor House and Woolmer Pond. This hoard was contained in two jars. From this hoard, which must originally have contained over 30,000 coins, 29,802 coins were obtained, mostly "third brass," but there were also some billion denarii. Of these coins 29,786 coins were catalogued. The hoard contained coins of the last sixty years of the third century, at the end of which it was hidden or, perhaps, lost by its owner or owners. But I find it difficult to believe that so many coins could have been collected by one private citizen or even by two such gentlemen. True, the times were unsettled, and the instinct to save one's money has always been strong in the human race, but the amount is, I think, altogether too big for it to have been the property of one or two men, and had it been the property of several men there would have been no point in collecting it and hiding it in one place. No, I agree with those who think that it was the army chest of the Emperor Allectus. Allectus was the usurping Emperor in Britain, and he was overthrown by the armies of Constantius Chlorus in 296–297. It seems almost certain that Constantius Chlorus landed in Hampshire and advanced inland to meet Allectus who came south from London, and the final battle may well have taken place in the Selborne area.

There was little peace for southern Britain from the end of the third century onwards. Until then the thoroughly Romanized districts of Britain, of which Hampshire was perhaps the most thoroughly Romanized of all, had enjoyed peace and quiet, and life for all but the slaves had gone very smoothly. But from about A.D. 280 onwards conditions began to change. The Irish began to raid the coasts of

Wales and Cornwall, and they planted colonies in Wales and perhaps also one or two in Cornwall, and there is a good deal of evidence that from now on there was much more unrest than usual among the Welsh. And at about the same time the Saxons began raiding down the Channel. Up until now the south of Britain had been in constant and close touch with Gaul and through Gaul with Rome itself. Her enemies had been far away to the north on the other side of the wall, and on the wall there was a strong army to deal with the raids. But now the frontiers began to change. From now on the wall was only one of the frontiers and by no means the most important. From now on the enemies of Rome were busily engaged in cutting the province of Britain off from the Continent. From now on the Romans in Britain had to defend themselves from all sides. The forts of the Saxon shore were not built at this time, but it was at this time that Britain first came to rely on sea-power. It was at this time, too, that the Roman leaders in the north, finding that the reins of the Imperial Government in Rome were not held so tightly as of old, since communication was more difficult, began to throw off the yoke and to set themselves up as Emperors on their own. And this, of course, must have made the life of ordinary citizens very much more difficult. Carausius (287–293) who was the Roman admiral in command of the galleys at Boulogne, revolted and made himself Emperor in Britain, and since he was with his fleet too strong to be quelled he managed to hold his own Imperial Purple for seven years, until he was murdered by his first minister Allectus. Britain under Carausius was severed from the Roman Empire proper, but Carausius was a great man and under him Britain seems to have enjoyed seven years of real prosperity. Carausius did not stop the raids of the Saxons down the Channel, but he attacked the raiders on their way home and thus secured a good deal of their booty. To do this he must have used ports on the south coast and he would have fortified these ports. He would have used Southampton Water and its associated inlets—no seaman of outstanding ability, as Carausius undoubtedly was, would have been blind to the advantages of that region—but we do not know which of the many possibilities he did use. For that matter we do not know when the great forts of the Saxon shore were built. They were not all built at the same time, and it seems probable that their organization was undertaken in the reign of Diocletian.

Of the nine forts of the Saxon shore eight have been identified beyond a doubt. The ninth is uncertain. It may have been Portchester. There has been a good deal of argument about it, but that need not concern us here. There was a fort at Portchester; there was another at Carisbrooke in the Isle of Wight; and some people suggest that there was a third at Bitterne. Both Portchester and Carisbrooke were built in the fourth century, but Bitterne is certainly very much older than that.

Portchester is now a square walled area, measuring about two hundred yards each way and enclosing about nine acres. This was the Roman fort, but since Portchester served as a fortress or a prison from the twelfth to the nineteenth century, most of it has been obliterated. The medieval castle-builder used the old Roman walls as his outer line of defence, and built within them the keep and the inner baily. The medieval keep and inner baily stand in the north-west corner of the Roman square, and in the south-east corner is the medieval church and the graveyard. The Roman walls were built of flint concrete and were some ten feet thick, and they were defended by semi-circular bastions, several of which still survive. Like most Roman forts of the period, Portchester has yielded to the excavator very few remains beyond a few coins of the fourth century, in this case chiefly those of Maximin Daza (305–314).

Bitterne is a site of a very different character. Situated on the east bank of the Itchen opposite Southampton, this was the Roman Clausentum, and it has yielded any amount of Roman remains. But it is by no means clear what precisely was the character of the Roman place. That it was occupied by the Romans almost from the beginning of their stay in Britain seems certain (and there are those like myself who believe that this was the first permanent settlement of the Romans after the invasion; that this was Vespasian's bridgehead and base), and it seems probable that it was always to some extent a military station. But whatever it was it was certainly not a fort built to repel the Saxon raiders, though it was almost certainly used for that purpose during the raids. There are signs that the fortifications were built up or perhaps repaired somewhat hurriedly; milestones were found in the walls, for example. Its situation, on the tidal estuary of the Itchen just where it makes a semi-circular bend so that on the north, west and south it is protected by the water, leaving only the narrow eastern approach to be protected by ditches and walls and such other means as seemed advisable, must have appealed to the Roman commander of the Saxon raid era as strongly as it had appealed to that great general Vespasian.

To-day, of course, Bitterne is a suburb of Southampton. The might of Rome lies buried. And everywhere is that so. A short stretch of wall here and there, a stretch of road here and there. But of four hundred years of occupation there is left practically nothing. The might of Rome lies buried under the soil of the island she conquered. The Roman imposed his will upon Nature just as he did upon the peoples he conquered, but Nature, whose stamina is inexhaustible, conquered the conqueror. Yet though the might of Rome has left scarcely a trace, there is all around you in Hampshire evidence of earlier civilizations. The Celt and those before him on these hills did not attempt to impose their wills upon Nature: rather were they influenced by Nature. They moulded their works to conform to Nature's will. And their buildings remain to this day as do their roads.

But we must go back to Silchester.

The unmistakable outline of Quarley Hill

CHAPTER III

THE NORTH-WESTERN HIGHLANDS

SHORTLY after you leave Silchester, following the old Port Way, you begin to climb. You are leaving the pine lands and coming on to the chalk. And soon you are on the Downs, and about six hundred feet up, and with every step you go further into wild country, and further away from modern England. These hills—seven, eight, nine hundred feet high (though they seem much higher)—have not altered at all from the time when they were trodden by small men of whom we know nothing beyond the scanty information we have gleaned from barrow and stone circle. Their surroundings have altered. Themselves they remain unchanged, proud and strong and truly wild.

On the highest of them the chalk is bare. The grass grows thinly and in tufts and is dry. There are junipers, many of them, and thorns, and thickets of gorse. There is no cultivation. The only sounds are the singing of larks, which you may hear on any day of the year, and the bleating of sheep and the ringing of their bells. And all the while the voice of the wind.

But here you will find no human beings. An occasional shepherd, perhaps—much more occasional now than even ten years ago—and he will be glad to talk in his quiet drawl of the birds and beasts and sometimes (if you get to know him well, and that is not easy) of the signs that are everywhere of a great civilization long since dead. You will find that he has a great regard for the tumuli and the barrows that he sees around him—and an unshakeable belief in ghosts. He lives among them. They know him and go about their occasions. The townsman they know not, and the townsman, his senses blunted by mechanical noise and the urgency of modern life, the haste of the motor-car and the jumble of bus and tube, the chatter of typewriters and the shrilling of telephones, is unaware of more delicate, more

69 F

The Gibbet on Inkpen—now in Berkshire

silent things. It is not easy for a townsman to spend a night alone, without covering, on these hills. Even the gipsies shun them. You may see them occasionally, but as a rule they keep to the lowland.

Perhaps a shepherd, perhaps a gipsy; beyond them nothing. The hills stretch north-east to north-west in a half-moon, and run for some ten miles. May be in all that ten miles—and the area covered must be more than thirty thousand acres—there live six hundred men (I should doubt it) and of these six hundred very, very few walk the tops. This is wild country.

You can walk all round the half-moon. The chalk falls away from you steeply. You look down upon rich cultivated land—rich and cultivated again now, because of the stress of war—but before the war not so well cultivated as once it was and as it always should have been, for the big land-owners had gone or were going, and the National Farmers' Union and the Central Landowners' Association that attempted to take their places made poor substitutes. The guidance and the love that without reserve the big land-owner used to lavish upon his land and those who worked it cannot be replaced by the impersonal regimented guidance that comes from a central body necessarily divorced from intimacy. The land thrives upon love, upon intimacy with those that it supports. We face an era of still fewer big landowners, of still greater regimentation. This land, this great plain stretched out before you, is well cultivated now because we still live in the aftermath of war. Shortly it will, I fear, return to the state of lazy cultivation in which it passed the twenty years between the wars. But upon the hills you have nothing to do with the land so displayed below you. You are isolated, unaffected.

But it looks very beautiful stretched there before you like the masterpiece of a great painter. The Kennet runs across it, coming from Marlborough and passing through Newbury to join the Thames, in lower country yet, at Reading. You can see the plain stretching away towards the Thames, a plain of many greens and here and there well chequer-boarded in the traditional style. Above you the lark sings and away to your right is the music of the sheep bell. It is very quiet on the down tops, but the country spread before you is even more still; no sounds come up. And over it you watch the play of sun and cloud. Now these few fields are blue and those brilliantly green. You can watch the sun strike through there and there and there, and the blue leave the green. You can watch the rain come down there on your right and immediately below you are cattle lazing in the sun. And around you the wind is freshening, and the great clouds mounting the sky. Up here, even on hot days in drought, there is always a small wind to freshen you. Below you the fields give you a hard stare, and the woods lie bloated, metallic like solid lumps of lead. All the world is silent. Down there you know it is hot and smelly with moist tar, and petrol fumes heavy between the hedges, and there will be the blare of horns and the screech of brakes. Up here is a small wind to freshen you. Away to the northward, almost as bare but by no means as grand as these hills, are the Berkshire downs looking back at you across the vale of Kennet. Away, there to the west, is Wiltshire, which is the county of downs, the sire of all these chalk hills of Berkshire and Hampshire and Sussex and Kent. You cannot say where Hampshire ends and Wiltshire begins here at the northernmost limit of their boundary. But all that over there to the west where is that sky without colour is Wiltshire, and those black dots are clumps of beeches. Somewhere over there to the west—as somewhere over there on the northerly downs—is the Ridgeway, that great prehistoric trackway. Somewhere over there is Avebury. Not so very far away. Distance is nothing when you are on these hills. And behind you, all this to the southward, east and west, is Hampshire.

I am standing on Inkpen Beacon, a thousand feet high. And I am not in Hampshire at all, but in Berkshire. And that only goes to show how foolish are the maps. Not so very long ago Inkpen was in Hampshire. Spiritually, geologically, in every way but cartographically it is in Hampshire still: geographically, too (despite what the maps may say), for Inkpen is the natural frontier on the north. Inkpen belongs to the Hampshire downs and not to the Berkshire downs that are so very different from it in every respect.

And so to look on these wild hills I stand on the greatest of them. I am in Hampshire. The map lies; not I.

On the highest point of Inkpen stands a double gibbet. It is the third to be erected. The first was put up in 1676 for the hanging of a man and a woman, villagers of Combe. I do not know what happened to that gibbet, probably it just rotted and fell down, but the one that was erected in its place was struck by lightning, and this is the third. There are a number of stories about the man and the woman, and this is the one that I like best. The woman was a widow with two children. The man was married, and had for wife a vinegary female whose charms altogether failed to make up for the sharpness of her tongue and the foulness of her cooking. The widow on the other hand cooked well and was complacent. She and the man were lovers, but the wife found out. So one day the man took his wife for a walk along the downland track that runs through Walbury Camp, a track far more ancient than the Roman roads, and coming to the dew pond, that is now known as Murderer's Pool (and this dew pond I have never seen dry), pushed her in and kept her there until she should trouble him no more. And that evening he went to the widow, and being a coarse man and cruel (and without brains) he told her not in a whisper (as wisdom would have dictated) but loudly and with boasts of what he had done. The widow was frightened, and begged him to speak softly; and when he would not, told him that she had only just put the children to bed upstairs and that if he talked so loudly they would surely hear, might indeed already have heard. Whereupon the man climbed the stairs to see if they were asleep, and if not to murder them both. The younger was asleep: the elder was awake, but had wit enough to pretend that he was not, and the man returned to his paramour satisfied. And the next day the child told. And the villagers arose and made both man and woman prisoner. Combe then was in Hampshire. And the tale goes on to tell how it became a part of Berkshire. The villagers having taken man and woman, and secured them safely, sent to Winchester in order that justice might be done. But to Winchester men these hills were far away, and wild and useless. The Win-

chester authorities would not stir in the matter. And so
finally the Berkshire people were appealed to, and they
came and erected the gibbet and hanged the man and the
woman, one from each arm. And having gone to considerable trouble, and no doubt a little expense, Berkshire
claimed Combe as payment. And that is why Combe is in
Berkshire when it should be in Hampshire.

The real reason is, of course, quite different—and a little
less sordid. Owing to the difficulty in getting over the bad
roads to Andover, it was decided that Hungerford, which is
very much nearer and was accessible by a very much better
road, would be a more convenient centre for rating purposes. And so the village was transferred to Hungerford and
became a part of Berkshire. But that does not make it
Berkshire. The survey of 1882, revised in 1901, and published in 1903 under the direction of Colonel Johnston,
Director-General of the Ordnance Survey, said Combe was
in Berkshire. The villagers knew he was wrong. In the
General Election of 1906—Director-General or no Director-
General—they repaired to Andover to record their votes.
Combe is Hampshire. And even to-day the more elderly
villagers regard Combe as in Hampshire and themselves as
Hampshire men. I do not know that the younger men and
women have inherited the same fine spirit of independence
as their fathers, but I do know that most of them seem to
go to work in Hampshire.

I suppose that the capital of this highland area would be
Kingsclere. It is a sleepy little town, but quietly beautiful
in its magnificent downland setting, and there are some
delightful houses bordering its streets, and there is a really
fine Norman church, which has been rather too ruthlessly
restored. Kingsclere was a royal manor under the Saxon
kings, and there are charters and documents dating back to
the eighth century. With the Normans it passed to the
church, for William swopped the lands here for lands in
Winchester in order that he might build his castle in the
latter town. But the Norman monarchs came here a good
deal to hunt, and King John in particular was here often.
Kingsclere was busier then than now, and it was quite a
busy little place until about the middle of the nineteenth

century. Now the market is empty; comparatively few
motor-cars pass through, for this is not a main road, and
there is not a railway: an ideal place to live. But though it
is off the map for the tourist, and though its market is
empty, Kingsclere is not a name unknown to modern townsmen. On the downs are the famous Kingsclere stables,
where the great John Porter trained. On the perfect turf
of these downs many of the greatest of English thoroughbreds have galloped, and many a famous winner has been
sent to Epsom and Newmarket and Newbury from here—
among them Ormond, and Common, and Flying Fox.

I suppose that most people would call Kingsclere a
village and not a town, but I think that it well deserves to
rank as a town even though modern high-speed life passes
it by. It is the only town of the district. But there are some
very interesting villages dotted over these highlands. High-
clere boasts of its park, which it maintains is the loveliest in
southern England (and I would not argue about that) and
of course there is the beauty of wooded Sidown Hill towering above. This park used to be one of the country seats of
the Bishops of Winchester. The castle—it is comparatively
modern—is now the home of the Earls of Carnarvon.
Burghclere has a twelfth-century church and a twentieth-
century shrine. The church is small, but it has three lovely
doorways, two of them Norman and the third by our earliest
English builders. The Norman doorways are on either side
of the nave. The one you enter by has a big decorated arch,
the other is very small and has a tympanum scaled like a
sea-monster. The third doorway has graceful foliaged
pillars and an arch with rows of moulding. The other thing
that I like particularly about this church—it is altogether
one of the most charming in Hampshire—is the pulpit,
which is made of hand-wrought steel. The twentieth-
century shrine is the Oratory of All Souls, rising like a
tower between two wings, which are two houses of charity.
The notable thing about it is its decoration, the pictures
covering its walls, painted on canvas by Mr. Stanley
Spencer, who spent six years on them. They are not, I
think, beautiful. They are starkly realistic. I imagine that
they will shock most people at first sight, and after the

quiet of the old church they are as shocking and breath-taking as a cold douche. I suppose that they are meant to be disturbing; I think that they are meant to shake one out of complacence. They certainly succeed. The canvases are huge. They overwhelm. They should be seen. But not more than once.

Two of the hamlets must be mentioned, and ought to be visited, if for no other reason than that they are so isolated. Woodcot is a tiny place with lovely views. The church, which has some beautiful carving from Belgium, is very much overshadowed by the yew. This is a giant, very decrepit now, but still very much alive and good for many years yet. It is said to be the largest yew in Hampshire, and it has a girth of nearly thirty feet. The other hamlet is Binley, which Cobbett thought one of the most isolated places that he knew in Hampshire. It is a long time since Cobbett was here, but things have not altered much. The landlady of the little cottage inn—which is called The Hurdler's Arms, a relic of the days when the sheep controlled the life of all this area—is also the schoolmistress, and teaches her pupils in a little room adjoining the parlour. When last I was there she had but three pupils, little fair-haired girls. But perhaps Binley is not the most isolated of these little villages; perhaps that honour belongs to Tangley. There is a story that would support Tangley's claim at any rate. Tangley is on a spur of these hills, separated from the main body by a trough of lower ground (but not so low as all of it is about 600 feet high) and you should really come to it up the main road from Hurst-bourne Tarrant. At the entrance to Doles Wood is a minor road on the right, and this is the road that leads in a matter of three miles or so to Tangley. It is a road that should not be missed for it has all the way magnificent scenery. It runs along the edge of the wood and it climbs all the time. Beyond Eastend Farm the ground slopes away, but the road keeps pretty high all the way to the cross-roads formed by the junction with the Roman road from Winchester to Cirencester. The built-up causeway of the old Roman road can be followed easily and as straight as ever crow flew to Hampshire Gate, which is the boundary with

Wiltshire. And here you can look on the fine sweep of
Cathanger Wood (which is in Wiltshire) and all around are
downs. Ahead, sweep upon sweep, to Marlborough and
beyond: behind, sweep upon sweep, to Walbury and Inkpen and Sidedown and the bluff naked head of Beacon Hill:
you can see Danebury with its old crown of trees, and far
down the valley the tower of Andover's church: you can see
the unmistakable slopes of Quarley, and the lofty highlands
sweeping round Lobscombe; in the far distance you can see
the spire of Salisbury: and, turning again, there before you
is a panorama of western Hampshire, the downs by Winchester and Stockbridge, a great sweep rushing up to join
their sire in Wiltshire, the woods where the land falls away,
and here and there cornfields and plough. If anyone tells
you that Hampshire scenery is dull and of a sameness, take
him to Hampshire Gate, and make him eat his words.
Keeping straight on over the junction of the old Roman
road and the modern lane, you come very soon to Tangley,
and Tangley, though not architecturally beautiful, is a
lovely village. It is a hill-top village, perched among woods
above a narrow cleft in the chalk, and it is still remote.
Indeed, it is called by Hampshire folk God-forsaken Tadley.
And this is how the name came about. Some fifty years
ago a balloon descended in a cottager's garden here, and
the balloonist, having lost his bearings, walked up to the
cottage to inquire as to his whereabouts. But the manner
of his coming had struck terror into the heart of the Tadley
man. Had he not with his own eyes seen this man come
down from heaven? So he dropped on his knees, and in
answer to the request for the name of the village, cried:
"Oh! Lord Almighty, forgive us, this is God-forsaken
Tadley." Such things can no longer bother the good men
of Tadley, for the Royal Air Force has its clutches firmly
into all this country, and the most common sound is the
sound of aeroplanes. Hill-top villages—it has been my
experience—are inhospitable, and you might expect to find
that Tadley was so, for there is but little of the Saxon about
the people here. There is still much of the old forester blood,
and the men are small and dark for the most part. But
Tadley is not inhospitable at all. The men are slow of

speech with a stranger, but they are neither suspicious nor hostile. And the inn (still an *inn*) is welcoming and provides extremely drinkable bitter. Men lived in Tangley many centuries ago, and many centuries ago, before history was made, men worshipped where Tangley church now stands. The church has been rebuilt, but still retains some Saxon details. It is not a remarkable church: indeed to my mind at least it is relieved from mediocrity only by its font. This is lead: and though I am not sure that those who call it Jacobean are correct, I do know that it is the only one in Hampshire, and that there are very few in all England. The churchyard makes up for any failings on the part of the church. There is a remarkably fine yew, and there are also three great sarsen stones beside whose rough grey ancientness the great yew is but a babe in arms. Once upon a time there were certainly more of these great stones in the neighbourhood, and it is not altogether impossible that once there was a stone circle here.

To return to the hills. The rampart is all chalk, but inside the rampart, where the hills run here and there, so that you are for ever discovering some new and snug little valley, the ground is richer. The heart is still of chalk, but over it there has been laid during the passage of year upon year for many hundreds of years, some twenty feet or so of clay and flints. And over the clay, as year has climbed upon year, the grass has withered and been drawn in by the frosts, so that there is now a rich loam above the clay, and this loam is two or three feet thick in places. Here is soil as rich as you could wish. And here before the war was much derelict land. Agriculture in England then was dying fast. It was saved not by an Englishman, not by a Tory Government nor yet by a Socialist Government; it was saved by an Austrian ex-corporal. The fear of empty bellies moved our politicians to save the agriculture of England. And as soon as the danger of empty bellies is removed the House of Commons will forget about the rich soils of England once again. Wherever you go in these hills inside the rampart's edge you will find warm hollows, where the plough-lands run up —too frequently nowadays one must say *used* to run up— to meet the coppices just where the chalk breaks through

and gleams white above rabbit-bitten turf. Here where the
ground mounts up you will find primroses and violets, and
a little later still cowslips—cowslips that put their lowland
brethren to shame—and bluebells; and here a little later
still there will be masses of wild mignonette, and in the
shade tall foxgloves will stand, stately and dreaming. Here
the wild rose grows in profusion. And where the wild rose
grows there may you grow wheat. How soon will it be
before once again flowers bloom upon the grave of English
agriculture?

Here in these hollows where the wild flowers stand in deep
pools of yellow and blue; here where the hazels line the
edge, you may see finches and pipits, may lie and listen all
the day long to the sweet babbling of larks and to that
laziest of all sounds in nature, the coo-ing of wood-pigeons,
caught and thrown back to you by the hills, so that all the
air throbs with deep warm sound; here are whinchats and
here the yaffle, the green woodpecker of ornithologists, with
swooping flight from edge to edge, and laughing cheerful
cry. And on the tops are wheatears, and stone curlew and
curlew, and lapwings and many, many larks. The kestrel
hovers above and the sparrow-hawk beats among the thorns
on his occasional visits from below. Twice have I seen the
hobby with swift flight skimming some outhanging bluff,
and more than twice the noble peregrine. And here in
winter are great flocks of tits and finches, yellowhammers
and bramblings, great concourses of rooks and pigeons,
vast multitudes of starlings, and many, many fieldfares,
but redwings I have never seen on the tops. And here in
winter the buzzard will sometimes circle in majestic mastery
over the cold bare hills.

There are not many trees. Junipers and a yew or so—
the yew is the tree of Hampshire, and has been called the
Hampshire weed, but it is more at home a little further
south—and thorns leaning over at drunken angles forced
thus by the wind, and in the hollows hazels (though I never
regard the hazel as truly a tree) and perhaps some beeches.
There are oaks, but no great oaks such as you may find in
mid-Sussex, for the soil is too shallow and the hills too
exposed, the wind too strong. Here are no gigantic elms,

as in the Vale of Pewsey that runs between the downs
farther to the west; here are no gracious chestnuts. The
trees here are trees that mind not exposure, that can fight
the wind. This is an exposed country. The wind here is
master. It is not a luxurious country. Things grow here
because they are strong and proud in their strength. The
hedges are tall and broad and thick, but they are so because
they *fight* to shelter that beyond them from the wind: they
do not grow, as do hedges elsewhere, to offer shade and
relaxation. There is nothing luxurious about this land.
The wind is master, not the sun.

There is very little water. No river naturally enough, but
also no streams. Such water as there is comes from ponds,
the majority of them dew-ponds, and the largest of these
does not measure more than forty yards or so across. And
in all these ponds there are no fish, not even minnows,
which I find rather extraordinary since the dew-ponds of
the downs farther south hold fish in plenty, and I know of
one that holds fair-sized carp, which is also rather extraordinary. Toads here are very uncommon, and frogs are
few, though again on the downs to the south both are
moderately plentiful. But almost every pond holds newts,
and I know of one where the great crested newt, an imposing, even, in appearance, terrifying creature, breeds in
great numbers. And on the bare chalk I have seen lizards
sunning themselves.

This land, despite the fact that you see hawks and owls
about more frequently than in most parts of Hampshire, is
very highly preserved. Or rather it used to be up to the
outbreak of the second German war. The old landowners
have all gone—the landowners that might be called indigenous—and why I do not know. If you were to ask one
—or his descendant—the answer would certainly have
something to do with death duties. But that, I strongly
suspect, would not be the real reason. Anyhow they have
gone. And with their going went good farming. In their
place have come men whose money was made and is still being made in big cities: men whose only interest in the country
lies in the sport that the country can provide. Their manners
are the manners of the towns, their knowledge the know-

ledge of cocktail-parties and drawing-rooms (there are exceptions: I know two at any rate): they have no being here: they are foreigners. But I welcome them—even those who do not know the names of their gamekeepers (and if that sounds odd, it is true; I was asked to shoot with a great landowner not so long ago who had not the faintest idea of the names of any of his gamekeepers)—because they preserve the country-side as country-side, and because from them will spring (if the new order will allow landowners of any size) a new aristocracy of the country-side to take the place of that degenerate aristocracy that has left; and with this new aristocracy will come, if progress does not move too quickly in the meanwhile, a new prosperity for the country-side. And so I welcome them. I do not align myself with that large body of opinion (an almost entirely urban body incidentally) to whom the large-scale preservation of game is as a red rag to a bull. Some of their arguments have more than a grain of truth in them, I know. But I know, too, that in these days when Progress has the bit between her teeth, land which is not highly farmed or highly preserved is doomed to the tender mercies of the builder, the nightmares of the planner, or the untidy litter of the poultry-farmer. Nor have I any room for the "old school tie" attitude that regards with contempt this new aristocracy of the country-side. The old (with great and noble exceptions: and happily there are yet some in Hampshire) cared little for the country-side that was their heritage and their trust. I know that the large-scale preserver of game is also a menace to farming on occasions. There is more than one example in Hampshire. But they are few and far between, taking the country as a whole, and as a whole they are also large-scale preservers of the country-side. To them, therefore, I doff my hat . . . with the pious hope that they or their sons will one day ally their interest in sport to an interest in agriculture, and so will one day truly take the place of those that have gone, and of the emasculated associations that are at present endeavouring—and nobly against fearful odds—to fill the gap.

This, then, is land highly preserved in normal times.

Hares are everywhere. I have seen twenty or more in one field on an April evening. And rabbits—well, rabbits are everywhere. I do not know how many were shot anually before the war, but I should guess at some twenty thousand or so, and judging from a recent visit the gassing campaign had little or no effect on these hills. These rabbits are smaller than their cousins of the lowlands and rather darker in colouring. From the shooting point of view new blood is sorely needed. From every other point of view really energetic action is needed. Shooting apart, rabbits are pests and could all be destroyed with advantage; not only here, but everywhere throughout the country. I do not like rabbits. I do not even like their floppy ears and pretty white scuts. I regard the rabbit as a pest, a pest that does untold harm and has practically no food value. They benefit nobody but those that shoot or, as is the case in many parts of the country to-day, those that make big money by trapping. I confess that I like shooting rabbits. It is good fun. But I would gladly see every rabbit exterminated by other means. And pigeons—well, pigeons are everywhere. And at certain seasons their numbers are increased by vast hordes from the Continent. It is my belief that an increasing rabbit population means an increasing pigeon population, though I know I could not support that belief in debate. It is my belief, too, that the rat has increased vastly on these hills of recent years despite—or because of?—the preservation of game. The rat, of course, increases everywhere, for in his philosophy everything can be turned to advantage. But I believe that we materially assist the rat when we shoot owls and other predatory birds . . . and I believe that the rat, which has no single quality other than courage to recommend it, does much more damage than any predatory bird. This land is highly preserved and truly wild and free. But despite the richness of the soil in the hollows it is not rich land. On the other hand it is not really poor land—though some, thinking in terms of the lush water-meadows and fat dairy cattle and hard cash might term it so. It is just a remote land, poor and inconsiderable in terms of money and population, but rich in everything else.

And that is as it should be. It has been so since before history. We cannot say that the earliest human inhabitants of Hampshire came to these hills, for we do not know, but we do know that the earliest of British civilizations was on these hills, and from then onwards these hills are crammed with the history of England, even as is the rest of Hampshire.

The earliest human inhabitants of Hampshire of whom we have any trace are the men of the Old Stone Age. There may have been men in Britain, there may have been men in Hampshire, before Palæolithic man—we cannot say that there were not simply because we have no record of any such occupation—but Palæolithic man is the first that has left us undeniable evidence of his existence. He has left it in the form of rude stone implements, flints chipped into the rough shape of axes, borers, and other tools and weapons.

The men of the Old Stone Age used to be called the River Drift men (the name has, I believe, gone completely out of fashion) because these stone relics of their sojourn in Britain are found in beds of gravel, which have been formed by the drifting power of rivers and floods that washed the gravel down from higher levels. The beds that contain these stone implements in Hampshire are found capping the cliffs at Barton, Hordle, Stubbington, Hill Head, Lee-on-Solent, along the shores of Southampton Water, and in similar situations, often as high as one hundred feet above sea-level. There are other beds of implement-bearing gravel inland, along the course of streams or the courses of former rivers. Such beds are found at Winchester and Alresford on the Itchen, at Romsey and Stockbridge on the Test, at Christchurch and Fordingbridge on the Avon, at various sites on the Loddon, at Southampton and at Highfield, and at many other places in the county. Many of these gravel beds are more than one hundred feet above the present levels of the streams, and this means that the water must then have flowed at a higher elevation than at present.

In fact, the first thing that we must realize about the Hampshire of Palæolithic man is that it was very different from the Hampshire of historic times, not only in its geography but also in its climate. The whole county stood at least six hundred feet higher than it does to-day. The Isle of Wight was part of the mainland, overlooking the valleys of the Solent and Spithead rivers, and the much greater valley of the Channel river into which the Solent and Spithead flowed. The Isle of Wight was then, in fact, a range of wooded hills. The climate was then Continental. Probably the mountains of Wales and Northern England and Scotland had snow-caps and glaciers, and the country between the Isle of Wight and the mountains was probably treeless tundra. This was the country of the mammoth and the reindeer and the bison. Herds of reindeer in the winter, and vast herds of bison in the summer, grazed across the valley of the Channel. In the spring and through the summer the woolly rhinoceros and the mammoth ranged the woodlands. These were the quarry of Palæolithic man, and his movements must have been largely conditioned by the food supply, though they were also conditioned by the presence or absence of salt, and of course by the necessity of keeping within range of a supply of flints for his weapons. He was at any rate a nomad pure and simple. He had no permanent habitation. He followed the herds. And the only records of his existence that he has left us in Hampshire are his crude stone implements.

In mesolithic times the character of the fauna changed. Man also changed his weapons. Upper Palæolithic man had improved upon the weapons of Lower Palæolithic man. He had learned how to kill from a distance. We have no evidence of this in Hampshire, for we have no caves, but the cave-dwellers of Creswell and Paviland—and they probably only occupied their caves in winter—had learned to kill their reindeer and their wild horses with flint or bone or ivory-headed lances propelled from spear-throwers. Mesolithic man went further. He replaced the lance by the bow and arrow, the arrow being tipped by tiny microliths. It is just possible that he had also domesticated the dog sufficiently to use it in his hunting. All these people were nomads, moving about in small groups, family parties rather than tribes, in pursuit of game and fish, roots and berries, and other natural products, and collecting their flints in the same way, from the surface spreads left behind by eroded chalk or boulder-clay, or using nodules taken from old gravels. If there was no other source of supply available these people used pebbles picked up from the beaches.

New Stone Age or Neolithic man, on the other hand, raised a large proportion of his food by his own efforts. There is a very great gap between Palæolithic man and Neolithic man: a very great gap not only in time but also in achievement. It is not possible to put a date to Palæolithic man—you can say that he lived in Hampshire forty thousand years ago, if you like; it is as good a guess as any —but it is possible to put a date to Neolithic man. He lived in Hampshire approximately two thousand five hundred years before Christ. Now, there were two sorts of Neolithic man who lived in Britain, and they are distinguished by their cultures, chiefly by the ware they used. Megalithic man preferred the chalk and oolite uplands, and Peterborough man, who probably arrived a little later in time, preferred the river valleys. The two cultures are quite distinct, the pottery of the Peterborough people being much more barbarous than that of the western or Megalithic people. The culture of the western peoples derived ultimately from the Mediterranean, while the other had spread from the northern fringes of Neolithic Europe, carried by a poor fisher folk who were in many ways still more Mesolithic than Neolithic in their way of life. But these two peoples soon met on the downs of Wessex, and some fusion took place between the two cultures. The result of this fusion was the birth of a distinctive British pottery.

But though Neolithic man raised a large proportion of his food by his own efforts he was still essentially a nomad, though now a pastoral rather than a hunting nomad. He has, therefore, left but little trace of habitation behind him, though he has left "camps," which were certainly not built for defensive purposes, since the banks are much too slight to be of defensive value, but were probably the headquarters of cattle-raising tribes—stockades in which the herdsmen could confine their charges.

But if Neolithic man did not leave many signs of habita-

Ladle and Sidown Hills. On Ladle Hill
is an unfinished encampment

tion, he did leave for posterity many of his burials. The Long Barrow belongs to Neolithic man.

Long Barrows are mounds of earth or stone, varying in length between 75 and 300 feet, and in width between 45 and 100 feet. In height they are generally between four and twelve feet. Neither the height nor the width are uniform as a rule. Long Barrows tend to be higher and wider at one end than the other, and the higher and wider end is usually placed towards the east, north-east or south-east. There are several types of Long Barrow. Where large blocks of stone were easily obtainable these were used in the mound to make an internal chamber of stone, but in Hampshire only chalk and earth, and perhaps some wood, were used. The primary burials—barrows were often opened up by later peoples and other burials made in them—in Long Barrows were always by inhumation of the skeleton, which was usually placed in a doubled-up position and occasionally had with it an arrow-head or a pottery vessel.

Long Barrows are uncommon in Hampshire, which, considering the amount of chalk upland, is strange. Even stranger is the absence of any mining. Neolithic man was not content to get his flint in the manner of Mesolithic man. He was an accomplished and disciplined miner, and he worked the chalk on a grand scale. Grime's Graves in Norfolk bear witness to his skill. These mines were the first to be explored in England and they have received more attention than any others. But mines have also been found in Sussex and Wiltshire. None have been found in Hampshire, though there is some evidence of mining activity near Medstead. It seems, therefore, that (having regard to the wealth of chalk available) there were regular mining communities, and that the flints were traded all over the country. Axes from North Wales were in Wessex in Neolithic times, which suggests a trade between communities separated by long distances, and this suggests a higher degree of civilization and organization than would appear at first sight.

About 1900 B.C. came fresh waves of invasion. These people came in by two routes: one from Brittany by way of Christchurch and so up the Avon and into the heart of

*Abbots Ann—the Thatch is
Wiltshire in treatment*

Wessex; the other from the Rhine mouth into eastern England, penetrating deep into the country by means of the Thames and the Fen rivers. It is often stated that the Beaker Folk belong to the Bronze Age, but they had, in fact, no higher civilization than the Neolithic peoples they found in occupation of the country. They brought no metals with them, but they did open up trade routes. And they buried their dead in a different manner.

These Beaker Folk introduced the Round Barrow. The Neolithic people who used the Long Barrows were a long-headed race. The Beaker Folk were a round-headed race. Dr. John Thurnam, the greatest of all authorities on barrows, summed it up thus: "Long barrows . . . long skulls; round barrows . . . round skulls." It is a generalization, of course, but it is accurate enough.

There are other forms of barrow. There are Bowl Barrows, shaped like a bowl inverted. These vary a great deal in shape and size. Some are only some five yards in diameter and a few inches in height; some are as much as fifty yards across and as much as twenty-five feet in height. They are the most common of our barrows, accounting for about 60 per cent of the total of all barrows in the country. They are, of course, merely a form of Round Barrow. In them there was a simple inhumation with a crouched skeleton. Another form of the Round Barrow was the Bell Barrow. This probably came about two hundred years later, say about 1700 B.C., and is a barrow with a ledge or platform between the mound and the ditch. In the earliest types the inhumation is a simple one with a crouched skeleton, but in the later ones there is a burial of cremated remains in urns. Disc Barrows are a further development of the Bell Barrow. They consist of a small central mound placed on a platform of considerable size, which is surrounded by a ditch, which has an outer bank. The distance from bank to bank may be as much as sixty yards. There is some evidence of a transition barrow, a barrow between the Bell and the Disc, in the New Forest. Ring Barrows are merely circular platforms surrounded by a ditch. They are most uncommon. There are a good many examples of ring-work in the country, but they do not all contain evidence of burial; not by any means, most in fact seem to have been designed for some quite different purpose. Another form of barrow is the Saucer Barrow. Personally, I am not at all sure that distinction from the Disc Barrow is justified, for it seems to me that these barrows may well be Disc Barrows with the central mound spread all over the platform. In the same way there seems to me to be no justification for the Pond Barrow, which is an inverted Bowl Barrow, and which was much more likely a habitation circle. But it must be admitted that they usually occur in association with barrows proper. Table Barrows are Round Barrows with flat tops. There are two types: one with a mound between one and four feet high and some twenty yards across; the other only a few inches high and anything between ten and twenty yards across. The latter type usually have a dip in the centre. Platform Barrows are very large barrows that look rather like Round Barrows with their tops removed. There are some excellent examples in the New Forest. Roman Barrows are usually large and steep. They may be oval but as a general rule they are rather like Platform Barrows, though higher and steeper and with flattened tops. Saxon Barrows are also of two types. The very large type with steep sides and conical in shape, in which the chiefs were buried, and very small ones, really no more than grave mounds, in which ordinary folk were buried and which are generally clustered close together.

The distribution of barrows is interesting and important. Nearly all the Long Barrows in Neolithic Wessex are on the chalk. There are many Long Barrows on Cotswold as well, and there is an almost complete absence of stone circles on Cotswold. This seems to suggest that the stone circle is of later date than the Long Barrow, which puts the date of Avebury and Stonehenge later than popular tradition would have it. Again there is a noticeable absence of Long Barrows from the New Forest. There are, as a matter of fact, very few Neolithic remains in Hampshire except on the chalk. Once chalk ceased to be an essential of life, the distribution map changes in the most striking fashion. Round Barrows are thick over Wessex as a whole, and very large Round Barrows are to be found in some numbers in the New Forest, and especially on the heaths near Beaulieu. All this must have been part of a great civilization dating from the early Bronze Age and centring round Avebury and Stonehenge.

It must not be thought that barrow burial belongs only to the prehistoric period. The Round Barrow has a very long history in Britain. Though they were first used in Britain about 1900 B.C., and are, therefore, commonly thought of as being prehistoric and belong to the Stone Age, they continued to be built until at least A.D. 650 and probably much later than that.

It is probable that during the Beaker period traders came to Britain fairly frequently, bringing with them bronze implements. They were the forerunners of a large-scale invasion from western Europe. These men had an aristocracy and military power, and they had in their employment craftsmen and merchants. They seized power on Salisbury Plain, and while under their rule trade was carried on on a very wide scale—gold from Ireland, amber from Jutland, trinkets from Central Europe, beads from Egypt, are found in their graves—under their rule also was developed a distinctive bronze industry that is recognizably British. This period of the Bronze Age lasted for almost a thousand years. During it there was developed a network of roads—some of them taken over from the earlier races, but many of them undoubtedly made in order to carry the trade of the ruling caste—but these roads were not roads in the sense in which we now use the word. There is no evidence of wheeled traffic in Britain before the late Bronze Age (but in this connexion it must be remembered that the only parts of a wheeled vehicle likely to furnish archæological evidence would be those parts made of metal; there may well have been wheeled vehicles made without the aid of metal at all) and so metalled roads were not needed. Though a sort of sleigh was probably used, most of the traffic was almost certainly carried on pack horses. Tracks were good enough for this purpose, and some of them remain to this day. Originally these tracks were not fixed; they travelled in a general direction rather than a fixed line. But

in the course of time some of them became fixed and well
defined and these are the tracks that we can follow to-day
for great parts of their length. Such are the great thorough-
fares of the chalk country, notably those linking Wessex
with Kent and Norfolk. The great Ridgeway, which does
not come within the Hampshire border, is perhaps the best
example. The Harrow Way, linking Salisbury with Dover,
enters the county just to the north of Andover, passes south
of Basingstoke, and then, bearing a little southwards, goes
through Farnham to reach the Hog's Back and the North
Downs. Portions of this trackway can still be followed and
I have walked them. There are at least two other ridgeways
in Hampshire, and both are easier to follow than the Harrow
Way. One enters the county near Quarley Hill, and then
travels eastwards to Danebury, Woolbury, St. Catherine's
Hill, Butser Hill, and so on to the South Downs. The other
runs from Winklebury westwards past the camps on Ladle
Hill and Beacon Hill and so to Walbury and Fosbury. Both
of these can be followed for many miles and make excellent
walks. And there are other tracks which, though they
cannot now be followed for any distance, strongly suggest
that once they were well used, as well used as the great
tracks that have survived.

I have just mentioned the camp on Ladle Hill. Camp is
not quite the right word. Hill-fort is better. These hill-
forts are among the most impressive of our prehistoric
antiquities. They do not properly belong to the Bronze
Age, but to the early Iron Age, and though they were undoubtedly used for defensive purposes they must have had
other uses as well. These are not properly understood and
give rise to a good deal of controversy. Hill-forts are impressive because of their size, the height of their ramparts,
the depth of their ditches, and because of the commanding
position in which so many of them have been built. Their
size shows that they must have been considered of great
importance by the people who built them. But the contrast
between these people, the size of their population, the stage
of development they had reached, and the size of these
forts has never been satisfactorily explained.

There are a great many hill-forts in Hampshire. Indeed,

there is scarcely a height that does not bear traces of a fort, and many of them are practically intact. Almost they are so placed as to afford a view on all sides, and many of them are very large. Hampshire cannot boast a Maiden Castle, but Hampshire has Quarley Hill, which is almost as impressive, and Walbury, which encloses an area nearly half a mile wide. And we have also Beacon Hill, and Bury Hill, and Woolbury Ring, and Danebury, and St. Catherine's Hill, and Old Winchester Hill, and Hengistbury Head, and many more besides. Each one is worth visiting, if only for the view. But as one stands on the crest of one of these old forts one cannot help but wonder what sort of a casualty list the Romans had. It is interesting, too, to see with what skill the builders used the lie of the land. Hengistbury Head is a good example of this. Here is an area well defined by the sea to the south and Christchurch to the north. All that was necessary to turn the position into a stronghold was to cut the narrow approach from the west. And this was done by cutting a couple of ditches and throwing up a couple of steep banks, which effectively seal off an area of several hundred acres. Another good example is that of Butser Hill. Butser is about 800 feet high, and on all sides except the south there is a steep drop of several hundred feet. Cutting off the approach from the south is a single ditch and bank.

Hampshire also provides evidence of the way in which these hill-forts were constructed, for in the county, in these north-western highlands, there is at Ladle Hill an unfinished example. Here you can see that the first thing that was done was to mark out the course of the ditch. The matter that was taken from the ditch went to the making of the rampart. The beginning of this work is preserved at Ladle Hill, for you can see the commencement of the ditch and the course that it was intended to take marked out in the form of a shallow trench. How this shallow trench was traced originally is not known, but it seems probable that it was first marked by a plough furrow. The work of digging the ditch was not done in a continuous line. That is evident from the remains of the proposed Ladle Hill fort, where the ditch is intermittent. Obviously separate gangs were at work on different lengths of the ditch at the same time, and when each gang had finished their length, the various lengths would be joined up and graded. Ladle Hill, from the size of the area that it was proposed to enclose, was going to be a very important fort indeed, so that it may be taken that the method of construction adopted was the latest and best method. One of the chief problems that faced the builders of hill-forts in chalk country was that of preventing the chalk ramparts from falling back into the ditch. You can see how they did it at Ladle Hill. Here the beginnings of the chalk rampart forms an irregular bank, and some way behind it are a number of small mounds that contain loose material—earth, small chalk blocks and so on. Obviously the method followed was to arrange the excavation in such a manner that a firm bed of relatively large chalk blocks was heaped near the edge of the ditch, while the turf, surface chalk and so on was taken well back from the ditch ready to be put on at a later stage. Excavations at Quarley Hill show that this method was followed there as well. But at Quarley Hill additional height was gained for the ramparts by adding to them surface scrapings from within the fortified area. Standing on Quarley Hill you can see how the ancient trackways (and the Roman roads, too) were sighted. They were sighted from skyline to skyline. The prehistoric surveyor laid his roads thus, and so did the Roman. Stand on Quarley Hill and you can look back to Cæsar's Belt on the distant skyline, a matter of eighteen miles away, and you can look forward a matter of a dozen miles to the great mound of Old Sarum on the skyline. And just by Quarley Hill runs the Roman road that we call the Port Way, on its journey from Silchester to Old Sarum. The Roman surveyor stood on Quarley Hill to lay his road, but I think that he did no more than verify the work of some other surveyor who stood on the same spot many thousands of years earlier.

The hill-fort on St. Catherine's must be the best known in Hampshire. It is easily seem from the train to Bournemouth, and every visitor to the ancient city of Winchester must at least look at the hill with its crown of beech trees almost at the highest point. St. Catherine's is not a big fort as hill-forts go in Hampshire, but it must have been an important one, for it was evidently sited with care. The north-eastern side of St. Catherine's Hill is connected by a narrow ridge with Twyford Down along which runs the ancient trackway to the South Downs. Closely following this ancient trackway is a Roman road and a modern road. This has always been an important line of communication, and the hill-fort is connected with it by a narrow ridge and also is situated so as to command it. Furthermore, it would be the first natural strong point of defence against an invader advancing up the Itchen valley from Southampton Water, a means of entry into England that has always been popular. The hill, too, is situated at the narrowest point of the Itchen valley. Northwards the Itchen drains a wide basin in the chalk highlands of central Hampshire. In prehistoric times this hill-fort must have been the central point of a wide area. In later times Winchester occupied the same position as a focal point of a large area. St. Catherine's is an early Iron Age hill-fort, dating from about 600 B.C. There was a settlement on the top before there was an earthwork or any fortification. But it was probably fortified at an early stage in its history. The introduction of the use of iron into Britain marks one of the landmarks in our history. The first men to bring the use of iron implements into the country were not exactly invaders so much as small groups of traders and settlers. Some of them came in by way of the Thames and the Wash, and made landings as far north as the Yorkshire coast. Others came from the north of France by way of the Hampshire Avon and Southampton Water, and penetrated far into Wessex. But before these people came there had been settled in the south of England certain Celtic peoples, who were in the late Bronze Age, but who probably kept in touch with the Continent and were not altogether different from the new-comers who brought iron with them. At any rate a hybrid culture resulted which is hard to define, and which is known to archæologists as Iron Age A. It is to this Iron Age A that St. Catherine's hill-fort belongs, and it seems probable that the defences on this hill and those on other hills in the south of England were thrown up against the next incursion of

Iron Age peoples. This occurred in the middle of the third century B.C. and was the invasion proper. This race known as Iron Age B came from the Marne district of France, and were a warrior race, crossing in small bands and bringing few or no women with them. These small bands established themselves among the Iron Age A people as an aristocracy. They introduced schools of metal craftsmanship, the schools which developed the Celtic art which was so grand a flower of the last years of our prehistory, the years immediately preceding the Roman conquest. They intermarried with the Iron Age A people and they brought over several other waves of their own people as well as giving sanctuary to many refugees from Cæsar's conquests.

About 75 B.C. came the last of the invasions of the Iron Age before the first Roman venture. This was the invasion of the Belgae, and is known as Iron Age C. The Belgae were not so very different from the people who were already here, and it does not seem that there was very much fighting. They were not conquerors by inclination nor warlike by habit; they, too, were really refugees. They were absorbed by the residents, intermarried with them, and brought with them into Britain softer ways than the old Iron Age A people had had originally. But the effect of that was not yet apparent when Cæsar first tried his hand at adding Britain to the Roman Empire.

We are back to the Romans again. And we had better return to the hills of the north-west border. On them are two of the largest hill-forts in the south of England; through them runs the green trackway that is called the Oxdrove. The Romans tramped these hills following the old trackways, and built here a road-house, which is now but a square of thorns, though the cottages are still called The City. Thus do country people perpetuate history. The Romans tramped these hills, but they built little and they cultivated less. After they left, these hills were nothing unless they were a hunting ground for Norman nobles. The land was too remote, too inhospitable. Too remote: nearly a hundred years after the emancipation of the serfs there were serfs on these hills. Too remote and too inhospitable. Even the buildings go to prove it. One church is more than five hundred years old; I should doubt if there is any other building that can go back half that time. The old manor houses—there were some once—have gone. Their successors are comparatively new farmhouses that have been enlarged mainly during the present century. Even the cottages—I have heard them called mean, but I do not think that they quite merit that title—are small and look as if they had been put together somewhat hastily, lacking altogether the sturdiness of the cottages further south, or in Suffolk or on Cotswold. None of the buildings—save that one church—has any air of permanence. It is as if the builders were overawed by the hills around them, as though they realized their massive strength, their everlasting nature, as though, cowed, they had said: "What is the use of building alongside these? For God's sake let's get the job finished and get out."

Here only the land is permanent, as it always was.

Only the land—and some of the men. There are men on these hills to-day who, by their names, by their looks, in their stature and their gait, proclaim their ancestry. Their forefathers held this land before ever the Romans came.

CHAPTER IV

THE VALLEY OF THE TEST

WHAT the Shires are to the hunting man, what the part-
ridge manors of Norfolk are to the shooting man, what
Everest is to the mountaineer, so are the chalk streams of
the south country to those that love to cast a fly. These
chalk streams have acquired a literature of their own; a
vast and varied literature, which ranges from the scientific
treatise, such as those of Mr. Shues, to the delightful
reminiscences of his schooldays by the Itchen at Winchester
by the late Lord Grey of Fallodon. But, to my mind, pretty
well the best of all the books of the chalk stream remains
Plunket Greene's charming *Where the Bright Waters Meet*.
And of all the chalk streams the Test is the most famous.
Indeed it is the most famous river in all England. G. S.
Marryat called it "the queen of chalk streams." That is an
understatement: queens are mortal. The fame of the Test
extends far beyond our shores to every corner of the world.
Wherever two or three anglers are gathered together there
is the Test in the midst of them.

The Test rises near Overton. Actually the source can be
seen from the main road. It is in a field adjoining Ashe
Place, which is about a mile and a half below the Deane
Gate Inn, and it looks like a small pond. In the abnormally
dry spring of 1938 there was no flow from this well-spring
and the stream did not commence to run until half a mile
or so lower down above Polhampton. That spring the
occupant of the lodge house at Ashe Place obtained water
by digging in the bed of the stream which normally flows
by his garden.

The river very soon shows its peculiar characteristic of
splitting into a number of different streams. It branches
near Polhampton while still very young; one stream running straight ahead through the meadow, the other straying
out into a green lane and skirting the hedge until it joins

its sister again at the Polhampton water-cress beds, close to a fine old farmhouse which is sheltered by some very fine sycamore trees. The other noticeable feature of the infant Test is the rapidity with which it assumes the appearance of a trout stream, if necessarily a trout stream in miniature. It is helped by the waters of several minor tributaries, and by the time it reaches Longparish it has become a river of considerable size. Thence onwards, with the help of other tributaries, some quite large and some very small, it grows continually in volume, sometimes widening out and running over magnificent open shallows, sometimes dividing into several branches, until in its middle and lower lengths it develops into a wide and deep and noble river.

From the angling point of view the Test may be divided up: the upper and middle sections being mainly devoted to the cultivation of trout, whilst from Romsey to Redbridge salmon are in some seasons fairly plentiful, and large trout and grayling are, every now and then, captured by experienced anglers in the grannom and mayfly seasons. Some of the prettiest fishing on the Upper Test is obtainable (if you have the money or the friends) in the neighbourhood of Laverstoke, but here, as in other parts of the river above Whitchurch, the average weight of the trout does not exceed 1 lb. The trout run a bit larger at Longparish and Bransbury Common, and from this point to Longstock they may be killed from $1\frac{1}{2}$ lb. up to $2\frac{1}{2}$ lb. and even occasionally a three- or four-pounder falls to the fortunate. Lower down, around Romsey, there are a few monsters—the Test record, a fish of 18 lb., was caught on the Broadlands water by Brigadier-General T. Hickman on 9 June 1922. Salmon fishing is confined for all practical purposes to the lower reaches of the river between Romsey and Redbridge. The heaviest Test salmon appears to be a fish of 38 lb. taken in 1889 by a Mr. Charteris, and in those days the fishing was not at all bad and many quite good fish were caught. To-day the salmon fishing can be disregarded, and if you want to know why, go and look at the river at Redbridge.

Considerable interest was taken in angling during the early part of the last century, and it was during this period that two famous clubs were formed on the Test. One of them was the Leckford Club, which held a very fine length of the river above Stockbridge, and the other was the Houghton Club which had a stretch of about ten miles immediately below the Leckford water. The Houghton (pronounced Hawton, if you are a Hampshire man) Club was founded in 1822. At one time the lower part of the water near the village of Houghton passed into the hands of a Dr. Wickham of Winchester, and for a while the club became known as Dr. Wickman's Club, but in 1892 the usurper became extinct, and the original Houghton Club came back into its own. It has stayed there ever since. I suppose that the Houghton Club is known the world over, but it is not generally known that it did not start as a trout fishing club. It started as a pike club, and the preservation of trout to the exclusion of pike and coarse fish was an afterthought. But there are still a good many pike in the water, and some quite big ones, despite more than a hundred years of continual and intensive persecution. The headquarters of the Houghton Club are the Grosvenor Hotel at Stockbridge. The club room is on the first floor and around the walls are colossal stuffed trout in cases. There are big trout in the Test, but some of these cases hold trout that are so big that one is inclined at first sight to imagine that they are plaster casts fashioned by some elderly member of vivid imagination *pour encourager les autres*. There are seventeen members of the Houghton Club, and the share that each member has to take up upon election is far from small. To fish the best reaches of the Test regularly you must be a wealthy man. I suppose it is worth it. It must be; would-be members grow white-headed before they are elected, and for some the sands of life run out before they are privileged to dip deep into their pockets.

There are grayling in the Test, too. The grayling is not indigenous to the Test. It was introduced some time early in the last century from the Wiltshire Avon. They throve remarkably in the middle and lower lengths of their new home, and at one time were so common that they had to be killed regardless of size. At first they seem to have been somewhat local in their habits, but now, though they are still fonder of the lower reaches than the rest of the river, they do occur throughout its length. The record Test grayling—and for the matter of that the record for any river in the British Isles rod caught (for a fish of $5\frac{1}{4}$ lb. has been taken in a trap in Shropshire)—is one of 5 lb. taken by Mr. G. R. Kendle in the Broadlands water in 1865. On the same day he had another of $4\frac{1}{2}$ lb. But nowadays they do not run to much more than $1\frac{1}{2}$ lb. and a two-pounder is thought to be a big fish. Grayling give good sport and are good to eat, but they are not welcomed by most trout fishermen in trout waters. So they are not welcomed in the Test, but they are likely to stay there for all that.

The Rainbow trout has also been introduced into the Test on more than one occasion, once by the Houghton Club itself. This was in 1899, when 300 fish of between 1 and 3 lb. were put down. A few were caught during the first season, but thereafter none, and so far as I know the same fate overtook all the other introductions. The fact is that the Rainbow will not do in unfenced waters. They spawn, they drop downstream, and they go on dropping downstream until they reach the sea, and then they drop out of sight altogether.

In the old days the bulk of the trout used to be killed during the grannom and mayfly seasons. It was then that the angler held high festival. There was very little fishing until the mayfly was up, and then for some ten days the water was flogged with might and main. And after that there was again scarcely any fishing. In those days, and up until about 1870 or so, fishing with large artificial flies was the normal method adopted on the Hampshire chalk streams, the most common patterns being mayflies and moths tied on large hooks. But many trout were also caught with the natural mayfly and the blow line. Eventually the dry fly method of fishing became general, flies became smaller and smaller, were tied on tiny hooks, and were cast from ten- or eleven-feet rods and smaller. And the trout became educated.

In the old days there were some very big bags and some very big fish. Men would get forty brace of trout in one evening at Longparish. Twelve trout of 5 lb. each and upwards in one evening on the lower Test was once the good fortune of an angler, and the same man had sixty brace in one evening just above Romsey not very much later. To-day a 5-lb trout is rare, and such a fish very rarely rises to a fly. And though there are still trout of 10 and 12 lb. in the lower reaches, they must be lured with a worm or some other delicacy frowned upon by the true trout fisher-man.

In other words the fishing on the Test is not what it was. The numbers of accomplished fishermen have increased, have increased enormously, and nowadays most parts of the river, outside the close season, are fished regularly and hard from Friday night until Sunday night, and there is a con-siderable amount of fishing throughout the week as well. And though the smaller ephemeridæ are as common as ever they were, the mayfly is certainly becoming scarcer year by year. The river is over-fished. There is no getting away from that.

But still anglers come from far and near to fish the Test— to the material benefit of those who live upon its banks. Excepting for a few clubs, the riparian owners either fish the water themselves or, and this is more common, let their rights to enthusiasts at the most fancy prices. If you have got to be a very wealthy man to join the Houghton Club, you have got to be a rich one to fish the Test at all; either that or very fortunate in your friends. A rod on one of the best beats of the Test is a luxury that can be enjoyed by very few, a rod anywhere is a luxury. The Test faces as a fishing river—or rather the riparian owners face—a doubt-ful future. Incidentally, the great increase in prices and the consequent increase in the difficulty of getting any fishing, has led to a great increase in the amount of poaching. Fish poaching used to be rampant on all the Hampshire streams. Izaak Walton refers to it, and in his *Compleat Angler* gives some account of the methods then in vogue. The methods have changed a bit with the years, and perhaps there was for a while in the middle years of the last century some falling-off in the amount of poaching, for fishing in those days was not the close preserve of the wealthy and was free from much of the snobbery that now invests it, on the Test at any rate. But I should doubt if it has ever really been absent from the rivers of Hampshire, and I know that it is now far from uncommon.

Personally—and I say this with a full knowledge of the opening that I give to those who would cry "sour grapes"—I would pay no fancy price for a rod on the Test, even had I the money to waste. I am a very keen fisherman and I know chalk streams that I would fish in preference to the Test every time (yes, I have fished the Test more than once) but it depends, of course, upon what you want of angling. My wants are very simple.

But, if I am not so keen on the Test as a trout stream, I love the Test as a river. It is altogether charming. It is a pleasant stream and it runs through pleasant country. It is a leisurely stream and quiet. When you first come to the banks—and if you are not a wealthy man, you come without reverence in your heart—the Test appears very much as any other chalk stream. But the more you know the Test, the more it grows upon you. It has that indefinable thing, atmosphere. If it is a stream to fish (and I will admit that there are those who maintain that it is the only stream to fish) it is also a stream to walk by, to laze by, to dream by, to sit by, to sleep by. It is a companionable stream and a friendly stream, even to those who, like myself, cannot afford to fish it. And I like the Test, not for the trout it holds, but for its friendliness. Its banks are peopled by ghosts. They are friendly ghosts for anglers, no matter what other faults they may have (and they have only one, in common with golfers, and that is a tendency to exaggeration) are at bottom friendly people. Almost everywhere along the Test you may, if you will but shut your eyes, see anglers in every costume from the queer garments of Izaak Walton's day to the easy, dirty, comfortable flannels of this present year of grace. And you may, if you will but listen very closely, hear them talk—or is it the slight breeze in the reeds?—and the talk has altered little since that day when Piscator first set off up Tottenham Hill. And if you keep your eyes open—and you not fishing—you will find the water wholly fascinating. Long glassy rides—I do not know a better word—with just an occasional break in the surface from a bed of weed. And when the sun is high, the

The old silk mill, Whitchurch

river-bed itself is lit up and every detail discernible, so that it is nothing but a great open-air aquarium. And then you may watch the great trout lying, motionless save for an occasional quiver of the tail, and the eels, very big eels some of them, worming their way through the weeds. Basket-traps are put down for these eels on the Houghton Club water. Eels journey downstream, so the traps face up-stream. Entrance is easy and exit difficult. I believe that the eels so caught bring in about £100 per annum. And here one day—but I do not know if it was actually on the Club water, for I am a bit vague about the Club boundaries —I watched a very large pike and saw him take a duckling. And here, if you will but listen, you may hear the strangely ventriloquistic cry of moorhen, and the contented quacking of duck, and the soft drowsy call of woodpigeon, and the wonderful melody of blackbird above the songs of warblers and the chirruping of buntings. The Test is a very charm-ing river, and is always more a river than a stream, for it has broadened into a stream quite close to its source and within a further mile or so has developed from stream to river. It wanders, winding in and out, dividing and meeting again, between quiet meadows and marshy flats, where sallow and mimulus, willow-herb and yellow-flag grow prodigiously; where cattle graze belly-deep in the rich growth by the river bank. It passes villages with old churches set decor-atively among the trees: it meanders past cottages that are quaintly thatched—the thatch in some reaching almost to the ground on one side—and have broad hedges and yew trees cut into every conceivable shape (and some whose meaning defeats imagination): it sweeps beneath charming old bridges: it runs through country that is rich in history.

Overton, at the head-waters of the Test, is a sad little place with beautifully old-world streets. Once it was a busy market town, with a great sheep and lamb fair; once there were here busy silk mills. It is one of the oldest townships in all Wessex, and the Parliamentary records that it was one of the first boroughs represented in the county. Its parliamentary rights have gone like its silk mills, and Overton that was so busy and important in the days of the coach languishes in the days of the railway. Once every

St. Mary Bourne, once famous for its "revels"

traveller to the West knew Overton, for it was the end of the first stage from London and fresh horses stood in the stables of the Poyntz Arms. The old hostel stood at the corner of the cross-roads, but to-day the schools stand in the place of the Poyntz Arms, and not one traveller in all the many hundreds that pour out of London on the western routes each week-end has ever heard of Overton.

But there is yet history in Overton. The church, which has been much altered and restored but still has traces of the ancient building, brings to mind the strange story of a sanctuary that proved to be no sanctuary. It was in the time of William of Wykeham, when one John Bentley, who was not an Overton man, killed, by accident it is said, a man and sought refuge in the church. After evensong he was engaged in conversation by the town cobbler, whose name was Spike (the name is almost too good to be true and I suspect that this Spike had a good deal to do with the business), and while he was talking he was suddenly pushed out of the church. Whereupon the townsmen, who had evidently been hanging about waiting for just this eventuality, set upon him and put him in the stocks, and ultimately sent him to Winchester. But the Bishop, on hearing the story, was very angry at the violation of the right of sanctuary, and sent men to Overton to inquire into the whole business and to punish the offenders. I have an idea that Spike regretted his part in the business. Overton, I fancy, has forgotten John Bentley, who took sanctuary in its church. But Overton remembers something of its ancient life, and each year in the neighbourhood at Christmas-time mummers perform a play that must be almost a thousand years old. It is a good thing to remember.

And Overton has more than a little to do with the Vine. The Vine was founded in 1790 when William Chute of The Vyne started a pack of harriers. The Poyntz Arms—named after Major-General Poyntz—then used to put up many followers of the hunt, including the Prince Regent. Chute himself was a character and a jolly good huntsman into the bargain. Of course, the country then was vastly different from that over which the present pack hunts—mainly it was common unenclosed and wire undreamed of. Even so,

"Nimrod" confessed: "I never hunt in Hampshire when I can help it"—and I have never thought so highly of Mr. Apperly since reading that. One famous hound of those days was Spanker, who was earthed in Chilton Wood after a twelve-mile point—and found five days later beside the dead fox. Not only did he recover but he hunted for many more seasons. Chute himself hunted longer than most men. When he got old he refused to jump, and, according to Æsop, "always got off and took hold of his horse's tail, who then drew him up"! The same authority has another nice story about the old man. On one occasion he asked a farmer to move a hurdle. The farmer, when he had done so, said: "Now you can come."

"Stop," replied Chute, as cautious as ever, "let me get off, and I will turn my horse over the ditch."

"But there is no ditch," said the farmer, "your horse will walk over."

"But I," said Chute, "fancy there is a ditch, and that is the same thing."

And he got off and solemnly followed his horse through the gap.

In those days the kennels were by the manor house; now there are different kennels. But the same country is hunted, though I doubt if the hunt can now boast such characters as the first master.

Hard by Overton, but a little lower down the Test, is Laverstoke. Laverstoke, thanks to the Portals, is park-like. But the scene of deep rural peace is somewhat rudely shattered by a high wall and policeman on duty at the arched entrance—policemen in the country are always a disturbing sight—and thus you know that you are at Laverstoke Mill, that famous mill where the Bank of England notes are manufactured. The method by which the notes are manufactured is a profound secret, the best kept secret in the world, though I suppose that the rough outline of the process is known. (I do not know it myself.) Hampshire has always given sanctuary to refugees from France—the young son of Charles the Simple, you may remember, was smuggled out of Laon in a truss of straw and brought to Athelstan's court at Winchester—and it was a refugee from

France who founded the mill at Laverstoke. His name was
Henri de Portal. He was a descendant of a Castilian noble
in the train of Elvira, daughter of Alphonso IV, on her
coming to France at the end of the eleventh century, who
founded a powerful family in Languedoc and Dauphine.
For more than two centuries the de Portals were Capitouls
of Toulouse, but with the Reformation of the Christian
faith they were among the first of the French noblesse to
suffer for their convictions. Within a century they had lost
power and wealth, and when Louis XIV broke faith and
revoked the Edict of Nantes they lost also lands and lives.
But three of the family escaped death and the torturers and
fled to England. The tale goes that when ruin and the
soldiers came to the Chateau de la Portalerie, an old nurse
hid the three children of the then head of the family—Jean
Francois, Henri and Guillaume—in an oven, the while the
house was being searched by the soldiers, and that they
were then concealed in wine casks and smuggled aboard a
ship and landed at Southampton. Nobody knows what
happened to Jean Francois, except that he died in London
many years later, but Henri certainly came to Southampton
and joined the Huguenot colony that centred round the
French church of St. Julian. He found employment at one
of the mills at South Stoneham, which was managed by
another Frenchman skilled in the manufacture of paper.
From this man he learned his trade, and it was while he
was here that he met the Squire of Hursley, Sir William
Heathcote. Sir William and the young Frenchman became
fast friends; and in 1710 the tenant of Bere Mill having
died, Sir William offered the lease to his friend. So to Bere
Mill near Whitchurch came young Henri de Portal with a
number of Frenchmen to help him. In 1711 Henri de Portal
became a naturalized Englishman—the document describ-
ing him as "Henry Portall, of South Stoneham, gentleman."
The mill at Bere prospered so greatly that in 1718 a lease
was taken of the neighbouring mill at Laverstoke. In 1727
Henry Portal obtained from Sir Gilbert Heathcote, uncle
of his great friend Sir William and then Governor of the
Bank of England, the right to manufacture the Bank's
notepaper. And here ever since—though actually the mill

was rebuilt by Sir Wyndham Portal—the business has been carried on. Two hundred years and more handed down from father to son must be something of a record for any business in England. Thus was founded the Portal family in England. There are many older families in Hampshire, but in modern times no family has been more conspicuous in Hampshire, and certainly none is more honoured. While they have been great in the life and service of the county, they have also been great in the life and service of the country. In Winchester Cathedral you may see the truly beautiful memorial to the two Portal brothers, Gerald and Raymond (of Uganda fame), whose short but notable careers in the Empire's service were typical of a great family. And in the late war another of the name performed great service in the direction of the activities of the Royal Air Force.

The church at Laverstoke stands between that village and the neighbouring village of Freefolk (which if you are a true Hampshire man you will call Frefvolk) and is used by both villages. It is a big church and new. It has some really lovely iron-work on the door, and inside there are two things of great beauty: the reredos, which is copied fom a medieval one, with eight painted panels, depicting the life of Jesus, four on each side of a central group of carved figures gathered about Our Lord on the Cross, with above them an array of golden canopies, the highest pinnacle of which reaches almost to the roof; and a delicately carved screen with lovely fan tracery, a rich vine band, and rood figures up above—as lovely a thing as you will see in any village church in England. But though both villages now use the new church, both retain their own old ones. That at Laverstoke stands in the park. It has been greatly restored, but it retains its old bell, dated 1624, and one or two old monuments besides those of the Portals, whose mausoleum it has become. There are two epitaphs in this church which I think deserve attention by all those who collect such things. One is with the beautiful marble bust of Kathleen Stewkley, who died in 1679. Hers is a face of charm and character and some humour, and the epitaph suggests that she was a lady of more than the average intelligence and learning. It does not seem to have given her an altogether happy life, for the epitaph ends somewhat bitterly:

> The dull oblige mankind
> And all their love engage,
> While 'tis a crime to be refined
> Above the present age.

The other epitaph is on the dignified wall-monument of Kathleen Stewkley's parents, John Trott and his wife, and it bears these lines:

> He wrongs the dead who thinks this marble frame
> Was built to be the guardian of his name,
> Whereas 'twas for his ashes only meant:
> His name was set to guard the monument.

That in its way is the equal of any of the many literary gems to be found in our churches.

Some two miles further down the river is Whitchurch, a town I rank very highly among the towns of Hampshire. It is an ancient town whose glories have long since departed. Once it returned two members to Parliament, once it had a very large market (it still has a market), once it was a post-stage and travellers came here from Newbury and Oxford to join the Exeter coach. To-day it is better known than Overton only because it stands on the main Newbury-Winchester road, and sees each week-end a surprising volume of traffic. But travellers do not stop in Whitchurch (though a large staff from the Bank of England came here during the war—and a few want to come back) for there is very little to see and pretty well nothing to do. And I think that that is a good thing for Whitchurch, for it means that the town can retain its quiet, quaint, grey beauty. I like it with its houses clustered in a sheltered hollow and climbing up the hill-side. I like it with the downs so near, and the river and the water-meadows and the woods. I like its freedom from road-houses and penny-in-the-slot machines. But there is for those who must see something, ancient or garish, in a town, nothing at all to see save two things in the mercilessly restored church. Both are unique. The belfry stairs are made of solid blocks of wood and cased in plain wooden walls about 500 years old and the walls are pierced by tiny traceried windows. The headstone of Frithburga was found in the wall of the north aisle in 1868, and it was then used for a ringer to stand on. It has the figure of the Lord with a cruciform nimbus, and the inscription: "*Hic corpus Frithburgae requiescit in pace sepultum*." Probably Frithburga was a nun from the neighbouring Priory at Wherwell, and that was founded in 986. But the stone may well be much older than that. That is all to see. But the imagination may play around The White Hart, one of the best and most comfortable hotels in the county (and one of the very few where nowadays the traveller is really made to feel welcome), which Kingsley portrayed in his *Two Years Ago*.

Just outside Whitchurch are the north gates of Hurstbourne Park. It is a fine park of over a thousand acres, running right down to Hurstbourne Priors along the Bourne valley. But though it is a fine park I think that Kingsley was suffering from one of his periodical fits of enthusiasm when he called it the finest park in the south of England—or, perhaps, he had not been to Arundel or Cowdray? The Bourne, which joins the Test at Hurstbourne Priors, a little below Whitchurch, is the first of the tributary streams on the north bank of the Test. Tributaries are generally ignored in favour of the main stream, but I do not think that they deserve to be, for invariably they contribute something to the main river, and not infrequently they are more beautiful than that they feed. Hurstbourne Priors—the natives, by the way, pronounce the first word *Ussebawn*—is a very ordinary village. It would be easy, having seen Hurstbourne Priors and the Bourne at its junction with the Test, to ignore the rest of the Bourne valley altogether. But it would be a mistake. The little Bourne—and a bit further up it is so little that it is called officially the Bourne Rivulet—is beautiful, and so is the country through which it runs.

St. Mary Bourne, which is the next village up the valley, is nothing very much to look at. A good deal of it is modern and not much of it is interesting though it remains sleepy and rural enough. But here the shallow Bourne, white with water-crowfoot, hurrying along between great yellow clumps of giant musk, against which you may sometimes catch the vivid blue flash of the kingfisher, is a stream to linger by, and a stream that sometimes holds quite decent fish into the bargain. In the churchyard is a great and venerable yew and in the church a Tournai blue-black marble font, the largest of the four that are in Hampshire, and the effigy of a crusader. And of the St. Mary Bourne of to-day that is just about all. But of the village of yesterday? Men lived here before history was conceived. Here Dr. Stevens found a whole series of grouped pit-dwellings— round dog holes, not in the least like what you or I would consider a human dwelling—with underground passages leading to them. He has given a full account of them in his *History of St. Mary Bourne*, and that is a parochial history that deserves to rank with White's *Selborne*. These pit dwellings must be amongst the earliest discovered habitations of man in England. Of the men who lived thus we know almost nothing, but we do know something of the men who lived in St. Mary Bourne a matter of a hundred years ago or so. For then St. Mary Bourne had revels. Dr. Stevens tells us that the boys used to blow their May-horns of willow-bark twisted in a spiral manner, the sweeps clattered shovels and brushes as they danced round their Jack-in-the-green, or rather Jill, for the walking bower usually held a "female of their order, the representative probably of Maid Marion of the olden times." And sports were held, running and jumping, and dancing, and single-stick and wrestling, the last two being the chief attractions for which —and for the half-guinea hat prizes—many famous wrestlers and backsword-playing champions came from far afield to compete. For these events there was an umpire— umsher in the old Hampshire dialect (and I heard the word only the other day, at Lord's of all places)—and of him Dr. Stevens wrote:

When the play became irregular or languid . . . suspended it for a time by calling "bout"; and after a short pause it was resumed on his calling "play." On an appeal, if successful, he called "blood," if not it was met with "no head" or "play on." In all stage matters his decision was final; although as one may imagine, in such society it was often violently cavilled at.

The manners of English crowds at sporting events, so frequently deplored in these days, do not appear to have altered so very much with the passage of time. The lot of the umpire is as it always was. The play, I do not doubt, was frequently irregular, but I cannot imagine single-stick in a village revel being languid. And it would certainly seem that it was on occasion as robust as could be, for did not one of the competitors die in Fareham lunatic asylum of "clouts on the head he had received on the stage"? The Rev. J. E. Jackson, writing in the *Wiltshire Archæological and Natural History Magazine* (Volume XXI, p. 334), says:

> They fought bareheaded, with the left arm fastened to the waist, so that they might not use it to ward off blows. To hit an opponent on the face was against the rules: but to hit him on the top of the head was the grand point, and the grandest point of all was to hit him so as to produce blood.

That certainly does not sound like a languid sport, but a sport leaving plenty of room for irregularities certainly.

A little further up the valley is Hurstbourne Tarrant. The village lies at the head of the narrow valley—though the Bourne, which may here be dried up, rises yet farther up just beyond Ibthorpe—and is much more conscious of downs and woods. It is an inviting village and the walks around are even more inviting. The valley sides here are so steep that if you walk (climb is a better word) up the churchyard you can look over the top of the shingled tower and spire of the church. I like this church, which is old (the walls are chiefly twelfth century and pierced with windows of many shapes and sizes), for its great round pillars and the old font, but particularly for its wall paintings, which, if indistinct (and that is only to be expected), can still in great part be traced with the aid of a little patience. Under the yew in the churchyard lies Joseph Blunt, who was the friend of Cobbett and a well-known local philanthropist. And also in the churchyard is the mausoleum of H. W. Prosser. I have heard this described as striking. I would not quarrel with the description; let us leave it at that. Henry Prosser was an eccentric—and in these days of regimentation that becomes wholly praiseworthy—but I think that it was a pity that he carried his eccentricity into the churchyard.

Overhanging the village is Hurstbourne Hill, with Doles Wood falling down over the slope towards the village. Doles Wood has been described most lovingly in Dewar's *Wild Life in Hampshire Highlands* and in his *Life and Sport in Hampshire*, and it remains to-day a most marvellous place in which to watch wild life. I do not know that it is officially a sanctuary (and I do know that it suffered as did all our woodlands severely during the war) and I suppose, therefore, that it is not. But it might well be. There are deer in this wood. I do not know how many or how long they have been there, or even if they form a permanent population or if they come and go. But there are deer—at times anyway. I have seen roe—a buck and three does together. They were there only for a moment and then gone, but the day was brightened by the sight. And on another occasion, just for a fleeting moment, a glimpse of a fallow buck. It is always something of a surprise to see deer. It should not be so in Hampshire, for Hampshire has a very large population of deer, but it is. It is the common belief that deer in England are now uncommon outside the parks (such parks as Richmond, for example), and the belief is so widely held and so frequently stated that we have become infected, unconsciously we believe it (knowing in our saner moments that it is quite untrue) and are surprised when we see a deer. But there are plenty of deer in Hampshire (and sometimes they turn up in the most astonishing places—so that I believe that they move from one suitable place to another and back again, crossing as they do so the most unsuitable tracts of country. Doles Wood, of course, is suitable, but I have within the last year seen roe crossing the main Winchester-Basingstoke road, which is surely the last place where one would expect to see deer: and during the very hard winter of 1940 deer came right up to my dining-room windows, and scavenged around my waste buckets in the stable yard), there are deer in Hampshire, yet though they are there, and one knows they are there, they are so shy and so incredibly clever at concealing themselves that they are rarely seen. And so whenever I see deer (except, of course, in Richmond Park) I am thrilled: and when I see them where I do not expect to see them, then I am thrilled indeed.

The main Newbury-Andover Road—the road by which we left Hurstbourne Tarrant—runs through Doles Wood, but for a main road in these days it does not carry much traffic, and a number of unfenced roads intersect the wood, but they are little used, and Doles Wood remains beautiful and entrancing. The wood was once a part of the great forest of Chute, which stretched from Clanville to Finckley and probably made contact with Harewood Forest. Much of it is wild and scrubby, and oaks grow above hazel under-growth, and there are silver birches and firs and ashes and hawthorns to bring the silver in the spring and red in autumn. And there are many birds. Rooks and wood-pigeons, of course. I do not know if rooks are on the in-crease or not (most elderly countrymen maintain that there were many more fifty years ago) but pigeons I have no doubt about. There are many more than there were twenty years ago, and many more come each autumn from the Continent. And there are plenty of jays. The jay is an unpopular bird. He likes other birds' eggs, and he warns all the world of your approach, and he likes fruit too. I have shot a good many jays in my time, but I like jays. I do not dislike their noisiness, and I love their colouring—if only they were not so fond of the fruit in the garden. And here, too, are a number of cuckoos and all the usual woodland birds that fill the air with sweet song. I have never seen any unusual birds here, but always plenty of birds—and per-sonally I think that we make too great a fetish of the un-usual the while we know too little about the usual.

We left the Test at Hurstbourne Priors, and we had better go back there, for if we follow the road on through or around Doles Wood we shall come again to Tangley and

the north-western highlands we have already explored. So
let us return to the unbeautiful village where Bourne joins
Test. Below the village the Test does all sorts of extraordinary things: is now broad, quite a mighty river, is now
narrow, divides and divides again, is now two streams, now
one, now three—so that I am never certain whether I am
following the parent stream or some wayward child. The
next village downstream is Longparish, which straggles
along the road to Stockbridge and which is very picturesque, and whose church contains an hour-glass. Longstock is by one of the most beautiful reaches of the Test,
and well fished by those that are fortunate enough. There
is much talk of fishing in the village, which is not surprising
when one remembers that almost all the village lives on the
people who come to fish. " 'Veish is the coriousest things':
and like all unfathomable things endowed with an irresist-
ible and unfailing charm," so wrote Mary Hawker in *Old
Hampshire Vignettes*. And we might as well leave the fishing at Longstock with that very wise remark, and turn to
another Hawker. Longstock is famous as the home of
Colonel Peter Hawker, the author of that shooting classic,
*Instructions to Young Sportsmen in all that Relates to Guns
and Shooting*, and the father of Mary. Thousands and
thousands of words have been written about Colonel Peter
Hawker and he wrote a good many about himself, for he
kept a diary from his sixteenth year. I do not propose to
add to them. Colonel Hawker was obviously a fisherman.
And obviously he was a very fine shot. But—infidel that I
am—I always find myself taking the gallant colonel *cum
grano salis*. Mr. Eric Parker has made a good defence of the
two wives, and especially of the second, and has undone
much of the wrong that Payne-Galwey did them, but all the
same I should like to know very much more about the two
Mrs. Hawkers. They must have been marvellous women.
Nor do we really know very much about the colonel despite
his diary, for that is really no more than a score sheet. And
his family were uncommunicative about him. I think that
he must have been a bit of a bore.

Behind Longstock lies Harewood Forest, or what is left of
it. Once it stretched for miles, but to-day it is not very big

and is cut in two by the main Andover-Basingstoke road. But it is still wild enough and there are many delightful footpaths and walks and the remains of the old Roman road. You can spend a day in Harewood without seeing a soul save, perhaps, a solitary woodman. The wild life of the place seems to be made up mainly of jays and woodpigeons and, in summer, wasps. There must be more wasps' nests here than in any other district of the same size in England! And here the red squirrel holds out, though the grey is, I understand, gaining ground despite the regulations for its extermination. There are said to be no deer in the Forest to-day, but that is not the case for I have found the slots of roe on more than one occasion. In the olden days this was a great hunting ground of Saxon Kings, so great that they had a "vill" or residence here, and two at least, Edgar and Ethelred the Redeless, made this their home, held their court and caused their Witans to assemble here. And it was in Edgar's reign that the incident occurred which is commemorated by the monument known as Deadman's Plack. The monument itself, a high stone cross standing on rising ground in a somewhat desolate corner of the Forest, is in no way remarkable. It was put up in 1835 by a Colonel Iremonger, then the owner of the Wherwell estate. The original inscription—there are a good many others now mainly dealing with the love affairs of itinerant townsmen—runs:

About the year of our Lord 965 Edgar surnamed the Peaceable, in the ardour of youth, love and indignation, slew with his own hand Earl Ethelwold, in resentment of the Earl having basely betrayed his Royal Confidence and perfidiously married his intended bride, the beauteous Elfrida, daughter of Ordgar, Earl of Devonshire, afterwards wife of King Edgar, and by him mother of King Ethelred II, which Queen Elfrida, after Edgar's death, murdered his eldest son, Edward the Martyr, and founded the Nunnery of Wherwell.

I like the wording of that inscription. But the story is plainly sordid.

Ordgar, Earl of Devonshire, had a daughter whose

"charms had so fascinated the eyes of some persons that they commended her to the King," whereupon Edgar (who was by no means blind to feminine charms: he was, indeed, a modern young man, for though he died at the early age of thirty-one he married three times and the lady commemorated on the monument was his third wife) sent his Hampshire Earldorman Ethelwold to inspect the maiden and, if her charms were all rumour said they were, to bring her to him. But Ethelwold (himself, I have no doubt, a bit of a lady's man) was quite enslaved by the charms that he saw, made no mention of his mission, did a bit of rapid courting, offered marriage and was accepted. He then sent word to Edgar that the lady's charms were not up to the required standard and settled down to a happy married life in Devonshire. But after a while Edgar heard that his Earldorman had married a most beautiful girl, and he sent demanding their presence at court. Ethelwold had not seen so far ahead as this and was very frightened indeed. He went to his wife and begged her to "administer to his safety by attiring herself as unbecomingly as possible." They arrived at court: and straight away Elfrida set about displaying her charms to Edgar and using all her wiles for all she was worth. Success, one gathers, was instantaneous. At any rate Edgar, "dissembling his indignation, sent the earl into a wood at Warewelle, called Harewood, under the pretence of hunting, and ran him through with a javelin." He then married Elfrida, who had certainly connived at her husband's murder.

When Edgar died—and his profligacy no doubt hastened his end—Elfrida was left with a son, Ethelred, and a stepson, Edward. An ambitious woman, and one not to quibble over trifles, she murdered the latter at Corfe Castle, stabbing him with her own hand under the pretence of offering him a stirrup cup. And so she made Ethelred King. Then, somewhat surprisingly, her nerve appears to have failed her—perhaps memories of her not inconsiderable crimes haunted her—for she retired from public life and erected a religious house, the nunnery, at Wherwell. Here she remained until her death, giving herself up to penances as whole-heartedly as she had once given herself up to licence. And here she

was buried—not so very far from the place where her first
husband was murdered by her second. "She was," says the
chronicle, "a beautiful woman: singularly faithful to her
husband."

And so to Wherwell. I like Wherwell—the Hampshire
pronounciation is *Urrell*—I like Wherwell with its thatch
and plaster cottages set deep in at the foot of its steep hill
covered with noble trees. Wherwell is really pretty and
quaint without being in any way "olde." Legend says that
the name is due to Queen Elfrida, the modern form being
a corruption of Whose Well. Another very popular idea is
that it is a corruption of Whore's Well. But as we know
that there was a village here long before Elfrida attained
notoriety and royalty, and also long before there were nuns
disporting themselves in the woods, it seems more probable
that the modern word is a corruption of hoar, and that the
place took its name from its hoar or ancient springs.

The first story of Wherwell that we know concerns Wifhilda. Wifhilda was, presumably, a maiden of considerable
charm, and she was a nun in the nunnery at Wilton. She
was persuaded by Wenfleda, who was King Edgar's aunt,
to leave the nunnery at Wilton and come and stay at her
(Wenfleda's) house "at Warewell." The tale says that Wenfleda acted on her nephew's instructions, but I doubt if even
Edgar could have known very much about Wifhilda's
charms, and I think that Wenfleda was not a very nice old
lady. Anyhow Wifhilda came and there was much feasting.
But she was impressed neither by the king nor the feasting,
and rejected the royal advances, which did not, I feel sure,
include any mention of marriage. As a result soldiers were
placed at the door of her room, but she escaped "through
the passage of a drain, and in the vill of Wharewell she was
entertained as a beggar in the hovel of a certain very poor
woman."

After the foundation of the nunnery by the reformed
Elfrida, the place became very popular with fashionable
ladies as a "rest cure," though the "cure" seems to have
been taken as a rule when they had incurred the displeasure
of their lords. So Cnut's queen Elfgyfn Emma spent some
little time here when she had annoyed her son Edward the

Confessor, and it was from Wherwell, according to the legend, that she went to Winchester to clear herself from calumny by the self-invoked torture of the red-hot plough-shares. And it was here, too, that Edward the Confessor, who does not seem to have been quite the gentle and even-tempered man that the history books would have us believe, kept his own Queen Eadgyth in retirement.

Up to the fourteenth century the nunnery was fortunate in its abbesses, and one, Euphemia, was certainly note-worthy. The nunnery buildings, which were on a low and marshy site, had defective foundations. The bell-tower collapsed and the whole place was in a dangerous condition. But Euphemia was not at all dismayed. She rebuilt the defective parts, and with her own hands laid the first stone of a new and better building. Although the chronicler assures us of her sweetness and piety he tells us that she had the spirit of a man rather than of a woman, and she does seem to have ruled the place with a rod of iron. But within a hundred years of her death the nunnery had acquired quite another sort of reputation. Bishop Pontoise com-mented upon the quarrels of the nuns, stressed the need for discipline and the need for silence. And later William of Wykeham, in order to avoid the cause for much gossip in the county, had to forbid that friars or any man, lay or cleric, should be given a night's lodging. The nunnery has gone but the reputation remains. At the Dissolution the place was given up, and to-day it is difficult to find a single stone of the old building, though if you go up through the churchyard you will come to two very ancient stone coffins and a seventeenth-century stone set in the wall telling of the "overacted zeal or avarice of King Henry" which des-troyed the nunnery in this place. But if the nunnery has gone altogether there are yet plenty of stories about it current in the neighbourhood. Ghosts are said to be common, and, of course, are always nuns (and I have met more than one man and one woman who believe that they have seen them), and it is also said that there are under-ground passages connecting this place and that with the nunnery grounds. But I do not know of anyone who knows where these passages, if they exist, actually are.

View from Hurstbourne Hill
with Doles Wood on the right

At Wherwell the Bullington stream, the only tributary on the east bank, runs into the Test. I am not certain just exactly where the junction is effected because the river here does all sorts of odd things, and equally I am not sure exactly where the Bullington rises. It rises somewhere beyond Micheldever, just about in the centre of Hampshire, by the grounds of Stratton Park, but it rises from many springs, and, as is the habit of chalk streams, these springs vary with the season. The Bullington is a lovely little stream—as the crow flies it does not cover more than six miles of country from its source to its fusion with the Test, though, of course, its windings and twirlings make its actual length a good deal more—and flows through gentle downland, with many villages clustered on its banks. None of these villages has any startling history, but all of them reach back into the dim past. Micheldever itself, the least important of them all (though I am always impressed by the railway cutting) has really ancient associations, for the camp at Norbury Ring is definitely pre-Roman and Saxon relics have been found all around. Of the other villages, Sutton Scotney has become rather tea-ridden, but Stoke Charity is as beautiful as its name and has a wonderful church, and Barton Stacey was before the war a village of character. It may be again, but the military had a long occupation and a railway line was built from Winchester to serve the huge camp and the country-side generally suffered from various activities as was inevitable. But the real charm of this little valley lies in the stream and the wild life that haunts it. Here are snipe and woodcock: snipe as plentifully as anywhere in Hampshire, and woodcock, in my opinion most definitely on the increase. Here are plenty of duck, and in the winter sometimes more than plenty: and here I have watched a family of tufted duck, the only time that I personally have seen this species on a narrow stream. Here I have caught a crayfish (and no doubt I was poaching): and here I have watched great crested grebe, resting no doubt on their way to the lake at Old Alresford: and here on Tidbury Common by Bullington village I saw a hoopoe feeding with a flock of starlings—and had another lesson on the misleading way birds are portrayed in the

Andover—Architecturally utilitarian

coloured plates of the bird books. If you look at the
coloured representation of the hoopoe you cannot but believe that the bird would be outstanding should you see it
anywhere in England. I know that I had always thought
so until I first saw it. Then I must confess that it was not so
very different from the starlings with which it was consort-
ing. It was bigger—about the size of a fat missel-thrush or
a little larger (but size in the field is misleading)—but it was
its shape rather than its colouring that drew my attention.
And had I not been looking at that flock of starlings very
closely (I was then very interested in the simultaneous flock
movements of birds, as indeed I still am) I do not know
that I should have noticed him at all. I am sure more pass
unseen in Hampshire and Sussex and Kent each year than
find their way into the records.

Just before the Bullington joins up with the Test it runs
through Bransbury Common. And here are snipe in plenty.
And here a few years ago the Dartford Warbler nested. It
ceased to do so about 1936, but in 1944 it returned and has
come back every year since. And all along this valley the
botanist will find enjoyment. On the downs he may find
round-headed rampion, and viper's bugloss, and the broad-
leaved and white helleborines, and burnt orchis and butterfly orchis and many others of that delightful family. And
in the valley are orchis too, and particularly the spider
orchis. And by the river-side where sedge and reed
warblers nest, great masses of glorious mimulus and golden
marsh-marigold and gay yellow iris and forget-me-nots and
pink-and-white buckbean. And over them flashes the kingfisher, the lark sings high above and the moorhen calls from
just around the corner, and everywhere is the persistent
double note of the cuckoo. The Bullington in comparison
with the Test is but a ditch—but what a ditch!

About a mile below Wherwell the Anton joins the Test.
There is good fishing in the Anton—trout and grayling—
though the fish do not attain such great weights as they do
in the larger river. The Anton rises near Penton Grafton
by Weyhill, and now the only place of note upon its banks
is Andover. Weyhill has a centuries-old fair, once famous
throughout the country and even over the water. There is

still a fair and some liveliness when it is held in mid-October but it is not the fair it once was, for the simple reason that it was a sheep fair and the sheep is an animal that finds little room in modern England.

Andover is not a beautiful place. It is modern. I have no objection to modernity, but in parts of Andover the present-day builder has been given a free hand and the result is just hideous. Though I have no doubt that the results of his labours will shortly fall down, they are as I write still standing, and so I am always glad to hurry through the town. It is so blatantly utilitarian. Yet actually Andover is very old, very, very old. The word *An* is the Celtic word for spring, and occurs in many places in the district—Abbots Ann, St. Mary Amport, Little Ann, East Anton, and the streams Anna and Anton. The word Dover is either the Celtic *Dever* (the modern Welsh word *Dwr*), which means a water-crossing, and which is also found in Micheldever, Brown Candover, Chilton Candover and Preston Candover, or an even more ancient word *eure*, which is, so I am told, a pre-Celtic word and perhaps the oldest word in our language and which meant simply water. You can take your choice (and I lean to the Celtic, which would mean "ford over the spring"), but you cannot get away from the ancientness of Andover, that is now so hideously modern. There was once a big Roman settlement in the neighbourhood, and pavements from Abbots Ann and Thruxton are in the British Museum, and also a wonderful store of Pewter plates and cups and dishes from Weyhill. But Andover's history really begins with the Saxons.

Edgar was apparently fond of the place. Edgar was a friend of Dunstan, who was the "big shot" of the time, and so the monkish chronicles whitewashed him well and truly and surnamed him the Peaceable. But Edgar's way of life caused comment even in those rough-and-ready days, and gave the ballad-mongers material long after Edgar himself had joined his ancestors. And one of these tales has Andover for a setting and is told by William of Malmesbury. Edgar, then on a visit to the town, heard from every one the praises of a local beauty. Edgar was never the one to pass by a local beauty, and his ideas of beauty were, I imagine, somewhat elastic. He therefore commanded that the girl should be brought before him. Now the girl was the daughter of his hostess, and this good lady was obviously many years in advance of her time, for she contrived that a slave should take her daughter's place. Edgar, not a very observant man, did not discover the fraud until the following morning. He then freed the slave and kept her until "he took Elfrida, the daughter of Ordgar, to be his legitimate wife."

Other kings also visited Andover. King John is supposed to have slept in the ancient inn (part of which is still an inn) called the Angel. Henry VII was here after Perkin Warbeck's rebellion. Charles I was here for a night after the second battle of Newbury, and James II on his retreat from Salisbury in 1688 just prior to his abdication. He had supper at the Priory House and the meal must have been a sad one for his companions were the traitors, Prince George who "drunk or sober had nothing in him," and Ormond, and James must have guessed that they were but waiting an opportunity to go over to Dutch William. George III was also here on his way to Weymouth. But the chief excitement of Andover seems to have come at election times. Then the doings were pretty wild, and money seems to have flowed as fast as the drink. There was much practical joking too, but that is not at all different from the general custom elsewhere at the time. And on the whole Andover seems to have been, as it is to-day, a respectable thoroughly utilitarian town throughout its history.

A little to the south of the town at Upper Clatford the Anna, which is also called the Pillhill, joins the Anton, and just before doing so passes at the foot of Bury Hill. On Bury Hill is a big early British camp, now nearly buried in the undergrowth and a great place for nesting birds. An archæological lecturer, telling his audience why the camp could never have been occupied because there was not a well, was pulled up by a farm labourer thus: "Did used to be well 'ere when I were boy: she were dangerous and she were filled in; I aided fill she."

A short way further up the stream is the village of Abbots Ann with its curious memorial garlands. The funeral custom, once common in many Hampshire villages, attached to the "blameless" life is still observed, and will one day no doubt be known as the funeral rite of Abbots Ann. Gilbert White, in his *Antiquities*, recalls how in Selborne church he could

> remember when its beams were hung with garlands in honour of young women of the parish, reputed to have died virgins: and recollect to have seen the clerk's wife cutting, in white paper, the resemblance of gloves, and ribbons to be twisted in knots and roses, to decorate these memorials of charity. In the church of Faringdon, which is the next parish, many garlands of this sort still remain.

Washington Irving, in his *Sketch Book*, called this "a delicate and beautiful rite." It now lingers only at Abbots Ann, but not in the same form as once at Selborne and Faringdon. For here both maidens and young men, spinsters and bachelors of whatever age, wear to the grave "the white flower of a blameless life." When such a one dies, his or her companions accompany the coffin to the grave carrying a chaplet or "virginal crown" and a pair of large white gloves on a wand. After burial these virginal crowns are preserved in the church. Though I do not think as Washington Irving, though I can see nothing particularly delicate or beautiful in the rite, I do hope that it will not be allowed to die out, for, to my mind, it is a most interesting memorial of times in England when chastity was even less common than it is to-day.

Beyond Abbots Ann is Monxton. Monxton is the prettiest village of the Anna group. On the ordnance maps the spelling is that used here, but it always annoys me terribly, for it should be Monkston, and I regard the "x" as ugly and unnecessary. I hope that we shall not follow the Ordnance Survey any further and come to write socks as sox (as some advertisement copywriters do already) or rocks as rox, but I fear that it is not improbable.

From Fullerton down the main river for some miles is the fishing of the Houghton Club. The water is kept most marvellously and the fish are large and well educated. But if the Houghton Club has a very good effect on the river it has as a whole had a bad effect on the countrymen of the district. As I have already said, you cannot join the Club unless you are more than ordinarily wealthy. That, I think, is a good thing. And the members most definitely bring money into the district. Unfortunately everyone for miles around knows that to fish this particular stretch of the Test needs money. On the downs away in North Hampshire the men are stolid and slow of speech and, as is proper, inclined to be suspicious of strangers. But they are at heart as thoroughly friendly and without meanness or cruelty or guile as men could well be. They take a man at his face value. And so in the other country districts of Hampshire. But not around Stockbridge. Here they care nothing for face value. They regard you closely and make a mental note about your financial standing in the world. They are friendly enough always; but more friendly if they think that you are rich. And that is not the way of the country-man. This attitude is not the fault—by which I mean the deliberate fault—of the members of the Houghton Club. First and foremost these gentlemen are fishermen—and that means that they are delightful men, for fishermen the world over, be they rich or poor, are simple and friendly souls, at least while they are by the water. It is the fault more of the countryman who, spoilt perhaps by a member or two in the boom years, is still on the look out for an easy penny. You cannot blame him, but it is a pity.

Stockbridge, which is the centre of all this fishing (though the village from which the club takes its name lies about two miles lower down the Test), is very attractive with its broad street and the steep hills rising at each end. I should think that almost every type of architecture from Tudor times onwards is to be found in this street, but the effect of the jumble taken together is most pleasing. Outside the club room of the Grosvenor Arms, Stockbridge has no note-worthy history. But it once had fame. It was one of the four "inconsiderable places" in the county that were de-prived of the privileges they enjoyed in returning members to Parliament under the old rotten borough system. Gay, in his *A Journey To Exeter*, has a verse about the town:

Sutton we pass, and leave her spacious down,
And with the setting sun reach Stockbridge town.
O'er our parch'd tongues the rich metheglin glides,
And the red dainty trout our knife divides.
Sad melancholy ev'ry visage wears;
What, no election come in seven years!
Of all our race of Mayors, shall Snow alone
Be by Sir Richard's dedication known?
Our streets no more with tides of ale shall float,
Nor cobblers feast three years upon one vote.

Gay did not exaggerate. Stockbridge was, in fact, the rottenest of all the rotten boroughs in the county, and that is no small claim to fame. There is a story that Steele, when he was canvassing the town, stuck an apple full of guineas and promised it to the first couple that should have an addition to the family nine months after he was elected. He did not get re-elected because he failed to keep his promise. It was an expensive business to get oneself elected as Member of Parliament for Stockbridge in the old days. In 1790 Captain Luttrell and Lord Imham spent £10,000 each on one election. Nowadays, though there is plenty of grumbling at the expense, all that really seems to be necessary are the promises, and the standard of observance does not appear to have altered since the time of Steele.

At one end of the town stands the oldest building in the place, or what is left of it. It stands in an old graveyard and it is the chancel of the ancient church, which was built about 900 years ago and pulled down in 1863. The old door ring is still there, and there are some wall-paintings, and a little old glass, and outside, by one of the west windows, there is a dial that was telling Stockbridge the time before the Conqueror came. But the thing I like best of all is the head-stone of the grave on one John Bucket:

And is, alas, poor Bucket gone?
Farewell, convivial honest John.
Oft at the well by fatal stroke
Buckets like Pitchers must be broke.
In this same motley shifting scene

How various have thy fortunes been
Now lifted high, now sinking low,
Today thy brim would overflow
Thy bounty then would all supply
To fill and drink and leave thee dry.
Tomorrow sunk as in a well
Content unseen with Truth to dwell:
But high or low or wet or dry
No rotten stave could malice spy.
Then rise, immortal Bucket, rise,
And claim thy station in the skies.

John Bucket was the landlord of the King's Head Inn, and sounds like a good one.

Beyond Houghton village the Test becomes three streams and not one, and I am never sure which of the two big branches (the third is merely a small stream) is the main river. At Bossington, which you come to just before Horsebridge, the Wallop Brook comes into the river. The Wallop Valley, which is called Wallop Fields, is wide and shallow between irregular hills (some of them very steep) and the earth is pleasantly red. I like Broughton (pronounced Brawton) better than either of the Wallops, perhaps because of the dovecote in the churchyard, but all three villages are thoroughly attractive, and both Broughton and Nether Wallop have friendly inns. Between these two is Nine Mile Water, and that is an astonishing name to find by a brook whose total length, counting every twist and turn, cannot be nine miles. I suppose that it is a corruption of Nine Mill Water, but even that I do not find very satisfactory. The only thing of interest to sightseers in all these villages is the pyramid in Nether Wallop churchyard. It is about twelve feet high, and it was set up in memory of an eighteenth-century "Doctor of Physick." It bears his coloured arms, and for some unexplained reason has red flames rising from the top.

In the eighteenth century Nether Wallop had a haunting. It was not a very good ghost and nobody seemed very clear as to what it did, what it was, or why it was. It showed itself by rattling the latch of a cottage door with irritating persistency. The tenant, being apparently convinced that it was not the wind (supposing that she had thought of so simple a solution), went to considerable trouble to prove that the rattling was due to some supernatural agency. She balanced bits of coal and of stick upon the latch and these "were constantly thrown off"; and she then, according to Gatehouse in his manuscript history,

> privately drew with a Brush and Paint, a Square of about a foot extent upon the Door, so as to inclose the handle of the Latch . . . the Lines being all exactly even and parralel, so that had any hand, or other Power touched the said handle, it must have appeared when the Day-light came: but nothing had ever affected the same. . . . She also privately caused ashes to be sifted about the Door, which must have detected any foot-step; but nothing of that sort appeared.

And Gatehouse got some of his family to witness this document and had it attested by the parson . . . so that the ghost must have made a considerable stir at the time. I do not know if the Nether Wallop haunting is still remembered by the inhabitants. When I asked an old man by the road-side about the ghost and if there were still ghosts in the village, he cocked a dark and bleary eye at me and said shortly: "Na, but there did ort be."

From Nether Wallop you can go to Danebury. You also can go from Stockbridge, and that is the easier way, but much the best way is from this village. The view from Woolbury, that is the hill on the Winchester side of Stockbridge, is the finer, but Danebury was obviously the more important of the two encampments. Indeed from the size of the fosse this must have been one of the most important townships in Hampshire before the Romans came. There have been improvements since then. The main roads, compared with the roads then, are wonderful, though the motorists still find cause for complaint: the railway runs through the valley, no more than half a mile away: aeroplanes roar overhead almost continuously. But over Danebury and the country round there is a sense of great age.

The people have changed, farming practice has altered, speed has conquered distance and almost overtaken time: there have been changes, too, on Danebury—the great earthworks are not what they were. But the hill remains just as it always was. Modern man standing on its summit must, despite the aeroplanes and railways and motor-cars, feel insignificant. That is the power of Danebury.

Two miles beyond Bossington is Mottisfont. Near here, actually at a little place called Brook, is a stream called the Farburn, which was used by the Abbess of St. Mary at Winchester to drive a mill and to supply fish when river-trout were unseasonable. I should think that the artificial reservoir made in the valley here was the earliest made in England. In a dry winter you can still see the great artificial dam about 25 feet high stretching away half across the valley, and the lake has now been partly restored and is a beautiful stretch of water of about 15 acres and reputedly swarming with trout. Mottisfont itself is beautiful with its tall trees and lush water-meadows, and just below Mottisfont another tributary of the Test comes in. Properly speaking this is, I suppose, a Wiltshire stream and not a Hampshire stream at all, for it rises well over the border. It is a pretty stream and it holds some quite good fish; it is larger than either the Anton or the Wallop; but it has not apparently got a name. The Ordnance Map does not give it one, and that must mean that it has not got an official name. And the locals have no special name for it. I have heard it called the Blackwater (a good many Hampshire streams are called that) and I have heard it called the Whitewater, and I have heard it called the Dun, and I have heard it called the Rife, which it certainly is not for Rife means "drain," which it is most definitely not. I should say that the Dun is the most likely, for there is a place on its banks called Dunbridge. But the main point of interest about it is its lack of title, and it would, perhaps, be a pity to take that away.

Three miles lower down the Test from Dunbridge—and the Test is now a big river—is Romsey. And Romsey deserves a chapter to herself.

CHAPTER V

ROMSEY AND THE ABBEY

ROMSEY to-day is not an attractive town. There has been much building of late and none of it is pleasant to look upon. It is quite a busy little place with its brewery (you are in "the Strong country" here, as the publicity manager of the brewery loses no opportunity of letting you know), its iron works and its corn and paper mills. I do not know anything about its iron works and nothing about its corn and paper mills, but I do like its beer. And in the square is The White Horse Inn, which is one of the very few in Hampshire that provides *good* food, a welcome and courteous service at reasonable prices. I have been there many times and always found that to be so, and it is a great deal more than I can say for most of the inns that I stay at in the county.

But though Romsey is an unattractive town taken as a whole—and you should never come into it from Winchester, but always from Salisbury; the Winchester entrance is positively hideous—there is scarcely a street in the town that has not got something pleasing or historic in it. The trouble is that the most of every street is so displeasing that one does not wait to explore as one should. There is, for example, the Conservative Club, once the Swan Inn, outside which there is a really beautiful piece of hammered iron-work. Fairfax used this iron-work as a gallows and from it hanged those of his soldiers who misbehaved themselves. And in the square is Matthew Noble's bronze statue of Lord Palmerston. Palmerston was born in Romsey and here he grew up. The fine white house Broadlands was there when James I used to come to the town, but it has been much enlarged, though I believe that, except for certain sanitary details and the matter of lighting and heating it is now much as it was in Palmerston's day.

And then there is Church Court, and it was here—as late as 1927—that the house known as King John's House was

127

found. A narrow alley leads to Church Court. On one side of it are eighteenth-century cottages, and on the other is a Tudor cottage of great charm with white wattle and daub walls held together by timbers, its four doors fixed by hand-forged nails, its oak hearth-kerb held by wooden pegs, its windows opening and shutting with Tudor hasps and catches. Set between these cottages is King John's House with its walls of flint and stone, some very fine windows and an ancient gargoyle. King John, we know, sent his little daughter Princess Joanna here with Christiana of Romsey as Governess, and we know that he charged the mayor and bailiffs of Winchester the sum of twopence a day for her maintenance. And we know that when she married the King of Scotland in 1221 the house in which she lived was given to the Abbey as a guest house. This is supposed to be the house, and King John is supposed to have built it as a hunting box. Perhaps he did and perhaps it is. It does not matter very much. It is beautiful anyhow. It has the original stone doorways, a beautiful but rather battered window with moulding inside and out, an oak roof with a Tudor kingpost, a three-handled stone mortar shaped by an axe seven hundred years ago, and, perhaps most marvellous of all its treasures, a set of blazoned shields, two portrait heads, and many mottoes cut in the plaster with the point of a dagger. The experts say that these drawings were done on the night of 13 February 1306, at the time when Edward III visited Romsey with his court. There is at any rate the crowned head of a king, and I suppose that it might just as well be Edward III as any other early king.

Not far away is the Abbey. And the Abbey straight away lifts the town from the commonplace and puts it among the elect. Coming from Winchester past bungalows and advertisements on shabby hoardings and under a very dirty bridge the Abbey looks less impressive than any parish church that you care to mention. But come from Salisbury, and from the hill above the broad wooded Test valley the church stands out, dwarfing the modern buildings that huddle so closely round it. Even so from the outside, once you are on a level, the modern buildings crowd in so closely that one might easily ignore the finest church in all Hampshire—perhaps in all the south of England.

But once inside and time stands still. Here is real beauty, the beauty of perfect proportion. Here is beauty without one single flaw. True it is that there are many different styles, but the people that built here were artists in love with their work and in love with God, and each style so fits into another that the building really is a whole. And the building is warm and welcoming; which is a great deal more than many churches are. The men that built here were in love with their work—everywhere you may see proof that this was so. The beautifully carved ornaments on capital and doorway, the wonderful carving of the corbels, no two alike: here is all the story of mankind, all its good, all its evil, all its loves, all its passions; here are kings and princes and martyrs crowned and in glory; here are priests cowled, some looking saintly and some looking vicious; here are beautiful women and here women with all the devilry in the world writ large upon their faces; here are faces alight with grace and the Truth of God; here are faces with the cruelty of the Devil, faces with avarice and faces with lust; and all about are rare designs, ball and chevron and scroll. Here is Norman work without equal in all England from the most elementary upwards; here is a pattern that shows classical influence most strongly, the while the honeycomb capitals in the ambulatory are said to be Saracenic in origin. Walk down from the east end and notice how each successive bay marks progress, the earliest perhaps Saxon or addition to original Saxon work, the latest—at the western end of the nave aisles—perfect Early English. Stand before the choir-screens and drink in beauty. Realize what men could do when God was more powerful than Mammon.

And yet of all this there is very little history. We do not know whose brain it was that was responsible for the idea. We do not know who put up the money. But we do know that the present building was built above and around a much older church, and that parts of the older church were incorporated in the new, and we do know that men lived just here before ever there was a church. As you stand in the centre of the nave, there lie under your feet the remains of a Roman villa, ruined and forgotten long before the first stone of the Abbey was placed in position. And it is possible that there is preserved in the church one other relic of those long distant times. In 1839, while a grave was being dug in the side aisle near the Abbess's door, the sexton found, at four feet deep, great masses of masonry, which were believed to be the foundations of an earlier church than the present Norman Abbey, and underneath this mass of masonry was a leaden coffin of extreme antiquity, which was lying north and south. That is not Christian burial. It contained the skeleton of a girl which the first breath of air crumbled into dust, leaving only a heavy plait of brilliant auburn hair (which is still preserved in the church) and which is almost as bright and shining as when the body was laid to rest, perhaps 1,600 years ago. It does not seem improbable that the girl lived in the Roman house.

And then when the floor was relaid towards the end of the last century, the foundations of most of the previous Saxon church were found, evidently left by the Norman builders to secure a solid base for their columns in the gravel bed on which the Abbey stands. If you lift the trap-door by the pulpit you can still see part of the apse that formed the east end of the Saxon church. The earliest Christian building, no doubt, was a wooden one built so the chronicler tells us by Edward the Elder. This church was replaced in 967 by the first stone church, and this church was in its turn pulled down about 1120 to make room for the Norman building that still stands.

There are other early signs also. In the east wall of the south chancel aisle, over the side altar, there is a Saxon carving in white stone representing the Crucifixion. It is done in high relief and there are many indications of an early date. For instance, Our Lord is beardless and the limbs are unbent; two attendant angels are placed on the limbs of the Cross; and below there are the figures of the Virgin and St. John, the soldier with the sponge and the vessel of vinegar, and the centurion with the spear. History relates that King Edgar gave a gilt crucifix to the Abbey. It seems very likely that this is that crucifix, despoiled of its jewels (some of the lead sockets remain), and if so it is in a wonderful state of preservation. There is yet another memorial of these Saxon times in the church. If you go out by the Abbess's door in the south wall you will find built into the west wall of the transept an almost life-sized figure of Our Lord upon the Cross. No one knows the exact date of this, but it shows strong evidence of Byzantine influence, and no example of this type of crucifix is found later than the eleventh century. These early representations of Christ upon the Cross are interesting for they have quite a different appeal. All modern representations show us Christ dead or dying. The appeal is to our pity, and so to our gratitude. The early representation—such as this one on the wall of Romsey Abbey—shows Christ alive. The head is erect and the eyes are open. There are wounds in the hands and feet, but there are no nails. The arms are outstretched but not in death, in the gesture of welcome. Christ calling you home. And from the sky above a hand points downward—the Father's hand. "This is my beloved Son."

I suppose that the history of Romsey Abbey may be said to start in the year 907. It was in that year that the Princess Aethelflaeda, the eldest grand-daughter of Alfred the Great, came with twelve companions to the island in the marshes (that is what the word Romsey means) to devote herself to the worship of God and the care of His poor. It was her father, Edward the Elder, who built her a church; it was here she lived and here she died, and here, somewhere, she lies in an unknown grave. The next that we know of Romsey is when another Ethelfleda was in residence, but not yet as Abbess, only as a nun. The Abbess at the time was a great and wise Irish lady named Morwenna (who became a saint), and it was in her charge that Edgar the Peaceful placed the unwanted daughter of his wife, the daughter of that Ethelwold whom he had murdered in Harewood Forest. Edgar began the rebuilding and enlargement of the Abbey about 966—that is, about one year after the incident in Harewood Forest, if the date upon the monument is correct. But I think that the date upon the monument is incorrect and that the murder of Ethelwold

took place about 962 or 963. Edgar married the beautiful
Elfrida in 964, according to E. W. Robertson, the most
reliable of the historians dealing with the period, and he
suggests that the marriage took place two years after the
murder. So long a lapse of time does not seem to fit in
with Edgar's character at all, until one realizes that the
lady was pregnant at the time, and that the daughter of
Ethelwold was not born until some time after her father's
death. There is some mystery about the whole affair, but
there can be no doubt that the child was destitute and that
she was placed in the care of the Abbess Morwenna by the
King, and there can be no doubt that she took the veil at
Romsey and was consecrated by Bishop Aethelwold before
Edgar's death in 975, when she would be eleven or twelve
years old.

The saintly Abbess Morwenna died about 993, but Ethelfleda, though already widely known, did not immediately
succeed her. The next Abbess was Elwina. This lady,
"prostrate before the Altar in prayer, was counted worthy
to hear a voice falling from heaven of the coming of the
Danes to the Monastery of Romsey on the next evening.
And she gathering up the relics and other possessions fled
with the sisters to Winchester." Here they were hospitably
received by the nuns of St. Mary's. "So Swanus, the king
of the Danes, with his son Canute, coming to these parts,
destroyed what was left with fire and sword." The mention
of Canute has caused the *Victoria County History* to date
Elwina's flight 1006, which was the date of the second great
Danish raid following the massacre of St. Brice's Day. But
I think that it must have been during the first raid for
otherwise it would mean that Morwenna was a lady of very
great age when she died and that Elwina was of a considerable age when she became Abbess and a very, very great
age indeed when she died. But in both raids the Danes paid
great attention to Hampshire. The Saxon Chronicle describes how, in 994, after besieging London without success,
the Danes "wrought the utmost evil that ever army could
do, by burning and plundering and by man-slaying, both by
sea and coast, and among the East Saxons, and in the land
of Kent and in Sussex and in Hampshire." The Chronicle

The River Bourne near Hurstbourne Priors

describes the raid of 1006 in graphic terms: "And then in mid-winter . . . throughout Hampshire, into Berkshire, and to Reading; and they did their old wont; they lighted war beacons as they went . . . they joined battle and they soon brought that band to flight, and afterwards carried their booty to the sea. But there might the Winchester men see an army, daring and fearless, as they went by their gates towards the sea, and fetched themselves food and treasures over fifty miles." Stirring times, and times of terror for the quiet men and women of the country-side.

Elwina was Abbess for only three years, and when she died (probably the horror of the Danish raid had a good deal to do with her early death) she was succeeded by the Holy Virgin Ethelfleda, beloved of the sisters. Now, this Ethelfleda and not the first one, the grand-daughter of Alfred the Great, is the patron saint of the Abbey. The Abbey originally dedicated in the honour of the Blessed Virgin Mary, but the name of St. Ethelfleda, virgin and abbess, was united with that of the Blessed Virgin in the dedication at a very early date. It has sometimes been thought that the lady was the first Ethelfleda, but there can be no reasonable doubt, I think, that it was the second and the *Romsey Psalter* was certainly in no doubt about it. And here is the account of the Saint. It is taken from a MS., which was once in the Library of Romsey Convent and is now in the B.M., MSS., Lands, No. 436. It is a fourteenth-century MS., which contains a chronicle of the Saxon Kings and the Lives of English Saints. Of these lives there are forty-seven and the sixteenth is entitled:

Here begins the account of Saint Alfleda and Saint
Merwinna, Virgins and Abbesses.

During the reign of Edgar, the illustrious and most Christian King of the English, there was a certain nobleman, by name Edwold, who, on account of his probity and tried fidelity, seemed to the King to excel all the rest of the courtiers of the royal service.

The King therefore gave to him in marriage Brich-giva, a young lady discreet in manners and handsome

Wherwell—somnolent Saxon Thatch

in form, and near of kin to his wife, Queen Elfrida. This lady had by him a large family of sons and daughters. Now, before the birth of her last daughter, in sign that she should be a child of light and worthy of God, the mother saw in a dream a ray of the glorious sun break forth above her head. In due time she gave birth to a daughter, re-born by the Holy Spirit through Baptism, by the Christian named Athelfleda. Who born and re-born was always pleasing to Christ, because the more she grew in age and stature, so much the more fully was she without desire for carnal pleasures. Which King Edgar hearing of, and not unmindful of the probity and fidelity of the dead Ethelwold, delivered the daughter Athelfleda, who was near of kin to the Queen, to the Blessed Merwenna, Abbess of the Monastery of Romsey, which he had constructed, to be brought up by her. After a time the Blessed Merwynna, having proved her to be active in the works of saintliness and obedience, recognized her as one who would undoubtedly profit under God's favour in the church. She therefore cherished her with the privilege of so great a love, that in going out and coming in, by day and by night, she desired to have her continually in attendance. And right well did Abbess Merwynna behave as a most sweet mother to Ethelfleda, and Ethelfleda as a most loving daughter to Merwynna. The one taught the way of the Lord in truth as a most modest mother, and the other, by entire obedience as a dutiful daughter, retained zealously what she had been taught. The one, as a torch of light, showed the way without error along a path of righteousness, the other, delighting in such a leader, followed without stumbling. The one on fasting days chastened her body by hunger, the other, whatever by abstinence from food she withheld from the body, she distributed to the poor in secret.

The King and Queen, pleased with her saintliness, with the consent of the Blessed Merwynna, caused her to be consecrated by the Bishop of Winchester, of good memory. And she lived henceforward under Abbess

Merwynna for some time, abundant in virtues, generous in alms, constant in watches, in speech vigilant, in mind humble, of joyful countenance, and kindly mannered to the poor. And that she might hide her saintliness and be able to help the destitute, she pretended at table among her companions to drink when she did not drink, and to eat when she did not eat, hiding in her sleeves the food which she was intending to bestow upon the poor.

Applying herself constantly to prayer, she loved the ecclesiastical and regular institutions, insomuch that she would never hear or say the canonical hours, as long as she lived the cloister life with the convent sisters, except within the church, nor would she omit any Hour on account of any secular business, nor be hindered by the greatest indisposition of body. In the church, the Blessed Ethelfleda in the singing and reading which were enjoined her was careful to fulfil her turn without a murmur. How acceptable to God her service was, he deigned to show by a glorious miracle. On her night for reading the lesson after receiving the benediction she approached the pulpit, but the lamp which she took in her hand to give light for the reading was extinguished, I do not say by chance, but by the providence of God, as the sequel showed. O, great grace of God! abundant mercy did not permit light in darkness to be without light. For such brilliance shone around the fingers of the right hand of Ethelfleda, the handmaiden of God, that it gave the clearest light to those around, and ministered to the reading very brilliantly. Nor did the heavenly splendour pass away before the lesson was entirely read by the servant of God, and the earthly light brought in. Wherefore it is to be ascribed to the finger of God that those fingers were illuminated, which, as is believed, were wholly free from unlawful touch.

It happened once on a time that her teacher went into a plantation of saplings, near to the house, where Athelfleda with the rest of the young girls was accustomed to study. Now whilst the mistress alone and without any witness was privately cutting the switches, the Blessed Athelfleda miraculously saw through the wall of the stone house, as through a glass, the saplings in the hands of the mistress cut for beating herself or her companions, which, tied up into bundles, she feared no less for them than for herself. But the mistress returning and bearing the switches, concealed and secretly, has scarcely crossed the threshold of the house when her scholar, having cast herself at her feet, exclaimed in a loud but firm voice, with many tears, "Do not, Mistress, do not beat us with the switches: we will sing and chant at your pleasure, willingly, as much or as long as you wish or command. When we gladly carry out orders, why do you beat us?" The mistress, wondering beyond measure how her scholar became possessed of her secret, said, "Rise up my daughter, rise up, and show me how you know that I have brought any switches." And she said, "I saw you under the tree whence you plucked them, and you still hold them under your cloak." It was found by careful enquiry that what was done by the mistress could not have been known by the scholar save through the Holy Spirit, who works in each one according to His will, and that the sight of this pierced the thickness of a stone wall, by the power of God, who caused the eyes of the man born blind to be opened, so that the blind could miraculously see.

Now the Blessed Ethelfleda made a custom of going every night outside the dormitory, where it seemed to her that she could most conveniently and secretly immerse herself naked in the cold water of a fountain or in the bed of a running stream, and stay in for so long as time permitted, chanting the Davidic Psalms, many or few, together with some prayers in addition. It happened once, that, on account of her good fame, the Queen called the blessed Ethelfleda to herself and kept her honourably in her chamber. She unwillingly made some little stay there, always fearful lest the deceitful pleasure of earthly vanities, which she often saw practised around the Queen, as the manner is, in dress, behaviour and other things, which are called by the gay, refinement, but which hinder from holy religion, should recall her mind from her holy purpose. On her first arrival, sitting on a terrace and looking round, she saw, near the chamber, a spring of fresh water. To this she went every night without delay, as had been her custom elsewhere, secretly, when the others in the chamber were sleeping, by door or by window, as seemed most convenient, and having undressed, she chanted and prayed in the water as long as was possible to her. At length, having returned, she was found in the morning in bed like the others, apparently sleeping as though she had done nothing else through the whole night. One night, however, when the Queen could not sleep for thinking, she saw the holy woman go alone and without witness from the room, and, not knowing her secret, she imagined her to be going out for immodest purposes at such an hour of the night, rather than for any other cause. The handmaid of God went out, and the Queen followed. The one, having made the sign of the Cross in the water, sprang in, and the other, perhaps seeing a sign in the heavens, was distracted with excessive amazement, and returning to the threshold of the chamber, screamed loudly and fell to the ground. Those who were by gathered round her in wonder, and took her into their arms, but she, utterly wanting her senses, tossed about in their hands, as if frantic. But, whereas the cause was quite unknown to the others, it was revealed to the holy virgin alone from heaven; who, thinking over the matter silently, immediately prostrated herself on the ground and mingled tears with her prayer without ceasing, until the Queen was restored to her former health, and said constantly, among the other words of her prayer, "Lord, direct my prayer in Thy sight, and lay not this sin to her charge, who knows not what she has done."

In course of time, when the Blessed Ethelfleda was renowned for miracles such as this, Saint Merwynna, the Abbess dear to God, departed this life to Christ,

and Ethelfleda, the handmaid of God, succeeded her in
the office of prelate, although not immediately. By so
much as she was placed above the others, so much the
more did she seem to be an example of humility and
saintliness. She delighted especially in exercising works
of mercy towards the poor, of which hear what happened. One of the bailiffs, to whose keeping the tene-
ments of the church were committed, who was her
household servant, placed in the coffers of the Abbess
for safe keeping, the whole payment which he was
bound to render in one year for his custody. The handmaid of God, however, whose care was ever of the poor,
withdrew from the coffers, little by little, and distributed to the needy all the money committed to her,
and when it became time for the bailiffs to render
account of rents received for the whole year to the
steward who was placed over them, the servant demanded back the money which he had delivered to the
Lady Abbess. But of the squandered money only one
farthing was found. The bailiff, in anxiety, did not
know what to do and the Abbess was placed in no less
difficulty. She blushed to make public her expenses,
and could charge them neither to her subtlety or ex-
travagance, and much less to the religion, which, above
all things, she desired to hide. What shall she do?
With whom shall she seek refuge? With Him assur-
edly, who is the Helper of those in tribulation and
anxiety, in whose service also the whole spending of
the money has been carried out. The Blessed Ethelfleda, purposing moreover with great earnestness to
defend the innocence of her young servant from in-
famy, directed her prayer to the Lord, in whom she
had ever placed her whole hope, with great confidence,
and said, "God who hast created all things out of
nothing, and has caused all things created by Thee
wonderfully to obey Thy commands, multiply on us
Thy mercy, Who dost not forsake those who hope in
Thee. I, indeed, have hoped in Thee, and Thou hast
not withheld from my desire. And now, so direct this
matter, that I shall not be confounded; and if not

hearkened to by Thee, I shall be put into exceeding confusion, like to those who begin a building, and, not having first reckoned the cost, are not able to finish, and so my enemies will laugh me to scorn. God, who multipliest the things which we have, and wonderfully restorest the lost, restore the money spent on the needy to the honour of Thy Name. For Thou hast said, 'What thou hast done to one of My little ones, thou hast done to Me.'" What more? The prayer ended, the coffers, previously empty, were found full of money, and the bailiff, having been called, the whole money was restored to him with great joy. The servant, in despair before, ran, without doubt, to his reckoning. The holy virgin, indeed, hastily directed her way to the church in order to render thanks to the most high God, who looked on her humility and snatched her from confusion, and said, "God, Thou filled the cruise of oil lest it should fail, and multiplied five loaves so that they sufficed for five thousand men, to this day Thou hast not forgotten to do marvellous things, but hast restored the money delivered to me and spent. Blessed be Thy Name, both now and ever, world without end. Amen."

After these things the Blessed Ethelfleda, renowned for miracles and full of virtues, departed this life 10 Kal November, going from the body of this life, from temporal pain to unfading glory. A great multitude of women buried the pious virgin outside the sacred oratory, as she herself had directed, for she did not appoint for herself a tomb in a more conspicuous place, whom vain glory had never prevailed on to err. As she had preferred a life of humility under regular discipline, so, in the time of her dissolution, she chose humble burial out of doors in the porch. And thus, Ethelfleda, an uncorruptible and glorious virgin, rested for some time in the same place in which she was buried, but, afterwards, miracles having increased, she was translated into the church with fitting honour, where Christ, on account of the merits of his spouse, bestows immediate benefits on those who ask, "to the praise and

glory of His Name, to whom be honour and dominion,
world without end."

Another old MS. speaks of her death in these words:
"After that she had by long well-doing freighted and re-
plenished herself with virtuous treasure and celestial riches
withall, she sayled safely out of this world and happily
arrived at the Heavenly porte."

By this time, of course, the Abbey had been rebuilt.
There seems to be little doubt that the sisters returned to
the place soon after the raid by the Danes—they probably
left again at the time of the second raid for a short while—
but they were certainly there and well-established by 1012,
for in that year Queen Emma (then still the wife of Ethelred
the Unready) gave lands to the Abbey. The charter is
printed in Kemble's Collections, and the words are:

> This year Aelgyfu gave or bequeathed thaes landaes aet
> Hwaetaedunae into Rummaesigae Christe and Sanctan
> Marian.

The year was 1012 and Aelfgyfu is Elgiva or Emma (the
word means, "the gift of the fairies"), and evidently the
royal help was continued after Emma had married Cnut
and the latter had become a Christian. Cnut succeeded his
father in 1017 and we know from a list of names in the
Hyde Register that there were in 1020 fifty-four nuns
in the Convent. It must then have been a flourishing
place.

Then for a matter of forty years and more there is no
history for the Abbey. We know that Edward the Confessor made a gift of lands, and we know that William the
Conqueror confirmed the ancient rights of the Abbey, for
there is a reference to this in a Charter of Henry I. This
was a period of quiet and prosperity for the Abbey, and
during this time much work was done on the structure.
History commences again in 1086, the year in which *Domesday* was completed, for in that year Christina, the daughter
of Edmund Ironside and the sister of Edgar Atheling and
also of Margaret, Queen of Scotland, took the veil at

Romsey. It was because she was there that the two daughters of Malcolm Canmore and Margaret, the King and Queen of Scotland, were sent to Romsey to be educated. Their names were Eadgyth (who was afterwards known as Matilda the Good) and Mary. It is not known in what year the girls came into the charge of their aunt, but they were undoubtedly at Romsey in 1093, for in that year William the Red came over from Winchester to see the Princess Matilda. The young lady was, of course, a person of great importance, for not only was she the daughter of the King of Scotland but she was also the representative of the old Saxon line. Whether William came to court the Princess or to carry her off is uncertain, but the aunt (who was probably the Abbess, though we do not know that for certain) was very worried about the whole affair and dressed her niece up as a nun and told the King that she was at her devotions, and William, after admiring the roses, rode away. It is an extraordinary story. William was not the sort of man who admired roses. And, though he had almost every known vice, women were not included in the catalogue. This is the only time so far as I know when his name is connected with that of any woman at all. And finally, if he had wanted to see the girl or to take her away or to do anything else, he would have done it. A small matter such as devotions would certainly not have stopped him. It is difficult to know what to make of the story, but my own guess is that he came in search of a wife, saw the girl and decided that his ordinary amusements were the better worthwhile.

Within seven years he was dead. Immediately his brother Henry, who was looked upon with favour both by the girl and the aunt, appeared upon the scene. But Matilda had donned the veil. There seems to be little doubt about that, for there was a well-staged inquiry to prove that she had never done any such thing. Anselm was a complacent bishop, and Matilda became "Good Queen Molde" of England. Romsey while she reigned enjoyed great prosperity and acquired great wealth. Royalty stayed within its walls, and it became even more a seat of learning, and a sort of University for the young of royal blood. Queen

Maud died in 1118 and two years later the building of the present great church was begun. Probably Henry I had a good deal to do with it, for there seems no doubt that his Queen had always held a great affection for the place and he was perhaps promoting her wishes after her death.

The next Abbess of note was Mary, Princess of Blois, and the youngest daughter of King Stephen. Her mother, Queen Maud, was the daughter of that Mary, who with her sister Matilda, later wife of Henry I, was brought up in Romsey. She was the favourite daughter and early dedicated to a monastic life. Like her grandmother she was sent to Romsey, though whether this was by her father or by Henry II is uncertain. It was not easy to be a Princess and an Abbess at the same time. In 1160 her brother William, Count of Boulogne, died and she became heiress to a great property. She became a prize in the royal game. Henry II, who was a man who brooked no opposition, urged Matthew of Alsace to marry her, and he, despite the strenuous opposition of Thomas à Becket came and carried her off. I do not think that she went willingly. The King was against her and she had no relatives left, and I think that she stood little chance. And she certainly never forgave Henry and did everything in her power to do him harm. The marriage took place in 1161, and it ended in 1169 when she left her husband and retired into the monastery of St. Austerberthe, where she died in 1182 at the very early age of forty-two, leaving two daughters who were afterwards legitimatized by the Pope.

I think that with the abduction of Mary, Princess of Blois, we may date the beginning of the decline in the prestige of the Abbey. The fortunes of the Abbey still continued to increase. Richard I was too busy elsewhere, but John helped the Abbey in a number of ways, and Henry III was very generous throughout his fifty-six years of reign. In wealth and in power Romsey continued to grow; but not in prestige.

It had been founded by a King's daughter; it had been fortunate early in its life in a very great and saintly Abbess, Morwenna; in her stead Ethelfleda, though she appears to have been canonized on the strength of one or two incon-

siderable miracles, gave to the foundation an enormous
reputation for sanctity; members of the royal family were
closely connected with it; it was a seat of learning as well
as a place of devotion. And then came the abduction of
Mary. Mary was succeeded by the Abbess Juliana. During
her abbacy Henry II brought over from France nuns from
the Abbey of Fontevrault. This took place sixteen years
after the abduction of Mary, and one can only suppose that
during those sixteen years there had been a steady decline
in numbers within the Abbey, and that there was a lack of
novices seeking profession. During the long reign of
Henry III there were no less than eight abbesses, and for a
period of almost a year there was no abbess at all. So many
changes in the rule of a great and influential institution
such as Romsey Abbey undoubtedly was cannot have made
for efficiency. Yet this was the golden age of monasticism.
There must have been something very wrong somewhere.
And there are signs towards the end of the thirteenth
century, when the Episcopal Visitations begin, that the
discipline of the Abbey had already grown lax.

The first visitation was made by Archbishop Peckham
in 1283. And this is what he had to say:

> Brother John, by Divine permission the humble ser-
> vant of the Church of Canterbury, primate of all
> England, to his beloved daughters in Christ the Abbes
> and Convent of Romeseyhe, salutation, grace and
> benediction.
> In a lily garden the Bridegroom is filled with delight,
> and finds pleasure in gathering lilies above all other
> flowers. It is therefore needful to enclose this garden
> by the defence of shrewd and sharp discipline, as the
> Paradise of God was enclosed by angelic care and the
> flaming sword, lest an entrance be opened to the ser-
> pent into the same, or to any sower of mischief, by
> which the pleasure of the Bridegroom should be turned
> to displeasure or less liking. The lily we believe to be
> the whole celestial and angelic ornament of virginal
> purity, which, by reason of certain matters found in
> our Metropolitan visitation lately held, in canonical

form, we desire to protect in perpetuity by the ready defence of injunctions.

First, therefore, we ordain that the Abbess for the time being choose a discreet council and change her companions every year so that by many testimonies the truth of her discretion may become known. Also that she bear in mind to behave as a mother of the society, and to cause herself to be regarded as such by all and each who require consolation, no less than is an earthly mother by her natural daughters. Let her therefore always seek to attract to herself the true affection of all without the accepting of persons, and so to show herself with saving probity to all alike that she be in no way noted for partiality. Let her, moreover, earnestly consider herself not as the mistress of the community's goods, but only as one who discharges the office of stewardess.

No abbess is to live finely and especially whilst the convent suffer want, and if the convent lack, the abbess is to show her sympathy, as a mother to her daughters, by doing away with her separate table and eating with the sisters, and any guests are to be refreshed at such times in the common hall.

Without the advice of the Chapter, she is not to appoint the steward, bailiffs or household servants.

If the abbess cannot be present at compline, the nun who is over the choir, with two of the more honourable of the nuns, shall inform her that compline has been said, and immediately all drinking in her chamber shall cease, and all lay people, whether of the household or guests, and also the religious shall leave, and at once the abbess shall say compline that she may be with the convent in the night watches, provided that she is not prevented by bodily infirmity; and in her chamber she shall have no lay people beyond two handmaidens.

The nuns are not to eat, when in good health, except in the refectory or abbess' chamber.

No man is to enter the nuns' chambers under the pain of the greater excommunication, but in the case of sickness the confessor, doctor, or relative may do so, in honourable company, and so avoid even the suspicion of evil.

Four officers are to keep the cloisters clear of any persons who come to gaze or chatter. A nun breaking silence with any man in the cloister is to be deprived of a pittance at the next meal. Such conversation is permitted only in the parlour or in the side of the church next the cloister, and to avoid unseemly conversation she is to have two companions.

Confessions are to be heard before the high altar or at the side of the church next the cloister.

No nun is to go out except in staid company, nor is she to stay with secular folk beyond three days.

The superstition accustomed to be observed at the Nativity and Ascension of our Lord, we condemn for ever.

Women are not to be admitted as paying guests without licence.

At the end there is a special injunction:

That a habit having arisen on the part of those going out, of eating and drinking on their return in the houses of layfolk and clerks in the town of Romseye, this is forbidden to the Abbess and sisters on pain of suspension from the monastery for a year.

Three coadjudicators are appointed for the Abbess— Margery de Verdun, Phillipa de Stokes and Johanna de Rovedoune—an unheard of proceeding and a great indignity for the Abbess. The instructions themselves are worded softly and kindly enough, but it is quite evident that the Abbey had gained a name for something other than sanctity. There must indeed have been some virulent gossip to have brought the Archbishop on a visitation.

The early part of the fourteenth century saw little improvement. Between 1298 and 1333 there were four abbesses, and the third of these, Alicia de Wyntereshulle, was murdered after only three months of office by poison.

Who instigated the crime was never discovered, but it was discovered that the whole convent—abbess, nuns, officials and servants—were guilty of fairly scandalous living. Then came an abbess who ruled for eighteen years (a very long rule compared with those of her immediate predecessors) and during this time we hear nothing very much about the Abbey, which can only mean that she pulled it together again. There were two visitations by Bishops of Winchester during this period but they do not reveal any great scandals, and the only injunction of note is that no nun shall have a curtain around her bed. That Sybil Carbonel pulled the Abbey together is shown clearly by the fact that at the election of her successor there were ninety-two nuns in residence and that the school was full of children of both sexes. Then came the Black Death. It has been estimated that the total population of England at the time was about five million and that about half of that number died. But it is not generally realized that the pestilence did not sweep over England but rather crept over the country with a terrifying slowness. It is known to have entered by a Dorset port, probably Weymouth, about the month of August 1348 and it did not reach Yorkshire until a full twelve months later. It reaped a particularly heavy harvest in the walled towns, in the monasteries and among the religious generally. It was a soil poison, but it must not be thought that it was not contagious. Far from that: "It was virulent, and so contagious that those who touched the dead, or even the sick, were incontinently infected that they died, and both penitent and confessor were borne together to the same grave." In Hampshire alone more than two hundred clergy perished. Romsey did not escape. The Abbess died, two of the Vicars died, and at least one of the Prebendaries. And there was a very heavy death-roll among the nuns. We do not know how many died in the pestilence, but we do know that there were ninety-two when the plague struck the town, and the next count that we have of the nuns in the convent can muster only eighteen, and the number never rose again above twenty-five until the final suppression.

If Henry II had put the Abbey on the downward slope,

the Plague and the troubles that followed in its train proved fatal to the great house.

No one could deny that the closing years of the Convent's existence were eventful. In 1472 Elizabeth Broke was elected Abbess. Six years later she asks Bishop Waynflete to accept her resignation. The Bishop had come to the Convent to inquire into certain stories he had heard (as a matter of fact the town must have been fairly buzzing with gossip), and what he found out must have made the poor man's hair stand on end. The Abbess confessed to perjury and to committing adultery with one John Placy. Her resignation was, of course, accepted. But there is some mystery about the whole affair, for the Bishop of Salisbury promptly absolved her, and her prompt re-election as Abbess does not seem to have surprised Bishop Waynflete at all. Elizabeth Broke was evidently popular with the sisters, and they probably thought that with her return to office their own shortcomings, which were not inconsiderable, were more likely to be overlooked. At any rate she was elected again. And the Convent promptly went from bad to worse.

On 29 October 1492 a further visitation was made on the instruction of Archbishop Morton. This showed that things were not as they should be outside the Abbey and that inside they were about as bad as they could be. But nothing was done. I cannot help but think that Elizabeth Broke was a woman of great charm and that she knew very well how to use that charm on those who conducted the visitations! But nine years later things had got to such a state that still another inquiry was ordered, and this was conducted by one Dr. Hede, a Commissary of the Prior of Canterbury. In 1492 it had been found that Elizabeth owed the sum of £1,000, and that she was more than friendly with the Rev. Bryce, the Chaplain of the Infirmary, that the nuns slipped out at night and frequented the taverns in the town, and that some of them slept in other and less desirable houses in the town of a night. But she remained as Abbess and Bryce as Chaplain. The inquiry of 1501 showed that things had not improved at all, and this time there were even rumours that Rev. Bryce was the father of a daughter, that men were admitted to the Convent at night, that the buildings were suffering from neglect, that the nuns wore their hair long, and that there was much drunkenness. Perhaps she might have been deposed again this time, but the next year she died.

Now, if ever, was the time for a strong abbess. Instead in 1502 the nuns elected by acclamation one Joyce Rowse, who was a sort of superior kitchenmaid. Within five years Bishop Fox had to issue a most severe injunction. He speaks to Joyce Rowse in very straight terms about drinking and eating to enormous excess, especially at night. He has to tell the nuns that they must not gossip with the townsfolk through the windows at night. He has to tell Thomas Leycrofts, the bailiff, that in future on pain of excommunication "he shall have no access to any chamber of the Abbess or nuns" and that he shall not send them letters or messages. And he has to tell William Scott that he shall not have "access to any nun or communicate with her through the kitchen window nor at any other place either in his own person or through some other person" on pain of excommunication. It would seem that Joyce Rowse had very much the same failings as Elizabeth Broke, and that the morals of the nuns had not improved. Eight years later Joyce Rowse resigned. Again we are left wondering why she was not deposed. Her successor was Anne Westbroke, a sacrist of the Abbey, and in the eight years of her office we hear of no scandals. Presumably she was not frail and presumably she was a stronger disciplinarian. She died in 1523 and Elizabeth Ryprose was elected in her place by acclamation. This, the last Abbess of Romsey, was a great woman. She had joined the nunnery more than twenty years before and so she knew all about the goings-on and all about the character of the women she had under her. Furthermore she does not figure as a scandalous character in any of the visitations. She put a stop to much that was wrong in the Convent, pulled it together, and was jealous of the high standing of her office. But it was too late. Henry VIII was short of money.

It is quite wrong to think that the suppression of the monasteries had anything to do with religion. Religion

148

was an excuse. The suppression was purely a financial manœuvre. It was, in fact, the first great experiment in Nationalization.

The first Act for suppressing the monasteries was passed in 1536. It dealt only with institutions with an income of £200 a year or less. The small, and therefore the weaker, members were to be attacked first. If this went well the bigger and stronger members would be dealt with in turn. One cannot but think that Henry was a little afraid of the effect upon public opinion. Romsey had an income considerably in excess of £200 a year, and was therefore not affected by the Act, but pressure was brought to bear on the Abbess as early as 1534. Elizabeth Ryprose put up a good fight, but she was forced to appoint receivers, and the men chosen were Thomas Foster and his son John. It was John Foster who played the major part in the suppression of the Abbey, and it was probably due to him that the Abbey's Rolls and MSS. were destroyed.

Henry was correct in his feeling that the suppression would offend public opinion. Eight months after the passing of the Act rebellion broke out in the north. "The Pilgrimage of Grace" was a big movement and for almost a year the Tudor dynasty was in danger of being overthrown. Some monasteries were reinstated by the rebels, and many of the King's visitors were attacked and roughly handled. But by the autumn of 1537 the King had regained control of the country and the work of suppression went forward. But he had learned a lesson. The larger institutions were bribed or threatened in the stead of another Act. Few remained by the end of 1538. If an abbot or an abbess proved true to the trust of office, he or she was deposed and a more amenable creature was appointed who immediately surrendered to the royal will. Such people received a pension, and so did the members of the institution, and some of these pensions were generous. The Abbess of Shaftesbury, for example, received £135, a considerable sum in those days. She had proved pliant.

Elizabeth Ryprose was not pliant. She seems to have done her best to alienate the property of the Abbey so that the King could not get his hands on it. There is a letter to

149   L

Cromwell which says: "The monastery of Romsey, hearing that they are in danger of suppression, are making leases and alienating their goods." And the writer wants to know if "he should stay them in this." We do not know what happened, for we have no record of the last days of the Abbey. But it is evident that Elizabeth Ryprose held out to the last and never surrendered her office voluntarily. Neither she nor any of the sisters received pensions as they would have done had the surrender been voluntary. The Abbey was forcibly suppressed.

The members of a suppressed monastery, especially those who held to their vows and did not give in to the temptations of the world, faced a hard life for which they were utterly unfitted. Some of those with wealthy relations or friends were no doubt given homes, but they would have been a very small minority. For the rest there could have been nothing but hardship and privation. We do not know what happened to the Abbess and sisters of Romsey after the suppression with one exception, that of Jane Wadham the sextoness. She obtained "capacity" and returned to the world. There is still a document extant relating to this:

11 June 1541. Commission to Cuthbert Bp of Durham, Nicholas Bp of Rochester, Thomas Bp of Westminster, . . . Horwood Attorney General and William Petre LL.D to enquire concerning the petition of Jane Wadham alias Foster, who states that after arriving at years of discretion she was forced by threats and machinations of malevolent persons to become a regular nun in the house of nuns at Rumsey, but, having both in public and in private always protested at this seclusion, she conceived herself free from the regular observance, and in that persuasion joined herself in matrimony with one John Foster "per verba de presenti," intending to have the marriage solemnized as soon as she was free from her "religion," and afterwards the same parties who had compelled her to become a nun induced the said John by their threats to become a priest; which notwithstanding as soon as the said Jane was released from her vows, the marriage was

solemnized in facie ecclesiae and they lived together
for some-time as man and wife, till certain malevolent
persons aspersed their marriage as contrary to laws
divine and human and caused her husband to deny his
marital obligations. The commissioners are authorized
to pronounce the marriage valid, if they so shall find it.

They did find the marriage valid. And John Foster, the
same man that had done so much to bring about the suppression of the Abbey, and his wife lived quietly at Baddesley of which parish he became the incumbent. But there
was a rhyme about him current in the neighbourhood, and
this too has survived in an old MS.:

> Mr. Foster of Baddesley was a good man
> Before the marriage of priests began,
> For he was the first to marry a nun,
> For which he begat a very dude son.

So ended the Abbey of Romsey. And with it a great
chapter in English history. In its early days it had been
great because of its piety. Later it had become great as an
educational establishment. It was great, too, because of its
wealth, and influence; great because among its members
were many representing the greatest families in the land,
many of noble and even of royal birth. It fell because of a
social change and the greed of a king, but it fell also on evil
times because of the immorality of some of its members.
Romsey was for some while a bad and vicious house, one of
the few in the country, for it is quite wrong to believe all
the many stories that unjustly are fastened on the religious
houses of England. The system was not a bad one at all.

Altogether Henry VIII suppressed 1,100 religious houses.
What did he get out of it? He got the sum of £140,745
6s. 2d., which is the equivalent of about three and a half
million pounds to-day. Quite a nice little nest-egg. But
the whole business was a shameful and criminal one. It
condemned many good and innocent men and women to
immense suffering of all kinds. And it put a sudden stop to
much valuable work, especially educational work. It is

probably true that there were too many religious houses in England, but that was not the reason for their suppression. The number might well have been reduced and the monies distributed among those left for the carrying on of educational and devotional work. But Henry wanted the money. It was for that reason and that reason only that he ravaged the inspired work of centuries.

After the suppression of a monastery the buildings were as a rule demolished or greatly reduced. This happened at Romsey. At the Dissolution the additional, which had been built for the convenience of the townsfolk, and the Chapel of St. George were pulled down, and so were the Decorated Dedication Chapels, which had replaced the earlier Norman Lady Chapel. But the fabric as a whole remained untouched. Why this was so is not known, but I think that the townsmen must have had a good deal to do with it. There was no other church in the town, and they had an affection for this one—so great an affection that on 20 February 1544 they bought the building for £100. Some repairs were done, rather roughly, and this explains the interposition of the Decorated windows at the east end. They were brought back to fill in the arches, and the work was not done very well. The present lovely positioning is due to a late vicar, the Rev. E. L. Berthon, who cut out the windows and lowered them into their present position. He asked the Government of the day for some assistance in this work for he considered that the work was such that it required more than local skill and that as Romsey Abbey was so beautiful a church it should rank as a national monument. He did not get the assistance for which he asked—there are no votes attached to repairing an abbey—and so he did the work himself with local help only. Not one pane of glass was damaged. To this vicar and the love and care he expended on the Abbey, the town and every visitor owes much, for throughout his time at Romsey he laboured unceasingly to restore the Abbey, and without any help save that of the townsmen who have always loved their church exceedingly.

In 1544 Queen Mary made a gift to the church of some of the vast quantity of plate that had been seized by her father. But the greatest of the old treasures did not come back until 1900. This is the Psalter, now in a glass case in the Ambulatory at the east end. Described as "The Romsey Psalter" this was advertised by Bernard Quaritch Ltd. in a catalogue, and fortunately the notice was seen by the Dean of Winchester who told the Vicar of Romsey, and the Psalter was bought by public subscription and restored to the Abbey. The volume consists of 304 pages of vellum and was written by an English hand about 1440. It seems probable that it was written by a Franciscan scribe, and this suggests that it was not for use in the choir of a Benedictine Abbey, but was rather the private property of some sister in the Abbey. The work is not, I understand, that of a first-class craftsman—and that is a good thing for had it been it would never have returned to its true home—but even so it is beautiful. And that is true even of the old calf gilt binding, which is much more recent (though still very old). The only record of the Psalter's travels from the time it was stolen (presumably at the Dissolution) is the name T. H. Lloyd on the fly-leaf.

Palmerston would be, I suppose, generally accepted as Romsey's most famous son, but I am not at all sure that the most successful was not William Petty, the son of a clothier in the town. Most of our knowledge of William comes from his will, which was also his autobiography. He was the son of a poor tradesman in a small way of business; he died an extremely wealthy man. After a period at the grammar school William Petty went to sea. He was not a good sailor and went to the Jesuit College at Caen for three years. Then he decided to study medicine, and the next we hear of him is as an assistant to the Professor of Anatomy at Oxford. A few years later he is with Cromwell's army in Ireland as a "physician" . . . "gaineing by my Practice about 400£ pr annum above my paid Sallery." Two years later "Perceiving that the admeasurement of the lands forfeited by the forementioned Rebellion and intended to regulate the satisfaction of ye soldiers who had suppressed ye same was most insufficiently and absurdly managed, I obtained a Contract date the eleventh of December 1654 for making ye sd admeasurement and by God's blessing so

performed ye same as that I gained about 9000£ thereby."
Petty was not the man to let an opportunity slip. On his
Irish estates he opened up lead mines and greatly increased
the trade in timber, and in Kerry he started iron-works and
a pilchard fishing industry. But he had less orthodox ways
of making a fortune. He made a great deal of money by
exhibiting Ann Green at Oxford. Ann Green, a murderess,
was condemned to death by hanging. After hanging for
half an hour she was cut down and sent to the dissecting
room, and there she was found to be still alive. It was Dr.
William Petty who attended her, and after her recovery he
cleared all expenses, medical and legal, and as well as getting further excellent advertisement pocketed a considerable sum, by charging fourpence a head to all who came to
look at her. At the Restoration he made his peace with the
Crown as successfully as he had done everything else. He
refused a title himself, but the Shelburne title was be-
stowed upon his widow. Their sons died childless, and the
title and the fortune passed to their daughter. It was her
grandson who became the first Marquis of Lansdowne.

Palmerston was born and brought up at Broadlands.
Politics kept him away from Romsey for many years, but
Broadlands was ever in his mind and he liked and missed
hunting with the Forest hounds and with Assheton Smith.
He kept a string of racehorses also, which were trained in
the county and always named after the farms and other
places near Broadlands. The exception was his mare that
won the Cesarewitch, which was named Ilione, a word no
one could pronounce correctly. Palmerston was also fond
of shooting, and there is this note of his about one of his
gamekeepers: "Thresher . . . spends his nights at the ale-
house, in order that the poachers may spend theirs in my
coverts. Conceive five guns killing sixteen pheasants in
Yew Tree, and beating the whole wood thoroughly?"
Evidently the character of the Hampshire countryman has
not changed a great deal. The greatest Foreign Minister
that Britain has had since the Napoleonic Wars was always
a Hampshire man and a sportsman, and the woods and
streams of Romsey were never far from his mind.

Three miles to the east of Romsey is the little village of

North Baddesley. Here also is a memorial of Palmerston. On a tombstone in the churchyard is the name of Charles Smith and just below it the name of Lord Viscount Palmerston is clearly visible. Smith was the son of a local smallholder and a confirmed poacher. One night he and an accomplice were caught by one of Palmerston's underkeepers, Robert Snelgrove by name, and Smith, to give his accomplice time to get away, fired when the keeper was close at hand and wounded him seriously in the thigh. Both men got away, but many months later Smith was caught, and condemned to death at Winchester Assizes. Palmerston did his utmost to get the sentence reduced to one of imprisonment but failed, and Smith was duly hung. The tombstone was paid for by Palmerston and the man's family was cared for by the Foreign Secretary for some considerable time.

But there is more than this rather sordid story in North Baddesley. Outside the village is a manor house and a tiny church. The rather quaint brick tower was built in 1674. The timber porch is fifteenth century, and the door has a curious sliding bolt for a handle. Inside the church is simply beautiful and quite unspoiled. The font is probably Norman; there is some glass six hundred years old; there is a glorious screen, the gift of Lord Chief Justice Fleming, who lived nearby, and he is believed also to have given the beautiful pulpit. Under the pulpit is a fifteenth-century chest with a rounded lid carved solid from an oak. And in the chancel is a richly carved fourteenth-century tomb, and in the window above is a fifteenth-century glass with a gold T in it. Both the tomb and the initial belong to Galfridus de Tothalle, Knight Hospitaller and rector here for more than fifty years. For this was the headquarters of the Hospitallers in Hampshire after they had been driven from Godsfield near Alresford by the Plague.

The Knights Hospitallers, like the Knights Templars, were a semi-military religious organization, properly known as the Knights of the Order of St. John of Jerusalem. The members wore a black cloak with a white cross upon the left breast (the Templars wore a white cloak with a red cross upon the left breast) and became known as Hospitallers from the first hospital founded by them at Jerusalem for the relief and assistance of pilgrims. The branch hospitals which they founded afterwards in Europe were known as Commanderies or Preceptories, according to their rank and were bound to the same kindly care of pilgrims and wayfarers. North Baddesley was a Preceptory, and it lasted as this for almost four hundred years. The place was suppressed in 1541 (it owned much valuable property and must have been coveted greatly by Henry VIII), but the estates were restored by Queen Mary for a short time and then finally suppressed by Queen Elizabeth.

The Knights Hospitallers occupied a very important place in the life of the country from the twelfth to the sixteenth century. This is not generally realized nowadays because we have forgotten how great a part pilgrimage played in the life of the people. The Hospitallers did more than protect, so far they could be protected, pilgrims to the Holy Land, though that was their chief business. They protected also pilgrims within the country. Only the rich or the very strong could make the pilgrimage to the Holy Land, and so the mass of the people made other pilgrimages, shorter in extent. Rome was the chief of these, and pilgrimage there started as early as Anglo-Saxon times. There was also the shrine of St. James at Compostella, and in the fifteenth century pilgrims for this shrine usually embarked at Southampton, and that meant work for the Knights at North Baddesley. But there were also many shrines in England that attracted very large numbers of pilgrims. That at Canterbury has become known to everyone and there is even a reputed Pilgrim's Way running from Winchester to Canterbury. No doubt some Hampshire people did visit the shrine at Canterbury, as no doubt a few visited the shrines at Walsingham and other places. Possibly a few even got as far afield as Ystrad. But most of them naturally visited the shrines in Hampshire. Canterbury was the shrine visited by the people of London and Kent and perhaps East Sussex and Surrey. Chaucer's Pilgrims were travelling from London and not from Winchester. I should doubt very much indeed the existence at any time of a Pilgrim's Way from Winchester to Canterbury. There is certainly practically no evidence for it, but we will come to that later on. But there can be no doubt at all that there were three shrines at least in Hampshire that attracted very large numbers of pilgrims before and after the murder of Thomas à Becket. They were the shrine of St. Swithun at Winchester, the shrine of St. Judocus also at Winchester, and the shrine of Our Lady of Grace at Southampton. Almost certainly there was also a regular pilgrimage to the Priory at Christchurch, for had not the church been built with the aid of the Divine Carpenter? And to St. Swithun's the people would bring their sick and feeble, for the Saint was well-known for his miraculous cures. It was these pilgrims that the Knights Hospitallers at North Baddesley cared for and protected so far as they were able. Many of them were so poor that they could not afford lodging of a night, and so would sleep in the woods by their way. There are a number of such places commemorated by name all over the county, as, for example, Pilgrim's Place near Micheldever and Pilgrim's Copse near Tisted. And though to-day the Knights Hospitallers have been forgotten yet their name still lingers on in place names in the neighbour-hood—Knight's Wood, Zion Hill, Little Prophet's Wood, White Cross field and so on.

Three miles below Romsey is Nursling where once there was a monastery, made famous by St. Boniface, who went from there to Germany which he converted almost single-handed to Christianity. This Hampshire man is very much better known throughout Germany than he is in Hampshire. This monastery was destroyed in one of the Danish raids and never rebuilt. Below Nursling again is Redbridge and here the Test flows into Southampton Water, and here the Abbey had a saltern.

Redbridge itself is just plainly horrible. But here at high tide the Test has noble proportions (at low tide there is plenty of mud and plenty of smells) and here I have seen a herd of forty swans, which for a place that is not a swannery is not so bad. There must once have been a plethora of bird life here, for here one winter's day, in sight of Southampton and its docks and with the funnels of some great liner—I rather think that it was the *Queen Mary*, but I know nothing about ships—I saw three pinkfooted geese. One does not expect to see wild geese in such a setting. But there are still redshank and ringed plover, and here I have seen the curlew and the sanderling. And in the stream there are fat grayling and slob trout and, still, some salmon. But Redbridge itself is horrible.

CHAPTER VI

THE NEW FOREST

To the average Englishman the word "forest" suggests extensive woodlands, darkness and quiet with glades between the tall trees. It so happens that the particular forest which is called "New" is extensively wooded, and that some of these woods are dark and quiet, but that is a coincidence due to the activities of the Forestry Commissioners. The New Forest is in general a land of fairly open character—about as different from the forest of popular imagination as the Serpentine is from Lough Neagh—and I have known more than one visitor on his first visit to express great disappointment. But the word forest is not intended to convey the meaning "wooded country"; that is a modern connotation. Properly, the word means "a wilderness," a space of uncultivated country. It is identical, I think, with the Welsh word *gores* or *gorest*, which means "waste or open ground." The word has survived in the English tongue, almost in its original form, as "gorse," which is essentially a growth of waste land.

But the word soon came to have a different, a more specialized, meaning. In the introduction to *Select Pleas of the Forest* (Seldon Society Publications, XIII) we find:

In medieval England a forest was a definite tract of land within which a particular body of law was enforced, having for its object the preservation of certain animals *ferae naturae*. Most of the forests were the property of the Crown, but from time to time the kings alienated some of them to their subjects. . . . But although the king or a subject might be seised of a forest, he was not necessarily seised of all the land it comprised. Other persons might possess land within the bounds of a forest, but were not allowed the right of hunting or of cutting trees in them at their own will.

And so throughout Norman, Plantagenet and early Tudor times the word meant an extensive area of waste-land, which to serve its purpose contained within its boundaries woodlands and pastures for the beasts of the chase.

There are still a number of forests in England—the Forest of the High Peak, the Forest of Dartmoor, the Forest of Exmoor, for example—and, for that matter, there are still a number of minor forests in Hampshire, truncated remains of much larger areas, such as Woolmer, Alice Holt and Bere, but only the New Forest has retained much of its original state. In its scenery, in its wild life, in its vegetation, in its laws, even in its people it stands alone. It has character. There is no other part of England like it.

Our history books tell us that William the Conqueror made it. The story is one of the traditions of our youth. We all know how the Conqueror's passion for hunting was so great that, to make room for the deer he wished to hunt, he laid waste a large area of fertile Hampshire, driving out the inhabitants, demolishing churches and houses and villages, destroying everything in his unbridled passion for sport. The history books are based on the old chronicles.

The earliest of these chroniclers was William Gemeticensis, who was a Norman and chaplain to the Conqueror. He says: "Many, however, say *ferunt autem multi* that the deaths of Rufus and his brother were a judgment from heaven, because their father had destroyed many villages and churches in enlarging the New Forest." That is vague enough in any case—"many villages and churches"—and there is in any case grave doubt if Gemeticensis ever wrote the thing at all. But the further away you get from the event the more precise does the information become. William Mapes, the chaplain of Henry II, is exact: "The Conqueror took away much land from God and men, and converted it to the use of wild beasts and the sport of his dogs; for which he demolished thirty-six churches and exterminated the inhabitants." Thirty-six churches, you could not wish for more exact information. William of Malmesbury says that the Conqueror destroyed churches and exterminated the inhabitants for "more than thirty miles." Orderic says that it was "more than sixty parishes."

Florence of Worcester maintains that before the Conqueror laid hands on it the land was "full of the habitations of men and thick-set with churches." Henry of Huntingdon says: "He ordered the churches and villages to be destroyed and the people to be driven out." The Winchester chronicle says: "for the space of thirty miles, the whole country, which was fruitful in a high degree, was laid waste." And Knighton says: "to make room for his beasts of chase, he destroyed 22 churches, some say 52, together with villages, chapels, and private houses, and formed New Forest, which he called his garden." That, too, is precise enough. But Knighton was under the impression that William II made the Forest!

It is a nice story, but it is not true. The fact is that the chroniclers—not without cause—hated the Normans so much that they were willing to believe anything they heard, and eager to invent good resounding tales of their own. The facts give them and the history books the lie.

It took William I twelve years to subdue the English to his liking, and it was not until 1079 that he ordered afforestation. The great survey for *Domesday* was made in 1086; and so we have a record of the Forest just seven years after the "laying waste." I am aware, of course, that the record in *Domesday Book* so far as the New Forest is concerned is in a very exceptional and suspicious condition. Anyone who studies the facsimile with care must be aware of that. There are many inter-line entries and so on, and it seems certain that a good deal of it was written in at a later date. It must be regarded with suspicion for that reason, but I have never heard it suggested that it is a deliberate forgery. It remains by far the most complete and authentic record that we have. And *Domesday*, it must be remembered, would have been compiled by a clerk, and most probably by a cleric, so that the clerical side of things would have been the most likely to have been exaggerated to the discredit of the Conqueror. But what does *Domesday* tell us? It tells us that the churches at Brockenhurst and Milford were still standing, that corn was still being ground at the mills at Bashley, Burgate and Milford, that Saxon thanes still had a number of holdings in the Forest, even that some of the manors were assessed at a greater value than they had been in the time of Edward the Confessor.

William Cobbett, a man of remarkable common sense and no less remarkable prejudice, saw clearly the ridiculous nature of the accusations of the monkish chroniclers. You will find this in his *Rural Rides*:

I shall have occasion to return to this New Forest, which is, in reality, though, in general, a very barren district, a much more interesting object to Englishmen than are the services of my Lord Palmerston, and the warlike understandings of Burdett, Galloway, and Company; but I cannot quit this spot, even for the present, without asking the Scotch population-mongers and Malthus and his crew, and especially George Chalmers, if he yet should be creeping about the face of the earth, what becomes of all their notions of the scantiness of the ancient population of England; what becomes of all these notions, of all their bundles of ridiculous lies about the fewness of the people in former times; what becomes of them all, if the historians have told us one word of truth, with regard to the formation of the New Forest, by William the Conqueror? All the historians say, everyone of them says, that this King destroyed several populous towns and villages in order to make this New Forest.

Western Grove, 18th Oct. 1826.

I broke off abruptly, under this same date, in my last register, when speaking of William the Conqueror's demolishing of towns and villages to make the New Forest; and I was about to show, that all the historians have told us lies the most abominable about this affair of the New Forest; or that the Scotch writers on popu-lation, and particularly Chalmers, have been the greatest of fools or the most impudent of impostors. I, therefore, now resume this matter, it being, in my opinion, a matter of great interest, at a time when, in order to account for the present notoriously bad living of the people of England, it is asserted, that they are

become greatly more numerous than they formerly
were. This would be no defence of the Government,
even if the fact were so; but, as I have, over and over
again, proved, the fact is false; and, to this I challenge
denial, that, either churches and great mansions and
castles were formerly made without hands; or, England
was, seven hundred years ago, much more populous
than it is now. But what has the formation of the New
Forest to do with this? A great deal; for the historians
tell us that, in order to make this Forest, William the
Conqueror destroyed "many populous towns and
villages, and thirty-six parish churches." The devil he
did! How populous, then, must England have been at
that time, which was about the year 1090, that is to
say, 736 years ago! For, the Scotch will hardly contend that the nature of the soil has been changed for
the worse, since that time, especially as it has not been
cultivated. No, no; brassey as they are, they will not
do that. Come then, let us see how this matter stands.

This Forest has been crawled upon by favourites,
and is now much smaller than it used to be. A time
may, and will come, for enquiring how George Rose
and others, became owners of some of the very best
parts of this once-public property: a time for such
enquiry must come, before the people of England will
ever give their consent to a reduction of the interest of
the debt. But, this we know, that the New Forest
formerly extended, westward, from Southampton
Water and the River Exe, to the River Avon, and
northward from Lymington Haven to the borders of
Wiltshire. We know also that the towns of Christchurch, Lymington, Ringwood, and Fordingbridge,
and the villages of Bolder, Fawley, Lyndhurst, Dipden,
Eling, Minsted, and all the other villages that now
have churches; we know, I say (and, pray mark it),
that all these towns and villages existed before the
Norman Conquest, because of the Roman names of
several of them (all the towns are in print), and because an account of them all is to be found in *Domesday
Book*, which was made by this very William the Con-

queror. Well, then, now Scotch population liars, and you Malthusian blasphemers, who contend that God has implanted in man a principle that leads him to starvation; come, now, and face this history of the New Forest. Cooke in his *Geography of Hampshire*, says, that the Conqueror destroyed here, "many populous towns and villages, and 36 parish churches." The same writer says, that, in the time of Edward the Confessor (just before the Conqueror came), "two-thirds of the Forest was inhabited and cultivated." Guthrie says nearly the same thing. But let us hear the two historians, who are now pitted against each other, Hume and Lingard. The former (vol. II, p. 271) says: "There was one pleasure to which William, as well as all the Norman and ancient Saxons, was extremely addicted and that was hunting; but this pleasure he indulged more at the expense of his unhappy subjects, whose interests he entirely disregarded, than to the loss or diminution of his own revenue. Not content with those large forests, which former kings possessed, in all parts of England, he resolved to make a new Forest, near Winchester, the usual place of his residence; and, for that purpose, he laid waste the county of Hampshire, for an extent of thirty miles, expelled the inhabitants from their houses, seized their property, even demolished churches and convents, and made the sufferers no compensation for the injury." Pretty well for a pensioned Scotchman; and, now let us hear Dr. Lingard, to prevent his Society from presenting whose work to me, the sincere and pious Samuel Butler was ready to go down upon his marrow bones; let us hear the good Doctor upon this subject. He says (vol. I, pp. 452 and 453): "Though the King possessed 68 forests, besides parks and chases, in different parts of England, he was not yet satisfied, but for the occasional accommodation of his court, afforested an extensive tract of country lying between the city of Winchester and the sea-coast. The inhabitants were expelled; the cottages and churches were burnt; and more than thirty square miles of a rich and

The "Cat and the Fiddle", Hinton Admiral

populous district were withdrawn from cultivation, and converted into a wilderness, to afford sufficient range for the deer, and ample space for the Royal diversion. The memory of this act of despotism has been perpetuated in the name New Forest, which it retains at the present day, after a lapse of 760 years."

Historians should be careful how they make statements relative to places which are within the scope of the reader's inspection. It is next to impossible not to believe, that the Doctor has, in this case (a very interesting one), merely copied from Hume. Hume says, that the king "expelled the inhabitants"; Lingard says "the inhabitants were expelled." Hume says, that the King "demolished the churches"; and Lingard says, that "the churches were burnt"; but Hume says, churches "and convents," and Lingard knew that to be a lie. The Doctor was too learned upon the subject of "convents" to follow the Scotchman here. Hume says, that the King "laid waste the country for an extent of thirty miles." The Doctor says, "that a district of thirty square miles was withdrawn from cultivation, and converted into a wilderness." Now, what Hume meant by the loose phrase, "an extent of thirty miles," I cannot say; but this I know, that Dr. Lingard's "thirty square miles" is a piece of ground only five and a half miles each way. So that the Doctor has got a curious "district," and a not less curious "wilderness"; and, what number of churches could William find to burn, in a space five and a half miles each way? If the Doctor meant thirty miles square, instead of square miles, the falsehood is so monstrous as to destroy his credit for ever; for, here we have nine hundred square miles, containing five hundred and seventy-six thousand acres of land; that is to say, fifty-six thousand, nine hundred and sixty acres more than are contained in the whole county of Berks. This is "history," is it? And these are "historians"?

The true statement is this: the New Forest, according to its ancient state, was bounded thus: by the line going from the river Exe, to the river Avon, and which

Highland Water, Brockenhurst

line separates Wiltshire from Hampshire; by the river
Avon; by the sea from Christchurch to Calshot Castle;
by Southampton Water; and by the river Exe. These
are the boundaries; and (as any one may by scale and
compass, ascertain) there are within these boundaries
about 224 square miles, containing 143,360 acres of
land. Within these limits there are now remaining
eleven parish churches, all of which were in existence
before the time of William the Conqueror; so that if he
destroyed 36 parish churches, what a populous country
this must have been! There must have been 47 parish
churches; so there was, over this whole district, one
parish church to every 4¾ square miles. Thus, then,
the churches must have stood, on an average, at
within one mile and about 200 yards of each other.
And observe, the parishes could, on an average, contain no more each than 2,966 acres of land. Not a very
large farm! So that here was a parish church to every
large farm, unless these historians are all fools and
liars.

I defy any one to say that I make hazardous assertions: I have plainly described the ancient boundaries:
there are the maps: any one can, with scale and compass, measure the area as well as I can. I have taken
the statements of the historians, as they call themselves: I have shown that their histories, as they call
them, are fabulous: OR (and mind this or) that
England was at one time, and that too, 800 years ago,
beyond all measure more populous than it is now. For,
observe, notwithstanding that he describes this district as "rich," it is the very poorest in the whole
kingdom. Dr. Lingard was, I believe, born and bred
in Winchester; how then could he be so careless; or
indeed, so regardless of truth (and I do not see why I
am to mince the matter with him), as to describe this
as a rich district? Innumerable persons have seen
Bagshot Heath; great numbers have seen the barren
heaths between London and Brighton; great numbers,
also, have seen that wide sweep of barrenness which
exhibits itself between the Golden Farmer Hill and

Blackwater.   Nine-tenths of each of these are less barren than four-fifths of the land in the New Forest. Supposing it to be credible that a man so prudent and wise as William the Conqueror; supposing that such a man should have pitched upon a rich and populous district wherewith to make a chase; supposing, in short, these historians to have spoken the truth, and supposing this barren land to have been all inhabited and cultivated, and the people so numerous and so rich as to be able to build and endow a parish church upon every four and three-quarter square miles upon this extensive district; supposing them to have been so rich in the produce of the soil as to want a priest to be stationed at every mile and 200 yards, in order to help them to eat it; supposing, in a word, these his-torians not to be the most farcical liars that ever put pen to paper, this country must at the time of the Norman Conquest have literally swarmed with people; for, there is the land now, and all the land too; neither Hume nor Dr. Lingard can change the nature of that. There it is, an acre of it not having, upon an average, so much of productive capacity in it as one single square rod, taking the average, of Worcestershire; and if that land were, as these historians say it was, covered with churches, and people, what the devil must Worcestershire have been? To this, then, we come at last; having made out what I undertook to show; namely, that the historians, as they call themselves, are either the greatest liars that ever existed, or that England was beyond all measure more populous 800 years ago than it is now.

Cobbett was by no means the first person to mistrust the historians, but I think that his attack on them is by far the most stimulating. And he is right. The historians are not telling the truth.

The Forest is very, very old. Before William came it was known as Ytene, which is not a name indicating fertility. There were oaks and hollies here before the Conqueror's day. This soil, so wretchedly thin—thick clay here, loose sand there, some gravels and some marls—could never have thrown anything beyond furze and rush, heather and bramble and trees, was never fertile. William, indeed, did little more than enlarge the boundaries of the Forest, and reafforest some fifteen thousand acres or so, that the Saxon with much toil had wrested from the barren heaths around him—that, and pass laws to keep what he had done.

It is generally said that the laws William passed to keep, so far as possible, his Forest were even harsher than the laws of the Danes. They were, of course, the laws of a Conqueror, of an absolute Monarch. But I am not at all convinced that they were harsher than the laws of Cnut. Cnut delivered the *Canon of Forest Law* at Winchester in 1016. Grave doubt has been cast upon the authenticity of this document, and there are those who maintain that the code is a forgery. I am not an authority on such matters, and I should, I suppose, bow down to those who are, but I must say that I can see no reason at all why William should have troubled to forge—to invent, for that is what it amounts to—an earlier code of laws. And even if he had had need to resort to some such deception, he could not have imposed it on the people who lived in the forests. They would have known at once, and the chroniclers would have known as well. But the chroniclers did not know. Be that as it may: William's laws were harsh enough. He did not mind some of the land being cultivated (was not corn ground at certain mills?). He did not mind the Forest people running their pigs in the woods at acorn-time. But he that killed a deer died. He that shot at a deer—and missed—had his hands cut off. He that disturbed the deer had his eyes taken from him. Such were William's laws. And for them was William hated.

Perhaps it was for his laws that the Forest came to be known as William's Forest; perhaps he actually called it the New Forest. But I think that that name dates from Robert of Gloucester:

Gane of hondes he loved y nou, and of wilde beste
And hys forest and hys wodes, and most ye nywe forest.

But at any rate it was William that made it Crown property.

William the Conqueror, when he died, bequeathed his crown to his second son, William the Red, realizing that his eldest son, Robert, Duke of Normandy, was too gentle a spirit to rule a recently conquered country. William Rufus was not a pleasant person. William of Malmesbury describes his personal appearance: "He was small and thick-set and ill-shaped, yet having enormous strength. His face was redder than his hair, and his eyes were of two different colours. His vices were branded on his face." William Rufus was a sadist and a homosexualist and one or two other things as well. As his father before him, he used the Forest as his playground. He enforced the Forest laws with the greatest stringency against peer and peasant alike, and he must have been hated in the Forest as his father, who certainly was not liked, had never been. And his excesses outside the Forest caused him to be hated no less, and particularly by the church, for he had a habit of refusing to appoint new abbots and bishops as sees fell vacant, appropriating their dues to his own use. It was not long before he had united the whole country, Norman and Saxon, against him and many plots must have been hatched to kill him. And it was in the New Forest he died, slain by an arrow.

A stone, known to all England and, I should guess to three-quarters of America, as the Rufus Stone, marks the fatal spot. It is a singularly uninteresting and unimpressive memorial, being encased in cast-iron to protect it from the attentions of those picnickers and tourists who would scratch their initials and worse upon its surface. (And some have even scratched upon the iron, which just shows how vital this scratching business is. We are an odd nation!) Upon the cast-iron case is reproduced the inscription which was written upon the stone (by the way, it was not put up until 1745) by John, Lord Delaware:

Here stood the oak tree on which an arrow shot by Sir Walter Tyrrell at a stag glanced and struck King William the Second surnamed Rufus on the breast of which he died instantly on the second day of August anno 1100.

169

King William the Second surnamed Rufus being slain as before related was laid on a cart, belonging to one Purkis, and drawn from hence, to Winchester, and buried in the Cathedral Church of that city.

That the spot where an event so memorable might not hereinafter be forgotten the enclosed stone was set up by John Lord Delaware who has seen the tree growing in this place.

And so here, or hereabouts, there died unmourned the most savage of all our kings.

This is the story told by the chroniclers, who, if they disagree on some points of detail, are agreed upon the main outline. King William and a small party composed of his brother Henry, Robert FitzHamon, Sir Walter Tyrrell, William de Breteuil, and a few others set out to hunt in the morning. They hunted all that morning and afternoon: and as the sun was going down a stag bounded past, and the King shot and slightly wounded it. As it ran he watched it, shading his eyes with his hand. Then another deer broke cover and one of the party (popularly believed to be Sir Walter Tyrrell: William of Malmesbury says that at this time the King was alone with Tyrrell; Vitalis says that there were others present) shot an arrow, which lodged in the King's breast. He tried to pull it out, but it broke off short in his hand, and he fell dead without uttering a sound. Immediately the party fled in all directions. Henry galloped to Winchester to get himself proclaimed king before anyone could put in a word for brother Robert, to whom incidentally he had sworn fealty. De Breteuil followed (but not, perhaps, as quickly as he might have done) and declared the rights of Robert, then in the Holy Land. Sir Walter Tyrrell made for the sea-coast, crossing the Avon near Ringwood, and went to Normandy. The others presumably went home. The King lay where he fell until a charcoal burner, named Purkis, put the body into his cart and brought it into Winchester. (There are still Purkises to be found in the New Forest, and some of the name are still charcoal burners. The track that this first of the family to attain fame followed, is called King's Lane and is visible at Otterbourne where it is now lined with the houses of the well-to-do.) And the next day, very hurriedly, William Rufus was buried unmourned and without prayers.

That is the story. And when I was at school the history books and my history master regarded the matter in the light of a fortunate accident. But I think that there can be no doubt that it was murder, deliberate and well-planned murder.

Everything points to it. One may disregard the dreams of the monks before the event (and an astonishing number of monks appear to have had bad nights just before the event), for these are obviously the embellishments of the chroniclers. But I do not think that one can ignore the fact that news of the King's death was current in France *before* he had died: nor do I think one should ignore the fact that Fulcred preached a sermon about the King being killed by an arrow the day before the King was killed by an arrow. And is it not an extraordinary thing that Henry caused no inquiry to be made into this business of his brother's death? That he was content to see his brother pushed under ground as rapidly as possible and no questions asked?

It was murder beyond a doubt. But it will never be known who was the murderer. Tyrrell certainly was not. His hurried departure for France has been taken as an admission of guilt, but it was probably due only to his anxiety to bring the glad tidings to Normandy as quickly as possible. He denied having pulled the bow many times afterwards (when he was well out of danger) and he even denied it on his death-bed. De Breteuil must be acquitted also. He had the courage to ride into Winchester and proclaim Robert, and that ride must have taken more courage than we can properly estimate in these days. So we are left with FitzHamon or Henry or some person unknown. It may have been some person unknown (arrows shot by unknown hands had accounted for Richard, William's brother, and Richard, his nephew, in the Forest, and William himself was not without enemies in the Forest) but I think that it is very unlikely. So important a task as the assassination of a king would not be entrusted to just anyone. The person selected would have been known to the monks, who obviously knew that the killing was scheduled for early August, and there would have been no need to conceal the name of an unimportant person. So we are left with FitzHamon or Henry. FitzHamon disappears from history. He may have retired on a fat pension granted by a grateful Henry, or he may, having served his purpose, have been put out of the way by a grateful Henry. I do not think that FitzHamon can be acquitted. But, personally, I think that the saintly Henry must start favourite. He acted with remarkable promptitude: there was no hesitation about his ride to Winchester: there was no suggestion that search be made for the murderer, that anyone may be punished: he had no qualms about breaking his oath to his brother: he had no qualms about marrying a nun. Henry, I fancy, was not so saintly as his chroniclers would have us believe.

We do not hear so much about the Forest for some five hundred years after the murder of William Rufus. Henry I, not perhaps surprisingly, seems to have avoided the area. Richard I seems to have abolished the penalties of death, blinding and maiming for Forest offences. John visited it a good deal and seems to have enlarged the boundaries considerably. Henry III gave a new turn to Forest legislation with his Charta de Foresta, which is a marked step along the road from barbarism to civilization, and which lays down definitely that in future no man shall lose life or limb for a poaching offence. Henry also did away with the barbarous custom of cutting the knees of dogs to prevent them hunting, and substituted the practice of "lawing"; that is the cutting off of the claws of the forefeet by the skin. Furthermore, he ordained that this should be done in a particular place, which seems to indicate that it was to be done only by a competent man authorized for the work. From this time on Forest legislation mellowed. Edward I gave a general pardon for all past offences, and ordained that in future a deer-poacher must be taken red-handed before it was lawful to imprison.

Edward I made two perambulations of the Forest. The first in the eighth year of his reign showed the boundaries at that time to be roughly: from Southampton Water on the east to the Avon on the west, the northern boundary being defined by a line drawn from Ower-bridge on the east to North Charford on the west, and the southern boundary being the sea from Southampton Water to the mouth of the Avon. Presumably those were the boundaries set by John. In the twenty-ninth year of his reign he made another perambulation, and for some reason which is not apparent he caused very considerable restrictions to be made in the boundaries. The boundaries set by this second perambulation remained until the twenty-second year of the reign of Charles II, and then they were confirmed.

But the most important change in the status of the Forest first becomes apparent in the reign of Henry III. From the time of Cnut until the death of John the most important thing about the forest is the venison. The protection of the deer overrides everything else. But we find Henry III taking a very considerable interest in the vert. He is interested in timber, in firewood, in pasture, in pannage. In the time of Edward I we find that the vert is given precedence over the venison, and that has continued until the present day. More and more do we find that the vert has increased importance; more and more do we find the importance of the venison lessening. To-day the venison has virtually ceased to have any importance at all.

Yet, if there is little actual news of the Forest during these five hundred years, there can be no doubt that it was cared for all the time. The oaks were used for the building of ships for the Royal Navy—some built with Forest oak fought against the Armada—and Elizabeth passed a law to prevent the felling of trees for charcoal. It was called "an Act that timber shall not be felled for burning of iron." Actually "sea-coal" had already at that time largely superseded "bavins" and "fire-coal" (charcoal) for domestic use, but charcoal was still used to a very great extent for the smelting of iron. Obviously Elizabeth was concerned to conserve a supply for the building of ships. She also instituted a system of enclosures to protect growing timber in the Forest. James I carried on this idea, and he also went in for planting, for he ploughed up areas of land, gathered the acorns and dibbled them in.

But it was in the Stuart times that the Forest fell on evil days. And it was James I who started the rot, for if he arranged for some planting he also gave a good deal away. The Stuarts are regarded with affection as a romantic family. This reputation is built up, I think, largely on the strength of the execution of Charles I, the puritannical dictatorship of Cromwell (the forerunner of Hitler) and the gaiety of Charles II. There is a very great deal to be said for all the Stuarts—and especially for Charles II, who was in fact a very great king, the last great royal ruler of England, and perhaps, taking everything into consideration, the greatest in our history—and there is very little that can be said for Cromwell, who was a traitor (his success should not blind us to that fact; success does not excuse), a tyrant, a sadist, a fanatic, and the first exponent of Nazidom. But there is no getting away from the fact that the Stuarts were so romantic and so kingly, that they were always short of cash. James I gave away the "morefalls" (that is, the windfalls) to various people to whom he owed money—and he even went so far as to pay his officers in trees instead of money. Charles I was always in debt and he granted the New Forest as security to some of his creditors. Cromwell was too busy bumping off Catholics, putting babies to the sword, and making money to bother about the New Forest. Charles II was as spendthrift as his father. He granted the young woods near Brockenhurst to various maids of honour at his court, presumably in return for services rendered. One young lady, Frances Wells by name, petitioned the King "to bestow upon her and her children for twenty-one yeares the Morefall trees in three walks of the New Forest," and she also wanted seven or eight acres of ground and ten or twelve trees wherewith to build her a house. Charles referred this petition to the Lord Treasurer, who strongly disapproved of it, and wrote upon the margin: "I conceive this an unfit way to gratify this petitioner." No doubt Frances Wells was gratified in some other way. But a year later we find one Winifred Wells, perhaps a sister of Frances, perhaps Frances herself

using another name, granted for her own use the King's
Coppice at Fawley and New Coppice and Iron's Hill
Coppice at Brockenhurst. On this occasion the King
ignored the Lord Treasurer and issued a Royal warrant on
his own account. Evidently the Wells family produced
highly attractive and complacent daughters, who contributed materially to the gaiety of the Royal Court.

Evelyn's *Sylva*, which was published in 1665, had caused
Charles II, who must have been in funds for the moment,
to enclose three hundred acres as a nursery for young oaks.
But Charles was never in funds for long, and his prodigality
and that of his predecessors had its inevitable effect. The
New Forest in the reign of James II was pretty well in
ruins. Keepers were not paid wages, and so re-imbursed
themselves by cutting and selling timber. And, as was only
natural, they did not bother themselves, and so rot attacked
the trees, which, having no shelter-belts to protect them
from the great winds of the Channel, suffered greatly.
William III in 1698 authorized the planting of 6,000 acres
in enclosures, and a further 200 acres annually for twenty
years. Before the work was properly under way there came
in 1703 a great gale. Woodward states that four thousand
of the "best oaks" were blown down in this storm. That is
certainly an exaggeration, for the "best oaks" would be the
last trees to suffer in such a storm, but there can be no
doubt that tremendous damage was done. In 1707 the
number of trees returned as fit for shipbuilding was 12,476;
a century before the number returned for the same purpose
was 123,927. It has been suggested that the latter number
is suspiciously high, but that must remain a matter of
opinion. It has also been suggested that the standard required for shipbuilding may have altered a great deal in the
intervening century, but there is no evidence to support
that, I think. No, it must be taken as evidence of a remarkable decay in the fortunes of the Forest. And yet in this
same year 1707 we find an order being given that three
hundred trees should be felled annually in the Forest for
shipbuilding. This does not of course include those trees
which would be felled for other purposes. It shows a truly
remarkable ignorance of the elementary principles of

forestry, and even of the most elementary principle that one should live within one's income.

It was not in fact until the beginning of the nineteenth century that a proper system of planting was introduced, the enclosures were drained, shelter-belts of Scotch firs were planted on the exposed sides of the nurseries, and the nurseries themselves were properly cared for.

And what was the Forest like at the beginning of the nineteenth century? This is what Mudie had to say about it:

But besides what we have enumerated, there are so many hovels, with minute patches of ground, which have been taken possession of owing to the indifference of the keepers, and are now held by prescription. These encroachers are, generally speaking, persons of very questionable character, who live most wretched and abandoned lives, and procure much of their miserable subsistence by plunder; while they are ready to enter with eagerness upon any smuggling or plundering expedition to which there may be the slightest temptation. In former times, we believe that this description of population was much more abundant than it is now. One cause of this is the check that has been given to smuggling, another is perhaps the greater vigilance of the keepers, and we wish we could confidently add that a third cause is the increased morality of the humbler classes of the population. We sincerely wish and in part believe this; but it is a point upon which it is difficult to come to a firmly established opinion. According to former reports, persons, not in a state of absolutely pecuniary destitution, were in the habit of stealing localities in the forest, which they did by means of hovels, the parts of which were prepared in other places, and brought to the forest and erected in the course of a single night. When once the hovel was erected, and a fire kindled, the keepers could not eject the tenant without the formality of a legal process; and both his ease and his safety were against his having recourse to that. It was a trouble for which he realized no particular advantage; and, as the persons who trespassed upon the forest in this illegal manner were as ready to become murderers as thieves, he was not safe if he interfered with them. This was a wretched state of things, certainly, but that it was the state of things is but too well known. It seems a general law of human nature, that, if a man either remains in the wild forest or returns to it, there is no alternative to his being or becoming a ferocious savage.

Mudie was writing (if he wrote the book himself, which is extremely doubtful) for the "upper classes." The times were ripe. Enclosure was in the air; the oppression of the peasant was in full swing. His book must have been extremely popular with the landowning classes at that time, and with all those who hoped to become landowners through the enclosures. And no doubt there was a grain of truth in some of the things he said, for the custom of enclosing land round a hovel was practised by a well-known Forest character in this century, and almost succeeded, would have succeeded had the man had the wit to keep his mouth shut.

But there is another side to the question; and for that we must turn to Cobbett. In the *Rural Rides* the entry for the 18 October 1826 is a very lengthy one, and one that would be worth quoting in full did the space permit. Here, however, are extracts from this entry:

To come back now to Lyndhurst, we had to go about three miles to New Park, which is a *farm* in the New Forest, and nearly in the centre of it. We got to this place about nine o'clock. There is a good and large mansion-house here, in which the "commissioners" of woods and forests reside when they come into the forest. There is a garden, a farm-yard, a farm, and a nursery. The place looks like a considerable gentleman's seat; the house stands in a sort of *park*, and you can see that a great deal of expense has been incurred in levelling the ground and making it pleasing to the eye of my lords the "commissioners." My business here was to see whether anything had been done towards the making of *locust plantations*. I went first to Lyndhurst to make inquiries; but there I was told that New Park was the place, and the only place, at which to get information on the subject; and I was told further that the commissioners were now at New Park; that is to say those experienced tree-planters, Messrs. Arbuthnot, Dawkins, and Company. Gad! thought I, I am here coming in close contact with a branch, or at least a twig, of the great THING itself! When I heard this I was at breakfast, and of course dressed for the day. I could not out of my extremely limited wardrobe afford a clean shirt for the occasion; and so off we set, just as we were, hoping that their worships, the nation's tree-planters, would, if they met with us, excuse our dress, when they considered the nature of our circumstances. When we came to the house we were stopped by a little fence and a fastened gate. I got off my horse, gave him to George to hold, went up to the door, and rang the bell. Having told my business to a person who appeared to be a foreman or bailiff, he, with great civility, took me into a nursery which is at the back of the house; and I soon drew from him the disappointing fact that my lords, the tree-planters, had departed the day before! I found, as to *locusts*, that a patch were sowed last spring, which I saw, which are from one foot to four feet high, and very fine and strong, and are, in number, about enough to plant two acres of ground, the plants at four feet apart each way. I found that last fall some few locusts had been put into the plantations of other trees already made; but that they had not *thriven*, and had been *barked* by the hares! But a little bunch of these trees (same age), which were planted in the nursery, ought to convince my lords, the tree-planters, that if they were to do what they ought to do the public would very soon be the owners of fine plantations of locusts for the use of the navy. And what are the *hares* kept *for* here? *Who* eats them? What *right* have these commissioners to keep hares here to eat up the

178

trees? Lord Folkestone killed his hares before he made
his plantation of locusts; and why not kill the hares in
the *people's* forest; for the *people's* it is, and that these
commissioners ought always to remember. And then
again, why this farm? What is it *for*? Why, the
pretence for it is this: that it is necessary to give the
deer *hay*, in winter, because the lopping down of limbs
of trees for them to *browse* (as used to be the practice)
is injurious to the growth of timber. That will be a
very good reason for having a *hay-farm* when my lords
shall have proved two things; first, that hay, in quantity equal to what is raised here, could not be bought
for a twentieth part of the money that this farm and
all its trappings cost; and, second, that there ought to
be any deer kept! What are these deer *for*? Who are
to *eat* them? Are they for the royal family? Why,
there are more deer bred in Richmond Park alone to
say nothing of Bushy Park, Hyde Park, and Windsor
Park; there are more deer bred in Richmond Park
alone than would feed all the branches of the royal
family and all their households all the year round, if
every soul of them ate as hearty as ploughmen, and if
they never touched a morsel of any kind of meat but
venison! For what, and *for whom*, then, are deer kept
in the New Forest; and why an expense of hay-farm,
of sheds, of racks, of keepers, of lodges, and other
things attending the deer and the game; an expense
amounting to more money annually than would have
given relief to all the starving manufacturers in the
north! And, again I say, *who* is all this venison and
game *for*? There is more game in Kew Gardens than
the royal family can want! And, in short, do they ever
taste, or even hear of, any game, or any venison, from
the New Forest?

What a pretty thing here is, then! Here is another
deep bite into us by the long and sharp-fanged aristocracy, who so love Old Sarum! Is there a man who
will say that this is right? And that the game should
be kept, too, to eat up trees, to destroy plantations, to
destroy what is first paid for the planting of! And

that the public should pay keepers to preserve this game! And that the *people* should be *transported* if they go out by night to catch the game that they pay for feeding! Blessed state of an aristocracy! It is a pity that it has not a nasty, ugly, obstinate DEBT to deal with! It might possibly go on for ages, deer and all, were it not for this *debt*. This New Forest is a piece of property as much belonging *to the public* as the Custom House at London is. There is no man, however poor, who has not a right in it. Every man is owner of a part of the deer, the game, and of the money that goes to the keepers; and yet any man may be *transported* if he go out by night to catch any part of this game! We are compelled to pay keepers for preserving game to eat up the trees that we are compelled to pay people to plant! Still however there is comfort; we *might* be worse off; for the Turks made the Tartars pay a tax called *tooth-money*; that is to say, they eat up the victuals of the Tartars, and then made them pay for *the use of their teeth*. No man can say that we are come quite to that yet: and, besides, the poor Tartars had no DEBT, no blessed debt to hold out hope to them.

So much for Cobbett on deer and commissioners. Now read Cobbett on the land:

We had come seven miles across the forest in another direction this morning; so that a poorer spot than the New Forest there is not in all England, nor, I believe, in the whole world. It is more barren and miserable than Bagshot Heath. There are less fertile spots in it in proportion to the extent of each. Still it is so large, it is of such great extent, being, if moulded into a circle, not so little, I believe, as 60 or 70 miles in circumference, that it must contain some good spots of land, and if properly and honestly managed those spots must produce a prodigious quantity of timber.

But though he is not in two minds about the land, he can-

180

Ibsley on the River Avon

not make up his mind which is the worse, the new aristocracy (what we should call to-day the *nouveau riche*; and the country suffered from much the same thing after the First German War) and the Crown officials.

> This forest has been crawled upon by favourites, and is now much smaller than it used to be. A time may, and *will* come, for inquiring *how* George Rose, and others, became *owners* of some of the very best parts of this once public property.

And again:

> Poor, however, as this district is, and culled about as it has been for the best spots of land by those favourites who have got grants of land or leases or something or other, still there are some spots here and there which would grow trees; but never will it grow trees, or anything else, *to the profit of this nation* until it become *private property*. Public property must, in some cases, be in the hands of public officers; but this is not an affair of that nature. This is too loose a concern; too little controllable by superiors. It is a thing calculated for jobbing above all others; calculated to promote the success of favouritism. Who can imagine that the persons employed about plantations and farms for the public are employed because *they are fit* for the employment? Supposing the commissioners to hold in abhorrence the idea of paying for services to the public; supposing them never to have heard of such a thing in their lives, can they imagine that nothing of this sort takes place while they are in London eleven months out of the twelve in the year? I never feel disposed to cast much censure upon any of the persons engaged in such concerns. The temptation is too great to be resisted. The public must pay for everything *à pois d'or*. Therefore no such thing should be in the hands of the public, or, rather, of the government.

Cobbett, as one would expect, held strong views on the

River Avon at Fordingbridge

Forest, strong views on the deer, strong views on the officials, but you will find nothing in his pages about the Foresters. There is a good deal about the poverty of the land, about the lack of fertility, but there is nothing about the poverty of the Foresters. Cobbett was a most observant man. Throughout his travels he notes the poverty or prosperity of the peasants of the districts through which he moved, remarks their distress or well-being. He makes no such remarks about the condition, physical or financial, of the commoners of the New Forest. Had conditions been such as described by Mudie it is quite inconceivable that they would have escaped the notice of such a man as Cobbett, quite inconceivable that having noticed them he would have refrained from commenting upon them. Mudie was writing for a special public, and one can only come to the conclusion that he had little regard for the truth. He (or his employers) wanted something and they did not mind how they got it. But from the fact that Mudie was prepared to distort the truth, and even to print downright lies, from the fact that he was prepared to attack the commoners in such violent terms, while Cobbett concentrates on the officials and the deer, makes it plain that all was not well with the New Forest at the beginning of the nineteenth century.

In 1848 a commission was appointed, which inquired into the rights of the Foresters, and finally produced order out of chaos by allowing, disallowing and amending the various claims that were showered upon it. The Blue Book which contains the report of this commission—its full title is *New Forest, Register of Decisions on Claims to Common Rights by the Commissioners acting under the Act of 17th and 18th Victoria Chapter 49*—was published by H.M. Stationery Office in 1858, and remains to this day (and I hope always will remain) the authority on the rights possessed by the Forester. The few copies that survive are greatly treasured by the Foresters, who also greatly treasure the few rights, in themselves of small value, that are theirs by virtue of its authority.

And what are these rights? They are rather complicated and deal with a number of things. The preamble to the

Register of Decisions on Claims to Common Rights
says:

Now we, the said Charles James Gale, James Bar-
stow, and John Duke Coleridge, to avoid unnecessary
repetitions in each case, do hereby declare that each
allowance of any rights is made subject to and that the
same is to be exercised and enjoyed according to the
Laws and Assize of the said Forest, and that in all
cases where a right is allowed subject to a payment,
such payment is to be made to our Lady Queen. And
that every right of common pasture may be exercised
and enjoyed at all times of the year, except during the
fence month, that is to-day, the twentieth day of June
to the twentieth day of July yearly, and the time of
the winter hayning, that is to say, the twenty-second
day of November to the fourth day of May yearly,
during which times we declare that there is no right in
all the unenclosed wastelands of our Lady Queen
within the said Forest for all their commonable cattle,
levant and couchant, in and upon the lands in respect
of which the allowance is made.

And we do hereby declare that common of pasture
for sheep is allowed only in cases where it is expressly
mentioned.

And we do hereby declare that every right of common of mast is to be exercised only in time of pannage,
that is to say, on and from the twenty-fifth day of
September, up to and on the twenty-second day of
November yearly, in all the open and unenclosed
woods and woody lands of our Lady Queen in the said
Forest, for all their hogs and pigs, levant, couchant, in
and upon payment, unless otherwise expressed, yearly,
to or for the use of our Lady the Queen, for every hog
or pig exceeding the age of one year, fourpence, and
for every hog or pig under that age, twopence.

And we do hereby declare also that every allowance
of turbary is of the liberty of having, digging, cutting
and taking turf in and upon the open wastes of our
Lady the Queen within the said Forest, by the view

and allowances of the Foresters of the said Forest, and of carrying away the said turf from the said places to and into the messuages mentioned and described in this our Register for the necessary fuel of the said messuages to be therein burnt and expended. And that every allowance of fuel and fuel wood is an allowance of the quantity described of good fuel wood yearly from the open and unenclosed parts of the said Forest by the view and allowance of the Foresters of the said Forest as reasonable and necessary estovers for the necessary firewood of the messuages mentioned and described in this our Register, to be burnt and expended therein.

And we do hereby also declare that every allowance of a claim of marl is of a right to have, dig, take and carry away from the open and accustomed marl pits in the said Forest, a schedule whereof is set forth at the end of this Register, by the view and allowance of the Foresters of the said Forest, sufficient marl for the necessary marling of the lands in respect whereof the said marl is allotted and adjusted to be exclusively used thereon.

It is a wonderful language, this English of ours. What it all means is that the rights of the Forester are concerned with the pasturage of ponies, cattle and sheep; with the turning out of pigs during the pannage-time, which is the season of acorns and beech-mast; with the cutting of turf, furze, heath and fuelwood for burning; with the digging of marl for the purpose of marling his land. Originally these rights were granted as some sort of recompense for the damage done by the king's deer. To-day there are not so many deer (though there are a great many more than is popularly supposed: it is quite inaccurate to say that the deer are few in number) and the damage they do is negligible. But the rights remain and are jealously guarded. They are not, by the way, vested in individuals but in property, being attached in each case to some particular holding, which may be a manor or a cottage or even a piece of land with no house upon it. When a tenant dies, or leaves the holding, the rights pass with the property to his successor. May it always remain so.

The next event of importance in the history of the Forest was The Deer Removal Act of 1851. This followed the report of Lord Portman's Commission of 1850, and marked a new era in the history of the Forest and the lives of the Foresters. The old order under which the Forest had been created as a home for the deer of the king, had gone for ever. Henceforward other interests predominated. No longer are the deer considered as of importance. Timber and agricultural interests move into the first place, and, since deer are inimical to both they are to be removed. The Act was implemented pretty thoroughly, but all the deer were not removed by any means. The Act was rushed through. There was no proper consultation with the people of the Forest. The Act itself was not unpopular, for the deer were a nuisance to the commoners in more ways than one. The Office of Woods seized upon this, stressed the damage done by the deer, and omitted all other considerations and the thing was done. When it was done, the Crown was given permission to enclose ten thousand acres for the plantation of trees, which ten thousand acres were to be thrown open as soon as the trees were sufficiently grown, and another ten thousand acres were then to be enclosed. The full purpose of the Act was not realized at the time of its passing, but it was not long before it was realized not only by the poorer commoners but by all those who held commoners rights. There was a tremendous outcry. The fault was that of the Office of Woods, who administered the Act in the most dictatorial fashion. There were appeals and petitions galore (no fewer than eight petitions were addressed to the House of Lords in 1867 alone) and in the end an inquiry was held, largely as the result of the drive and organizing genius of Mr. Eyre, who was beyond doubt a born rebel. As the result of this inquiry came the New Forest Act of 1877. This Act made three major changes, and these changes, of course, led to many minor adjustments. First, it abolished the ill-defined and disputed power of the Crown, and defined beyond question the rights of the sylvicultural department to future enclosure. Second, it protected the commoners in

the exercise of their admitted rights from all sorts of
annoyances; from the application of obsolete restrictions
(such as the winter hayning), from the sale of commonable
land without compensation, and so on. Third, it reconsti-
tuted the ancient Court of Verderers on an elective basis
with altered franchise expressly to become representative
of the commoners and to protect their rights and privileges.
In fact, the Act met all the complaints of the commoners
and redressed all their grievances. But all the same the
Act took some little time to settle down. It was not a
good job of Parliamentary draughtsmanship, and it left
a good many points open to various interpretation.

Gerald Lascelles, who came to the New Forest as the
official of the Office of Woods (in the post which is now
known as Deputy Surveyor) had an uncomfortable time to
begin with. He came as a young man, and at the time when
readjustments were being made. The commoners had just
won a bitter battle against the Department. There were
wrongs to be righted. The Department had not shown
itself conciliatory in the past and had ridden roughshod
over many accepted privileges. It is not altogether surprising that the commoners lost no opportunity of irritating
the officials whenever they could. Lascelles was, of course,
the chief sufferer from all this. But he was the right man
in the right place. It is not often that the Government of
this country makes such a wise choice for such a position
as this at a time of difficulty. In his retirement Lascelles
wrote his reminiscences, and in this most entertaining book
he leaves no doubt at all as to his views on policy and
people, but during his term of office he kept his counsel and
worked so well that he left behind him a memory that is
not yet forgotten as a great gentleman and a just officer.

Lascelles draws clear distinctions between the small
commoner, the landlord, and the new middle-class that was
then flocking into the New Forest, and always championing
the commoner. For the commoner he has nothing but
liking and respect, so long (as Kenchington points out) as he
keeps his place. For the landlords he has a natural class
sympathy, tempered with a good deal of scorn for their
championing of rights that were of little value and which

he regarded as inimical to the Crown. For the new middle class his attitude is a mixture of contempt and irritation. Some of his comments are scathing: some terribly biased, but allowance must be made for his position in this respect. Of the Verderers' Courts, pointing out that they are the most ancient in the land save only for the coroners', he says:

> The old court had represented both Crown and commoner alike, and assisted the Crown ably in maintaining and preserving order in the Forest. A verderer, too, who was elected for life by the full County, took an oath of allegiance to the Crown. This did not at all suit the book of the promoters of the 1877 Act, whose object it was to set up a body which should override and oppose the Crown, and gain full powers over the Forest in favour of the commoners alone.

And again;

> The ancient oath of the verderer, which dated back to Norman times and rather resembled the oath of allegiance taken by a member of the House of Commons, was abolished, so that the members of the new Court should be troubled by no scruples when they attacked the interests of the Crown.

It will be seen that the interests of his department are identified with the Crown by Lascelles, and that any opposition in defence of their rights and livelihood by the commoners is regarded by him as little short of treason. This is going a bit far.

Again he has some sharp things to say about official verderers:

> A new and nondescript member of the Court was added, who was called the Official Verderer. He is nominated by the Crown, which thereby gains a solitary representative in the Court, provided the Official Verderer takes the view that he is in any way pledged

187

to support the Crown. But his duties are entirely un-defined. . . . Some Official Verderers have interpreted their obligation in one way, others in quite a different manner.

This description of the Official Verderer might hold good to-day, when the gentleman is sometimes appointed for no apparent reason at all, but of the men of Lascelles' day it can not be said to be anything but another example of bias. The only Official Verderer for whom Lascelles had any room was the Official Verderer who would do as he was told by the Deputy Surveyor.

During the first period of settling down there was a good deal of litigation, notably the famous "Sawing Engines Case," and this litigation practically ran through the commoners' funds. The commoners found, as others have found before them and others since, that it is no good taking a Crown department to law. The public purse is deep and can always be refilled, and there are the Law Officers at beck and call. Lascelles rejoiced at the "Sawing Engines Case":

One good effect, however, was produced; com-promised as it was, this miserable case led to the expenditure of a considerable sum by each side.

The amount which the verderers had to pay used up nearly all the capital with which they had been started under the Act of 1877, to hold on behalf of the com-moners. There was no little disgust among that body when they heard that their capital had vanished. But the lack of funds to fight with had a wonderfully peacemaking effect, and was most serviceable in keep-ing the litigious section of the verderers out of court . . . for a time at any rate.

And that is true. The lack of funds caused at first an armed neutrality and later a reasonable working arrangement between the verderers and the department.

But trouble soon broke out afresh. This time over the roads. Here the New Forest was in a special, indeed a quite extraordinary, position. The commoner maintained that the old Forest tracks, fords and crossings were quite good enough for him as they had been for his father. He had no need for macadamized roads, for bridges, for culverts. The only heavy traffic in the Forest, he pointed out, was the heavy timber-haulage of the Office of Woods. He did not see why he should pay for the upkeep of roads he did not need. Let the Office of Woods pay for their own transport costs. And if new roads were needed for the new gentry that were flocking into the district (many of them to houses, lodges and cottages that had been put on the market by the Office of Woods) then that was not anything to do with the commoner. He did not want the roads and he had not asked the new gentry to come. Lascelles describes all this as being but a further manifestation of disloyalty to the Crown, as an attempt to evade obligations by throwing the whole burden on to the Crown. It was, of course, nothing of the sort. Deadlock was reached, and there would have been trouble—there was trouble in one or two places—had not the New Forest Highways Act provided that the Crown would put the old roads into sound order and build the new ones. Thereafter they would be maintained by the Road Boards. Even at that one part of the Forest, around Ringwood, refused to play. However, soon after this roads became the responsibility of the new County Councils, and the problem was resolved.

This was the last of the trouble; of the open trouble at any rate. In the Forest now everything is peaceful. But that does not mean that everyone sees the Forest in the same light. The present Deputy Surveyor is D. W. Young. He is a man of broad views and at the same time has very good scientific qualifications. He is exceptionally popular in the Forest, and especially so with the commoners. I think there would be general agreement that of all the Deputy Surveyors he is easily the best. I think there would be general agreement that, quite apart from his professional interest in the district, he has the interest of the Forest very much at heart. But you have only to read him to see clearly that there is, as he sees it, still a great deal of opposition to the Crown officials and their policy from the commoners.

One of the causes of dissatisfaction is the planting of pines. Young's view of pines is:

> With but little protection the whole forest would become a pure pine forest by natural regeneration within a century. The pines, however, are an offence to Commoners and a large section of the public. The Forestry Commission has undertaken to keep their extension in check. For the moment their existence, even in enclosures, is only tolerated. We are approaching a time, however, when their crowns will flatten out and let shafts of light on to their red stems. The ugly ducklings will then have become swans, and the public attitude towards them is likely to be very different. This will ease matters in some respects but may complicate them in others. Exploitation of such trees will be jealously watched.

That the pines are an offence to commoners and a large section of the public is perfectly true. There are a number of local bodies which constantly campaign for the absolute extirpation of pines throughout the open Forest. These people realize well enough that the pine has a great commercial value as pit-props, and they realize that there must be some in the enclosures, but they would rather, if they must be planted, that is, if conifers must be planted, that only larch and Douglas pine were planted, for neither of these spreads so rapidly. Then the use of Scots pine for shelter belts causes a great deal of annoyance, for the Scots pine seeds easily and is planted in just the positions that made seeding in the open Forest easy. There is also more than a little feeling about the planting of single species stands. There are many people who would like to see conifer and broad-leaved species in mixed stands. Personally I would like to see all the conifers extirpated. There are plenty of places where they could be planted without offence—the great Forestry Commission plantations in Wales and Scotland, for example.

The commoner dislikes the Forestry Commission on principle. It is not unreasonable. Most of the commoners come of families that have been here in the Forest for centuries, and the officials are all new so far as they are concerned. The commoner has a long memory. And this is his home. He is particularly bitter about the "lawns." That there has been a rapid and severe deterioration of the lawns and grazing grounds during the present century, and especially during the past twenty-five years, is beyond question. I have myself witnessed it. I have watched the brambles and the gorse, the poor thin heather, the thorns and the seedlings, I have watched them all spreading over the grazing grounds. Some of the smaller ones have altogether disappeared now. And I should say that there is not a single lawn in the whole Forest which has not suffered encroachment from scrub, which is not now a poor shadow of the place it was when I was a boy. This sad deterioration is not due to the Forestry Commission alone. There are many factors connected with it. But the majority of commoners see only the officials, and there the blame lies, despite the personal popularity of the Deputy Surveyor. The commoners fought the Office of Woods when they would enclose the lawns, and the commoners won the fight. Now the lawns are disappearing again, and they see only the Forestry Commission in the place of the Office of Woods. There is a firm belief that the Forestry Commission means to have the lawns. They cannot get them by enclosures, so they will destroy them, and when they have gone they will plant their pines. That is the opinion of the commoner. They see the scrub, the thorns, the seedlings, the heather, the gorse, always creeping further and further on to the lawns; they do not see any attempt being made to cut them back. They know (and this is incontestable) that they could be cut back. They know that if they did the cutting themselves there would be trouble. They draw their own conclusions.

The commoners also dislike the shooting licences. These shooting licences bring in a considerable income to the Forestry Commission—I believe that the sum is something like £1,500 per annum—and the commoners maintain that there is a fixed resolve on the part of the officials not to do anything that might interfere with the cover. They main-

tain that the keepers have definite orders not to cut the
furze, not to burn the spreading thorn scrub. I do not
know if there are in fact such orders in existence. I do
know what the commoners think. I quote from Dr.
Kenchington's book. He is repeating a conversation with
an old commoner: "We be like Red-Indians on a reserva-
tion, hampered all ways, and there they all bides, polite
enough, ready enough to promise to 'do something' or 'to
see what can be done'! That ends in nothing, and the
commons be getting wuss and wuss! They sits around
waiting for we to die off, so's they can have it all, to do as
they like wi'." I must have heard the same thing said, if
not quite in the same words, hundreds of times in the past
twenty-five years. And not only from the old commoners,
I have heard it often enough from young men and women
as well. The commoners—there is absolutely no getting
away from it—are not happy about the way the Forestry
Commission is treating their Forest.

Now, what are these commoners? Are they any different
from the general run of Hampshire countrymen? Yes, they
are. Very different.

I think that one of the queerest things about the Forest is
that you so rarely see a Forester. You see their ponies, and
their pigs, and their cows, but you very rarely see them
(or if you do you do not somehow connect them with the
Forest, you do not say "that is a Forester"). What you
see are the tourists, and the middle-class residents. You
may, perhaps, and only then if you are very forthcoming
and a very good mixer quite free from class-consciousness
(and most of the middle-class residents are very far from
being that), you may perhaps know the cottagers in the
immediate neighbourhood—within a radius of a hundred
yards, say—but beyond that, no. There is no sort of bond
in the Forest between landlord and tenant as there is in so
many parts of the country, and as there still is to some
extent elsewhere in Hampshire. The rich here have no
control over the poor. The poor are not beholden to the
rich as they are elsewhere in England: they turn out their
livestock on the *Nation's* land. Elsewhere in England the
rich, the landlords and the big farmers, and the not-so-

rich, the small farmers and the retireds, know a good deal
about the men who hedge and ditch and plough and milk.
In some parts—as on the Cotswolds—there is a considerable intimacy between landlord and labourer, some linger-
ing of the feudal system left when son follows father on the
same land and in the same family's employ. And there is
much to be said for the feudal system—or rather the feudal
tradition—in the country and among country people. But
there is none of it in the New Forest. More often than not
the rich man (I am speaking comparatively, of course; I
mean the man with a car, and normally with a servant) has
no knowledge whatever of the cottager at his gate, and is
completely uninterested in him. And the cottager, though
he knows *all* about the rich man, is completely uninterested
in him and his possessions and his doings. There is no bond
between the two. The Forester has remained a race apart.
And he is so quiet and unobtrusive that he escapes notice
and has, thus, escaped standardization.

A race apart. On Saturday nights in Lymington you will
know the truth of that. They crowd the streets: they drink
beer in the pubs and talk and play darts. They shout and
jostle and sing in the lights of the naphtha flares. For just
about four hours they have a burst. But by ten o'clock the
flares are put out and the stalls vanish, and the Forest
people return to the Forest. They come into Lymington
for a burst, and they have a burst. But all the while they
remain apart.

A race apart. They have a gipsy look about them. But
they are not gipsies. They have the same pride, the same
dark, fiercely eager look, but they have not a jot of that
false humility with which the true Romany has learned
through centuries of persecution and outlawry to cloak his
pride. There is nothing of the beggar about them, nothing
of the outlaw. They are solid as the Romany is solid, but
as the Romany is not they are also stolid and silent. Stolid
and silent; yes, and secretive and unfriendly. If you go into
a country pub in England, countrymen will include you in
the conversation—that is hospitable. But, even in Lymington on a Saturday night these countrymen will exclude you
from their conversation. They will talk in lowered voices

and glance at you every now and again just to see that you are not listening. That is the form of their independence. It comes, I think, from living in dark and silent places and knowing the spirits that live among the tall trees. Yes, but it also comes from the Celtic blood. These people are very like the small dark people of the mountains of Cardiganshire in many ways. Yes, it comes from the Celtic blood; but also from a thousand years and more of smuggling and poaching, from a thousand years and more of avoiding and wearing down strangers and their laws. There is here in the New Forest a people that has never been conquered—just as the people of Central Wales have never been conquered— a proud people living on their ancestral soil. They have never been conquered. And I do not think that they will be conquered by the Forestry Commission.

And what of the country they live in?

The New Forest consists of some ninety thousand acres of what the guide books call "virgin forest country," and of these ninety thousand acres some sixty thousand are open to the public. According to the most recent map issued by the Ordnance Survey, Beaulieu and Buckler's Hard and Lymington and Sowley Pond and Ibsley Common are not, as one always imagined they were, in the Forest, so I am not quite sure about the figures I have just given. The open country, whether officially in the Forest or not (and all Forest people, despite the Ordnance Survey, regard Lymington as in the Forest), which is accessible to the public, is probably a good deal more than sixty acres in extent.

I have no intention of writing a description of the beauties of the New Forest. The Reverend William Gilpin, one time Vicar of Boldre, wrote the only one that I have ever found in the least satisfying (though there have been any number of books written about the Forest), and his effort ran into two bulky volumes. It was published in 1741, and is now to all intents and purposes unobtainable. But Mr. Gilpin, to my mind, did his job well and in a pleasing manner, and I could not emulate him if I would. In any case beauty lies in the eye of the beholder, and while I find complete satisfaction in certain parts of the Forest and consider these places to be as beautiful, or more beautiful, of their kind than any other places in England, I rarely find any one to agree with me. For example, I like Thorney Hill, and could sit and look back over the dip that holds the railway to the woods by Burley and Red Rise all day and never be bored. And maybe I am alone in that liking, for Thorney Hill is usually conspicuously free from humans.

The Forest has every type of scenery, but mainly it is of the heath type. There are places where the landscape has all the freedom of real moorland without any of the rigours of real moorland climate. (That is not to say that the New Forest is never cold; it can be the coldest place in the south of England, and the snow can, and often does, lie deep and drift as on true mountain moorland.) There are woods as deep and dark and lonely as any in England. There are open glades and pretty streams. There are bogs and marshes. And there are combinations of all of these, so that you may see reeds and rushes and heather and gorse and trees jostling cheek to jowl; and I know of no other district in England where this is so.

But the real beauty of the Forest lies in its colouring. This is quite beyond description and apparently, judging from the pictures I have seen, also beyond the skill of artist to capture. In spring there is nowhere in England so soft: in high summer no woods so green. But the real glory is in autumn. Here then are all the browns and reds and yellows and rusts that ever were in the imagination of artist, and all in perfect harmony. Here are beeches with their boles moss-grown (moss, by the way, grows only on the northern side if the tree is at all exposed) and their leaves a burnished copper; here are oaks in russet dress and birches in lemon: and here is bracken a rich crimson and here the purple heather and the dead ling, a rich burnt amber, fitting carpet for glory.

That is one aspect of the Forest. There is another. In places it is becoming suburbanized. Villas are creeping in from Bournemouth and Ringwood, Romsey and Southampton, New Milton and Sway. Mon Repos and The Nook, Bella Vista and Wetu, are insinuating themselves where they have no right to be, and with them come manners (or lack of them) and customs that are alien to the ancientness of the Forest. The fault lies in the ownership of the Forest. It is no longer—despite popular belief—Crown property. Long ago the sovereign exchanged the New Forest (together with the Forest of Dean and one or two smaller areas) for the annuities of the Civil List. The New Forest is, therefore, National Property. It belongs to you and me as well as to everyone else. But so queer are the workings of England, it is, being a national property, much less subject to popular control than are properties that are privately owned. The Town and Country Planning Act gives local authorities considerable control over the use and development of private property. But local authorities have little or no voice in regard to national property. This is regarded as strictly the concern of one or other of several absolutely water-tight government departments. National property is, in fact, a bureaucratic monopoly. Government departments are really concerned with one thing only—the financial aspect. They very rarely show intelligence, beyond immediate financial intelligence, and never initiative, and they are quite unapproachable. And so I expect building, and for the most part shabby and unsuitable building, to continue in the New Forest. It can be prevented, so far as I can see, only by adopting the New Forest as a national park.

But building is not the only deadly disease that has the New Forest in grip. There is the week-end cottage menace. More and more the Forest cottages are being bought by rich townsmen for week-end homes, or by retireds for permanent homes. And this danger, which the Forestry Commission could easily prevent is, I think, even more pressing and even more deadly than the building of jerry bungalows and shabby four-by-twos. If you are to preserve the Forest, you must preserve the Forester and his means of livelihood. Without him the thing is nothing, a sham. You might as well asphalt the paths, stick bandstands here and there, and boating lakes and dodgems, and have done with it. It would still be a park; it would, indeed, be more truly a national park.

Every Forest cottage bought by "gentry" and enlarged

or "improved" is a cottage less for the commoners. The commoner who might have lived there and contributed his work and sense and living and spirit to the Forest that is his home has to go elsewhere. That is bad enough. But worse; the owners of these improved cottages contribute nothing at all to the life of the Forest. They do not keep stock (a few hens in a pen at the end of the garden is not keeping stock), they contribute nothing to the communal life of the Forest, they do not even spend their money in the Forest; they shop in Bournemouth or London; they dress away from the Forest; they live away from the Forest in spirit.

The "capital" of the Forest is Lyndhurst, which is a contraction of Linden Hurst, meaning The Wood of Lime Trees. Once, so I have been told, Lyndhurst was a beautiful straggling village set in the midst of magnificent timber. Even I can remember it when it was not too bad. To-day it is quite the most hideous place in the whole Forest, and would take high place among the hideous places of Hampshire. Lyndhurst lives on tourists. It is quite honest about it, which is more than can be said for many other places that do the same thing. Broadway is the crowning example in all England, and that is in its favour. There is not much of "Ye Olde" about Lyndhurst. But the village is thoroughly unpleasant. The hotels, no one could call them inns, do not, with one exception, give you a welcome, though they do give you quite good food. The exception is The Crown, which does appear quite pleased to see you and may even remember you if you return at a later date. The shops are unfriendly—and frequently rude. Lyndhurst likes the charabanc trade—quick and easy and generally foolish—and does not want anything else. Luckily, beyond the Verderers' Court, and Leighton's painting and Burne-Jones's windows in the modern church, there is nothing to see in Lyndhurst and therefore no reason to stop.

But the Verderers' Court should be seen, not because there is anything particular to see, but because it is part of history. In ancient times the officials of the Forest were numerous. They included a lord warden, agisters, regarders, verderers, keepers (who were also called Foresters)

Lymington Harbour

and verminers. The freeholders of the Forest were called *Swains*, and the word still lingers on in the pure Saxon word *Swainmote*. But for the most part the old names are going. Only agister and verderer hold out, and they, I fear, are waging a losing battle. *Swainmote*, commonly called the Verderers' Court, is held five times a year in the King's House at Lyndhurst. It sits in a long dark ancient room filled with old furniture and lined with stags' heads. It is a more friendly court than the usual magisterial court, more informal, and it is highly respected in the Forest. Its business nowadays is, I suspect, highly varied. It does still deal with the old laws of the Forest—which are mainly concerned with trespass and the poaching of deer (and the arresting of anyone found at night in the king's wood with blackened face)—it does still deal with pigs and pannage. And nowadays it must deal, I imagine, much more frequently than of old with rights of way, for the Forestry Commissioners do not like rights of way. I wish it also had the power to deal with red-brick bungalows placed in unsuitable positions.

In the dark room of the Verderers' Court there hangs, just below the stags' heads, a piece of rusted iron, which is known as Rufus's Stirrup, and through which, it is said, all dogs had to pass to escape "lawing." The practice of "lawing" dogs commenced, so far as one can make out, in Henry III's reign. The great mastiffs kept by the Foresters were a continual source of trouble, owing to their depredations among the deer. So *expeditation*, or lawing, was introduced, the mastiffs having three claws struck off each of their fore-paws and being thus rendered harmless to the deer. To-day you can keep any dog you like in the Forest, and he may keep his full complement of claws. And Rufus's Stirrup dates from the sixteenth century, anyway.

All these laws originally hinged on the deer. To-day you will not see many deer in the Forest. Indeed you may spend days and weeks in the Forest without seeing a single deer. But there are deer in the Forest. I do not know how many there are; I do not think that anyone does. I know that the Deputy Surveyor tried to make a census of the deer not long ago, and gave it up as a bad job. Six thousand were said to have been destroyed after the Deer Removal Act, and it has been said that two thousand were left, I should think that that was quite probable. It may well have been more. The New Forest is a big place and deer are clever at taking advantage of cover. Official statements say that two hundred are killed annually now. This is achieved by deer drives. It may be taken as certain that in every drive more deer escape than are shot. It may also be taken as certain that no drive is perfect, that many deer double back in the undergrowth and are not seen at all. The buckhounds, even in normal times, provide good sport, but they do not kill many deer. Taking all this into consideration, I should not be surprised to find that there were more than two thousand deer in the Forest to-day. It is generally agreed, anyway, that they have increased of recent years.

Five species, or varieties, occur in the Forest—the red deer, the roe deer, the fallow deer, the Japanese deer and the Manchurian deer, the last two being varieties of the Sika. Of these the red deer is now the most uncommon. It is rare to get a sight of one, and this has led to statements that they no longer occur in the Forest. That at least is not true, for I have seen them on more than one occasion recently. The red deer is a big animal, especially is this true of the stag, and it is rather wonderful to see how easily they make their way through the thick undergrowth and by the trees and the speed at which they can travel in such country. So used have we become to thinking of the red deer as the animal of the open highland country in Scotland that we have forgotten that it is really a woodland animal, and that here in the New Forest among trees and thick undergrowth it is in its true surroundings. It is interesting also to watch the complete disdain with which the red deer treats the fallow deer. I have more than once seen the two species together, and the red has ignored the presence of the others, passing among them as if they were not there at all. Some of these Forest stags reach a great size, bigger, I feel sure, than the red deer of the Highlands, but they very rarely produce good antlers judged by Scottish standards. Albinos occur in the Forest red deer. One white stag has haunted the Lucy Hill neighbourhood for many years now;

though I have not personally seen it for some four years it was alive in 1945.

The fallow deer of the Forest differ somewhat from the fallow deer of our parks, and even from the fallow deer at large in other parts of Hampshire (the fallow deer is not an uncommon animal in Hampshire, though so rarely seen by the ordinary traveller) and especially in their antlers. The normal antler form in the fallow is palmated, but the deer of the Forest show a marked tendency towards the many pointed form of antler common to the red deer. There is a difference, too, in colouring. Among the fallow deer of our parks there are two varieties of colouring, the one with dark backs and lighter underparts, and the other light with white spots on backs and sides and yellowish-white underneath. The light deer scarcely change colour at all with the seasons; but the dark type changes to the light colour with white spots in the summer, changing back again for the winter. The divergence from the normal in the antlers of the fallow deer of the New Forest has led some authorities to trace their descent from the great fallow deer of the shores of the Sea of Marmora rather than from the fallow deer of Asia Minor. I am not competent to judge of such a point. But I do not think that there is a great difference between the dark deer, which are the typical wild deer, and the light deer, which are the typical park deer. The two occur on the same ground, for instance in Richmond Park and in many of the woods of the southern counties (including the New Forest), but they keep separate and do not apparently ever interbreed, though they do interbreed at Whipsnade. In the New Forest, where both types occur, though the dark is the most common, there is a most definite segregation, and I have never seen the two mixed in a herd. This seems to suggest something more than a mere variation in the same species. In the parks the fallow deer is noticeably gregarious. In the wild the species is less gregarious than the red deer. You will rarely find a large herd. Small parties are the rule and the sexes keep together from the beginning of the rut until the early spring.

Hutchinson in his book on the New Forest expresses doubt as to there being any roe deer left in the area. That is absolute nonsense. There are plenty of roe in the Forest and indeed throughout the woods of Hampshire and the south of England. But the roe is a very shy animal and mainly nocturnal and so rarely seen. During the daytime they lie up in the thickest cover they can find. They feed at nightfall and again at dawn and they usually drink before doing so, and if you can find one of their drinking places then you will be certain of seeing deer. For the most part the roe of the New Forest move in small parties of five or so, but on the feeding grounds several parties will sometimes gather together, separating again for the day. In northern Hampshire the parties are often larger and I have seen a company of twenty-seven on the move at one time.

Both the Japanese deer and the variety known as the Manchurian occur in the Forest. They are at large in several parts of the country, and especially in the woods of Hampshire and Surrey, but they have only come into the Forest of fairly recent years, and they are not present in great numbers. It is said that they will interbreed with the red deer (which I find very difficult to believe) and also with the roe deer, particularly in Dorset. I have no evidence to support either assertion.

The other large mammal which is to be seen in the New Forest, and to be seen in very large numbers, is the New Forest pony. The New Forest pony is a wild animal in the sense that it is free to wander where it will, and that it receives little or no care. The ponies run free at all seasons of the year, but they are rounded up periodically for branding or for the sales, for they all belong to the Foresters. The foals are branded at the round-ups according to the brand of the mare with which they are running at the time of branding. The stallions must be approved by a committee before they are turned out into the Forest (a stallion not approved cannot be turned out) and so the breed is kept fairly sound, having regard to all the interference and modern conditions very sound indeed.

The ponies create a great deal of interest. Each winter they figure in the columns of the daily Press, described as underfed and starving. There are about 1,800 ponies in the Forest at the present time, and none of them, it is safe to say, is starving or in any danger of doing so. The annual letters are written by people with a great love of animals, but with little knowledge of the Forest pony. They are also written, more often than one would guess, by people with no love for animals and no knowledge at all of ponies or Forest conditions, but with a great love of seeing their names in print. The Forest pony may look thin in comparison with the sleek hacks and hunters, but the breed is naturally small and spare and wiry. It is also incredibly hardy and adept at finding food.

But it is not, it must be admitted, as hardy as it used to be. And this is due to the interference of horse-lovers who have "improved" the breed. This "improvement" commenced about 1880. Since then the breed has undergone a huge change. The true native type has been destroyed (and cannot now, I think, be recovered) and the animal has been removed from true relationship with its habitat. It is a very great pity.

The New Forest pony that had been evolved by Nature through the ages was a small, stocky, rather hairy, and very hardy, moorland pony standing about eleven hands. This pony knew all about the Forest. He had no need of winter housing, no need of winter feed. He was thrifty and clever, and he could winter perfectly well on the rough grazing provided by the Forest. Shaggy and small, this native breed had more in common with the Kalmuck and Tartar ponies than with southern breeds, and they were alone except, perhaps, for the Shetland in this respect among the native breeds of Britain. In the winter they eat the holly and the young furze tops. Gorse, of course, belongs to the pea family and has a nutritive value. It is a very valuable food for cattle and for sheep—it was used for this purpose by all the older generation of Foresters, and is still used by some—but the problem is to reduce it sufficiently so that the animals may not have to face the prickles. The old breed of Forest pony knew how to do this without help. The old Forest pony had a thick growth of hair on his face—he wore a beard—and with this armour he would face the thickest gorse. Moreover, before he ate the gorse, he would trample it under foot. This was the breed that provided the pack ponies for rural transport; this was the breed that was used by the smugglers of the New Forest. This was the breed that had been here since time immemorial. It was not very good-looking, perhaps, but it did know its job and it was ideal for the conditions.

Its looks killed it. When the new middle class began to move into the New Forest with the industrial revolution, they wanted something smarter. They set about "improving" the breed. They introduced Arab stallions. Now, I have nothing but admiration for the Arab. It is a magnificent animal, and its value in the cross is beyond question. But not in all crosses. The surest way of ruining the Shetland would be to introduce an Arab cross. But such considerations did not worry the new rich of the nineteenth century. The Arab was used. The breed became taller and lighter and spindlier, and weaker. They became much better looking, it is true. They became much more showy. They looked good as saddle ponies, and in the traps. But they had lost the stiff stocky strength and toughness of the old breed, and they had not gained the thoroughbred bone of the Arab. And even more than that, though that was bad enough, they had their temperament ruined. The placidity of the moorland pony was gone, but instead of the mettlesomeness of the thoroughbred Arab, there was only a cross-grained nervousness. They acquired the irritability of spinsters just past the marriageable age. It was a tragedy. The sale for the pits—for which a great number used to be bought every year—was quickly lost. And it was some time before a substitute was found. But a substitute was found. There was a good trade in ponies up to the beginning of the First German War. My own small village of Burley sold more than 3,000 pounds' worth in 1913, and that was not an exceptional year. It was an average year's trading. But the First German War and the introduction of popular motoring killed the pony trade. There was still some sale for the light-weight ponies that made good saddle-horses, but that was not a big sale and it was almost entirely out of the Forest. That lasted until the slump of 1930. After that there was a little export trade to such places as Mexico and Chile. But the pony business was more or less dead. It started to die with the introduction of Arab blood. There was one great effort to get out of the Arab rut and to breed back true to type. It was made by Lord Lucas, Colonel Cecil and Miss Blackmore. It is much to be hoped that they will find successors.

There are also a few wild donkeys in the Forest. I do not know how many. I do not know to whom they originally belonged, nor when they ceased to have attention from their owners. But there has been a herd frequenting the Rhinefield area for some years now, and the change in habit since taking to a free range has been most interesting. During the day these animals are never far from cover, and are usually to be found in thick undergrowth. They feed like the deer—at nightfall and again early in the morning. I have never found them easy of approach, but they are not more than wary. They are not shy in the same way as are the deer. Judging from the number of foals, six, that I saw this year, 1945, breeding is quite satisfactory.

But we were in Lyndhurst. And Lyndhurst is a place that one should leave as soon as one can. Luckily it is a place that it is very easy to get away from: roads run in every direction and all of them, with the exception of the Southampton road which loses any semblance of beauty at Lyndhurst Road, pass through fine woodlands.

If you take the Cadnam-Romsey road and turn left just after passing the Kennels you come to Minstead. No one should leave the New Forest without visiting Minstead, for the village has a church that is quite unique. Somewhere or other I have read a description of Minstead Church in which it was dismissed as an "ecclesiastical villa." I have heard it described as hideous and I have heard it described as beautiful. Personally I have seen many more beautiful churches than Minstead, but it is certainly not hideous. To my mind it is lovely—not for any beauty of architecture or setting, but solely because it is so exactly right. I cannot imagine Minstead without just that church, nor that church without Minstead. And is that not exactly what one should feel about a village church? And Minstead Church, small and white-washed and set upon a little hill in the fashion of many Forest churches, has a welcoming, homely atmosphere so that it is difficult to leave it. Or so I find.

Architecturally it is a positively astonishing jumble of styles. Originally it was Norman (it is first mentioned in 1272) and it has a truly remarkable Norman font. The chancel arch is Gothic but built in some part with rounded Norman stones. The north doorway is transitional. The porch is seventeenth century, the tower eighteenth. There is a southern transept of about the year 1800 and the remains of a fifteenth-century chancel screen. And there is the great three-decker pulpit. The whole might so easily be horrible—and blends perfectly. And then there are the family pews of Castle Malwood and Minstead Lodge. (It was at Castle Malwood that Rufus was supposed to have lodged the night before he died.) These pews are enormous, more like rooms than pews, for they have fireplaces and are backed by large windows. Once in them the worshippers are hidden from the congregation, but not from the eye of the preacher. And in the vault under the chancel lie Comptons. Comptons have been squires and rectors of Minstead for more than two hundred years. One Canon Compton was rector for fifty-six years, and no less than five have held the living. And among them lies one that was not a Compton and had no connexion whatsoever with the family—an Earl of Errol. This gentleman died so heavily in debt that his creditors seized his body to prevent its burial (though what good they thought that that was going to do them I cannot imagine, unless they thought that they might sell it to one of the hospitals), and the then squire Compton, an old man, heard of it. He went over to the Earl's house and sat by the body and prevented it being taken away; and the next day brought it to the manor and gave it burial in his own vault. That was true Christian friendship. The spirit of that old Compton lingers in Minstead to-day. It is a spirit that is hard to find in this modern England of ours.

The churchyard has fine yews and good headstones, and is one of the most peaceful, in the sense of restful, places that I know. Below is the village green; and the village green, so rapidly disappearing elsewhere in England, re-

mains the integral part of almost every Forest village.
Upon it men play cricket (and cricket is Hampshire's game),
upon it men meet their sweethearts, upon it men feed their
cattle and their pigs and their geese, around it men discuss
this and that, and live and love and die. Across the village
green of Minstead as I sit in the churchyard I see the Trusty
Servant Inn, its sign bearing the same picture as that at
Winchester College with the same doggerel verse, which
runs:

A Trusty Servant's portrait would you see,
This "emplematic" Figure well survey,
The Porker's Snout not nice in diet shows
The Padlock Shut no secret he'll disclose.
Patient the Ass his master's wrath will bear
Swiftness in errand the Stagg's feet declare:
Loaded his Left Hand apt to labour saith:
The Vest his neatness Open Hand his faith.
Girt with his Sword his Shield upon his arm
Himself and Master he'll protect from harm.

Back to Lyndhurst—to get out again as quickly as possible by the road to Beaulieu. This road runs to the right
of Bolton's Bench, which is an ancient tree-covered barrow,
and through a gorse-covered common which merges into a
heathery moor. Away to the right is Pondhead Inclosure,
where in early summer the rhododendron blooms set off the
oaks and the bluebells, though more purple than blue, are
lovely. If you cross the moor to your left you come to Long-
water, where the stream, that a little later on is worthy the
name of Beaulieu River, is bordered in spring with masses
of marsh-marigolds. A little further on to the left is Matley
Wood, and the road crosses Matley Bog where, in the spring
again, the redshank rouses all the world of birds at every
fancied danger. Beyond Matley Bog and away to the left
is the softly rounded mass of Denny Wood bordering moorland, and beyond Denny is a patch of marshy ground en-
circled by a dyke—and this patch is brilliantly orange in
autumn, and in autumn I have seen the wood sandpiper
and in spring the green sandpiper here—and this patch is

called the Bishop's Ditch. It belongs, I believe, to Winchester College. The story goes that the form of the original grant was "as much land in the New Forest as the Bishop of Winchester, on his hands and knees, could crawl round in a day." The Bishop was a keen sportsman, chose the best bit of snipe-shooting in the Forest and crawled solemnly round it, accompanied presumably (but in an upright position) by the Cathedral solicitor. It is a good story and conjures up a pleasing picture. But probably there was once a fish-pond here. Just beyond the Bishop's Ditch is Woodfidley. The Foresters have a proverb about Woodfidley rain: if rain clouds are seen at Lyndhurst coming from Woodfidley, then it will Woodfidley rain, in other words it will rain steadily and drenchingly all day long. Woodfidley, I think, must have some great power over the clouds for the same proverb holds good for Brockenhurst and Beaulieu, which lie pretty well in opposite directions from Woodfidley itself. Woodfidley is a great place for butterflies. It was here, as a small boy, that I caught my first white admiral and my first silver-washed fritillary and my first (and only) pale-clouded yellow. Now I no longer collect butterflies, but I still like watching them in Woodfidley.

Returning to the main road where we left it at Matley Passage, we pass on the way to Beaulieu through some two or three miles of heathland before coming into woodland again and so to Pannerley Gate, which is, I believe, the official boundary of the Forest, and so following the stream of Beaulieu (for it is still no more than a stream) we come to Beaulieu itself at the head of a wide open reach.

Beaulieu might well be spoilt. If Broadway has any excuse, then Beaulieu has every excuse in the world. It has history, and a river, and a beautiful name. Well might it prostitute its charms for the tourist in the manner of many another English village. But Beaulieu is unspoilt and honest, and cares nothing for tourists.

There was an abbey here once. The one and only abbey founded by King John, and founded, so it is said, because of a dream. It was in 1204. A deputation of Cistercian monks had had the temerity to appeal personally to the king for relief, and John, in a fit of rage at their impudence, had ordered them to be trampled to death by horses. But that night the king dreamed; and dreamed that he himself was brought up for trial, and condemned, and flogged. The dream was so real that when he woke his body bore traces of the punishment he had received. Being advised that this nocturnal visitation was a sign that the Deity was not altogether pleased with him, he ordered the monks to be released and, as a token that he was really sorry, he founded the abbey at Bellus Locus, which was to become one of the proudest and one of the most powerful of all English abbeys. John died long before it was completed. And despite his subsequent career I do not think that he ever forgot that dream, for he had himself buried between two saints, a sort of additional insurance against a painful life after death. The abbey was completed in forty-five years—very quick work—and was dedicated in 1249. On that day the abbey was visited by Henry III and his queen and a long train of nobles and prelates, and their entertainment cost Hugh, the first abbot, a nice round sum. Beaulieu Abbey was built with stone brought from the Isle of Wight in carts across the causeway which then existed, so it is said, between the island and Lepe. I understand that the causeway is regarded as a legend by most of the authorities. Personally I do not think that it is a legend. I think that that causeway was a fact. As with Holy Island to-day, I believe that at low tide you could still, in 1204, and probably a good deal later, walk across to the island. Pope Innocent III granted the abbey very important sanctuary rights. Here came Anne Neville after her husband, Warwick the Kingmaker, had been killed at the battle of Barnet; and here came Perkin Warbeck, the pretender to the throne in Henry VII's reign. Warbeck was a thorn in Henry's side for fourteen years, but after his disastrous campaign in Cornwall in 1497 he decided that he had better put himself beyond Henry's reach and under the protection of the Pope. Two years later he was persuaded to surrender, and paid for his trust on the scaffold. At the Dissolution there was a good deal of trouble because of the number of criminals and debtors who lived in the grounds with their wives and families, the sanctuary rights then being freely used by gentlemen from all over the country. In 1537 Beaulieu died and Henry VIII used the stones to build Hurst Castle.

Perhaps this abbey deserved its fate. The men that built it built in love and awe and wonder. But later came abbots who were, perhaps, more worldly, too worldly, and by their scheming helped to bring about the downfall not only of this abbey but of religious institutions of the same kind throughout the country. The Cistercian Order arose at a period of earnest revival, and as a protest against the laxity and worse that ruled in Benedictine and Cluniac houses. Their rule was austere. The meanest and coarsest of garb, a rough white woollen garment, had to be worn by the monks for work during the day, and the same garment served as a nightgown. The rule of silence was strictly enforced, and everything was very simple. The new order had a most marked effect in raising the standard of living— to use a modern phrase—in the monasteries of the twelfth and thirteenth centuries, but it had also its great weakness, a weakness that had become most marked by the time of Henry VIII. It was alien to its organization. It gave no allegiance to the bishops, owing allegiance only to the parent abbey at Citeaux. This gave to ambitious and politically minded abbots great scope for scheming and so became a source of disunion in the national church.

But the Cistercians were beautiful builders—Tintern and Fountains bear witness to their skill—and they were great lovers of books. Little remains above the ground of the great Abbey of Beaulieu, but that which does is most beautifully preserved. The late Lord Montagu of Beaulieu spent years in making the place intelligible to the visitors. He loved the place and his love still dominates it. He is buried in a secluded corner of the cloisters, a fitting resting-place for one who realized to the full his obligations as a landowner, in days when the majority of his kind thought not of what they owed to their property, but what their property was good for in hard cash.

Little remains of the infirmary and the dorter and the chapter house, but the splendid dignity of the original abbey can be judged from the lay brothers' house, which is still standing. Thirty years or so ago this upper room was in ruins, the haunt of jackdaws and owls—I have myself collected eggs in it—now it is used as a meeting-place and is one of the most beautiful rooms in all the country.

Another part of the same building is used as a museum and many of the treasures excavated from the ruins can be seen here. They include a double "heart-coffin," a reminder of the time when parts of the body were buried in various places so that the whole might miss none of the prayers of the congregation.

The most complete part of the building remaining is now the Parish Church. In one way, at least, this church must, I think, be unique. Its orientation is not east and west, but north and south; which is explained by the fact that it was not originally a church at all but the refectory of the abbey. It still resembles a refectory rather than a church for all the smell of incense, and it is, taken all in all, rather a cheerless building. But the early English lancet windows and the thick buttresses are interesting, and the pulpit is remarkable. This is of carved stone and is truly beautiful. Originally, of course, it was not a pulpit but the rostrum from which one monk read some uplifting homily the while his brothers chewed a frugal meal in silence. It is approached by a stone stairway actually built within the thick wall. There are eighteen steps of uneven height worn by the passage of many feet through six hundred and fifty years, and the monk as he climbed them (and the parson to-day) was visible all the way through an arcade of moulded arches.

The details of the abbey are to be found in an excellent guide which the old man at the gate will sell you for sixpence. The money goes to the upkeep of the place, and few who have walked round it and drunk of its peace and drawn of its inspiration will think the sixpence money wasted.

Beaulieu once had a witch named Mary Dove. This lady, who lived in the eighteenth century, was something of a quick change artist. She was, as became a lady of her profession, pretty good on a broomstick, but she was also expert at becoming a black cat or a barn owl or a hare. The old man at the gate will talk about her with pleasure, telling you a new story each time you go, but if you ask him if it is true that on a summer's evening you can hear the monks singing their vespers (and this is believed by almost everyone in the village) he will not answer you a word, but will just smile at you, a slow and secretive smile.

Lower down the river—it is now a river proper—is Buckler's Hard. Buckler's Hard is well out of the Forest according to the Ordnance Survey, and is not regarded as part of the Forest by any author I have read. I do not care. The hamlet, if it existed, was in the Forest in the Conqueror's day, and the hamlet, despite the maps and the authors, is in the Forest to-day in every way—spiritually, physically, geographically—in every way save cartographically.

A lot of people visit Buckler's Hard every year. A few—speaking comparatively—come in yachts; the majority come in motor cars or on bicycles. Quite recently they have built a car-park to house these vehicles, and by so doing have undoubtedly saved the hamlet from much harm; and they have built the cark park well away at the end of the lane that leads down to the cottages and the river. One should be grateful for the car-park—and I am—and yet I remember how shocked and hurt I was when first I saw it, which was utterly inconsistent since when I visit Buckler's Hard I do so more often than not by car. But that car-park, with its uniformed attendant, seemed to bring into the little, kindly elfin hamlet some of the blaring, hungry spirit of the great cities. And I loved Buckler's Hard. I love it still—and the car-park.

This was a great place once. In the days of Adams, the shipbuilder, it held its head high among the shipbuilding yards of England. Here from Forest oaks they built great ships: *Illustrious* of seventy-four guns, *Europe*, *Agamemnon*, *Vigilant*, and *Indefatigable* of fifty-four, *Greenwich* and *Sheerness* of forty-four, *Swiftsure* and *Euryalus*. And of these, *Illustrious*, *Agamemnon*, *Swiftsure* and *Euryalus* fought at Trafalgar. They were built here, and as you look at the tiny hamlet and the narrow winding stream that seems incredible. And looking at the glistening yachts with their bright paint—yachts that would be mere toys beside those ancient men-of-war—it seems utterly incredible that having been built they could ever have reached the open sea. Yet they did. They were towed down the winding creek by men in row-boats. That could have been no easy task, for the fairway twists and turns in every direction and a large spit of shingle and mud stretches out from Needs Oar Point. But not content these ships were then towed, still by men in row-boats, all the way round to Portsmouth. The slipway from which these ships were launched is still there. And so is the master builder's house, which is now an hotel. The lettering on the hotel is beautifully small and unobtrusive—and the place has, I understand, a very high reputation. I can only say that I have been there on three occasions, and never have I been in a hotel where I have felt less wanted—but then, of course, I only required lunch and a drink. I must have struck it on off days.

And Buckler's Hard to-day? To-day pretty well as in Queen Anne's day. Just one street. A broad street with grass verges running down a gentle hill to the blue waters of the Beaulieu River—and beyond the green wooded shore by Exbury and the gulls flashing white against the green. And on each side of the street a row of cottages with leaded lights and green or brown mullions and transoms, and built of that delightfully rich brick that was made when Anne was queen. There are ten cottages on each side of the street, and one of them—on the left-hand side as you go towards the river—has a chapel. Just one small room, but so simply beautiful that it takes a long time before one can leave. And at the bottom of the road, just by the ancient slipway, is a fir tree, so correctly placed that I am sure it was planted purposely to set off the place. And usually by the fir tree there is a very friendly donkey, who must be getting very old indeed now, for I seem always to have seen that donkey in that place right from the time when I was a small boy. And from each cottage front-door runs a neat stone-bordered path across the grass verge to the wide street. Neat. Neat is the word that describes Buckler's Hard, I think. Beautifully neat and trim and spick and span (but not consciously so) and still, to-day, ship-shape. And that is right and proper.

212

Entrance gate of Carisbrooke Castle, I.O.W.

Addendum

I understand that this hotel changed hands in 1945. I should like to make it clear that my three visits were all made before that date and that no reflection upon the proprietors or management is intended.

From Beaulieu, taking the road to Brockenhurst, one comes to Hatchet Gate and so, officially, into the Forest again. Just beyond the Gate, and a little off the road on the left-hand side, is Hatchet Pond, which is a great place for birds, especially in the winter, for it is a fair-sized sheet of water. The country hereabouts gives the impression of being high ground—it is in point of fact only just in excess of a hundred feet above sea-level—for it is exposed and has a truly moorland aspect and is swept by the salt breezes from the Solent. From here you can look across Hampshire to the low line of the Isle of Wight, only about seven miles away as the crow might fly, but seemingly miles and miles away; and on a fine day, with the sun lighting the chalk cliffs where the Needles thrust boldly into the sea, I know no more satisfying view in all England. All the country south of the Beaulieu-Brockenhurst road as far as Norley Inclosure, and from Beaulieu Rails on the east to Dilton Gardens on the west is heathland. Most people call it Beaulieu Heath, but few know it as Hatchet Moor, and I have heard it called Greenmoor and Lady Cross Moor (on the north side of the Brockenhurst road is an old house called Ladycross) but I call it the blasted heath, for the time when I got to know it best it was blackened and desolate from a heath fire, and the stray clumps of Scots pine standing up here and there made it seem all the more lonely. On that occasion I walked the two miles across it from Hatchet Pond to Boldre and in all the walk saw not a single soul and only four birds—two crows, a heron and a gull. I have been many times since and seen many people walking and on horseback, and many birds, including the Dartford Warbler, but that walk has remained in my memory, and always for me Beaulieu Heath will be a lonely and desolate waste.

About a mile and a half after leaving Hatchet Gate the road runs into woodland, then through woods (some of them planted as part of the afforestation scheme carried out in William III's reign) all the way to Brockenhurst. Brockenhurst is very old. The name is Saxon, meaning badger's wood (and there are still plenty of badgers in the neighbourhood), and the church is one of the two mentioned

Taverland Manor, I.O.W.

in *Domesday*. Yes, Brockenhurst is old: men lived here before the Conqueror came, even, I think, before the Romans came. But there is nothing very old about Brockenhurst to-day. The old church, which is built upon an artificial mound at the top of a little hill, has a Norman doorway on the south side, a chancel arch of very early and plain Norman work, and a square font of Purbeck marble which must be very nearly as old as the chancel arch. It is otherwise not a remarkable building. In the churchyard is a magnificent yew, reputed to be (is there any churchyard yew not so reputed?) one thousand years old, and the trunk of a really mighty oak. There is also a "colonial" grave-yard where lie buried many New Zealanders who came here during the First German War. And here also is the grave of "Brusher" Mills. Mills, a local man, was famed through-out the Forest as a snake-catcher. He was also a hermit and a great drinker of rum (he drank one whole bottle each evening) and as he rarely, if ever, washed, he had his own peculiar aroma.

Standing in the churchyard one can imagine old Brocken-hurst, and the name of the old village inn, the Rose and Crown (the Tudor badge) conjures up history. But modern Brockenhurst has nothing to do with history. There are fast trains to Waterloo, and a good many first-class season ticket holders, though one could not call this "first-class" country as one can parts of Sussex and Kent and the whole of Surrey. But the good train service has meant luxury hotels and a good golf-course and riding stables and so forth. Brockenhurst lives on visitors, but manages to do so in a fairly dignified manner, and so remains a pleasant place. And Brockenhurst has an industry, the famous Forest Toys, which will no doubt revive now that peace has returned. There is also a business—the hiring of hacks. Brockenhurst is the Hyde Park of the New Forest. You can see—mainly at the week-ends—all the funny sights that you can see in Rotten Row, and some funnier. And Brockenhurst, so I have been told, is the snobbiest place in the New Forest—and that, let me assure you, is saying something.

Yet Brockenhurst is not altogether divorced from the

Forest. Not so very long ago the Forest used to come right into the village, for, so we are told, herds of deer would race up the village street when nights were dark, and all the village dogs would be roused and would rush from their kennels after them and perhaps pull one or two down. No deer come to-day. Brockenhurst stands in the midst of lawns. The men who hacked down the trees to make room for these lawns did so to make light, to clear a way from danger, so that they might live in the open light and have knowledge of what was coming. And to-day beyond the lawns the Forest stands as it has always stood, watchful and dark. And one day it will, I am sure, creep in again and swallow up Brockenhurst and the big hotels and the stockbrokers. It stands there waiting an opportunity.

South of Brockenhurst lies Boldre, which is in the Forest, and Lymington, which should be but is not officially. You can go by the main road and turn off at Batramsley Cross; or you can go by following the Lymington River, which is really Highland Water (and should here be called the Boldre; Lymington River proper begins below Boldre village), on foot from Brockenhurst by Perry Wood, and Whitley Ridge, past the ford at Royden Manor, and alongside Newlands Copse. And this is much the best way, though difficult walking at times, for the main road is like every main road in England, dangerous and hideously noisy. The Boldre has never had its praises sung, so does not, I suppose, contain fishable fish, but it is pretty and peaceful and winds and twists in the most delightful manner, and finally lands you at Boldre.

Boldre is quaint—in the modern meaning of that word. The thatched cottages should really be beautiful but are only quaint. Boldre, though not yet fully graduated as "ye olde," is well on the way. I do not like Boldre village, but I do like Boldre Church, which is a very lovely mixture of Norman and Early English. Here Parson William Gilpin ministered for thirty years, and here he wrote *Forest Scenery*. Gilpin was a contemporary of Gilbert White, but his literary efforts are not nearly so well known, largely, I think, because his style is not so simple. Certainly he knew a good deal about natural history and he might, had he had the fortune to meet Pennant, have done for the New Forest what White did for Selborne. His epitaph states that he and his wife expected with "new joy to meet several of their neighbours" in "joyful immortality." Gilpin, from all accounts, did a good deal for Boldre and was popular with his parishioners. When he came he found the village "utterly neglected by their former pastor, and exposed to every temptation of pillage and robbery from their proximity to the deer, the game, and the fuel of the forest, these poor people were little better than a herd of banditti." Evidently he cleared all that up. But he did not confine his attention to the poor. It is on record that a wealthy farmer in the neighbourhood, who had considerable fame as a lady-killer, was taken to task on many occasions by the worthy Mr. Gilpin. These warnings had no effect, and finally the vicar banned him in the spiritual court. Sentence of excommunication was suspended only on condition that he performed penance in public. This he and his latest lady friend, clad in the white sheets that were the recognized penitential garments, duly did in the presence of an enormous congregation, and lived in peace with the vicar thereafter. The Church had power and commanded respect in those days, but William Gilpin, in addition to being an author and a naturalist of no mean ability, must have been a man of very strong personality. He deserved, I think, a greater fame than has fallen to his lot.

His, however, is not the only literary connexion that Boldre can boast. Warner, who wrote a history of the county, was curate here. And Southey, whose fame must surely be based on the quantity of his writings rather than on their quality, was married in Boldre Church in 1839 to Caroline Bowles, who, if she never wrote as voluminously as her husband, did write one book, *Chapters on Church-yards*, which has a charm that no book of his ever attained.

About two miles south of Boldre lies Lymington. Lymington, though officially outside the Forest, is spiritually well in the Forest and has a firm connexion with the Forest extending over many centuries. Despite its coastal trade, its yacht-building industry, Wellworthy's, and the ferry to the Isle of Wight, Lymington is a thoroughly sleepy place

all through the week, and absolutely dead on a Sunday.
Each day for about an hour before noon and for another
hour in the afternoon it has a spasm of business, for in those
hours the gentry of the neighbourhood come in to do their
shopping. Then Lymington looks busy and wealthy with
its wide main street filled with big cars. And those two
hours a day (Lymington is a really good shopping town,
with one of the best bookshops in the whole of Hampshire—
a good bookshop, by the way, is a most reliable index to a
town) and perhaps the yacht-building keeps the place alive.
But Lymington *lives* only on Saturday nights, for on Saturday nights the Forest people come in to do their shopping,
and then for some four hours the town is noisy and crowded
and exciting—a mixture of market-town and sea-port and
fair, a mixture which I find infinitely alluring. All the way
down the wide street there are stalls, and the stall-holders
shout; and some try to bully the passer-by and looker-on,
and some try cajolery, and some mix the two in the most
bewildering manner. And among the stall-holders are
cheapjacks from all over the country—one man (he sells
wrist-watches) I have seen in Guildford and Devizes and
Leicester and St. Albans—selling the most astounding
things. And the street is crowded and the naphtha flares
play strange tricks with the faces of the men and the girls.
It is a grand place on a Saturday night is Lymington, and
I hope that the Saturday stalls will survive in this age of
regimentation. But Lymington is a grand place anyhow.
I hardly ever go there, but I wish that I lived there.

North from Brockenhurst the road runs to Lyndhurst,
and one should take that road even though it means going
to Lyndhurst because it runs through some magnificent
scenery: beeches with smooth trunks and oaks gnarled and
lichened, graceful birches and dark hollies stand out above
the bracken, and everywhere there are little winding paths
wandering off in the most seductive manner through the
bracken and the gorse and brambles into the woodland
depths. It is better, indeed, to leave the main road, with
its uninviting prospect, and to follow one of these paths.

The one I like best is on the right-hand side not long after
leaving Brockenhurst, and I like it best in June. The trees

meet overhead and out of them as I pass wood-pigeons flap suddenly, making the most prodigious noise. There are always rabbits just round the corner (even now after the blitz conducted for six years by the Ministry of Agriculture) rabbits that sit up and have a look at you before lolloping lazily into cover. And in June the bracken is fully open and foxgloves stand tall beneath the oaks. The bracken has many colours in the light of a June sun, now green, now white, now grey, now blue, as they reflect the sky through some gap in the trees. Bracken can be a pest, very frequently is a pest, and men spend their lives inventing machines that will crush it, and tear it, and prevent it spreading. But bracken, horrible as it can be on agricultural land, is the perfect setting for oaks. Some way along this path of mine you come to acacia trees (and there are not many in the Forest) and then suddenly to heath and great clumps of gorse, and then down again into another wood of oaks, where foxgloves flourish exceedingly. And on this walk you may well see deer.

So may you on another which you can take from the Brockenhurst-Lyndhurst road, and which is, I think, the best of all the fine walks in the Forest. This means leaving the main road and following the course of the winding stream (here correctly called Highland Water) as it runs beneath the side of Black Knoll Heath and skirts New Park Inclosure. The path leads through Queen's Bower, and Queen's Bower is enchanting with its little streams—three join together here—and its little wooden bridge and huge shady oaks and the bracken that is waist-high in the season of the year. I do not know why it is called Queen's Bower, and I have not met anyone who does know or has been able to put up any but the obvious suggestion—that some queen liked the place very much and used to come here with the maidens of her court. But which queen? And why no record of her coming? I feel that, if a real crowned queen had favoured this spot, there would have been a record of it somewhere. But there is none, and I like to think that it was a Forest queen—a simple but beautiful maiden who held her court, a court composed of suitors not maidens, here. It is in any case well named. And it is a great place for moths and butterflies, and consequently a great place for collectors armed with baggy nets. I have been told that that monarch of the woodlands, the Purple Emperor, lives here, but I have not seen one. But some of the trees bear notices upon their trunks, "NO SUGARING ALLOWED," which must annoy the entomologists very much, though I do not suppose that they take much notice of it.

The stream runs between little sandy banks, and is clear and shallow and amber-coloured above a gravel bed, so that one can watch the shoals of tiny fish darting here and there at incredible speed, with every now and then a larger fish swimming lazily among them, a liner among the dinghies. And here every now and again I have watched the water-vole busy searching the banks, and seen the kingfisher flash by, and more than once I have come across signs of the otter, though it never seems to me a proper stream for an otter. Here there are oaks on either side, their roots drinking in the stream, their branches meeting and lacing overhead, reflected as a maze in the water beneath. But a little later beeches replace the oaks and the stream, still perfectly clear, runs deeper, eating the sand away from the roots, so that they stand out as great knotted sinews, providing in nook and crevice shelter for many beetles and here and there a home for a vole. In some places the banks are crowned with bracken and in others with smooth moss-covered turf, and in these latter places you may see the signs where the deer have come down to drink—and perhaps, if you are very lucky (and sit very still indeed) you may see a deer drinking. That is luck that has not yet come my way. A little later there is a ford where the stream runs over a smooth gravel bed, and rounding a bend widens into quite a broad and quite a deep pool. This is the place for dragon-flies. Country children—and a good many countrymen—call them "horse stingers," and regard them somewhat fearfully. My knowledge is a little greater than that, for I know that they do not sting and are harmless, but beyond that very elementary fact I know, to be frank, very little indeed about dragon-flies. Indeed, the only species (I believe that there are about forty species to be found in Britain) that I can be quite sure of recognizing is

Pyrrhovoma nymphala, the large red damsel-fly, which is very much the same thing as saying that the only butterfly one can name correctly is the large cabbage white or the only bird the house sparrow. But I feel sure that this pool attracts a good many species. In addition to the large red damsel-fly I have seen a small cousin; and I have seen blue ones of varying shades and sizes, and blackish-green ones and black-and-yellow ones, though at different times of the year. And once by this pool in June, when I was a boy, I caught a dragon-fly of a kind that I have never seen since. It was, speaking from memory, quite small, only about an inch in length. But I can remember its colouring quite well. It was a beautiful emerald green and it had an orange moustache, and it had orange spots on its wings. I was very pleased with it and took it home with me and showed it to my schoolmaster, who was then staying with us to collect insects in the New Forest. He was also very pleased with it, and I did not see it again.

A little beyond this pool the path reaches the Lyndhurst-Christchurch road. And here you have the choice of two walks. You can go on up Highland Water to Highland Water Inclosure and through Puckpits and over Withybed Bottom to the Ringwood-Cadnam road—and that is a beautiful walk; or you can turn left down the main road, which here runs through open country with heath and gorse and hawthorns and the trees away behind. This is the easier of the two and leads to some of the most famous features of the Forest.

Where the trees come down to the road again, there are two gates. That on the left leads into Vinney Ridge Inclosure and is comparatively dull; that on the right into Knightwood, and this is the one to use. In Knightwood stand three of the Forest giants—the Eagle Oak, the Knightwood Oak, and Peter's Oak, though this last is actually in Holiday Hill Inclosure. Each of these trees has attained the dignity of special mention on the Ordnance Survey map (the only other tree to achieve such a distinction being the wholly disappointing Naked Man), and of them the Knightwood Oak is by far the most magnificent. It is supposed to be the oldest and largest oak in England,

and as its girth at shoulder-height is twenty-two feet, I think that it is quite likely all that it is claimed to be. They make me feel small and insignificant, these trees. They make me think that this life of ours, about which we take so much trouble and make so much fuss, is really a very small matter. They make me realize how foolish is this hurry, this frantic hustle after money, this savage struggle for existence that civilization has made of life. This great tree was here, though no more than a seedling, when Stephen was ruling a troubled kingdom. It was here, a mere boy, when John was signing the Magna Carta. It was here, nearing maturity, when Edward I was settling things in Wales. It was here, a sturdy man, when the Armada sailed to destruction. It watched its neighbours and its friends being cut down to make the ships to fight Napoleon. It watched its friends fall before the fury of the storm and the cold precision of the axe. It heard the news of Waterloo and Inkerman, and Lucknow, and Mafeking and Ypres and Verdun. In its old age it heard of Dunkirk and Tobruk, of Caen and Falaise, of Stalingrad and Cassino. In its old age it heard the whistle of bombs (a very large number fell in the New Forest) and the drone of bombers on their way to Coventry, and later the same drone on the way to Hamburg and Cologne. It has seen kings come and go and dictators rise and fall. It has watched year upon year men make love in just the same way and in much the same words. It has watched year upon year all those things happen that we, each generation of us, consider new and exciting, new and terrifying. And each year in October its leaves come spinning to the ground. They have done so now maybe eight hundred times. I have a feeling that it will be shedding its leaves long after I have joined the many thousands that have died since it was born.

Leaving Knightwood you enter Mark Ash Wood—again I would like to know the derivation of the name—and here are grand beeches. Mark Ash should really be visited in early spring, before the leaves hide the symmetry of the trees, or in late winter when the buds clothe the wood in a red haze. Wise in his *New Forest* wrote:

The true beech-forms, their boles spangled with silver scales of lichen, and the roots grasping the earth, feathered with the soft green down of moss. But not in individual trees lies the beauty of the forest, but in the masses of wood. There, in the long aisles, settles that depth of shade that no pencil can give, and that colouring which no canvas can retain, as the sunlight pierces through the green web of leaves, flinging as it sets a crown of gold round each tree-trunk.

Mark Ash Wood could not be better described.

If you bear right-handed through Mark Ash you come into Boldrewood, which is the home of ruined oaks and woodpeckers, and also of splendid conifers and fallow deer. And through Boldrewood you come to Mogshade Hill. Here you may go on to the main road from Ringwood to Cadnam or turn left-handed and cross Bushey Bratley, which is moorland, into Oakley Inclosure. Oakley is enormous. I do not know if it is the largest of the Forest Inclosures, but I imagine that it must be. It is intersected by innumerable paths and rides, and is the easiest place in the world to get lost even if you know the Forest well. My sister and I, when in our teens, once got lost in it for some hours, and we should have known where we were, for we then lived on the edge of it. We spent a long time walking down tracks that got narrower and narrower and finally lost themselves in bracken; we stumbled in and out of bogs, and crossed tiny meandering streams, without having any real idea of the direction in which we were travelling (the sun is not of much use in Oakley); and then suddenly (and certainly when we least expected it) we joined a track we both recognized. We certainly were not frightened, but I think that we were both a little uneasy. I know that I was, for I felt during that walk the *hostility* of the Forest—and I have had that feeling once or twice since. I know that I was very glad to see that track and to know just where I was.

In Oakley, on the edge towards Berry Beeches, is the Old House. I do not know the exact story of the Old House, or even if there is a story at all, but it has the reputation of being haunted. I have been told that it is haunted by a beautiful young girl and also that it is haunted by a horrible old crone. I have been told that the young girl was murdered and that the old crone committed suicide. I do not know. I think that the house has probably acquired its reputation because it is very lonely and very dark among the conifers. But I have seen two old women, true gipsies, cross themselves as they pass, and somehow, though I know that the Romany is superstitious, I have never regarded the race as religious. Certainly the haunting does not prevent them from visiting the place for the magnificent daffodils that grow there in the spring.

Oakley, too, has deer. I have seen all the species here, red, fallow, roe, and both sorts of Japanese, at various times. And it was here, once in the wood by Lucy Hill, and once just outside the wood by Burley Moor, that I had my best two views of the white stag, a magnificent animal, at least in memory. And it was in Oakley that I made one of my best friends—a tinker of the name of Arigho, who has since taught me a great many things that I should not know.

About a quarter of a mile south of the great Inclosure of Oakley lies the village of Burley. Burley has altered enormously of recent years, and not, I think, for the better. Twenty years ago, even ten years ago, it was a very pleasant little village—a mixture of retireds and cottagers. The retireds came here because they liked the country and wanted to live as well as they might on smallish pensions and with largish families. They liked the quiet and the facilities for riding and the rather comic (but very cheap) golf-course, and the fact that it was some way from a station, and had an extremely leisurely and infrequent privately run bus-service. In those days everyone knew everyone—including the one or two excessively rich, but still pleasant, people that lived in the neighbourhood—and though I cannot pretend that everyone got on with everyone else, they did not do so badly. But now Burley has been discovered. Progress has arrived. Houses were springing up all over the place just before the war, and were not always as tasteful as they might have been. The golf-course was discovered by Bournemouth—but fortunately a movement to enlarge the club house and to add a bar and a card room was defeated by the local members. And to-day Burley, though infinitely preferable to Lyndhurst or Brockenhurst, is undoubtedly suburbanized. Perhaps as a defence against this, perhaps because of it, Burley has suddenly become frightfully "pukka." And the cliques that are one of the most noticeable features of Golders Green have a good footing in Burley—a great pity.

One walk from Burley is through Burley Street to Picket Post. The best way to do this is to keep to the main road, for by so doing you get the magnificent view over Vales Moor and Crow Hill, a view that one would expect to find in Yorkshire or Devonshire but not in Hampshire. Crossing the main road at Picket Post, you keep for maybe half a mile to heathland, and then drop down to Linford Inclosure and through Linford Inclosure to Linford Brook. The streams in this part of the Forest—Linford Brook, Dockens Water, Latchmere Brook, and Ditchend Brook—feed the Avon and run westwards. They are in some subtle manner different from the streams further south in the Forest, all of which run east and south; they move more purposefully, as if fully conscious of the part they play in the life of a great river. And in this part of the Forest the ground is more hilly and the Inclosures fewer and less imposing in size, though not necessarily in timber, than those south of the Ringwood-Cadnam road. This north-west corner of the Forest is less well known, is indeed pretty well unfrequented. It does not boast a single village of size, and the farms are few and far between. The moorland, most of it three to four hundred feet up (which is a good height for the Forest) is really wild, and it is here that one may expect to see wild life in some profusion, though during the war the R.A.F. were rather busy all around this part.

The four streams—they run roughly parallel and, as the crow might fly, are about a mile apart with high ground in between—are much favoured by birds. Curlew nest on Hampton Ridge and above Black Gutter Bottom. The raven has visited here quite recently and the hen-harrier. The buzzard has come back. Snipe breed in the bottoms and so do the redshank; and every heath carries a maximum population of small birds. And this part of the Forest is also favoured by the roe deer and the Japanese deer. It was always pretty well open here, for there are plenty of signs of man's habitations before the Romans came. Just off the Ringwood-Cadnam road are three groups of tumuli —one by Stoney Cross and the other two between that point and Picket Post. In Roe Wood Inclosure, above the Linford Brook, are the remains of an early British Camp; and in the Sloden Inclosure, above the Dockens Water, is the remnant of an early British earthwork, which (there is not much left of it) may also have been a camp once. And there are tumuli on Hampton Ridge and Janesmoor Plain and by Anses Wood. Before the Romans came this part of the Forest was well populated, at least as well populated as it is to-day. And it was in this part of the Forest that Heywood Sumner made his important discoveries of Pottery sites.

Another walk from Burley is by way of Burley Beacon and over the railway line that runs from Brockenhurst to Ringwood. Almost anywhere over the railway line you can turn left and walk on to Holmesley Ridge, which the local people call Thorney Ridge or Thorney Hill. You cannot turn anywhere—there are no defined paths—because there are unsuspected bogs dotted about here and there. If you turn at the right point you come on a small pond to which a surprising number of birds come at all seasons of the year, and which holds some magnificent crested newts. As you walk along Thorney Ridge you will, in the nesting season, put up lapwing after lapwing, and they will sough around you with plaintive cries, tumbling about in the most astonishing manner, as they think that you are getting too near to their nests. And in winter they are here in flocks together with vast, but ever passing, congregations of starlings. This heath is a great place for adders, and my favourite hunting-ground for them. Occasionally I have found the much rarer smooth snake here also, but this is not quite the right sort of country for him, and just back over the railway on Goat-pen is a more likely spot if you are interested in snakes.

Leaving Thorney Hill you pass Holmesley House, as pleasantly situated as any in Hampshire, and enter

Holmesley Inclosure. Holmesley Inclosure is said to be the haunt of purple emperors, and has a nice little stream which seems to go nowhere and to do nothing, and an occasional kingfisher; otherwise it is very dull. Leaving Holmesley and climbing steeply over the corner of Goatpen Plain, you cross the main road—at the week-end a very dangerous crossing indeed—and enter Wilverley Inclosure, and walking through this you come out on the Burley-Brockenhurst road by the Naked Man. Every one in the Forest knows the Naked Man, and every one who comes to the Forest wants to know it, and quite a few make a point of going to see it. So compelling is a name! The Naked Man is a landmark. It has achieved the distinction of a mention on the Ordnance Survey, though few of the tourists that go to see it do so for that reason. Most of them must be very disappointed, for the Naked Man is nothing like any naked man that I have ever seen. It is just an ancient oak that has been struck by lightning, and it looks very much like any other ancient oak that has been struck by lightning. It is not worth stepping off the road to see. From the Naked Man you can walk over moorland, dipping and rising and in some places very boggy indeed, all the way into Brockenhurst.

There is one other walk from Burley to Brockenhurst which is well worth taking. This is to pick up the Ober Water on Burley Lawn, and to follow it by Red Rise, and over the main Bournemouth road, past Aldrigehill Inclosure to its junction with Highland Water at Brockenhurst. At first sight the Ober Water may seem a dullish stream. It runs through bog and heath and gorse and not through much woodland. It holds fish (bigger fish than you would guess) and the kingfisher and the heron know all about its fishing capacity, though few humans fish it. It is just a Forest stream that the cattle drink from, and the ponies and the deer of a morning before we are up to see them. But if you are interested in birds then you will walk along this stream not once but many times. For some reason that I have never been able to fathom, this is a favourite place for the birds on the autumn migration and again on the spring journey. And near here, actually on Red Rise, I have seen the blackcock quite recently. It is not a beautiful walk, the Ober Water is not a beautiful stream, but this can be one of the most interesting and exciting walks in the Forest.

As the reader may have guessed, I am very fond of the New Forest. I have known it from boyhood. Here I knew as a very little boy Brusher Mills, here I met W. H. Hudson, and was given a lasting interest in many things by that strange but lovable character. Here I have made friends with gipsies and tinkers, with Foresters and keepers; here I have seen things that I should not have seen; here I have collected butterflies and snakes, beetles and flies; here I have watched birds and deer; here I have learned the talk of the Romani, and the ways of the Romani; here I have walked and slept and dreamed. I think that I can say that I know the Forest as well as most people. I think I have walked most of it. I think that I have drunk beer in all its pubs at some time or another, though Harry Mills at the Crown and Stirrup remains my first love in this direction: this is a real Forest inn. But even so, I would not say that I know the Forest. It would take more than a lifetime to explore the whole of the Forest as thoroughly as possible— and I have still, I hope, some little time to go. But no man will ever know the Forest through and through. The Forest will always remain apart from man, will always remain largely unapproachable and beyond complete understanding.

In that, and the fact that the main roads that run through it are good roads, lies its greatest protection. The people that use the main roads are in a hurry to get to the joys of Bournemouth and in too great a hurry to do the Forest damage. But all the same, something more than the present rather haphazard system is needed—if the Forest is to survive and take its proper place in the life of the country. Personally, though I do not agree with all that the Forestry Commission does, I have nothing but gratitude for the Forestry Commission and for the wonderful way in which the Deputy Surveyor has managed a difficult horse. But for him the place would have been either a ruin by now or a stockbrokers' playground. That it is still the New

Forest is very largely due to his tact and determination. But something more is needed. And that something—there can be no doubt about it—is that the Forest should be turned into a Nature Reserve. Leave the present people in charge, but give them the power to prevent building, the power to protect, and the power to preserve more than their actual Inclosures.

Nunwell—Home since the Norman Conquest of the Oglander Family

Chapter VII

THE ISLE OF WIGHT

THE best way to reach the Isle of Wight is by the ferry from Lymington. It is not, if you are coming from London, the quickest way—that is from Portsmouth to Ryde—and it is not the easiest way, for you have to change at Brockenhurst for Lymington. But there can be no doubt at all that it is the best way. Lymington is a delightful old town to leave from and Yarmouth is a delightfully pretty little town to arrive at, and the crossing is lovely all the way. Furthermore you get a proper view of the island by coming this way. One's first view of the island, coming in by way of Ryde or Cowes, is a shock. The place looks rather like Streatham Hill or Balham, a conglomeration of late Victorian houses with a lot of new brick stuck up around them. And one's first journey into the island from either of these towns is also rather a disappointment. The whole place seems to be a collection of tea-houses, and hotels and boarding houses and guest houses and holiday camps—a place on the make. You do not get that impression if you come in by way of Yarmouth.

But the island has not always been a holiday centre. For many years it was an outpost, subject to all the vicissitudes of outposts the world over. The Romans under Vespasian conquered it about the year 43. Under the Romans it enjoyed peace and a considerable prosperity, and some of the Roman remains in the island—notably the villa at Brading—are very fine. The Roman name for the island was Vectis, and this name has nothing to do with the modern name of Wight, which comes straight from the Saxon name Weet. The name seems first to have been applied to the island at the time it belonged to the kingdom of Kent. At this time the island, in common with the rest of Britain, was in a most unsettled state, and it did not remain in the hands of the Kentish chieftains for long. Cerdic, who had established the kingdom of Wessex, in-

229   R

Winkle Street, Calbourne

vaded the island in 530, conquered it and slaughtered most of its inhabitants. Incidentally Cerdic is a most interesting character. He led the West Saxons to a kingdom, but his name is not West Saxon or any other sort of Saxon, and the direction of his invasion of Hampshire and the first founding of the kingdom of Wessex seems to have come from the west and not, as one would expect, from the east. The name is a Welsh name, and all the names of his descendants are also Welsh—and the Welsh are the same people as the Britons, who were conquered by the Romans and after the Romans had left came back to enjoy a brief reign before the coming in force of the Saxons. Just what Cerdic was doing in this galley (there can be no mistake about the name; all the chroniclers agree, and they get the Saxon names right when there are Saxon names to use) has never been decided. It seems probable to me that he was the son of a Saxon father and a British mother, and that the mother was the stronger character of the two and brought up her children as they should be brought up, with British names and with British ways of thought. I think that the marked success of the kingdom of Wessex can best be explained thus: that it was not entirely alien to the native way of life and thought. Cerdic's kingdom lasted until 661 when the island was conquered by Welfere, King of Mercia, and handed over to the South Saxons. This regime lasted for about fifteen years, and was then brought to an end by Cadwalla (another Welsh name) who was a direct descendant of Cerdic. The new Wessex sovereignty lasted for a century, and was stopped by the Danes in 787. This was the beginning of a long period of Danish supremacy, though it is not known if the Danish rule was uninterrupted. They seem to have used the island as a base and a storage centre for the booty they got on their raids on the mainland. But I think that at times they were driven out—always to return—for there is the record of another Danish landing during the reign of Alfred the Great. At any rate in 1001, during Athelred's reign, they again seized the island, and this can only mean that they were driven out in the meanwhile. And this time they stayed until the end of the Danish regime in Britain.

There was trouble again during the reign of Edward the Confessor. Earl Godwin was outlawed, and during his outlawry he twice plundered the island and generally made himself a nuisance to the Crown. This seems, indeed, to have been a favourite sport of outlaws, for the same thing happened in the reign of Harold. The outlaw this time was Tostig, and he plundered the isle and murdered many of the inhabitants.

Internal peace came with the Normans. William the Conqueror gave the lordship of the island to William Fitz-Osborne. This man was favoured by the Conqueror above all the other barons, and was made Earl of Hereford and Seneschal and Marshal of Normandy and England. His rule of the island did not last long, for he was killed in Normandy in 1070, but in the short time he was in control he made a number of far-reaching ordinances. It was he who introduced the modified form of the feudal system that subsequently prevailed in the island. He, too, was the founder of the Benedictine Abbey of St. Mary at Lyra, in the diocese of Evreux in Normandy, and he gave to this abbey six churches in the island, and some lands, and the tithes of the demesne land of the island lordship. He also gave lands to certain gentlemen in his train who had served him faithfully. One of these gentlemen was Richard d'Orglandes, who was given land at Nunwell, and so began the history of the most ancient and most revered of all the island families—the Oglanders of Nunwell, who are still residing at Nunwell, though the direct line father to son died out in 1874, when a cousin succeeded Sir Henry Oglander.

William FitzOsborne was succeeded by his son Roger. Roger seems to have been an ambitious and rather foolish man, for five years later he took part in a conspiracy against the Conqueror (the very last man to take liberties with), and as a result of this rashness he spent the remaining years of his life in prison. The lordship of the island passed to the Crown, but William himself seems to have visited the island only once, in 1085, when he came to arrest his brother Odo. The lordship remained in the royal hands until 1101 when Henry I gave it to Richard de Redvers, who had married the daughter of William FitzOsborne. He, too, held it only for a short time, for he died in 1107, and was succeeded by his son Baldwin. Baldwin also was unlucky, for he backed Maud in the civil war, was driven from the island, and did not return until 1153, an ailing man who died two years later. His son Richard enjoyed his lordship for the comparatively long period of seven years, during which he enriched the Abbey at Quarr and gave to the town of Newport its earliest charter. His young son Baldwin, who succeeded, died within the year, to be succeeded by his brother who also died young. The next in succession was an uncle, William de Redvers, more usually known as William de Vernon, and with his succession the luck changed.

In the meanwhile, however, a very important grant had been made by the Conqueror and confirmed by Rufus and Henry I. This was the gift of half a hide of land at Quarr to Walkelyn, Bishop of Winchester, who was then building the great church of St. Swithun at Winchester. With the grant went permission to dig stone for the building operations. The stone quarries, of course, had been worked for a long time before this. The Romans almost certainly had a building of some sort here, and they almost certainly dug stone in these quarries, but the fame of Quarr stone—the stone that you can see in the grand Norman transepts of Winchester Cathedral—commenced with Walkelyn and Winchester.

William de Vernon held the lordship of the island for thirty-two years, and was about the most able of all the overlords of the island. He was one of the barons who forced John to sign Magna Carta. There is plenty of evidence that he and the king did not see eye to eye on many points, and de Vernon, fearing that his lands would be confiscated by the monarch, transferred the lordship of the island to Hubert de Burgh, who had married his daughter Joan. When Hubert died without issue, de Vernon obtained his estates back by paying a fine to John of 500 marks and leaving his grandson as a hostage with the King. It was this grandson who succeeded him at his death. He seems to have been a remarkable youth in every way, but he continued the unfortunate tradition of his family and held the overlordship but five years. He left two daughters, one of whom became a nun. The other was Isabella, who was in time to rule over the island. But in the meanwhile the lordship was exercised by her mother, who carried out the duties very well. Isabella married the Earl of Albemarle, and was thus Countess of Albemarle, Countess of Devon and Lady of the Isle of Wight, and a most powerful personage altogether. She ruled the island for ten years, living at Carisbrooke, where she maintained a court that was only exceeded for splendour by the Royal court. She was most generous to the Abbey at Quarr, but she did not brook interference and when she did have a quarrel with some of the monks she demanded and got back some of the lands that she had given them. On her death-bed she sold all her powers and privileges to the Crown for the somewhat inadequate sum of 6,000 marks. There was a good deal of surprise at the time and the deed of sale was freely declared to be a forgery. It was investigated in Parliament, and not unnaturally found to be above suspicion—it would have been a bold man who would have found that Edward I had been guilty of forgery!—and so ended the history of the independent lords of the Isle of Wight.

The change was not altogether bad for the inhabitants. It made the various bishops and big clergy take some part in the defence and upkeep of the island and that was to the good of the islanders, who had hitherto had to meet all this sort of expense themselves. But, inevitably, it led to friction between the various big tenants of the island and the Crown on such points as the nature of the service they should give in return for their tenure of lands. There was thus some unsettlement. But from one point of view, and this the main one, there could be no doubt that the change was most beneficial to the islanders.

Conditions had altered both here and abroad. I think that there can be little doubt that the sale of the lordship of the island was brought about as a result of great pressure from the Crown, and I think that there can be no doubt that the safety of the country was the overriding consideration of Edward I. When the Duchy of Normandy belonged to the British the island was not of great strategic importance. But the Duchy had been lost, and the French were now great and confirmed enemies of the English Crown. At the beginning of the thirteenth century the French had brought war to the coast and towns of Hampshire, and it was evident that if at any time the Isle of Wight should be captured and held by the French then the strategic situation would be completely altered and the whole safety of the country would be in peril. Edward I was a far-sighted man and he acted wisely, for the acquisition of the island meant that he could call on the men of the island and on the men of the mainland for its defence. Furthermore, he organized a regular system of watchers with signalling stations and beacons. There were thirteen beacon stations in the East Medine and sixteen in the West Medine. In other words in the time of Edward I the Isle of Wight had its Home Guard. This was merely a start. For more than two hundred years the island had been free from invasion, but now it was continually troubled by the French, so much so in fact that it became necessary for all the male inhabitants to be trained in the arts of war, and the saying that "every island man is a soldier" soon became pretty well true in fact. Even stricter measures were taken for security. There was a close connexion between the island and France in religious matters. In 1340 there was a French abbot and two monks at Appledurwell, and as we were then at war with France and the French had but recently landed and captured Southampton and set it on fire, it was thought to be unwise to allow French monks on the island and they were removed to Salisbury. Armed men were stationed at twenty-nine points round the island and a militia was organized under Sir Theobald Russell of Yaverland. Just in time; in the same year the French landed at Bembridge, but were driven back by the militia whose leader was killed in the moment of victory. For the rest of the century the French were continually making raids on the island. So many of them—for the most part brief incursions for pillage and rape—that they have not been fully recorded. They came to be regarded almost as a matter of course. But in 1377 there was a raid on quite another scale. Then the French landed in force. They captured and

destroyed Francheville, which when it was rebuilt was
known as Newtown, they captured and burnt Yarmouth,
and they captured and utterly destroyed Newport. They
had the island at their mercy and they might well have
made it a French possession if their leader had not lost his
head. Flushed with success he attacked (against the advice
of his officers, it is said) the castle of Carisbrooke. All the
remaining men in the island (there had been great slaughter
during the course of the French advance) were gathered in
the castle which was commanded by Sir Hugh Tyrrill, and
the French attack was repulsed with great loss of men. So
great a loss, that they took to the boats and returned across
the Channel. Yet there was little food in the castle, it was
quite possible to cut off the water, there was little chance
of succour coming from the mainland in time, the place
was almost bound to have surrendered in the course of a
few days. A wise commander would have sent a boat back
to France with the news and a request for many more men,
and sat down and waited. History might well have been
very different if this French sailor had behaved in a different manner.

Another descent by the French was made in 1404. This
was, I think, a more deliberate attempt at invasion and
conquest than the very successful raid of 1377, for the
leader was a nobleman, Waleram, Count de St. Pol, and he
had under his command 1800 fighting men and many
Frenchmen of noble birth, who brought their own fighting
men with them. He embarked at Harfleur and sailed
straight across to the island, where he landed unopposed.
The people of the island, quite unable to fight such a large
and well-equipped force, retired inland, and the Count
seems to have been so confident of success that he set about
creating knights among his followers and even dividing up
the rule of the island among them. One of the island priests
came to him on the first night of the landing and proposed
terms for ransom, and he made the terms sound so reasonable that the Count considered them. In the meanwhile a
boat was sent to Portsmouth for assistance. The following
day a conference was held about the terms for ransom, and
during the conference the island received the help from the

mainland and the islanders themselves organized. The Count realized that he had been outwitted and took to his boats again. He was not a man of the calibre of the unknown sailor who thirty years before had wrought such havoc with a small force. He might have conquered the island, but greed led him to consider a ransom (he could not have come for such a purpose with so large a force) and when the reinforcements arrived, though his forces were strong enough to offer battle with every hope of success, he retired rather than fight. This was the last attempt at conquest. But there were many more raids on the island. In 1418 the French landed and drove off a good many cattle, but suffered heavy losses in so doing. They came again in 1419 with "a great navie, and sent certain of their men to demand tribute in the name of King Richard and Queen Isabell." The men of Wight replied that the king was dead, and that the queen, sometime his wife, had been sent home to her people without any condition of tribute, "but if the Frenchmen's minde were to fight, they willed them to come up, and if no man should let them for the space of five hours, to refresh themselves, but when that time was expired they should have the battayle given to them." This very sporting offer was declined and the French sailed home again. Then for more than a hundred years there were only scattered raids by French pirates (and apparently by Cornish and Welsh pirates also) and the next French attack did not come until 1545. Then they brought with them a great navy—150 large ships, 25 galleys, and 50 other vessels and transports—and anchored off Brading, the fleet stretching almost as far as Ryde. The object of this attack was not the Isle of Wight, but Portsmouth, where the British fleet, hopelessly outnumbered, lay. But the British would not come out of harbour, and so the French commander landed men on the island and they set about burning and pillaging in the hope that the sight of the fires would spur the English on the mainland to offer battle. The English on the mainland did nothing of the kind, but the islanders gave a very good account of themselves and inflicted heavy casualties on the French by attacking small parties of them from ambush. The French, however, did do a great deal of damage on the island. It was during this invasion that Wolverton, near Brading, was burnt and sacked, and never rebuilt, so thoroughly did the invaders do their job.

This was the last invasion of the French. It frightened the British Crown sufficiently to make them take steps that should have been taken long before to strengthen the island defences. As a result the forts at Cowes, Sandown, Freshwater and Yarmouth were built, and almost every parish in the island was provided with artillery. Incidentally it was the artillery in the fort at Cowes that seems to have given the name to the town, for the noise of the discharge was supposed to resemble the lowing of a cow.

> The two great cows, that in loud thunder roar,
> This on the eastern, that the western shore.

All traces of the eastern fort have long since disappeared. But the remains of the western fort now form part of the Yacht Club.

During the Civil War, the people of the island were wholeheartedly for the Parliament. The Earl of Pembroke, who was a Parliamentarian, was in command of the island for several years, and in 1647 he was succeeded by Colonel Hammond. Two months after Hammond's appointment Charles, who was residing at Hampton Court, suddenly left that palace and went to Hampshire hoping to find there greater security. Then he crossed to the island and placed himself in the charge of Hammond. There was a good deal of bargaining first. Hammond was the nephew of the Dr. Hammond, who was the King's Chaplain, and there seems to have been an idea that Hammond would treat him well. Indeed, Charles only crossed after he had received Hammond's assurance that he would "do him all the duty and service in his power." For a few weeks, indeed, the King appears to have been treated as a guest by the Colonel, but that worthy had sent messengers to Cromwell as soon as the King was on the island and he knew that he could not get off again, and the period as a guest did not last long. Charles was a prisoner. And Hammond got the thanks of Parliament and a present of £1,000 and an annuity of £500 for himself and his heirs. A lot of money in those days. It paid to betray your word and your king. Charles remained a prisoner on the island for thirteen months, and then on the night of 29 November 1648 was removed by an armed force to Hurst Castle on the mainland, and thence in close custody to London to lose his head in Whitehall.

That was the last event of historical importance in the history of the island as an island. From the Stuart period onwards the Isle of Wight is merged wholly in the county of Hampshire.

But Charles was not the last monarch of Britain to live in the island. Queen Victoria made this her home for many years and here she died on the evening of 22 January 1901. Queen Victoria's seaside home was Osborne House at East Cowes. And the house is to-day a memorial to the Queen and, in no small degree, to the Victorian Age, which was the most famous and, for some people (a small minority actually), the most prosperous in the history of Great Britain. The house was built in 1846. The apartments are lofty and simply crammed with furniture and curios, bric-à-brac, pictures, ornaments, and statuary. The Durbar room is a mass of teak carving and ornamental plaster work, which always makes me feel ill, but the ceiling (if you can tear your eyes from the rest) is handsome enough. But the rest! There is a peacock over the mantelpiece and there is a fish with gold and silver scales and horrible shiny eyes, and everywhere there are glass cases filled with examples of Eastern workmanship. They are symbols of a power that has departed. But I have an uneasy feeling that the potentates that presented them did so with their tongues in their cheeks. In the dining-room there hangs a portrait of the Queen as a young mother with Prince Albert at her side and her children around her. It is the happiest portrait of Queen Victoria that I have seen, and the Prince Consort looks almost human. In the floor there is a brass plate showing where her coffin lay in state. In the grounds, which are now a bird-sanctuary, and which are on the whole very beautiful (especially the wilder parts) there is the Swiss Cottage where the Royal children played at house-keeping, and which is now a small museum. It, too, is too full of ornaments and bric-à-brac, but there is a lovely model shop with the name Spratt over the door and the words "Grocer to Her Majesty." The toys, in fact, are the best part of the whole.

When she lived at Osborne House, Queen Victoria used to go to church at Whippingham, which is a small village close to the house. It has a church that is a positive jumble of everything in the way of style and lack of style. It stands on a little hill overlooking the River Medina, and you reach it through a lych-gate built of Indian teak and an avenue of cypresses. There was a church here in the Norman times, but the present building was built by the Prince Consort. As a building it would be quite unremarkable if it were not so very ugly. But the memorials within are extremely interesting. Many of course are to do with the Royal Family. There is the marble tomb of Prince Henry of Battenberg, who was married in this church to Princess Beatrice, and there is the pew given in memory of his mother by Edward VII, which has wall tablets with medallions of the Prince Consort, the Duke of Albany and Princess Alice, and another tablet with a charming cherub on it in memory of the two children of the Empress Frederick. There is also a memorial window to Princess Elizabeth, the daughter of Charles I, who died as a prisoner in Carisbrooke Castle. And a great many more, among them one to William Arnold, the father of Thomas Arnold of Rugby, the high priest of Victorianism.

Queen Victoria brought great prosperity to the Isle of Wight. Of that there can be no doubt. Before the building of Osborne House, before the coming of Cowes as the sea-side home of the Royal Family, the island was left pretty well alone. It was no more popular than the centre of the New Forest. When the Queen died there was a rash of Victorian building all along the north coast and at Ventnor and elsewhere. Everyone who was anyone came to the island if not to live—and it was a little difficult to get at and away from for that—then for holidays. Yes, she brought great prosperity to the island. And as an island of quiet beauty she ruined it for ever.

The Isle of Wight is small, smaller than the smallest

county in Britain. The total area is only 147 square miles. It is only 22 miles from the Foreland in the east to the Needles in the west. It is only 13 miles from Cowes in the north to St. Catherine's Point jutting out into the English Channel in the south. I have walked across it many times from north to south, and a few times from east to west and west to east. I have also walked all around it twice, once starting from Cowes and moving clockwise, and once starting from Ryde and moving anti-clockwise. I have walked it in other ways also. I would not say that I know it well —certainly not as well as I do the New Forest or the area round Winchester or that round Alton—but I do know it fairly well.

Through the centre of the island, from east to west, there is a range of lofty hills, which give, as chalk downs should, good pasturage for sheep. I can even remember, as I can for the downs of the mainland, when sheep used to graze them in numbers. They are really high, these downs, and they give views over every part of the island, over the Channel to the south, and over the mainland to the north. This central range of hills is the dominating feature of the island. Otherwise the surface of the island is much diversified, more so, I should imagine, than any other part of Britain of similar area. On the coast the land is in some places very high—St. Catherine's Hill is 781 feet, and is only topped by St. Boniface Down which is 789 feet—and this is especially so on the south where the cliffs are very steep and where landslides have brought down great masses of rock which lie scattered about on the foreshore. On the northern side the land slopes down to the sea in easy stages (though you might not think so from a casual visit to Ryde), but at the western end again, by the Needles, the cliffs are steep and precipitous. In fact the height of the cliffs of which the Needles form the extreme point are 600 feet in most places, and many of them are perpendicular and some of them overhang, with many deep caves and fissures, which were once beloved by smugglers.

Though I personally prefer the central downland, I know that the most beautiful feature of the island is its coastline. You should traverse it from west to east, crossing from

Lymington and starting from the Needles. Then there is Alum Bay with its coloured cliffs, and Scratchell's Bay with deep caves (which I used to explore as a small boy) and the remarkable "Grand Arch." Freshwater Bay, about the most unspoilt of all the island resorts, and the world-famous Blackgang Chine of immense depth. And then St. Catherine's Point, which was a landmark for all the early mariners making the crossing of the Channel, made the more conspicuous now by the white lighthouse on the summit. Between Chale and Ventnor stretches the Under-cliff, a geological extravaganza that is renowned all over the world. Here, a tumbled mass of rocks and cliffs, you can find tropical flowers amid the maze of trees and bushes. It really is beautiful, but at the same time I find it rather melancholy. There have been landslides here recently—indeed there are landslides all the time—and in 1928 a succession of big falls blocked the road on the Gorse Cliff section of the Undercliff, and necessitated the building of a new road to Chale by way of Niton. Beyond Ventnor is Bonchurch, where Swinburne is buried, and the Landslip with Luccombe and Shanklin Chines at the north end. Shanklin Chine cuts through the cliffs of Sandown Bay, which ends in the Red Cliff and Culver Cliff, beyond which lies Whitecliff Bay, whose cliffs are nearly as remarkable as those of Alum Bay. All this part of the coast is fine and worth visiting, but the northern shore is less remarkable unless you happen to be a student of the more degraded forms of Victorian architecture.

Everyone who is really interested in getting to know something of the island should walk round it, and then take the round the island trip, which is operated from Ryde at a very reasonable cost, so as to see the coastline from another angle. But living in the island is another matter, I fancy. Many famous people have done so, of course, from the Royal Family to Keats, Swinburne, Tennyson and so on. (And many other famous people have lived here somewhat against their will, for Parkhurst Prison, which was once a Borstal Institution but is now restored to its place as one of the leading convict prisons of Britain, is situated but a mile or so from Newport.) All of them, if unconsciously, have helped to spoil the island. Once the Garden Isle, it is now purely a tourist resort. It suffered a good deal of bombing during the war, and as much from five years of occupation by the British Army, but it is coming back into its stride very quickly. And that means coming back to fleets of charabancs and swarms of tea gardens, and holiday camps, and huge hotels. The main revenue of the island is the tourist trade. It is in fact *the* revenue of the island. And the island not unnaturally makes the most of it. You can still find places in the centre of the island that somehow missed the Victorian blitz, and they are wholly charming. But they are few and far between. You can still find island men and women who talk of the men and women who visit the island from the mainland as "overners." But they are few and far between. The island is given up to the tourist trade. It is that that they concentrate on. And you cannot blame them; it's their business and their sole means of livelihood.

That they have made a success of it cannot be denied. But in the process they have destroyed the individuality of the Isle of Wight. Blackpool also lives on the tourist trade. But Blackpool is chock full of individuality. The islanders go about their business in rather a different manner from the men of Lancashire or the men of the Isle of Man. They are earnest in their desire to make as much money as possible while the sun shines. But while the men of Lancashire and the Isle of Man are every whit as earnest in their desire to do the same thing, they are cheerful about it with an infectious vulgar cheeriness. Nothing of that sort here. The shadow of Victoria and Albert lies over it all. The islanders seem to be regretting the necessity that drives them into the tourist industry. Over the whole island, despite the lovely colouring and the beautiful sunlight, despite the freshness of the breeze on the downs, there is a melancholy.

Nothing can alter the island now. The tourist trade has come to stay. They might as well make the best of it. They might well throw away the well-bred regret, come out of the shadow, take a leaf from Blackpool's book or from the book of that other Garden Isle.

Chapter VIII

PORTSMOUTH AND SOUTHSEA

THE shortest crossing from the Isle of Wight to the mainland is from Ryde to the Clarence Pier at Southsea. But it is more interesting to stay on the boat and to go to the quay at Portsmouth harbour. Portsmouth was severely bombed on many occasions during the war. At the time of writing no rebuilding has been done, and, as there are all sorts of plans in existence for a new and better Portsmouth and Southsea, I can only deal with the town as I have known it.

I have said that the best thing to do is to stay on the boat from the Isle of Wight and to get off at Portsmouth harbour. I might have said that the best way to come to Portsmouth at all is by sea. For then you do get a view of towers and spires and roofs jumbled together over water that is thoroughly attractive. Once you are in the town you are apt to miss this attractiveness in the maze of rather dirty streets. Portsmouth was never built as a town, never planned. It grew gradually and always haphazardly. It is incomplete, an accident among towns. It has fine buildings —notably the old Guildhall—but for the most part the building is undistinguished and gives the impression of being hurried. Indeed, once off the water front, it is a thoroughly unattractive place. But near the water front, at least in certain corners, it is quite picturesque. Portsmouth has now an opportunity, thanks to Hitler, to become what it always should have been, a gracious and well-designed naval base with outlying residential quarters. There is now a grand opportunity for imaginative town-planning.

You will always hear talk of "Old Portsmouth." I wonder if there has ever been a time when there has not been an "Old Portsmouth"? No one seems to know when the place actually started. I suppose it may be said to have begun with the building by Roman engineers of Portchester, from which it is said that Vespasian sailed to the siege of Jerusalem. He may well have done so, for Portchester was undoubtedly an important Roman naval base. Incidentally, it is a strange thought that this Roman soldier and his son Titus, should have brought the civilization of Rome to these islands, and then sailed from these islands to destroy utterly a much older civilization on the other side of the then known world. But you can, if you like, give to Old Portsmouth a very much greater antiquity than this. There are those who maintain that there was a port here long before the Romans, even some who maintain that the place was built at the same time roughly as Rome, which was about 753 B.C. And if you believe that, then you are at liberty to give the town as much antiquity as your imagination will run to.

For myself I am content to start with the Roman galleys of Vespasian. They undoubtedly came up the long creek to the grey walls of Portchester Castle. There is a rumour, that finds favour in some quarters, that one of them brought Pilate, then an old man harassed by conscience, but that, I think, may be left as rumour, and rumour we know to be a lying jade. There is also another story: that one of these Roman galleys brought St. Paul himself and landed him below Portsdown Hill. There is at any rate a quay called Paulsgrove. But there are some things that are certain about these early days. In Old Portsmouth in the declining days of the Roman Empire lived the Count of the Saxon Shore, the man whose impossible duty it was to protect the coast from Wight to Wash from the Saxon pirates. Henry of Huntingdon tells us how the town got its name. According to him, in the year 501 two Saxon ships came to the place under the command of a Saxon pirate named Port and with him his two sons, Bieda and Maegla. They routed the Britons (who fought with great bravery) and so the place became known as Port's town. I fancy the name is somewhat older than that. But as the Romans had used the place as a naval base, so did the Saxons, and so later did Alfred in his battles against the Danes. And from that time onwards Portsmouth

244

has been connected as closely as can be with the British Navy.

Indeed, to describe Portsmouth properly I should have to write a history of the British Navy, and that is a thing that I do not want to do, and could not do even did I wish. A sketch must suffice.

In 1101 Earl Robert landed at Portsmouth "twelve nights before Lammas, and the king marched against him with all his forces." Twenty-two years later great Henry II "proceeded to Portsmouth, and stayed there over Pentecost week, and as soon as he had a fair wind he sailed for Normandy." Ten years later, when the king had gathered together a large fleet at Portsmouth there was a great fright "when the ships were anchored on the shore, ready for the King's voyage, the sea being very calm, and little wind stirring, the great anchors of one of the ships were suddenly wrenched from their hold in the ground, as though by some violent shock, and, the ship getting under weigh, to the surprise of numbers who tried in vain to stop her, set in motion the ship next to her, and thus eight ships fell foul of each other by some unknown force, so that they all received damage." That was, of course, but the first of many recorded disasters. But it is not until 1213 that we hear of any building of harbour works. On May 20th of that year King John, who used to embark packs of fox-hounds from Portsmouth, wrote to the Sheriff of Southampton ordering him with all speed "to cause our docks at Portsmouth to be inclosed with a good strong wall, in such a manner as our well-beloved and faithful William, Archdeacon of Taunton, will tell you for the preservation of our ships and galleys; and likewise to cause penthouses to be made to the said walls, as the same arch-deacon will also tell you, in which all our ships' tackle may be safely kept." This started a lot of building. Edward IV began the round towers at the harbour mouth, Richard III continued them, and they were finished in the reign of Henry VII, who was urged to complete them as soon as possible by Fox, the Bishop of Winchester.

In 1545 the French raided the Isle of Wight, and the English fleet was gathered to meet them. The ports of the

Sandown Bay from Shanklin Down, I.O.W.

huge *Mary Rose* were open and she heeled over and sank, drowning seven hundred men, in the sight of Henry VIII who was standing on Southsea Common.

> All over, and the cry of mun, and the screech of mun! Oh, sir! up to the very heavens! And the King he screeched right out like any maid, "Oh, my gentlemen! Oh, my gallant men!" And as she lay on her beam ends, Sirs, and just a-settling, the very last souls I seen was that man's father and that man's. Iss! Iss! Drowned like rattens! Drowned like rattens!

And speaking of Henry VIII, old Martin Cockrem adds:

> Oh, he was a king! the face o' mun like a rising sun, and the back o'mun! So broad as that there, and the voice o'mun! Oh, to hear mun swear if he was merry, oh, 'twas royal!

Just previously to this disaster there had been an addition to the harbour works. Leland came to Portsmouth and found the harbour defended by "a mighty chaine of yren, to drawe from towre to towre." The ancestor of the great booms of modern days. Leland goes on:

> About a quarter of a mile above the towne is a great dok for shippes and yn this dok lyeth part of the ribbes of the Henry, Grace of Dieu, one of the biggest shippes that hath been made *in hominum memoria*. There be above this dok crekes in this part of the haven . . . there is much vacant ground within the towne walls. There is one fair street in the toune from west to north-east . . . King Henry VIII at his first warres into Fraunce erected in the south part of the toune three great bruing houses with the implements to serve his shippes at such tyme as they should go to the se in tyme of warre . . . the toune is bare and lyttle occupied in tyme of pece.

In 1552 Edward VI held a review here of the whole navy, including galleys, pinnaces and rowboats, with the exception of two at Deptford Strand and the *Henry Grace de Dieu*, which was at Woolwich. The navy then consisted of fifty-three vessels and was manned by 7,780 seamen, marines and gunners. And that, considering the population at the time, was a very big navy indeed. But, rather curiously, Portsmouth played no decisive part in the Armada battles.

On 5 October 1623 there was great rejoicing in Portsmouth over the landing (which meant the safe return) of Charles and the Duke of Buckingham from their expedition into Spain. A gilded leaden bust of Charles was put up in the High Street, and for many years no officer, soldier or civilian was allowed to pass it without doffing his hat, yet strangely in view of this demonstration of loyalty Portsmouth never declared for the King in the Civil War. And five years after the rejoicing at the return of Charles and Buckingham there was throughout Portsmouth a hue-and-cry for the murderer of Buckingham. Buckingham was the most powerful man in England and the favourite of two monarchs. John Felton was a gentleman "of good carriage and reputation," a lieutenant, who had suffered wrongs at the hands of the Duke. The deed was done at The Spotted Dog with one blow from a shilling hunting-knife. Felton was hung at Tyburn and gibbeted on Southsea Common. He made no attempt at escape and indeed boasted of his deed, believing that he had done his country a service—as in fact he had.

When the Civil War broke out, Portsmouth was the strongest and best fortified town in the kingdom. Colonel Goring (a somewhat doubtful character) seized the town for the King (actually before the King was ready to act) and immediately Sir William Waller laid siege to it and soon forced its surrender. On 7 September Goring surrendered on very easy terms, threw the town key into the harbour (from which it was dredged two hundred years later) and departed for Holland where he spent his time trying, not very hard, to raise recruits for the Royalist cause. The loss of Portsmouth, says Clarendon, "struck the

King to the very heart." There was some little excitement at the end of 1648, however, for a party of some four hundred sailors came ashore, protesting their loyalty to King Charles, "and certain persons well affected to His Majesty placed two hogsheads of beer in the Market Place," and the sailors did not lose the opportunity. So well did they fare that the whole lot of them were turned out by the soldiers without a shot being fired.

On 21 May 1662 Charles II was married in the Garrison Church to Catherine of Braganza. Pepys, of course, was there. He followed "in the crowde of gallants" and duly inspected "the present they have for the Queene: which is a saltsellar of silver, the walls cristall, with four eagles and four greyhounds standing up at the top to bear up a dish." Pepys was here again in 1668, and on this occasion he did his best to slip off without his wife, saying nothing to her overnight. But Mrs. Pepys knew all about her husband and outwitted him. Says Pepys: "Waked betimes, and my wife at an hour's warning is resolved to go with me; which pleases me, her readiness." And it is from the diarist, too, that we learn how bad the plague was in Portsmouth: "Sylvester of Gosport is not able to get on with the chain he is making for the harbour mouth being unable to come to work on account of the plague; the plague very bad at ye point."

And now to Queen Anne. It is not often that we can trace a proverb to its source. But here we can and the source is in Portsmouth. The story is told by Saunders:

Portsea may be said to have sprung into existence about the early part of the 18th century. Anne had always paid great attention to the fleet, and made great additions to the dockyard. Being on a visit to the Commissioner's house in the dockyard she was instrumental (in 1707) at the suggestion of her consort, in saving from destruction the houses in the west dock field which the workmen had built. They named the street Prince George's Street in compliment to Prince George their benefactor. Bonfire Corner commemorates rejoicing over their success. Perhaps Queen Street was named after Anne. "Pray can you tell me if Queen Anne is dead?" Most of those who use this phrase are unconscious of its origin, and our townspeople would, as a rule, apply it to one Alice Melville, better known as "Queen Anne," who for more than thirty years was notorious for her filthy habits, her falsehoods and her abusive tongue.

In 1702 Sir John Gibson was Governor of Portsmouth, Anne was ruling England, and Marlborough's victories were making Britain triumphant. The deposed James was a pensioner on the bounty of a French king, and a bitter spirit of religious and political intolerance was rife. It was as dangerous to be a papist as it was to be a Jacobite. Portsmouth was at this time a garrison of great importance, great fleets coming and departing from it, the gallant Sir George Rooke its representative in Parliament. Now there was at this time in London a youth who was destined to rise to importance and honour in the place of his adoption. This young man resolved to turn his back on great cities, and to seek his fortune in the Hampshire seaport. Travelling by coach was in those days too expensive for his limited means, the road waggons were too slow, so with youth and a good pair of legs he started his journey on foot. As he wended his way through London he was attracted by a great concourse of people, and the heralds were proclaiming in the usual form, "The Queen is dead; long live the King!" At the drawbridge outside Portsmouth the young man was questioned by the sentinels as to his purpose and intentions: and in proof of his having come from London he tells them of the death of the Queen. This at once aroused suspicion, for they were unaware of the event, and he was marched off under escort to Gibson, the Governor of the garrison. The governor raved furiously at what he believed to be a seditious report, for though outwardly professing attachment to the ruling power, causing the band to play loyal tunes, and sporting the orange cockade ostentatiously, he was suspected of sympathy, not for the House of Hanover, but for a king "t'other side of the water." The stranger was ordered to be kept in military custody. This was scarcely done when a mounted messenger arrived, bringing with him official confirmation of the royal decease, and ᵗhe prisoner was at once brought back and released by the governor with profuse apologies, and the youth whose first experience of Portsmouth was of this rough and uninviting character, rose to opulence, and became the founder of a great and respected family. This young traveller was Mr. Carter, afterwards Sir John Carter and Mayor of Portsmouth.

Gibson had at this time become unpopular. His hard nature, harsh treatment of small offenders, and the cruel punishment of the picquet or wooden horse which he was so fond of administering to the soldiers under his command, caused him to be disliked. And though professing tolerance for religious matters, and even going so far as to identify himself with denominational religionists in their deputations, he was suspected of being secretly their enemy. A political trimmer and unscrupulous partisan, he had at election times placed soldiers at the town gates to prevent burgesses who lived at common, and who were supposed to be adverse to his party, from entering to record their votes.

An opportunity had now come for resenting these acts, and the townsfolk would ask each other in the hearing of this Jacobite governor, "Pray can you tell me if Queen Anne is dead?" The saying is common even now, and Portsmouth people may answer the question in the affirmative, as applying to Queen Anne, who died at St. James's Palace in 1714, or to the "Queen Anne" who died in the Portsmouth Union House in 1868.

In 1757 Admiral Byng was brought to Portsmouth—he was insulted and reviled in every town and village on the road—to be tried on board the *St. George* and shot on board the *Monarque*. Byng, I think, was a badly used man.

Voltaire about summed up the whole sorry business when he said that the admiral had been murdered "to encourage the others." Two years later some soldiers, who had been filling cartridges at Southsea Castle, left some of the powder lying about, and this exploded the next day and did considerable damage in the town and caused a few deaths.

All this while the dockyard had been growing by leaps and bounds. A good deal of it was built by convict labour —for a time the Tichborne claimant was thus employed— and convicts built Fort Cumberland, by the entrance to Langstone Harbour away to the east. This fort was part of a scheme for coast defence that the Duke of Richmond failed to carry through the House, for the Speaker gave his casting vote against it. Gibbon satirized the whole business in two lines:

> To raise the bulwark at enormous price
> The head of folly used the hand of vice.

George III paid a visit to the dockyard in 1773. Twelve ladies of Portsmouth begged for the honour of rowing the King from the dockyard to a man of war, and the King afterwards said that his boat had been *manned* by twelve of the finest women in Portsmouth.

Three years after this the rope house was set on fire (and completely burnt out) by one John Aitken, commonly known as "Jack the Painter," who was a political fanatic. The fire did not stay in the rope house, but spread to neighbouring buildings, and altogether it was a disastrous conflagration. A good many people lost their lives in the blaze. It was then found that it had not been an accident. How suspicion fell on Jack the Painter has not been told, but there must have been a smart piece of detective work for the man was found at The Raven Inn at Hook near Basingstoke, and captured as he was getting out of a window. He was brought back to Portsmouth and hanged at the dockyard gates in 1777 upon the mizzen mast of the famous *Saucy Arethusa*. His skeleton, which was gibbeted at Blockhouse Point, at the mouth of the harbour, was afterwards pledged for drink by some sailors, and one of his fingers, mounted in silver, and used as a tobacco stopper, is in the Portsmouth Museum.

But executions were common in Portsmouth in those days:

On Saturday, August 14th, 1782, David Tyrie, a clerk in the Navy Office, was hanged, drawn, and quartered on Southsea Common for trying to sell naval secrets to France. A free fight took place for portions of his body; "the blood spouting over the spectators; the miscreants cutting off his fingers for tobacco stoppers, and leaving the unburied remains exposed to the sea-fowl on the beach. His head was kept as a show for many years by 'Buck Adams,' the keeper of Gosport Bridewell, who publicly claimed it, placed it in a bag, and carried it home under his arm."

We were a robust people in those days. Five days after the execution of Tyrie, the *Royal George*, a ship of 108 guns, whose poop lanterns were so large that the men used to get inside them to clean them, sank at her anchors at Spithead "whereby 650 seamen, 250 women, many officers, and Admiral Kempenfelt were drowned." There were many at the time who claimed that this was work in revenge for Tyrie, but that is nonsense. Why the *Royal George* sank will never be known, but certainly it had nothing to do with Tyrie, though it may have had something to do with the orgy that was in progress on board.

This was by no means the last of the many naval tragedies that Portsmouth people have witnessed from the shore. On May Day 1797 the whole town was shaken as if by an earthquake when the *Boyne* blew up at her moorings in Spithead after sending shot from her loaded guns in all directions among the fleet and even as far as Stokes Bay. And there were others—but to chronicle them all would be to write a history of the navy, and that is a thing I said I would not do.

With famous ships there have been also famous men. Almost every famous British sailor has been connected with Portsmouth at some time in his career. Anson came back here from his famous voyage round the world. Sir Edward Pellew brought in the *Cleopatra*, the first French prize captured in the "old war time." Lord Howe came here with his prizes after the glorious First of June. And within three years the very existence of the Navy (and Britain) was put in peril by the great mutiny at Spithead. From this port sailed Bligh on his tragic voyage in the *Bounty*. Hawke, Keppel, Boscawen, Rodney, St. Vincent, Nelson, Jellicoe, Beatty, all of them, admirals and empire builders alike, knew every foot of the anchorage and every place of entertainment in the town. Nelson came here many times. In 1784 "a blackguard horse" ran away with him on Southsea Common, and nearly killed him. If it had, so it is said, there would have been no Trafalgar and no Battle of the Nile. I doubt it. Nelson was a great man—but he was not the only great man in the British Navy. There would have been someone to take his place. Opportunity makes the man. And have you ever thought what we should think of Nelson had there been no war with France during his service? Would we even have heard of him? We would not. Do you know off-hand the name of the admiral who commanded the British Fleet in 1880? Or even of the admiral who commanded the British Fleet in 1929?

But Nelson is connected with Portsmouth for ever, for here his body was brought back, and here lies the *Victory*. Admission to the *Victory*, by the way, is free. So little is free in this country nowadays that the point is worth noting.

The Garrison Church has been called the Military Cathedral of England. Originally it was the Domus Dei Hospital, an almshouse founded by Peter de Rupibus, Bishop of Winchester, in the thirteenth century. It has had an eventful history. In 1449 Bishop Adam de Moleyns, Bishop of Chichester, who was also a great statesman in the manner of the prelates of his day, was seized by certain soldiers and sailors, and after a dispute about "the abrygging of their wages, they fil on him and creulli there kilde him." At a later date it was a store for arms. Later still it was the governor's house, and the green outside is still called Governor's Green. Here Charles married Catherine of

Braganza. The present church, considerably renovated in 1866 but with much of the old fabric remaining, is the old great hall and chapel of the almshouse. The renovations were not, as might be expected from the date, in keeping; architecturally the place is pretty dreadful. But one should not regard it as an architectural specimen (you can regard it as an architectural monstrosity if you like), but rather as a national mausoleum. It is, indeed, filled with memories and memorials, and before the war there were here many tattered banners recalling heroic deeds all across the world done at a time when we were busy gaining an Empire for ourselves. The carved stalls and the stained glass windows are, every one of them, a memorial to some brave soldier, and there are here names that will be famous when the British Empire has joined the Roman in the vault of history—Wellington, Nelson, Moore, Hill, Outram, both the Napiers, Raglan, Clyde and so on and so on. And here also is a memorial to Captain John Mason who founded New Hampshire across the Atlantic.

The Cathedral Church of St. Thomas is the old Parish Church which was built to the memory of Becket soon after his murder in Canterbury Cathedral. It was partly rebuilt in the seventeenth century, and very considerably enlarged in 1936. It suffered badly during the raids on Portsmouth, and is now being partly rebuilt and again enlarged, and stone for the purpose is being sent from every British colony and all the Dominions. There are, or were, a great many interesting memorials in this Cathedral, but to me the most interesting thing about it is the history of a smell. By the middle of the nineteenth century the church was in a shocking state owing to the "improper custom," as Gilbert White called it, of intermural burial. In 1850, according to a report, people had to leave the building during a service owing to "the effects of the noxious effluvia." The evil brought its own remedy as the continual opening of the vaults and the excavation of fresh resting-places affected the not very secure foundations. Nobody died of the smell in the Cathedral Church, but a similar condition in the Garrison Church did cause two deaths.

There is history everywhere in Portsmouth, down streets, in old houses, on quays, in docks—the history of battles, of fire and plague, of murder, of famous personages. There is history too in the pubs. In *Frank Mildmay* we read: "Captain G . . . did not live at the George, nor did he mess at the Crown; he was not at the Fountain nor at the Parade Coffee house; and the Blue Posts ignored him; but he was to be heard of at the Star and Garter on the tip of Portsmouth Point." Really to know what the old pub days of Portsmouth were like we must read such books as *Jack Ashore* and *Ben Brace*. "With fiddles and a dance at the Ship, with oceans of flip and grog, and give the blind fiddler tobacco for sweetmeats and a half-crown for treading on his toe! £5 14s. 0d. for a day and a night at a public does not err on the side of moderation." The Fountain Inn is now no more: the old Blue Posts Inn, mentioned in Marryat's *Peter Simple*:

> This is the Blue Postesses
> Where Midshipmen leave their chestesses,
> Call for tea and toastesses
> And forget to pay for their breakfastesses.

was burnt down nearly a hundred years ago. And many another pub of fame went up in flames or down in rubble during the last war.

What days those must have been! When the sailors got married and the wedding parties returned from church they used to swab decks by washing down the tables with quarts of ale (it was not quite so expensive in those days) which they swabbed backwards as fast as the landlord could throw them. Do you remember the old song?

> I've a spanking wife at Portsmouth gates, a pigmy at
>   Goree;
> An orange tawny in the Straits, and a black at St.
>   Lucie.

In the old days every bar had straw laid down, which was

carefully sifted every morning, because the sailors usually pulled out a handful of gold and notes and when they were not over-sober some would quite likely drop on the floor and not be noticed. There is, too, the story of the Point landlady who badly wanted to show marriage lines, and insisted that one or other of three midshipmen who could not pay their bill should marry her forthwith. She was a strong character, in more ways than one, and the poor boys tossed for the honour, and got on board as soon as they could afterwards. Reading a newspaper in Jamaica not long afterwards one of them was heard to exclaim, "Thank God! My wife's been hanged!" The story reads strangely nowadays, but once that sort of thing was not uncommon not only in Portsmouth but in every naval port in Britain. Tales could be told—and I could tell a few myself, for I have read widely in the subject—of the under-world life of Portsmouth that would make exciting reading for those of strong nerves, but this is not quite the sort of book in which to tell them. Nor has all the under-world life ceased in the old town yet.

And the streets! Broad Street and High Street. Walk up them and think. The place is full of ghosts, if you be of the right temperament. Men lived here who would make Portsmouth famous even if there had never been a sailor in the place throughout its history. George Meredith; Jonas Hanway, a great reformer who is now chiefly remembered (if he is remembered at all) because he was the first man to carry an umbrella; John Pounds, the crippled cobbler; Sir Frederick Madden, who did much valuable work for early English literature; Brunel of tunnel fame; Simon Brown, who compiled dictionaries; George Cole the artist; Sir Walter Besant the novelist; and last, but not least, Charles Dickens, who was born in a small house in Commercial Road. Dickens is, therefore, a Hampshire man beyond question, but little of his fame belongs to Hampshire. Beyond the accident of his birth he is really a Londoner through and through.

Portsmouth now has grown. Its tentacles have reached out and grasped Cosham, Eastney, Fratton, Milton, Great Salterns and Hilsea. Over an arm of the harbour, reached by ferry, lies Gosport, which, though a separate town, is so much a part of Portsmouth in fact and tradition that it must be dealt with in the same breath. Gosport is the storehouse of the Navy. Everything the Navy needs is stored in the Victualling Yard. The shore sweeps round from Nicholson's Yard to Blockhouse Point and then over a bridge which is incidentally still a toll bridge) to Old Haslar Hospital, which is the Navy's hospital, and which was built in the eighteenth century. It is for a hospital quite a handsome building and it is entered through a pair of very handsome gates. But for the rest Gosport is far from attractive. A vast quantity of the houses are old, but they are also poor, and mean and shabby. The place has a melancholy look, like a man dying slowly from an incurable but not painful disease. Somebody renovated the church and ruined it in doing so, but fortunately left the timber arcades which are simply wonderful and a feature worth going a long way, even worth a trip on the crowded ferry, to see. And Gosport has one other claim to fame. Somewhere in the town Henry Cort of Lancaster set up his forge for iron puddling. In 1740, which was the year in which he was born, Britain produced only 48,000 tons of pig iron. Little more than a century later we were producing more than eight million tons, and that was due entirely to the experiments and the genius of Henry Cort. Yet Cort, as is so often the way with men of genius, died poor and broken-hearted. Someone else got the money and the honours. All that Cort got, and that so long after he died that he would not worry about it anyway, was a panel over the entrance to the Gosport public library—and the tale is that there was a real squabble over that since most of the people concerned had never heard of him and did not believe that he had done anything wonderful and that if he had he had not done it in Gosport.

On the other side, the Southsea side, there is Hayling Island and the Langstone Harbour, a lovely stretch of shallow water that is at last going to be used as an air base. Its only use to date has been for small boat sailing and for the occasional wild fowler, for here you used to get a wonderful selection of sea birds and sometimes some flocks

of wild geese. Hayling Island is very small—only ten square
miles in all, only four miles in length—but it is older than
history. Here is Tournebury which is a prehistoric earthwork, that was moated at some later date. There is a font
which is Saxon and a yew tree that may have been here
when the Normans came. And the bells of St. Peter's
North Hayling have been ringing for over six hundred
years. This is a wonderful church, and no one has ruined
it with renovations in the Victorian manner. The doorway
is fifteenth century, the arcade within is twelfth century,
the poppyhead benches are almost certainly fourteenth
century, and the font was carved at least in the twelfth
century. The whole fits too. There is a calm and dignity
about this church that is not to be found in many churches
in Britain. The great family of Hayling was the Rogers
family, and the name is still common on the island. They
were not great in the sense of nobility or of military fame,
their name does not resound down the years of history.
But they were the family of Hayling. The graveyard is full
of the stones that bear the name. There is a Thomas Rogers
with a marvellously carved wheatsheaf on his stone, and
there is John Rogers whose stone bears two weeping figures,
a woman in classical dress and a man in a tall hat with
mourning streamers. And there is Sarah Rogers, who died
in 1812, and whose tomb bears this epitaph:

> Ye virgins fair, your fading charms survey,
> She was whate'er your tender hearts can say,
> Let opening roses, drooping lilies, tell,
> Like these she bloomed, and ah! like these she fell.

Hayling, though it is always appallingly full in the summer
months, has not been spoilt. It remains a small island and
it makes no attempt to catch a tourist trade. You can go
to Hayling if you want to, and you can enjoy yourself with
what Hayling provides—which is a first-class golf course,
lots of sand, excellent bathing, some riding and little else—
and Hayling will be pleased to see you. But if you will not
come again, because there is not a super-cinema and a
super palais de danse and a fun fair, then Hayling will not

be sorry. It is a very pleasant place. And it is truly Hampshire.

That cannot be said for Portsmouth. Portsmouth is in Hampshire but not of it. Portsmouth has a peacetime population of more than a quarter of a million people. It exists solely for the armed forces. Its civilian population lives on the armed forces and by the armed forces. And the armed forces are always changing. It is like Aldershot, a shifting population with no roots in Hampshire and no connexion with Hampshire save that temporarily ordained by His Majesty's Government. Cricket is played by the county not on the town ground, but on the United Services ground. Only when the professional football team (the majority of whom have absolutely no connexion at all with the county) does well in the First Division does Portsmouth loom large in Hampshire eyes and hearts. And, when, as has happened once, Portsmouth wins the Cup—well, then, of course, Portsmouth is truly Hampshire.

CHAPTER IX

SOUTHAMPTON

BETWEEN Portsmouth and Southampton two rivers flow into Southampton, the Meon and the Hamble. I shall return to the Meon, a stream which deserves a chapter to itself, later on. The Hamble is a small river with an estuary out of all proportion to its length. It has two sources, the one rising at Durley and the other at Bishop's Waltham, which meet a little above Botley to form what is called Botley Creek, which is, in fact, I suppose, the Hamble River. The place is now a great centre for yachtsmen and the whole of the lower stream is dotted with pleasure craft, but there was history here long before the pleasure boats, for it was here that those two strange Saxons with the Welsh names—Cerdic and Cynric—gained their first foothold on our southern shores. Later came the Jutes and then the Danes, and then the French, burning and raiding. The little stream has seen much bloodshed. And history is still being made on its breast and on its banks. For here, anchored in midstream, lies the *Mercury*, in which boys are trained to be good sailors and good Englishmen.

The *Mercury*, a great grey ship, is the successor to a graceful three-master which was a tea-clipper in the African trade before becoming a training ship. In the First German War she was bought for service and she sank at sea. The *Mercury* owed its beginning to Charles Arthur Hoare. This great man provided a ship, a shore establishment and plant and paid for their upkeep for twenty-three years. After his death in 1908 the fate of the *Mercury* hung in the balance. It was saved by the courage and initiative of a famous cricketer, Commander C. B. Fry. Fry, on his own begging, was given the chance to run the ship for two years, and was promised that if he did so successfully it should not come to an end but would be made an Educational Foundation. Fry, and his wife, with great courage, succeeded in making

260

*The Cathedral Tower overlooking
the Camber Dock, Portsmouth*

those two years more than worthy of the *Mercury* tradition. The ship was saved solely because of their devotion and remains to-day providing some of the best personnel in all British shipping.

Indeed, the *Mercury* has a great and honoured name in both the Navy and the Merchant Service. Many of the boys who began life on the lower deck with a *Mercury* training have attained to masterships in the Merchant Service, and many to responsible warrant rank in the Royal Navy, while not a few have reached the Quarter Deck, and once there have shown themselves more than worthy of the honour that their capabilities and training has won for them. The reason for this great success is not far to seek. It lies in the training and that is due to the genius of the Commander. Fry believes, as did the founder, that to be of true service to his country a man must be absolute master of himself. And to be absolute master of himself a man must develop all that is best in his nature to the utmost of his power. The basis of the *Mercury* training is religious. And every taste for beauty and the arts is encouraged from the moment that it is perceived. If a boy is found to like poetry or drawing or music his liking is at once encouraged by every means by his teachers and the encouragement is direct. In particular is music encouraged and fostered. *Mercury* music has become famous. For some fifty years it has been taught by the same master. There are *Mercury* musicians throughout the services. To boys, who at the end of their training, have found themselves to be unable through some physical handicap to enter fully the career for which they have lived and worked so hard for so long, this musical training has proved a blessing indeed, for they have been able to enter bands in the Army, Navy and Air Force, and many of them have become bandmasters.

But everything is done for the boys. The playing fields are magnificent, there is a lovely little theatre, the church is lovely, and the building in which are the classrooms is light and airy. In the messroom every table has its flowers, and the recreation room has been made beautiful by panels painted by a true artist.

The æsthetic side of life, which is too often frowned upon

The Bargate, Southampton

in our public schools, is encouraged fully in this training ship, and the lesson might be learned with profit by many of our schoolmasters. C. B. Fry has served his country as few men have done. It is to be hoped that one day proper tribute will be paid to one who has great claims to be considered the greatest Englishman of his generation.

Botley, at the head of the river proper, is the centre of a strawberry growing district. Botley strawberries are famous for their taste and quality. I have heard Botley described as quaint. It is not hideous—yet. It has a remarkable number of inns, some of them pretty. It has one or two fine houses. But it has also a wholly remarkable collection of villas, shanties, bungalows, and cottages, an amazing amount of corrugated iron and wire netting which, like corrugated iron and wire netting everywhere, appears rusted and untidy. In fact the most remarkable thing about Botley is that it is not yet absolutely hideous.

And Botley had a parson named Richard Baker. In one hundred years—1803 to 1903—Botley had only two parsons. Richard Baker was here for fifty-four years, and the other one was John Morley Lee. You will find a good deal about Baker in the pages of Cobbett's *Rural Rides*. Baker hated Cobbett. He would not let the villagers ring the bells when Cobbett was released from Newgate, where he had been imprisoned for protesting publicly at Englishmen being flogged under a guard of Hanoverian soldiers. And Baker in his turn was hated by the villagers. Cobbett tells us how a legacy hoax once got the parson up to London:

Up went the parson on horseback, being in too great a hurry to run the risk of a coach. The hoaxers, it appears, got him to some hotel and there set upon him a whole tribe of applicants . . . wet nurses, dry nurses, lawyers with deeds of conveyance for borrowed money, curates in want of churches, coffin-makers, travelling companions, ladies' maids, dealers in Yorkshire hams, Newcastle coals, and dealers in dried night-soil at Islington. They kept the parson in town for several days, bothered him three parts out of his senses, compelled him to escape, as it were, from a fire, and then, when he got home, he found the village posted all over with handbills, giving an account of his adventure under the pretence of offering £500 reward for the discovery of the hoaxers.

Southampton has steadily been reaching out towards Botley, as it has been spreading in other directions. And now it can be taken for granted that there will be an even greater and more rapid spread. For Southampton was well and truly bombed during the war. The centre of the town has to all intents and purposes ceased to exist, and there has been a great deal of damage in other parts of the town as well. The centre will have to be entirely rebuilt and re-planned—and that is equally true of several other districts as well—and there will not be again the same crowding as of old. But it is equally certain that the population of Southampton will be as large or larger than that before the bombing. Outward spread is the only solution. The town can spread northwards in the Winchester direction. It is already, practically speaking, to Eastleigh (and Eastleigh already reaches, practically speaking, to Chandler's Ford), and it seems probable that Southampton will soon include Eastleigh as Portsmouth includes Southsea. There can be a little spread in the New Forest direction, but this is limited by the special position of the Forest in the life of the nation. The obvious direction, other than that towards Eastleigh, is towards Botley. Perhaps it will have the effect of tidying up that town.

Southampton stands on the peninsula between the Test and the Itchen. The site has been the abode of man from the very earliest times, but there is very little definite about life here before the coming of the Romans. There is plenty of legend dealing with pre-Roman times, and there is some ground—despite the views of modern historians for believ-ing that the first landings of the main Roman invasion were made about here. But once we leave the Chroniclers and come to the historians of the Roman period we are on surer ground. We know that there was a very considerable settlement here on the east bank of the Itchen where the modern Bitterne stands—the existence of this settlement is proved quite apart from the historians by many interesting relics—and it is generally believed that here was Clausentum. Within the settlement there have been found large numbers of coins, which cover the whole period from Tiberius to Arcadius (A.D. 37–408), proof enough that this town was established very early in the Roman occupation and that it was not abandoned until the final departure. But whether it was only a military post or a combination of military post and trading port is not quite so certain. We know little or nothing about the incidents which must have attended the departure of the Romans from this neighbourhood, but it does seem probable that for some time—perhaps more than a hundred years—before the evacuation the estuary and the whole of Southampton Water had been infested by Saxon pirates, and that for some considerable time before the Romans finally left there had been traders of Saxon origin here and that some of the Jutes (a more peaceable and mercantile people than the average Saxon of the period) had had a settlement here, not a settlement that they had won by force of arms but one that they had been allowed to establish by the Romans. Be that as it may, there can be no doubt that as soon as the Romans left, Saxons and Jutes began to pour into the area in numbers. From these peoples sprang the Kingdom of Wessex. It was here at the mouth of the Hamble that the two with the odd names, Cerdic and Cynric, first landed. Archæologically there seem to be some solid grounds for doubting the site as the original starting-point of the West Saxons, and some grounds for placing that site in the Thames Valley, which might also help to account for the Welsh names of the leaders. But in any case they did arrive at Southampton at some time, and I am myself of the opinion that in this, as in so much that has been questioned by recent authorities, the Anglo-Saxon Chronicle is telling the truth. And there can be no doubt that at a very early stage in its history Southampton was an important place, for it gave its name to the shire.

But Southampton emerges from the obscurity of legend and hearsay into the strong light of recorded history only with the arrival of the Danish raiders, that is in the ninth century. The Danes had an eye for a good waterway, and they were unlikely to overlook Southampton Water and all the many inlets that run into it. The Water was a gateway into the interior. The Danes came because from Southampton they commanded the ancient city of Winchester, then without doubt the richest town in Britain, and also because its situation on a peninsula—a position that they were always keen to take over—provided excellent means of defence and easy means of escape. Their first large-scale raid came in 857. Then thirty-five ships sailed up the Water, and landed their crews near the Hamble River. But this raid was beaten off. Three years later the Danes came again; and this time they made good their landing and captured the town. From there they pushed on to take and sack Winchester. But on the way back they were again defeated and only a remnant got back to the ships. Then Alfred the Great took over the town. Southampton must then have seen much ship-building activity, and there must have been many skirmishes in the Water and the surrounding creeks. So early was Southampton connected with ships and ship-building.

With the death of Alfred the Danes came again. And now there was no organized force to oppose them, and no leader of courage and imagination. In 980 Southampton was captured and most of the inhabitants put to the sword. And the next year the Danes came again and laid waste to the coast around. And finally came the great invasion, when Sweyn of Denmark and Olaf of Norway swept through the country. They captured London, they ravaged Kent, Sussex and Hampshire, and having done so, they settled down at Southampton, and here they waited for the Danegeld that Ethelred had collected for them. The history of Ethelred's attempts to ward off the Danes and the story of the treachery that led to his downfall have no part in the tale of Southampton, but it was at Southampton, after he had fled, that the Witan assembled and offered the crown to Cnut. That was in 1016. The Danes had always been connected with the town and it was fitting that here they should reap the reward of so much fighting and bloodshed. Nor did the connexion cease. For it is at Southampton that the legend of the tide and Cnut is placed. Nor is the connexion dead even yet. There is still a road in the town called Canute's road.

The connexion with the Danes, though their Empire was but brief, was destined to have lasting effect in the town's history. It was one result of the Danish conquest that there was an alliance between the English and the Normans. This alliance had a most profound effect upon Southampton, for it made the town the chief link between the two parts of William's kingdom. It became the great port for the arrival and departure of men and monarchs. All the kings came here and every great man. A great palace was built—it occupied most of the south-western corner of the town—and in it was accommodation for the nobles and their trains, and strong fortifications were built, some of which, the inside portion of the Bargate, for example, remain to this day. A massive castle was also built on a lofty mound within the circle of the walls, and a number of churches were set up, and in 1124 The Priory of St. Denys, which was a house of the Black (Augustinian) Canons, was founded.

It was with the Norman Conquest that Southampton came to prosperity, and the whole of the period from the Conquest to the loss of the northern French possessions was one of great and rapid development. I think that it will be sufficient to mention just two signs of this—the founding of a merchant guild and the granting of a charter. The merchant guild was founded at least as early as the reign of Henry I. It contained all the important burgesses of the town, and in the course of time it became—quite likely it was so from the very beginning—the governing body within the borough. Its ordinances are fortunately extant in a beautifully written manuscript of the fourteenth century, which gives a most interesting picture of municipal organization in the Middle Ages. Probably it was the guild that obtained the charter. Several minor grants of privileges were secured from time to time from this king and that, but it was John who, in 1199, was induced—no doubt in return for a very heavy payment—to concede to the burgesses the "farm" of the borough. For £200 per annum paid into the Royal Exchequer they were to be free from the pecuniary exactions of the sheriff, and independent of the financial organization of the county; and that was a much-coveted privilege worth paying a substantial sum to acquire.

But it must not be forgotten that Nature played a great part in the prosperity of the town as she does to-day. Though the possession of territory in northern France was a great asset, the town's prosperity was due really to its unique position. Its waters are safe and easy of access and very sheltered, and if that is an asset to-day, as it undoubtedly is, it was even more an asset in the days of sail and oar. The Isle of Wight, which lies across the entrance, acts as a rampart against the seas, and also diverts the course of the tide as it drives against the coast, thus producing an effect of prolonged highwater, the so-called "double-tide" for which the town is famous. This phenomenon was noticed long, long ago, for we find Bede writing:

> In this narrow sea, the two tides of ocean, which flow round Britain from the immense northern ocean, daily meet and oppose one another beyond the mouth of the river Homelea, which runs into that narrower sea, from the lands of the Jutes, which belong to the country of the Gewissas. After this meeting and struggling together of the two seas, they return into the ocean from whence they came.

The river Homelea is, of course, the Hamble. The tide wave which passes up Spithead checks the ebb of the tide that passed up the Solent, and so prolongs high water for some two hours, making Southampton pretty well independent of tidal conditions. After low water the tide rises for about two hours and then remains more or less stationary for about an hour. It then rises again for about three and a half hours. So, six and a half after low water it has risen to the *first* high water. Then it ebbs for about an hour, though the fall is only about nine inches, and then commences to rise again, reaching its former level (and sometimes exceeding it) in about seventy minutes. This is the *second* high water. The ensuing ebb continues for about three hours and a quarter, but is most rapid during the last hour. There is no difference at neaps in the level near high water. The advantage of all that is obvious. And in addition the port was connected to the capital by the Itchen, and was situated in the middle of the south coast and right opposite the mouth of the Seine, which is the front door to northern France. In fact, ideally situated for commerce; and it was not slow to take advantage of its advantages.

In 1205 the English lost their northern French possessions. It would be more correct to say that the English king lost his possessions in northern France, for the English gained a good deal more than they lost by the loss. At the time no doubt this was not realized. For Southampton the loss must have looked like the end of the seaport trade. There must have been a good deal of alarm and despondency among the tradesmen and merchants. And, of course, Southampton did fall from its position as the chief port of passage between the English and French shores. But England at the same time ceased to be an appendage of a continental empire, and became a country standing on her own feet. And a country almost continuously at war with the French. Southampton ceased to be a great port of passage and became instead a great fortress. She became the gathering-point of armies and the starting-point of fleets, and she became also a great ship-building centre. For almost two and a half centuries Southampton was a great stronghold, always threatened by the French fleets, many times attacked, and once actually captured and almost destroyed. That was in 1338. It happened on a Sunday morning, and a large fleet of some fifty ships, Norman, Genoese and Spanish, took part in the raid. The people fled and the raiders were able to do their work undisturbed. But the next day the people rallied, and drove off the attackers, but that was too late and the town did not recover from the devastation for many years. Contemporary chroniclers are full in their accounts of it. Even the Edwardian poet, Laurence Minot, devotes a section of his *Songs on King Edward's Wars*, which was written in

1352, to a detailed description of it. Minot was a staunch patriot, and he made out the best possible case for the people of the town and did his best (in the manner of the modern penny daily) to minimize the disaster, but the tale remains a poor tale.

> At Hamton, als I understand,
> Came the galayes unto land,
> And feel fast thai slogh and bread,
> But nought so makill als sum men wend,
> For or thai wened war thai mett
> With men that sone there laykes lett.
> Sum was knokked on the hewyd
> That the body thare bilevid.
> Sum lay stareand on the sternes,
> And sum lay knokked out thaire hernes.
> The galay men the sath to say
> Most nedes turn another way.

But the story is best told, I think, by Stow, the Elizabethan antiquary:

The 4th of October fifty galleys, well manned and furnished, came to Southampton about nine of the clock, and sacked the town, the townsmen running away for feare. By the break of the next day they which fled by the help of the country thereabout came against the pyrates and fought with them, in the which skyrmish were slain to the number of three hundred pyrates together with their captain, the King of Sicilie's sonne. To this young man the French king had given whatsoever he got in the kingdom of England. But he being beaten down by a certain man of the country, cried out "Rancon, rancon," notwithstanding which the husbandmen laid him on with his clubbe till he had slaine him, speaking these words, "Yea," quoth he, "I know thee well enough: thou art a Francon, and therefore thou shalt die"; for he understood not his speech, neither had he any skill to take gentlemen prisoners and to keep them for their ransome. Wherefore the residue of these Genoways, after they had set the town on fire and burned it up quite, fledde to their galleys, and in their flying certain of them were drowned. After this the inhabitants of the town encompassed it about with a great and strong wall.

There has, of course, been a wall before this. But the main fortifications had been on the landward side. Now they were taken to cover the seaward as well, for it was there, naturally, that the main brunt of the French attack had fallen. During the day the great "King's House" with all its subsidiary buildings had been almost wholly destroyed. Only the massive outer walls remained standing. It was decided not to rebuild the house, but to use the ruins to strengthen the fortifications of the town. So along the western front there was built that great wall, known as the Arcades, which is still standing.

But walls or no, Southampton suffered severely from that raid. The inhabitants feared to return, which was not altogether surprising, for two years later the French made another determined attack, though this time they were not successful. And, indeed, for the next thirty-six years, the town was only half inhabited. Two years' rent was due to the King, and the burgesses had to petition the King to release them from the burden of maintaining the fortifications. That was in 1376. The very next year proved the necessity for strong fortifications, for the French made a most desperate attack which was only beaten off by the heroic endeavours and consummate generalship of Sir John Arundel, who was for the brilliant manner in which he had conducted the defence, made Marshal of England.

The English, of course, were not doing nothing all this while. They were doing quite a lot. The Battle of Sluys was fought and won in 1340 and for a while at least we held command of the narrow seas. In 1345 Edward III collected 32,000 troops at Southampton and a big fleet, to which Southampton contributed twenty-one vessels and five hundred and seventy-six seamen. And in a few months all Europe was ringing with the news of Crecy. We are not told in our history books about what happened after the battle of Crecy, but the French certainly suffered a terrible retribution for their burnings. Later came another king to Southampton to collect another army and navy. Under Henry V prosperity returned to the town in sudden and great measure. Here it was that the two great ships the *Grace Dieu* and the *Holy Ghost* were fitted out, and here many smaller ships of war were built. And for five weeks in the year 1415 Henry V was in and around Southampton superintending the gathering and fitting out of an army of 30,000 men and the collection of one thousand five hundred ships that were to carry them across the channel to fame. It was from his "chastel de Hantonne au rivage de la mer" that Henry addressed his last letter to the French king before he embarked. And it was here, just before he sailed, that Richard, Earl of Cambridge, the king's cousin, Lord Scrope of Masham, and Sir Thomas Grey "lightly conspir'd" against him. Sir Thomas Grey, being a commoner, was condemned by a jury and executed immediately. The others were tried by a council of peers and condemned also. The Earl of Cambridge being of royal blood was allowed to walk to the place of execution just outside the Bargate, but Lord Scrope was carried there on a hurdle.

All through these years there had been great rivalry between Southampton and Portsmouth for the position of premier war port. Portsmouth won, and Southampton devoted its attention to commerce. Commerce had always played a big part in the life of the town; it now played the paramount part. The wine trade with Gascony became very important, and as early as 1215 it was second only to that of London. (In 1272 Southampton imported 3147 tuns of wine compared with 3,799 tuns imported by London.) In the fourteenth century the still more lucrative connexion with Venice was formed. Venice was then the great market for eastern goods, for the spices and perfumes, the silks and the carpets of Persia, India and Cathay. And every year with impressive ceremony a great fleet of galleys used to set forth from Venice bound for northern Europe laden with the wealth of Asia. The trade was reciprocal; on their return the Venetian merchants took with them the products of the lands they had visited, wool and cloth and leather from England and fine cambrics from Flanders. In 1378 a statute of Richard II allowed the Venetians to make Southampton their port of call, and from that time until the sixteenth century, when the eastern trade passed out of the hands of Venice, every year saw their great galleys riding at anchor in Southampton for some sixty days at a time the while their merchants did business. There are still relics of this time in the town's history present to-day; Costello and Mancini are good Hampshire names.

With the trade came added importance. Four annual fairs were established and in due course confirmed by Royal Charter. And the government of the town grew steadily in independence and dignity. In 1400 a charter gave judicial autonomy to the borough . . . cognizance of all pleas, claim to all fines and forfeitures. Another charter in 1445 raised Southampton to the dignity of a Corporation, so that its mayor, bailiffs and burgesses became persons in law capable of holding lands and prosecuting pleas. Two years later another charter completed the emancipation of the borough by elevating it to the rank of a county with a sheriff of its own. These great, indeed exceptional, favours were granted expressly and explicitly because the burden of defence fell upon the citizens of the town. The preamble to the charter of 1400 states that the additional privileges granted by the King were so granted "pro melioratione et fortificatione villae praedictae in frontem inimicorum nostrum notoriae situatae." Furthermore, honours were piled upon the mayor until he became a man of national dignity and importance. He was made the King's escheator, clerk of the market, mayor of the staple, steward and marshal of the King's household—though probably only when the king was in the town—and an admiral of England within the wide limits of the port of Southampton, which stretched from beyond Portsmouth in the east to beyond Lymington in the west.

But though these honours were mainly military, and hinged on the defence of the town, they sprang from the trade of the town. It was the trade that made the town important and worthy of expensive defence. The French raided plenty of other places, whose mayors did not receive signal honour. It was the import of wines and the export of woollens that made Southampton. Everything was done to stimulate the woollen industry. Special grants were made from time to time in the form of release from tolls and so forth, but the greatest stimulus came from the wars in the Netherlands, for they brought crowds of refugees to England and a large colony of them was established at Southampton, and a smaller colony at Winchester. In 1567 special permission was obtained for them to establish factories for foreign fabrics and new drapery. But this did not please the freemen of the guilds, and they obtained a special order that each Flemish settler "should keep and instruct two English apprentices for seven years, and after that should employ one Englishman for every two strangers." The materials that these refugees introduced were of finer texture than the goods of English manufacture, and were known as "rashes" or serges, and "sayes." They obtained a wide reputation, and for a time their export was considerable. Every effort, too, was made to see that there was sufficient skilled labour for the trade. In 1578 a "House of Correction" was established at Winchester for the punishment of the numerous "sturdy and valiant beggars" that roamed the country at this time. The employments listed for men included spooling and quilling of yarn, weaving of kerseys and serges, wool combing, cloth dyeing, making of hats, gloves and wool cards. And for the women the employment was spinning, carding and sorting of wool, carding of tatters' spools and the knitting of hose and dressing of flax. All unskilled workers were to be set to learn any of the above crafts and were to be kept for five years, three of which were to be spent in learning the craft and two more to pay the state for the board and lodging and instruction. The "House of Correction" was provided with a loom and a press, with a dye house and vats, and with a copper furnace. It sounds an excellent plan, but it roused a good deal of ill-feeling among the freemen of the guilds, and after about fifty years the place was abandoned.

In the meanwhile, however, a great change had come over the world. At the close of the fifteenth century and the beginning of the sixteenth, geographical discovery and scientific discovery, intellectual rebirth and religious revelation, and political transformation and social transition, succeeded one another with bewildering rapidity. The old order had grown up through more than a thousand years of slow development. It passed away almost overnight, with a suddenness and a completeness that has had no parallel in history. A new world was born. A new life swept through the western world. New and vast fields of enterprise and adventure were opened up in far distant quarters of the globe, and at the same time new and vast fields were opened up in the human mind and human spirit. The world had moved out of the Middle Ages into the Renaissance.

Southampton was affected more, perhaps, than any other English town by the death of the old world. Two features marked the change in English history. Firstly, the age-old ambition of English kings to possess French provinces and, if possible, to acquire the French crown, gave place to a policy which entailed the balance of power by diplomatic means in Europe and the extension of English influence and dominion in the newly discovered lands across the wide seas. Secondly, the opening up of the Cape route to the East moved the centre of gravity of the mercantile world from the Mediterranean to the Atlantic. Venice and the other city-states of Italy fell from eminence: Lisbon, London, Antwerp took their place. And to these must be added Southampton. For these changes had a profound effect upon the fortunes of the town.

The place was no longer of any value as a fortress, and the change in international trade, and particularly the cessation of the visits of the Venetian galleys (the last one came in 1532) deprived the town of one of its great sources of wealth.

In fact the age which saw the rise of England to a position of first-rate importance and power in the heirarchy of European nations saw the temporary decline of Southampton. We find Henry VII speaking of the town as "now lately greatly decayed." We find Henry VIII remitting some of the debt, a small remission for Henry VIII was always short of money and loved money even more than he loved women. We find Edward VI remitting a great portion of the debt, and later remitting it all save £50 per annum. All this is eloquent of the state into which the town had fallen. And during the great days of Elizabeth, Southampton was really a depressed area. But from then onwards improvement began. The wine trade began to come back. With the suppression of the monasteries there had been a great falling off in the consumption of wine. Mary granted to the burgesses the monopoly of the import of sweet wines, and she saw to it that any wool shipped to the Levant went from Southampton under penalty of treble custom. Elizabeth, who did not like depressed areas and who probably had an idea that Southampton might be a valuable place in the event of war with Spain, confirmed the grants made by her sister and increased them to include all wines from the Levant and Kandy. The corner had been turned.

In 1620 a group of religious refugees gathered at Southampton and from there set sail in the *Mayflower* and the *Speedwell* for America. The departure of the Pilgrim Fathers marked the beginning of an emigration unique in the history of the world. Within the next twenty years twenty thousand Englishmen crossed the Atlantic, and many of them sailed from Southampton. And the discovery of the Newfoundland fishing grounds made Southampton the chief market for the fish and oil that were brought to England, and its ships played a very big part in the new trade. Indeed, so important did the town become in this connexion that the mayor had to take note of all offences or crimes committed on the soil of Newfoundland by the crews of boats sailing from Southampton.

There was a further slump at the end of the eighteenth century, when the population had sunk to little more than a thousand and only thirteen ships were using the port. But with the nineteenth century Southampton rises again and we enter upon the modern history of the town. Actually the rise began some while before this, but it was not due this time to any form of external trade. Under George III the town was for more than sixty years a popular watering-place and health resort, rivalling Brighton on the one hand and Bath on the other. And with this sudden incursion of fashion the town began to grow. And in 1803 its prosperity was established on the surer basis of maritime enterprise and commerce. In that year a bill was passed through Parliament authorizing the building of docks. Ship-building began again. Large men-of-war were built at Southampton and Bursledon, and the invention by the owner of the mills at Stoneham of improved blocks and pumps for use on ships of war attracted more trade to the town. The revival of ship-building and the use of Southampton as a port of embarkation for the Napoleonic wars certainly woke up the town authorities to the possibility of improvements. Southampton began to construct docks and quays, and canals were planned to connect the town with Salisbury and London. These canals were planned in 1795 to avoid the attacks of French privateers. One channel was to link the Itchen with the Test at Redbridge and to be taken on to Salisbury; the Itchen Navigation was to be restored and linked with the Redbridge canal at Houndwell, and Winchester was to be linked with Basingstoke, and by the Basingstoke canal with London. The scheme was never carried out, partly because of expense and partly because naval victories cleared the Channel of privateers.

But in 1803 dock construction was contemplated. Up to this time there had been two piers, one near the end of the High Street, and the other about 180 yards further west. The harbour was exposed, and though the water was deep—15 feet at the spring tides—no very large ships could use the port for repairs because of the lack of dock accommodation.

The first proposal was to enclose about 200 acres of mud-land between the Test and the Itchen. This enclosure was to extend 600 yards seawards, and there were to be four docks of about 74 acres each, with a berth accommodation extending for about two and a half miles with about 140 acres for warehouses and sheds. Three of the docks were to open from the Itchen Channel and one from the south. It was thought that such a scheme would make Southampton an auxiliary port to London, and it was much stressed

The nave and east window of Netley Abbey

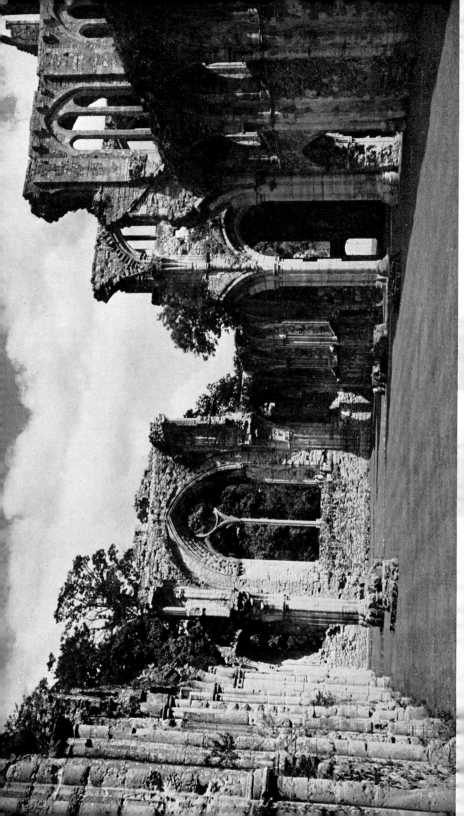

(as it had been in the Middle Ages) that the difficulties and dangers of the voyage round to London would be avoided. In 1836 a Dock Company was formed and the first stone was laid in 1838. The tidal dock was opened in 1839. This was then the largest in England, having an area of 16 acres, a depth of 18 feet at low water spring tides, and an entrance 150 feet wide.

From 1838 the construction of the South-Western Railway was in progress and this helped the development of business greatly, and the P. & O. Steamships first made use of the new docks in 1842. The inner dock was completed in 1857. All this time the construction of graving docks was going on and four were completed by 1879, and in this year also an extension was made to the Itchen quays which added nearly a third of a mile to the quay accommodation.

That this rapid extension was more than justified will be realized by the following figures:

1780. 13 vessels belonged to the port of Southampton. 5 were chartered for Jersey; 5 for Guernsey; the remaining 3 for Portugal and Malaga.

1798. Value of exports was £21,800. Duties paid thereon £900. Duty paid on imports £15,000. Duties on wines £12,000. Duties on coasting trade £9,000.

1840. Value of exports £130,000.

1841. Value of exports £560,000.

1860. About 300 vessels belonged to the port of Southampton. 30 for the West Indian trade. 50 belonging to the P. & O. Company. And the remainder to other companies.

And the effect that the building of the docks had on the town may clearly be seen from the following figures:

1803. Docks first contemplated.   Population 8,254
1836. Company formed.   „   23,534
1838. First stone laid.   „   25,200
1842. Outer Dock opened.   „   28,500
1851. Inner Dock opened.   „   35,305

St. Margaret's, Titchfield

1875. Itchen Quays opened.   Population   56,211
1890. Empress Dock opened.   ,,   64,405
1892. Transfer of Docks to Railway.   ,,   65,621
1911. Ocean Dock opened.   ,,   120,512
1934. Completion of 7,000-ft. Quay.   ,,   177,000

It will be noticed that the greatest increase in the growth and importance of Southampton has occurred since 1892, when the whole of the docks undertaking passed from the hands of the Southampton Dock Company to the London and South-Western Railway Company, which is now merged in the Southern Railway. From the moment that they took over, the Railway Company proceeded to increase the accommodation and to improve the facilities.

I think that it is worth while enumerating these docking facilities more fully, for they are a monument to private enterprise second to none in the world, and should be mentioned in these days, when private enterprise is in its twilight owing to the lack of it shown by so many of its chief supporters. It is due solely to private enterprise that Southampton now occupies the position she does among the great ports of the world.

OUTER DOCK.		
Water area	.	16 acres.
Length of quays	.	2,621 feet.
Width of entrance	.	150 feet.
Depth at H.W.O.S.T.		31 feet.
Depth at L.W.O.S.T.		18 feet.

In its early days this dock, the first to be opened at the port, berthed the largest ocean-going shipping in the world. It is now used almost exclusively by the Southern Railway Company's cross-channel mail, passenger and cargo vessels. A modern passenger station has been built with customs offices, buffets and waiting rooms.

INNER DOCK.		
Water area	.	10 acres.
Length of quays	.	2,575 feet.

This dock is open at High Water only. The Inner Dock is

connected with the Outer Dock by means of a lock. It was opened for traffic in 1851. This is the only non-tidal basin in the port, but owing to the advantage of the double tide the pair of single gates at the entrance can remain open for six hours each day.

EMPRESS DOCK.	Water area	.	.	18½ acres.
	Length of quays	.	3,880 feet.
	Width of entrance	.	165 feet.
	Depth at H.W.O.S.T.	39 feet.
	Depth at L.W.O.S.T.	26 feet.

This was the last extension to be undertaken by the Southampton Dock Company. It was opened by Queen Victoria on 26 July 1890 and is the largest of the four basins on the Docks Estate. It was possible even at that time to make a forecast of the position that Southampton was to hold in the shipping world, for, with the opening of this dock, Southampton was the only port in Great Britain at which vessels of the deepest draught could enter or leave at any state of the tide, and in spite of the increased size of the modern vessels now in service that is still true to-day. At Berths 24/25 at this dock, accommodation has been provided for the banana traffic, which is in normal times very heavy. To facilitate quayside working and to prevent damping and chilling of the bananas, a covered way 400 feet in length extends along above the quays, enabling the entire process of ship-to-rail working to be carried out in the dry. Discharge is effected by means of elevators from the ships' holds on to conveyor belts running longitudinally to the quay, and a five-ton gantry crane, which traverses the length of the berths, is utilized to place in position the discharging equipment.

OCEAN DOCK.	Water area	.	.	15½ acres.
	Length of quays	.	3,807 feet.
	Length of dock	.	1,600 feet.
	Width of entrance	.	400 feet.
	Depth at H.W.O.S.T.	53 feet.
	Depth at L.W.O.S.T.	40 feet.

The transfer of the White Star Lines New York service from Liverpool to Southampton in 1907 made further dock accommodation essential, and the construction of this deep-water dock was undertaken and finally completed in 1911. The largest vessels in the service can berth at these quays at any time no matter what the state of the tide. Electric cranes, ranging from 35 cwt. to 5 tons lifting capacity, with a radius of 65 feet and a height of lift of 100 feet, are installed along the 3,807 feet of quay. The four large single-storied transit sheds built along the quay are probably the most modern and convenient in the world and have a total length of 2,440 feet, each being 120 feet wide. In addition to the normal North Atlantic traffic dealt with in this dock, one berth is reserved for vessels engaged in the timber trade.

ITCHEN QUAYS.	Depth at H.W.O.S.T.	46 feet.
	Depth at L.W.O.S.T.	33 feet.
	Depth at H.W.O.S.T.	33 feet.
	Depth at L.W.O.S.T.	20 feet.
	Depth at H.W.O.S.T.	47 feet.
	Depth at L.W.O.S.T.	34 feet.
	Total length of Itchen Quays . . .	3,346 feet.
TEST QUAYS AND SOUTH QUAY.	Depth at H.W.O.S.T.	40 feet.
	Depth at L.W.O.S.T.	27 feet.
	Depth at H.W.O.S.T.	45 feet.
	Depth at L.W.O.S.T.	32 feet.
	Total length of quays	2,687 feet.
OTHER QUAYS.	Total length . .	1,992 feet.

The deep-water quays facing the rivers Itchen and Test provide more than one mile of quayside complete with modern dock equipment, transit sheds and rail facilities.

This accommodation is used a great deal by shipping, for the minimum depth of water alongside at L.W.O.S.T. permits all but the largest ships afloat to be safely berthed. Single-storied transit sheds line most of the quays, but there are three double-storied sheds serving the southern portion of the Itchen Quays. Electrically operated level-luffing cranes with lifting capacities up to 5 tons are a prominent feature of the quayside equipment. The South Quay, which marks the extreme southern boundary of the docks, where the rivers Itchen and Test meet to form the estuary of Southampton Water, comprises one berth and has a quay frontage of 460 feet. Large quantities of cargo are normally received here and there is a very large Cargo Shed.

DOCKS EXTENSION.	Depth at H.W.O.S.T.	58 feet.
	Depth at L.W.O.S.T.	45 feet.
	Depth at H.W.O.S.T.	53 feet.
	Depth at L.W.O.S.T.	40 feet.
	Total length of quays	8,014 feet.

The huge Docks Extension scheme was commenced in 1927 and the new 7,544 feet quay wall was finally completed in 1934. This quay extends westward in a straight line along the River Test towards Millbrook Point, and is separated from the old docks by the Town Quay and the Royal Pier. There is accommodation for eight of the largest ships afloat. The approach channel to this new quay is about two miles long, about 600 feet wide, and is dredged throughout its length to a minimum depth of 35 feet at L.W.O.S.T. Facing the quays are eight single-storied transit sheds, each 150 feet wide and varying in length from 600 feet to 900 feet. These sheds have been built in pairs and have proved extremely successful in dealing with large cargoes of general traffic. They are equipped with all the most modern appliances for dealing quickly with passengers and with cargo, and are provided with railway lines at the back and front, and bays for the simultaneous loading and unloading of road vehicles. At the rear of the sheds there are sidings capable of taking six boat trains. Connection to the main line of the Southern Railway is made at the eastern end of the Extension, but loop lines also make another con-nexion with the main line at Millbrook Station.

COAL BARGE ACCOMMODATION.	One Jetty for discharging coal from colliers to barges. Length 360 feet.
	Three basins for the accommoda-tion of lighters. Total area 5 acres.

That covers the wet dock accommodation of Southamp-ton. The dry dock accommodation is as follows:

DRY DOCK No. 1.	Opened in 1846. Length overall 401 ft. Length at floor level 378 ft. Width at entrance 66 ft. Depth of water over blocks at H.W.O.S.T. 19 ft. 3 ins. Depth of water over blocks at H.W.O.N.T. 15 ft. 9 ins.
DRY DOCK No. 2.	Opened in 1847. Length overall 281 ft. Length at floor level 240 ft. Width at entrance 66 ft. Depth of water over blocks at H.W.O.S.T. 14 ft. Depth of water over blocks at H.W.O.N.T. 10 ft. 6 ins.
DRY DOCK No. 3.	Opened in 1854. Length overall 523 ft. Length at floor level 501 ft. Width at entrance 80 ft. Depth of water over blocks at H.W.O.S.T. 24 ft. 2 ins. Depth of water over blocks at H.W.O.N.T. 20 ft. 8 ins.
DRY DOCK No. 4.	Opened in 1879. Length overall 479 ft. Length at floor level 451 ft. Width at entrance 56 ft. Depth of

water over blocks at H.W.O.S.T. 22 ft. 9 ins. Depth of water over blocks at H.W.O.N.T. 19 ft. 3 ins.

DRY DOCK No. 5 (Prince of Wales). — Opened in 1895. Length overall 745 ft. Length at floor level 729 ft. Width at entrance 91 ft. Depth of water over blocks at H.W.O.S.T. 31 ft. 9 ins. Depth of water over blocks at H.W.O.N.T. 28 ft. 3 ins.

DRY DOCK No. 6 (Trafalgar). — Opened in 1905. Length overall 912 ft. 3 ins. Length at floor level 852 ft. Width at entrance 100 ft. Depth of water over cill at H.W.O.S.T. 35 ft. Depth of water over cill at H.W.O.N.T. 31 ft. 6 ins.

DRY DOCK No. 7 (King George V). — Opened in 1933. Length overall 1,200 ft. Length at floor level 1,141 ft. 6 ins. Width at entrance 135 ft. Depth of water over cill at H.W.O.S.T. 50 ft. 6 ins. Depth of water over cill at H.W.O.N.T. 47 ft.

The King George V Graving Dock was opened on 26 July 1933 by his late Majesty, and is the largest dry dock in the world. It is situated at the western end of the Docks Extension Estate. The dock was built for the *Queen Mary* but it can accommodate vessels of even larger size, indeed anything up to 100,000 gross tons. It is provided with two travelling cranes, one of which has a lift of 50 tons. The main de-watering plant consists of four electrically-driven 54-inch centrifugal pumps, each of 1,250 h.p., and these can empty the huge dock in four hours.

That is a very brief and inadequate factual description of the port of Southampton. But it should be sufficient to show that it is a very fine port indeed. The growth of

Southampton's shipping during the last fifty years shows that this is generally recognized the world over.

So far as cargo is concerned, Southampton ranks at present fourth among the ports of Britain. I think that it is a position likely to be altered very soon, for there is now less conservatism in the world than there used to be, and provided that enterprise on the same lines that have made the port what it now is, which is the best and most up-to-date in the world, is allowed to continue more and more trade is certain to be attracted to a place that offers such outstanding facilities. These facilities are really outstanding. The geographical position of Southampton is a paramount advantage for a receiving and distributing centre, for immediately behind the port is a hinterland containing 16,000,000 people within a radius of 100 miles, and transport is efficient and speedy both by rail and road. And everything possible has been done to ensure that all types of cargo are handled with dispatch and safety. As a result, already, the produce of almost every exporting country in the world is in peacetime handled at Southampton Docks. Fruit, grain, meat, vegetables, timber, wool, skins and hides predominate in the extraordinarily varied list. Fruit of most varieties (I am of course speaking of normal times) is received in an uninterrupted flow throughout the year. South Africa sends to the Mother Country huge quantities of both deciduous and citrus fruit, and the bulk of this is discharged at Southampton. Then there is the banana traffic from Central America and the West Indies, and considerable quantities of fruit are also unloaded here from North and South America, Australia, New Zealand, Spain, Jaffa, France, the Azores, and the Channel Islands. Shipments of grain are also discharged throughout the year, and the importance of this traffic has been greatly accentuated by the establishment of the Solent Flour Mills on the Docks Extension Estate. Seasonal cargoes of timber—and there is ample storage capacity here—come from the Baltic and North American ports. But I think that it is as a port for the handling of perishable goods that Southampton is really outstanding. In addition to the huge quantities of fruit, there are large consignments of meat, chilled and frozen, and butter is imported from South America; tomatoes from the Channel Islands, also potatoes; bacon, hams and frozen salmon from North America; eggs and meat from South Africa; and meat and eggs and dairy produce from Australia and New Zealand. Throughout the year South Africa also sends to Southampton heavy shipments of wool, skins and hides, which are destined for the industrial centres of Yorkshire and the Midlands, and for re-shipment to the Continent. And that, it must be stressed, outlines only the most important goods that are received at the port.

The normal export trade consists mainly of manufactures from the big centres of the north and the Midlands, and of transit goods from the Continent. Iron and steel machinery, rubber products, and hardware from Birmingham, woollen and worsted manufactures from Yorkshire, cotton goods from Lancashire, lace from Nottingham, hosiery from Leicester, leather goods from Northampton, tobacco for re-export, all these are regular travellers through Southampton and they go to all parts of the world.

Though fourth—at the moment—in the list of cargo ports, Southampton is easily first, and has been for many years, in the list of passenger ports in Britain. Many factors have contributed to the winning of this position. The natural geographical advantages, the ability of the port to offer accommodation to the largest liners in the world regardless of the state of the tide, the open docks and quays which mean that passengers can be landed with the utmost expedition, and the fact that the journey to London is only an hour and a half by some of the most comfortable trains in the world, at least as far as smooth running is concerned. And on the top of all that the greatest care has been taken to look after the comfort of these passengers. As a result of the initiative and forethought of the Southern Railway about 20,000,000 tons of shipping enter the port every year, and from the port there are more regular steamship services to all parts of the world than are available from any other port in the world. It is a magnificent record of achievement. And one, that is not finished yet by any means.

At the time of writing it is not possible for me to give

the full story of the great part that Southampton Docks played in the war. At any rate that story deserves—and no doubt will get—a book to itself. But at least it can be said that no time in its long and eventful history has the port more fully proved its value as a national asset. At no time has it played a more important part in the history of its country.

As in the First German War, Southampton was Embarkation Port No. 1 for the British Expeditionary Force. The figures of the B.E.F. do not seem very impressive when compared with those later attained, but all the same nearly 800,000 troops were embarked for France together with some 375,000 tons of stores and equipment. The subsequent tragedy of 1940 when France collapsed and the miracle of Dunkirk saved the British Empire for just a while is too well known to need retelling. Southampton played a big part in the evacuation, and many thousands of refugees passed through the town from the Continent. There were, too, thousands of small craft, which escaped from the Germans and found shelter in Southampton Water. They were a sight never to be forgotten by those fortunate to see them, and to know the stories of courage that made their presence possible.

From then on Southampton played an ever-increasing part in the war effort. There was inevitably a period of comparative calm after the disaster of Dunkirk, at least in comparison with the bustle and haste that had gone before. Big trade more or less stopped as the menace of the U-boats caused the transfer of the big ships to western ports. All the same, smaller ships continued to arrive at and leave the port to carry on the country's business, although they had to do so under the eyes of the enemy and in the ever-present threat of invasion. But at this time the greatest activity of the port was in the repair of vessels damaged by enemy air action and by the U-boats. There were thousands of men engaged on this work, and from the beginning of the war until the end of 1944 no less than 10,000 ships were repaired at Southampton. No mean record; for this work had to be carried on under steady attack. From the middle of 1940 the Germans commenced a regular series of day and night attacks on the port and the town. The town, as I have already said, suffered badly, and the docks and all the waterside undertakings suffered severe damage. Sheds, offices, and other buildings were destroyed; quays, permanent way, cranes and other equipment was damaged; but at no period was work absolutely stopped.

As time went on, shipping operations were increased. Southampton was used for the Lease-Lend traffic. The raids still continued, and with the operations then being undertaken it was a matter of urgency that the work should not be dislocated. It was not. From early 1942 Southampton was once again a busy port; so busy that it might almost have been peacetime—only the raiders brought realization that all the activity was to do with something more serious than simple trade. Lease-Lend ships came regularly from across the world, and coasters came regularly with coal from Wales. The larger vessels were returned hurriedly in ballast (occasionally with a little priority export traffic) and the colliers were returned with salvage from bombed areas in the country.

In July 1942 came the attack on Dieppe. Many of the vessels used for this were dispatched from the port, and this was another big strain on its resources.

With 1943 came preparations for the invasion of the Continent. This was a huge job for the port, for all the requirements of the Services and many Government Departments had to be met at the same time as repair work on damaged vessels went on. Suitable berths had to be allocated for the embarkation of British, Dominion and United States troops, mechanical transport, equipment and stores; hospital ships, and ships for fresh water for the operation, had to be dealt with at quays suitable for their particular requirements. There were also of course all sorts of other factors to be considered such as the stocking up of large stores of coal to avoid undue strain on the railways at the time of actual operations, the provision of additional cranes and other dock equipment, additional rail sidings and connexions, and the organization of military personnel to supplement civilian labour to carry out this enormous programme. And all the time normal commercial operations were carried on, and only stopped when the operational needs demanded it.

Southampton also played a big part in the building of the famous "Mulberry Port." The work was, of course, spread out all along the coast, but Southampton had a very big part in it, for the Dry Docks were used especially for the "Phœnixes" and the "Bombardons," some of which weighed as much as five thousand tons. King George V Dock was largely used for this purpose.

With the approach of June 6th, troops, stores and ammunition poured into the docks—they had for long been a strange enough sight with hundreds of assault vessels—and during the thirty weeks up to the end of the year over 1,600,000 tons of cargo were dispatched. This represents nearly one and a half times the combined export and import trade for 1938, and it was dealt with in seven months. To make it possible, additional sailing points had been provided by the construction of hards, and special terminals had been constructed for the operation of train-ferry vessels. It really was a magnificent achievement, so huge, indeed, that it defeats the imagination. It is much to be hoped that proper justice will be done to it in book form soon. It might help to show the world that the British are at least as good and usually better than others when it comes to organization, even though we forget to tell the world about it loud enough for the world to hear.

Southampton town has been too badly damaged to warrant any description. Suffice it to say that before the war it had the finest approach, over common, of any town in England. The main street was spacious (it still is!) and clean. The shops were busy and prosperous and polite. There were a number of excellent wine bars. The citizens looked as if they enjoyed life. The Civic Centre was beginning to settle down and to stop looking an upstart. And down at the end of the main street you came suddenly on to the world. The streets were not so spacious and not so clean. The wine bars looked a bit mingy. But the whole place, if it did not quite live up to the luxury of the liners, was quite the cleanest and most happy port that I have seen—and I have seen quite a few here and there.

Southampton exercises, has always exercised, an enormous influence on the Hampshire behind her. But she has always remained in some measure apart from the county proper. It would be wrong to say that Southampton was not Hampshire. It is true that she is cosmopolitan, that you see here every colour and hear every tongue, but she is more of Hampshire than Bournemouth, more of Hampshire than Portsmouth. Southampton is Hampshire all right. But she is also the gateway to the world. And the front door to Britain.

Chapter X

BOURNEMOUTH AND CHRISTCHURCH

THE main line from London runs through Southampton to Bournemouth. A hundred years ago there was no Bournemouth. To-day everyone knows Bournemouth and its pine trees, and its health-giving facilities, and its opportunities for amusement. The story of Bournemouth is a romance of big business, but it will never be history, unless it be the history of a ruined coast-line. And the town, which has swallowed up Boscombe and Southbourne and stretched over the border into Dorset, and is about to swallow up Christchurch, has nothing to do with Hampshire beyond the fact that most of it lies within the county boundary. You will not hear many Hampshire voices in Bournemouth —you will indeed be lucky if you hear one—but you will hear plenty of Lancashire and Birmingham and any amount of Cockney, not only in the summer but throughout the year, for it appears to be the ambition of most of the business men of the north and the Midlands to live here when they have made sufficient "brass." And no one can blame them. Bournemouth is quite a nice place, but despite the fact that it holds a most important position in modern English social history, it can be dismissed immediately from any book about Hampshire. Christchurch, which is now its eastern suburb, cannot.

Christchurch—or Christchurch Twynham, to give it its full name—is as ancient as Bournemouth is modern. It is situated (or rather was originally situated) between the rivers Avon and Stour. The Avon is sixty-one miles long. It rises near Roundway Down, drains the chalk of Salisbury Plain, the green sands of the Pewsey Vale, and the tertiaries from Fordingbridge to the sea, and it flows within sight of Stonehenge and Old Sarum. The Stour rises in Somerset, flows through Dorset and unites with the Avon at Christchurch to form an estuary. It is fifty-four miles long. Rivers were roadways once. And we might expect to find that a locality so favoured was of great importance in pre-historic times. And so it was. There are great earthworks on hill and cliff, and there are tumuli of Stone Age and Bronze Age all over the neighbourhood. Guarding the estuary is the ancient earthwork on Hengistbury Head with its double dykes. And a mile or so north of the modern town is Katterns Hill (now called St. Catherine's Hill) and on this plateau there was an early British hill town, with outlying ramparts and watch towers. In fact that is what the word Katterns means—*Kader Ryn*, the fort of the run or rivers. And later there was a Roman camp here, probably a camp set up by explorers.

In history the first mention of the place is in the *Saxon Chronicle*. Here, after the record of Alfred's death in 901, it is stated that Ethelwold the Aethling disputed the succession and the choice of Edward the Elder by the Witan, and that he seized Wimborne and Tweoxna. Tweoxna was then the name of Christchurch, and it means roughly "the town on two rivers." It was one of the *burhs* or stockaded towns built by Alfred as defence against the Danes, and from Ethelwold's point of view a place of considerable importance. The revolt soon collapsed, but Ethelwold gave trouble in the neighbourhood for another five years before surrendering and signing the peace of Yttingaford (the modern Iford) in 906.

The main town of Christchurch is built in the form of a capital L, and in the centre, near the angle, are the ruins of a medieval castle, which was built by the de Redvers, Earls of Devon. The castellan's house, roofless and partly destroyed, stands by its moat stream which is supplied by the Avon. This is a rare example of Norman domestic architecture and one of the most perfect in England. The house is rectangular, covering an area of eighty feet by fifteen feet. Though the roof has gone, the walls, except where the north-east turret has fallen, are almost intact. There are two storeys and the great gable is almost perfect. Part of the stairs remain and so does the circular chimney, which is said to be the earliest domestic chimney now existent in England. We owe what is left to William Jackson, Vicar of Christchurch. Up to the end of the eighteenth century this wonderful Norman building was almost perfect. Then its destruction was begun, and the whole building would have disappeared but for the efforts of the vicar, who so aroused public opinion—no easy matter in those days—that the work of destruction was stopped and the ruin left. It is often thought that the roof fell in, but this is not so; it was taken off by an eighteenth-century builder. Across the castle yard is an artificial mound about twenty feet high and on this mound are the east and west walls of a massive keep. The walls now are about thirty feet high and ten feet thick, built of uncut stone, and they give a very good idea of the strength of a Norman fortress. The castle was built in the twelfth century. King John on at least two occasions visited the place and held his court within the walls, but most of the other royal visitors have preferred the hospitality of the Priory. Indeed the castle has no connexion with any important event in our history. There was a massacre here in the troubled reign of King Stephen, but except for this the troubles of the Barons and the Wars of the Roses passed it by, for it stood on no great road, and the only other warlike activity it has witnessed was a slight skirmish which was quite indecisive in the Civil War.

It was inevitable that a church should be built. Originally the church was intended to be on St. Catherine's Hill. But whatever was erected there during the day was found to be cast down during the night, and the materials mysteriously transported to a place about a mile to the southward. After this had happened several times, it was realized that a church could not be built on the hill, and building was commenced at the place indicated. Immediately the workmen were joined by another. He was a model workman, for he worked all day but was never present when pay was to be drawn nor at mealtimes. Work proceeded apace, and then one day it was found that one of the beams was a foot too short. The strange workman placed his hand upon it, and instantly it fitted—and thereafter the strange workman was seen no more. The

Place House, Titchfield

carpenter's Son had helped to build the church, and so at the workmen's demand the church was named Christchurch. The beam is in the church to-day, projecting from a ledge where it has been placed out of the way of initial-cutting visitors, and the guide will tell you the story with eagerness. He believes it. The same legend, minus the beam part, occurs in many parts of the country, though in some places the Devil is held responsible for the casting down.

The church (or rather, churches, as will be shown presently) with its adjacent monastery lies directly to the south of the castle, and between it and the estuary. It is said that a monastery existed here from the earliest times, and at least from Athelstan's time. In any case the castle was no defence for the church or the monastery, and it is clear that when the ecclesiastical settlement was made no raiders from the sea were expected. We do not know when the first settlement was made and the first church built, but it seems evident that it was after the Danish troubles, after the Viking forays. Our oldest reference is *Domesday Book*, which records a monastery in existence, which held estates in Hampshire and the Isle of Wight during the reign of Edward the Confessor. And as regards the manors in the Isle of Wight, *Domesday Book* states that they had "always belonged" to the monastery at Twynham, which can only mean that in 1086 the exact year of the grant had been lost.

William Rufus gave the monastery to his chancellor, the famous Ralf Flambard. And it is to Flambard that we owe the Priory Church. Ralf, who was nicknamed Flambard or the Torch (by which name he is known to English history), was a priest of common birth, who made himself so indispensable to William that he became the latter's chief minister. He it was who devised the plan by which Rufus became "every man's heir," and he was no whit behind his blackguard master in any of his many evil ways. He was, in fact, a most unpleasant character. But Flambard built Durham Cathedral and Christchurch Priory. His motives were certainly not of the purest, but we are here concerned only with the result. Durham was his

Hengistbury Head, shielding Christchurch,
a great port in prehistoric times

masterpiece. But the Priory Church is quite enough to make me think of Ralf the Torch with gratitude.

Flambard's idea for dealing with Christchurch was to hold the revenues until a sufficient sum had accumulated to enable the church to be reconstructed. In the meanwhile the canons, though they received no pay, received their keep gratis. The canons, who had a shrewd idea that a goodly portion of the revenues went into Ralf's pocket, resisted strongly, but Flambard, who knew a number of ways of persuading people that he was right, had his way. He pulled down the old Saxon monastery, but before he could do much with the rebuilding, Rufus was murdered, and Henry I deposed the unpopular minister and gave the monastery to de Redvers. Ralf went to the Tower. The saintly Henry (and you know my opinion of Henry already) later sacrilegiously seized the building funds. The monastery was reduced to five canons, and it was at this point that Henry gave it to Richard de Redvers. At about the same time Flambard made his peace with Henry (I have an idea that the king had need of his brains in the matter of raising money) and was appointed to the bishopric of Durham. Somehow he and de Redvers came together, and the matter of the rebuilding of the Priory was brought up. Henry was unwilling or unable (but had he been able he would still have been unwilling) to refund any of the monies that he had taken, but de Redvers was willing to endow and Flambard was very willing to co-operate. There can be no doubt that beneath all his wickedness Ralf the Torch had a great fondness for Christchurch. It is not generally realized that he was not a Norman, but a Saxon or maybe even a Briton, and a man of the New Forest at that, for *Domesday Book* shows that he was one of the ejected landowners of the Forest. Had Rufus not been murdered we might never have seen Durham Cathedral as it is to-day, but we might well have seen an even more magnificent Priory Church. Richard de Redvers placed his chaplain, Peter de Oglander, one of the great Isle of Wight family, in charge of the monks, and it was under his rule and that of his successor that parts of the church and the convent were roofed over. The arrangement seems to have been that as much of the monastic revenues as possible should be placed to the fabric fund, and this was supplemented by gifts from de Redvers of rentals, lands and fees. In fact the new era of endowments may be said to have started here at Christchurch. Flambard, until his death in 1128, supplied the architectural genius and carried out experiments here for his greater work at Durham.

In Stephen's reign there was an important change. Hitherto the monastery had been in the hands of seculars, but from this time the Augustinian rule was introduced, and it became a house of canons regular under a prior. In order to achieve this the senior canon was made the Bishop of Chichester, and one Reginald, who is remembered as a benefactor and who is buried in the central passage of the nave just in front of Prior Draper II, the twenty-sixth and last prior of Christchurch, was brought in as the first prior. In all, the Priory lasted for three hundred and eighty-nine years—from 1150 to 1539—and though there were some scandals (the canons once plotted robbery on a large scale) the place does not seem at any time to have become so lax as some of its neighbours. At the Dissolution the Priory was surrendered without much demur to Henry VIII's commissioners by Prior John Draper who was described as a "very honest and conformeable person" and who was granted a pension of £133 6s. 8d. per annum. The commissioners seized the Priory treasures among them

> jeullys and plate, whereof some be mete for the Kings Majesties use: as a littel chalys of gold, a gudely large cross doble gilte with the foot garnyshed with stone and perle: two gudely basons doble gilte, having the kings armys well inamyled

and the buildings were pulled down and the estates given away to laymen, while the living was made over to the Cathedral authorities at Winchester.

The most noticeable feature of the church to-day, apart from the tower which is really beautiful seen across the Avon, is its great length. This is explained by the fact that the present church is not one church but the remains of three. The choir was the Priory Church proper: the nave was the parochial church: the Lady Chapel was the manorial church. Strictly speaking, I suppose, only the choir should be called Christchurch, for the others were dedicated to the Holy Trinity and the Blessed Virgin. As a parish church the buildings must form one of the largest —indeed I should say easily *the* largest—in England. Architecturally the building is a mere jumble of styles—as a whole it cannot compare with Romsey Abbey though the setting is infinitely finer—but so long as you do not look for an ordered architectural scheme (if you do you will find the Priory disappointing) you will find many magnificent features from the rough horse-shoe arcading in the crypts to the sixteenth-century work in the chantries. There are some priceless gems in the Priory Church and interspersed with them some absolute atrocities. Viewed from the outside I think that the whole is a little disappointing because of its great length which is unrelieved by a central tower at the union of the gable and flat roofs. It seems incomplete. This is, of course, because it is really three churches rather roughly joined together. In fact the stump of a central tower (which would make all the difference) still exists, uniting the Norman nave with the older choir and monastic church. It is well seen at the juncture of the nave and transepts where the rounded and massive Norman arches rise high above the early English clerestory of the nave. The tradition is that the central tower fell early in the thirteenth century, and destroyed in its fall the existent monastic church containing the Redvers chantry. A little later this monastic church was rebuilt as the present choir, and it actually contains the crypt and tombs of the earlier building. The eastern end was originally an apse, but a little later the Lady Chapel was added through the interests of the Montacutes and Wests, the manorial lords. This most easterly portion of the church was squared off at its eastern end, and connected with the nave by the north and south choir-aisles, which are outside the monastic choir. It was at about this time that the chantries were added, and alterations were effected on the eastern side of the north transept, and about now, too, the present western tower was built. From the monastic seals and certain stone bosses in the church it would seem that the central tower consisted of a low square stump capped by a spire surmounted by a cross and ball. Each corner of the cruciform church is represented as bearing small finial towers, most of which have disappeared. So you get the unrelieved length of 333 feet with a tower at the extreme western end of 120 feet, which is inserted into the nave rather than attached to it. The whole looks rather like a gigantic railway engine, as somebody (I forget who) once said.

If you look at the outside closely you will find all sorts of important alterations. The eastern side of the north transept was once apsidal like the south transept. The north front of the north transept still retains its beautiful arcading and tracery, especially round the turret tower, but the Norman round-headed windows have been destroyed, and a huge ugly window inserted at a higher elevation. Again, in the nave north wall the old Norman windows have been remodelled on the early English type in keeping with the upper clerestory, but the intervening lights of the triforium still retain their rounded shape. The north porch, which is the principal entrance to the church, is a grand massive structure of two stories, elaborately ornamented. Before the present tower was erected by the Montacutes, whose armorial bearings may be seen on the spandrels of the west door, the west end of the nave must have been magnificent. High up on the face of the tower, which destroyed the west end of the nave, there is in a canopied niche an image of the thorn-crowned Saviour in benediction. This is considerably older than the tower itself, and originally it stood over the western porch.

Yes, the whole thing is a muddle. The Norman turret with interlaced arcade and diaper tracery will bear comparison with anything in the country, and alongside is a remarkably ugly window, which though it cannot detract from the beauty of the lacework, ruins the effect of the whole. There is much Norman work, characteristically massive, but at the same time of a grace that is very rarely found in work of this period. The twisted pillars of the triforium and the curious ornamentation (unlike anything else in the country) above the main arches are evidence of an inventiveness not usually found in builders of the Norman period.

Separating the choir from the nave and transept there is a very fine, but much defaced, stone rood screen of the fourteenth century. This screen repays close examination for it grows and grows on the observer until there comes suddenly realization what a very beautiful thing it is. Quatrefoiled panels with shields below the canopied niches are separated by buttresses, and each empty niche has a vaulted roof and there are tiny creatures creeping and flying along the buttresses. The whole thing is wonderfully rich, and too often passed by with but a casual glance.

I have heard it said that the fifteenth century choir is the finest part of the church. It is certainly beautiful and magnificent at the same time. One should spend a long time looking at the roof. One could spend weeks looking at just this and no more and always one would be seeing something new. From the roof hang bosses and pendants supported by angels in gold and colours, bearing monograms and shields and flowers. Every time I go I see something new in this roof, and never yet have I found anyone to decipher it all for me.

And then the canons' stalls. There are thirty-six of them. At first sight the carving is rough and ready. At first sight only. In each there was originally a "miserere" seat, and the details of every one of them are worthy of the closest examination. They must have been the work of a lifetime for the medieval craftsmen, and it seems that they were so in love with the work that they could not bear to stop, for the wealth of carving in the "miserere" seats flows over the ends of the benches, and on to the arm rests, and even from under the pinnacled parapet the faces of animals and birds, the portraits of kings and queens and bishops look down. Yes, they are worth the closest examination, for these craftsmen were no respecters of persons and they held up to satire the world in which they lived. They reveal in a curiously blunt (and unedifying manner) the humour of the

monk and the monk's attitude to the religion he professed.
Here is a fox, the symbol of cunning, preaching from a
pulpit to a flock of geese; here is a goose bringing a gift to
a friar; here is the parish clerk symbolized as a cock; here
is a buffoon; here is a man with his trousers held up by a
nail driven into his back; here are dogs and fowls and foxes;
and here is Richard III, carved with remarkable fidelity,
in the company of two grinning devils. Evidently Richard
III was not popular in Christchurch. Here are all the
emotions known to the human race. Here is every type of
countenance. Here is almost every vice. And here are a
few of the virtues.

Remarkable, too, are the chantries. The finest, I think,
is the Salisbury Chantry. It was erected for the burial of
the Countess of Salisbury and her son Cardinal Pole, but it
was never used for that purpose. This chantry is architecturally very similar to the Fox Chantry in Winchester
Cathedral, being late Perpendicular work with Renaissance
embellishments. The countess died because Henry VIII
was not the man to forgo revenge. She was imprisoned for
two years and then, though over seventy, was brought to
the block and executed. She, fully conscious of her innocence, refused to kneel and the rhyme runs:

> Salisbury's countess, she would not die
> As a proud dame should . . . decorously.
> Lifting my axe I split her skull
> And the edge since then has been notched and dull.

There are many other monuments. One is to Shelley: another to Sally Williams, who died of grief and took twelve
years doing it. And in the churchyard is a brick tomb of
1641 with these lines:

> We were not slayne but raysed,
> Raysed not to life,
> But to be buried twice
> By men of strife:
> What rest could living have
> When dead had none?

> Agree among you,
> Here we ten are one.

So far as I know the lines have never been explained. I believe that the generally accepted solution is that the ten men were drowned in a shipwreck off Christchurch Harbour, and first buried without the consent of the owner in other ground, being reburied here because of his resentment. It does not sound at all like a good solution to me. But, by far the strangest relic is in the visitors' book. In the year 1907 is the signature "William R.I."—the Kaiser. In 1917 there came a stranger to the church who asked to be allowed to put his signature next to that of "his friend the Kaiser." It was a strange request for 1917, and it caused a bit of a stir. But in the end the request was granted. The signature is that of Louis Raemaekers, the man who was hated throughout Germany, the man whose savage cartoons helped to make Germany hated throughout the world.

But, of course, everything in the church is dwarfed by the reredos, which is just as wonderful as it is unique. There are many who think that it is the finest in England. I can only say that I have not seen anything approaching it either here or abroad.

The original plan of the unknown artist was to combine the genealogy of Christ and the scenes of the Nativity. As in a Jesse window, the lowest group shows the reclining figure of Jesse on a most majestic scale, David with his harp is on the left hand and Solomon on the right. The branches of the vine, the symbol of the stem of Jesse, intertwine with the lower figures and end at the feet of Mary of Bethlehem. In the upper group the Heavenly Child is seated on Mary's knee, a rather odd-looking little figure, while the Wise Men offer their gifts. There is an ox and a donkey looking on, and in the background there are shepherds with their sheep looking upward and listening to the message of the Heavenly Host. The buttresses dividing the niches are covered with tiny figures of saints most delicately carved, but the niches themselves are empty. The vigour of the carvings is really astonishing, astonishing

that so much strength can be allied to so great elegance.
What the effect must have been when the niches were
filled, each and every one of them, with silver figures,
defeats the imagination.

I have described this reredos in some, though insufficient,
detail. Yet I am not sure that one should pay any attention to detail at all. It stands there, pale and luminous, a
background to a condensed architectural history of
England. So wonderful is it in its pale bright beauty that
it is enough to regard it humbly from afar, without bother-
ing about the loveliness of the detail. It is a thing to
worship, not examine.

It is a white church, this Priory Church. Long ago the
walls were coated with lime, so thoroughly coated that in
1805 they sold the wash from the walls for five pounds.
To-day the remains of the lime and the liberal use of soap
and water keep them white: and keep this church cheerful,
which is a great deal more than can be said for many an
ancient church.

Christchurch is beginning—as is inevitable—to suffer
from the proximity of Bournemouth. In summer it is quite
a gay place, and the main street is usually crowded with
people on their way to Bournemouth or to the sandhills
down at Mudeford. And along the river are gaily painted
house-boats, and small yachts and motor boats and canoes
and rowing boats. There is an air of joyful and healthy
festivity. But it is in winter that I like Christchurch best.
Then the streets recapture a little of the past. The river is
deserted save for a small boy or two fishing with a worm
on a pin, a man or two trying to do better. Then there are
the shore birds to watch; and there are many that come to
this estuary, and some of them rare travellers from distant
corners of the world. And then the bats that through the
summer have wheeled and darted through the twilight
above the old castle and over the water are at rest, and, if
you wish, you may examine them at rest. For if Christchurch is a wonderful place for the migrant sea-birds, it is
no less a wonderful place for the bats. There are twelve
species native to this country, and you may watch ten of
them on any fine summer evening, and find ten of them in

hibernation of a winter's day if you are of a mind. They
are in keeping with Christchurch of a winter's day, for then,
too, the little town sleeps and forgets the feverish excitement of Bournemouth's summer; sleeps as do the bats to
gather strength for the hunting of next summer.

CHAPTER XI

WINCHESTER

No CITY in all England—except London, and London is a county of houses and mean streets, and no city—is so full of history, so crowded with memories as Winchester. Here history lives. It does not matter where you go in Winchester, you step into the past, a past most beautifully preserved by the present. Indeed in great measure the past in Winchester is the present. It pervades everything—the Cathedral, the numerous churches, the strong and vital ecclesiastical life, the Castle Hall, the municipal activities and judicial functions, the streets and squares and alleys—everything.

Winchester is a city that has been ruled as a city for more than a thousand years. It is fully conscious of its associations, fully conscious of the part it has played in English history. It has retained even in these mercenary days its dignity; and retained, too, many of the features and customs of ancient days. Here the Curfew first rang, and must then have sounded as the knell of national aspirations: here each evening the Curfew rings yet, a reminder for all who care to listen that nations rise again. This is a sentimental association. There are other features in Winchester to-day that belong to the roots of our history, and are retained in all their picturesqueness, not because they are picturesque but because they have maintained their original usefulness—the Cathedral Bedesmen, the Brethren of St. Cross, the Almsmen of Beaufort's Order of Noble Poverty, and so on. There is much that is old in Winchester: little, thank heaven, that is "ye olde."

Everywhere there are the dry bones of history. By themselves they are dull, but in relation to their surroundings, severally and together, they give to Winchester a haunting quality which I personally find immensely attractive. In the Cathedral you stand not only in the presence of God, but also of those men who were the rulers of England in the days when England was unknown by that name, was but struggling to become a nation: in the presence—the bodily presence, for here their bones lie—of Cynegils, that rude chieftain, whom Birinus the missionary converted to Christianity; of Egbert, the statesman, who first welded together the many warring elements, and made of them the beginnings of a nation; of Cnut, the great Dane, who ruled so wisely and so gently. These are great names, too easily forgotten. And Winchester has others. Here, within Wolvesey Walls, we may walk where Alfred walked with Asser and Plegmund. Alfred did not make England, but here in Wolvesey he conceived the great record of national history, the greatest record excluding the Old Testament that has ever been carried out, the *English Chronicle*. That alone would be enough to secure undying fame for Winchester. But there are yet memories galore, memories that in comparison with those of Cynegils and Alfred and Cnut seem recent; memories of the Conqueror and of Rufus, of William of Wykeham, of Henry I, of Matilda and Stephen, of John, of Henry VIII, of Philip of Spain, of Cromwell, of Charles II. Here the first Curfew rang and here *Domesday* was compiled. Here Waltheof, the last hope of Saxon England, was executed, and here the first English Public School was founded. These things stand out. As background, for those that have the imagination to see, are Celtic tribesmen and Roman legionaries, are Saxon berserkers and Danish vikings, are Saxon thegns and Norman barons, are abbots and priors, friars and pilgrims, merchants and gildsmen. Here indeed is a city venerable and rich in association.

To-day, following the motor-roads, you are in Winchester before you see it. The town lies in a hollow and the hills rise so steeply that even the Cathedral is hidden. But the city should be seen from one of the surrounding hills, if the full measure of her age and the full measure of her beauty is to be realized. Stand upon St. Catherine's Hill and look upon Winchester as the sun sets beyond the farther range of hills. Do so if you possibly can upon an October evening, when a mist is rising from the valley and joining hands with the smoke of many chimneys. You will look upon a city of mingled red and grey, and you will see the Cathedral with its heavy tower, and Wykeham's College partly hidden in trees, and the Hospital of St. Cross. You will see it all through a silvery-grey haze that obliterates the slate roofs, and makes of ancient and modern a harmonious whole. You look down upon the birthplace of this England of ours.

Of the original Winchester, the early British town of Caergwent—the Roman Venta Belgarum—we have no record beyond the name. Nor is there much in the way of definite record for some two hundred years after the Roman occupation. During this time the Pict and the Scot in the north, Angle and Jute and Saxon in the south, were fighting for the country; and when at last some order had arisen out of chaos, the Celts had for the most part been driven away (or at least driven from the river valleys) and the Teutons ruled the roost.

Two Germanic tribes had settled in Hampshire. The Jutes had spread westward along the coast from Kent (but they had probably had trading stations hereabouts in Roman times) and conquered the Isle of Wight; one of these Jutish tribes, the *Meonwara*, settled along the easternmost of the Hampshire valleys, the Meon Valley. Side by side with the Jutes came a fiercer tribe, the *Gewissas*, under the leadership of Cerdic and his son Cynric. I have already remarked upon the extraordinary fact that these Saxon leaders should have Welsh names. Cerdic and Cynric made a number of raids along the coast and up the rivers, and were sometimes successful and sometimes defeated, but ultimately they vanquished the local inhabitants and their allies. That was at Charford on the Avon in 519. Cerdic became the King of the West Saxons, ruling over a territory that probably corresponded pretty closely with the Hampshire of the present day. Our authority for all this (except the boundaries) is the *English Chronicle*. Recent research has thrown a good deal of doubt on some of the statements contained therein, and a weighty body of opinion now maintains that the Saxon penetration probably took place along the Thames Valley. Personally I am inclined to

regard the *English Chronicle* as serious history—the com-
pilers lived a good deal nearer the events than we do—and
to accept the idea of penetration from the coast. Not that
it makes much difference now—the point is that there
ultimately evolved a West Saxon Kingdom, fiercely
heathen.

When, at last, Christianity did reach the West Saxons,
it came not from Canterbury but from Rome through a
special mission headed by Birinus. The story of Birinus
has been told by Bede, and (in modernized form) runs thus:

At that time, during the reign of King Kynegils, the
race of West Saxons, anciently termed Gervissas, received the faith of Christ, which was preached to them
by Birinus, who had come to Britain at the instance
of Pope Honorius. His intention had been to proceed
direct into the heart of the land of the Angles, where
as yet no teacher had penetrated, in order there to
sow the seeds of the faith; for which purpose, and by
direction of the Pope himself, he was consecrated
Bishop by Asterius, Bishop of Genoa. But on arrival
in Britain, and coming first into contact with the
Gervissas, he found them everywhere to be in a state
of the grossest heathenism, and so he considered it to
be more profitable to preach the Lord to them, rather
than to go farther to seek a field to labour in.

Actually at the time, A.D. 634, Cynegils had his capital
at Dorchester on the Thames, and it was there in the following year that he was baptized. But Bede implies that
Birinus himself converted Winchester and dedicated a
Christian church there, for he tells us that Birinus placed
his bishop's stool at Dorchester and after years of hard
work,

having erected and dedicated many churches, and
having by his pious ministrations called many to the
Lord, he departed himself to Him and was buried in
that city, and many years after, by the instrumentality
of Bishop Hedda, his body was translated to the city

of Venta and placed in the church of the Blessed Apostles Peter and Paul.

Birinus landed in 634 and converted Cynegils in 635. Cynegils did not erect the church at Winchester, but he founded a monastery there in 643 (the year in which he died) and endowed it with all his lands for several miles around Winchester—a memorable endowment, for some of this land in and about the parish of Chilcomb has remained in the unbroken possession of the church ever since—a matter of some fifteen hundred years. The church itself was built, according to the *English Chronicle*, by his son Cenwalh in 648. (This was not the first church to be built in Winchester. One of the very first churches in England must have stood in just this spot, for we have handed down to us descriptions of a church built by the Roman Lucius in 164. It was destroyed by the Emperor Diocletian at the time when he threatened to destroy Christianity.) Birinus's body and his bishop's stool remained at Dorchester until 676, when both were removed to Winchester. The bones of Cynegils and Cenwalh are traditionally preserved in two of the mortuary chests above the side screens of the choir in the Cathedral, but I am not sure where the bones of St. Birinus are supposed to be. It is from this time, too, that the first mention of the modern name of the city dates, for Bede refers to it as "the city of Venta called by the Saxon people Vintanceastir." And from this time the written record of Winchester runs unbroken to the present day.

For a hundred years or so nothing of importance happened in Winchester. But in 802 Egbert became King of Wessex. Egbert had been at the court of Charlemagne, and he made good use of what he had seen there. A great warrior and a great statesman, he soon impressed the neighbouring states and chieftains, and at a Witan held at Winchester in 827 he proclaimed himself king of one realm which he called Angle-land. So Winchester became the birthplace and capital of England. And so the inscription on the wonderful statue of Alfred the Great, which was erected in 1901, and which reads "To the founder of the Kingdom, Nation, Winchester and the English name" is not strictly accurate, wonderful man though Alfred was. Egbert's remains also are preserved at Winchester in the Cathedral. The inscription on the mortuary chest reads:

Hic rex Egbertus pansat cum rege Kenulpho
Nobis egregia munera uterque tulit.

Egbert was a great man and a great ruler. And he was the founder of a great line of kings—Ethelwulf, Alfred, Edward, Athelstan—each one of whom did much for Winchester and much to make England great. Ethelwulf was very generous to the Church. He granted to her one-tenth of all the royal lands, a grant which has frequently, but erroneously, been described as a grant of tithe. The deed of gift was executed in the Cathedral Church at Winchester, in the presence of the Witan and solemnly laid upon the altar. The original is still preserved in the British Museum. Ethelwulf was a pious man but his reign was anything but peaceful. The Norsemen had begun raiding in Egbert's time, and all through Ethelwulf's reign they came, burning and ravaging and destroying. Ethelwulf died but the attacks went on, and in 860 Southampton was burned and the raiders came up the Itchen and sacked Winchester itself. They did not get away scathless, for Osric the Earldoman with men from Hampshire and Berkshire put them to flight and "had possession of the place of carnage." All the same it was a distressed country, harried to despair by the ceaseless fighting, that Alfred came to rule in 871.

What is a woman that you forsake her,
And the hearth-fire and the home-acre,
To go with the old grey Widow-maker?

Yes, the Widow-maker was busy in England when Alfred ascended the throne of his fathers. But in barely five years the Danes were beaten and peace restored, and though the Danes lived on the one side of Watling Street they lived amicably enough with the Saxons on the other. Alfred set about making his country safe. He built *burhs*, stockaded towns along the coast, and he built a navy of ships "full

*Looking towards the Entrance Gate
and the street, Winchester College*

nigh twice as large, swifter, and steadier and higher" than the long boats of the Vikings. But at heart Alfred was a man of peace, and at his court at Wolvesey he encouraged the pursuits of peace. It was here in the course of eighteen years that he gave to the people law and good government, and it was under his guidance and loving care that Winchester became the home of all the learning and all the arts known at the time. I do not think that it is generally realized that under Alfred Winchester rivalled the earlier splendour of Aachen in the time of Charlemagne, that his court was known all over the civilized world (a small world then, it is true) and had a reputation that has certainly never been approached by any other English court before or since. To Winchester came learned men from every quarter. St. Grimbald, the Prior of St. Bertin's in Picardy, for whom a new minster was to be built in the capital; John the priest, a man of great skill in the arts and a man of great learning; Asser the scribe, Alfred's friend and biographer. And there were others also. The *Chronicle* tells us most graphically of the arrival of a little company of learned men from Ireland in 891:

Three Scots came to Alfred the King, in a boat without oars or rowers, from Hibernia, whence they stole away, because they desired for God's love to be in foreign parts, they cared not where. Their boat was made of two skins and a half, and they took with them food for a sen-night. And about the seventh night came they to Cornwall to land, and thence they went up to Alfred king. And their names were Dunslane, Maccbethu, and Maelinnum.

Alfred, as Kitchin so aptly puts it, made "Winchester the centre of all the learning of the age, the home of the learned, and the little city may well be proud of its place as mother of the intellectual life of the English people." I do not think that that is an exaggeration. And Winchester is still the home of many learned men, and is still a seat of great learning.

But it must not be thought that Alfred was merely the

w

Winchester Cathedral from the college

director of all this. That he was a man of genius, and that he guided the efforts that began the development of the English mind and language is true. But he was more than the guiding spirit; he was also the chief workman. He wrote himself in English and with a remarkable freshness. And he translated freely and vigorously; he gave to the English people a guide to civil life, a geography, a religious philosophy. But his greatest work was undoubtedly the *English Chronicle*, which besides being one of the great histories in the world, is also the mother of the English literary language. This, the first prose book written in English (it was in part penned by Alfred himself) was by his orders chained in the Cathedral Church so that all who could read might read "of adventures and of laws, and of battles, of the land and kings who made laws."

Alfred's last work—the erection of the Newan Mynstre at Winchester—was left unfinished. He had planned it and bought the land, and chosen Grimbald as the first abbot, when he died. "The delight of his people and the dread of his enemies," he was buried in the Cathedral Church. But the fear of his greatness was too strong. The story goes that the canons of the church were frightened, and affirming that his ghost walked and gave them no peace, besought his son Edward to transfer him to the New Minster then building. This was done. Then in 1110 the New Minster was removed to Hyde, and the bones were taken away and reburied in the new Abbey Church. Lastly, in the eighteenth century, the remains of Hyde Abbey were pulled down by the corporation of Winchester to make room for a new Bridewell, and the bones of the noblest and greatest of all English Kings were lost for ever. A little more care, I feel, might have been taken.

Of the new Minster that Alfred founded in the open churchyard on the north side of St. Swithun's Church, and of St. Mary's Abbey, the Nunna-minster, which he founded to the north-east of the Old Minster no trace now remains. The former has been completely swept away, but of the Nun's Minster a few names still remain—Abbey Passage, the Abbey House, the Abbey Mill, which was the mill attached to the Nunnery. For a very long time these three minsters which filled up the south-eastern corner of the city were by far the finest group of buildings in England, and near by was the Palace of Wolvesey, which was at once castle for the defence of the town, school, court of justice, and royal dwelling-house. And of Wolvesey there are still ruins.

I wonder how many of the thousands of visitors to Winchester realize that in medieval times there were two castles within the city walls? There was Winchester Castle, near the West Gate, which was the royal headquarters, and there was Wolvesey Castle, in the south-east corner, which was the episcopal residence. The King's Castle was a Norman building. But Wolvesey Castle, though it was practically rebuilt in the twelfth century by Henry de Blois, was one of a series of official buildings which have stood on the same site since the earliest times. The fact that a Roman pavement of some distinction has been found within the castle precincts shows that it was a house of some considerable importance long before the Saxon kings of Wessex made it their principal palace.

Leland, writing in the sixteenth century, says: "The castelle or palace of Wolvesey is welle tourid and for the most part waterid about." That may seem surprising nowadays. Yet the name by its termination, "*ey*," indicates that the site was an island, and as a fact the river still flows along the eastern wall, and there is still a water-course on the western side. It must once have been a place of great strategic strength. How did it come to be the seat of bishops instead of the palace of kings?

When Cynegils was king at the time that he was received into the Christian Church he was living at Dorchester on the Thames. That was because there was then some idea that Mercia might be annexed to Wessex, and Dorchester was a conveniently central place from which to watch events. Later the royal seat was moved to Winchester as being more central for the government of Wessex only. The bishop moved too, to the monastic house which was attached to the church that Cenwalh built. This was natural because the bishop (Hedda) was adviser to the king in matters ecclesiastical and secular, and the nearer he was to the palace the better. For some time the king and the bishop both lived at Wolvesey, but gradually Winchester became more than the capital of the kingdom of Wessex; it became the seat of kings whose overlordship was recognized as far north as Northumberland. But though the King's authority extended so far, the bishop continued to work only in his own diocese and to live in the royal palace. The King with his added work came to Wolvesey less and less to live, and gradually the building came to be recognized as the residence of the bishop only.

We do not really know what the buildings here in Saxon times looked like. There is in the eastern wall, near the southern end, flint work arranged in the herring-bone pattern which is taken by most antiquaries to be Saxon work, and that is the only bit of Saxon work remaining. The oldest remains now left in the ruins of the castle, save for that small portion, are those of the work of Henry de Blois, who was appointed bishop by his uncle Henry I.

Henry de Blois, one of the most remarkable men of his or any other age, was a grandson of the Conqueror, being a son of the Conqueror's daughter Adela by Stephen Count of Blois. He was originally a monk in the great Abbey of Cluny. This Abbey had immense influence throughout Western Europe because within its walls men received an education that fitted them for almost any job of importance, secular or ecclesiastical. Henry de Blois was such a man. The *Gesta Stephani* says that "Henry, Bishop of Winchester, ranked higher than all the nobles of England in wisdom, in policy, in courage, and in wealth," and another writer says that "he collected treasures both of nature and art." He constructed the treasury in his Cathedral, and he was the first man to collect and enshrine the bones of the early kings and bishops. In 1126 he exchanged the cowl of the monk for the mitre of an abbot, and went to Glastonbury, and it was while he was here that he began to be connected with English politics. Three years later, on the death of William Giffard, he was appointed bishop, but he did not resign his abbacy, but continued to hold both until his death. A few years after his appointment to the see of Winchester he began to build his castle at Wolvesey, or rather to re-build the existing castle. You have only got to look most casually at the existing ruins to see that most of the material has come from some other building. For a long while it was thought that the stones from the Saxon building were re-used. But Nisbet proved conclusively that they were not, that the stones came from the Abbey at Hyde. De Blois and the Abbot of Hyde did not agree, and naturally the Abbot did not get the best of any quarrel with the bishop.

It was at Wolvesey that the Council called by de Blois, acting as Papal Legate, to consider the imprisonment of the bishops of Lincoln, Ely and Salisbury by Stephen was held. This was in 1139. Two years later a conference was held near Winchester at which de Blois agreed to accept Matilda as the rightful sovereign, although Stephen was his brother. However, soon after Matilda had been recognized there was a misunderstanding between the Bishop and the Queen over money. Matilda would not give way, and de Blois left her court at Oxford and returned to Winchester. Matilda followed and took possession of the Royal Castle on the hill, summoning the bishop to attend her. His reply, "I will prepare myself," was carried out in no uncertain manner. He was busy converting his palace into a strong fortress, and he was not quite ready for the hostilities which were then certain to break out and which he had done a good deal to help on the way. De Blois, in fact, thought he had backed the wrong horse, and he now sent for all those who supported Stephen. The *Gesta Stephani* says that "the siege was, therefore, of an extraordinary character, such was unheard of in our days. All England was there in arms with a great conflux of foreigners; and their position against each other was such that the forces engaged in the siege of the Bishop's Castle were themselves besieged by the royal army, which closely hemmed them in from without." But the Bishop won and Matilda's short reign came to an end. On the death of Stephen, de Blois went to Cluny, where he had already sent some of his most valuable possessions. He was a most prudent cleric! One of the first acts of the new King, Henry II, was to order the demolition of the castles of the

313

bishops, and those of the Bishop of Winchester were expressly mentioned. The charges for carrying them out are mentioned in the Pipe Rolls for the year 1155–6. Henry II was taking no chances with the brother of the late king. All the same the demolitions do not appear to have been carried out very thoroughly (perhaps de Blois was still too powerful) for in the seventeenth century we find that the Parliamentarians thought the walls of the Bishop's Keep strong enough to warrant the use of gunpowder to prevent them being held by the Royalists. And the fact that the bishops continued to live here until Bishop Morley again used the old materials to build a new palace proves that it was still perfectly habitable. Quite apart from that, Cardinal Beaufort entertained Henry V here just before the Battle of Agincourt, so it must then have been in very good repair, for Henry V was not the sort of man to put up with poor lodging.

When Bishop Morley erected his great palace facing College Street he left his successors more than they could cope with, for it must be remembered that the Bishops of Winchester were also responsible for the upkeep of Farnham Castle. So Bishop North (1781–1820) pulled down the main portion and only left a wing. Now the Bishops of Winchester are back again in Winchester, living in that wing which during the time that they were living at Farnham was used as a Church House for the Diocese. The modern palace was built from a design by Christopher Wren. His front has gone, but part of his work remains with the Tudor Chapel which has a new east window of great beauty, the work of Christopher Webb. But when we talk of the modern palace we must remember that some at least of the materials with which it was built came from the Conqueror's Palace which was burnt down in 1102, and that some more came from de Blois' Castle. We might remember too that it was here, though not in this actual building, that Philip of Spain and Mary Tudor spent their marriage night.

But we must return to Alfred and the story of Winchester. Alfred was succeeded by his son Edward the Elder. Edward reconquered the *Danelagh* and made England whole again, and it was he who built the New

Minster and had his father's body moved there from the Cathedral. And here, in due course, he himself was buried. And so king succeeded king, Athelstan, Edmund, Edred, Edwy, until we come to Edgar the Peaceable and Magnificent.

We have already come across Edgar in other parts of Hampshire. The monkish chroniclers were never tired of praising him, his virtues, his piety, his magnificence, his generosity to the Church. To them he was a second Solomon. We know that he was a licentious, evil-living man (so of course was Solomon to a large extent), but he seems to have ruled fairly wisely on the whole, though the great Dunstan probably had more to do with that than had Edgar. But Edgar and Dunstan, great as they undoubtedly were in their separate ways, pale to insignificance before Athelwold, saint and builder, who emerges as the dominating figure of the times. Athelwold did a great deal for Winchester. The Danish raids and the continual fighting over more than a century had left the monasteries in a low state. The monastic way of life was not yet established in England, and the places were staffed by non-resident canons. Athelwold gave the canons (most of whom were married and many of whom were not content with a single wife) the choice of accepting the Benedictine rule or departing. We do not know what happened to the ladies, but some of the canons undoubtedly chose religion and discarded their wives, and those that were firmly under control were replaced by Benedictine monks who lived a celibate life in common. These monks brought with them spiritual zeal. Athelwold established a scriptorium in each monastery, and Winchester soon became the centre of a great school of manuscript illumination. Some of the treasures of this school are still to be seen in the British Museum, the library of Winchester Cathedral, the Bodleian Library at Oxford, and at Rouen.

And Athelwold built a new cathedral. He did this about 963 and in the process enlarged the original Saxon church of St. Swithun. The life of St. Athelwold was written by Wolstan, a Benedictine monk and a singer in the Cathedral, in elegiac verse. He gives a full account of the Saxon

315

building, its crypts, its windows, the weathercock which crowned one of the towers, and the organ of which he declared, "like thunder the iron tones batter the ear that everyone stops with his hand his gaping ears"! But Athelwold did more. He gave to Winchester a saint. Swithun, the humble bishop of Egbert's day and perhaps the tutor of Alfred's boyhood, had died in 861, the year after Winchester had been sacked by the Danes, and was buried beneath the turf outside the old Minster. He was buried thus at his own wish. Athelwold raised the remains, enshrined them in a splendid tomb, and brought them into the new Cathedral, which was dedicated to his memory. St. Swithun soon became a popular saint, and pilgrims flocked to Winchester from all over the country. The legend by which he is best known probably arose a good deal later. It is, in any case, a legend by no means peculiar to him. There are at least five other saints in the British Isles credited with some control over the weather (though none of them are quite so generous) and similar legends exist in Italy, Germany, France, Belgium, Hungary and Spain, and probably in a good many other countries as well. Funeral rites have had some connexion with the rain ever since man buried man, and dead men's bones have had some value as rain-makers in many a pagan religion. At the same time legend attaches many miracles to the moving of St. Swithun's bones from their original resting-place, and one of them seems to have had some confirmation. An old smith saw the saint in a vision and heard him rescind his order to be left in the churchyard, and prayed that the iron ring in the coffin might come out if this dream was true. The ring came out at a touch, but when the staple was replaced no one could move it again. During some of the excavations in the time of Dean Kitchen a ring and a staple were discovered just where the saint was reputed to have been buried.

Something of the building of Athelwold can still be seen —the well beneath the altar in the crypt, some fragments of stone in the feretory, and the massive wall on the south side of the Yard to the Slype. The Roman origin of the Cathedral suggested by Rudborne is not of course to be

taken seriously, but a good deal of Roman work has been
found at one time and another and the possibility of an
early Christian church here cannot be discounted. It was,
after all, a Roman town.

Athelwold completed one more gigantic task. He trans-
formed the channels of the Itchen and brought the waters
—and the fish—through the monastery and the town by
fresh channels. Wolstan wrote:

Lucque
Dulcia piscosae flumina traxit aquae
Successusque laci penetrant secreta domorum
Mundantes totum murmiere coenobium.

Such a man was Athelwold—saint, revivalist, builder,
engineer, lover of the arts. He died in 984 and was buried
in the crypt of the Cathedral he had built. We hear very
little of Athelwold. But he was a very great man in very
many ways, a very much greater man than many who
have greater fame in English history.

Trouble came with the accession of Ethelred the Redeless, a man of loose morals and loose counsels. He may be
ignored, but we cannot ignore his Queen Emma, the
daughter of Richard Duke of Normandy, for she was the
central figure in Winchester history for more than fifty
years. Beautiful, fascinating, clever, she was the wife of
two successive kings and the mother of two more. She was
a personality, if not a pleasing one. Ethelred on the day he
married her gave her Winchester and Exeter as a wedding
present. And when he died Cnut married her. Harold,
Cnut's son, took away her treasures and persecuted her:
and Edward the Confessor followed Harold's example. It
was in Winchester that she walked the ploughshares. But
the memory of her is kept alive to-day by the manor of
Godbiete. Queen Emma granted the manor to the Prior
of St. Swithun toll free and tax free for ever. And so within
the limits of Godbiete there developed a sanctuary in the
very heart of the city, where those who had offended the
law in one way or another might take shelter and remain
untouched, for "no mynyster of ye Kinge nether of none

other lords of franchese shall do any execucon wythyn the bounds of ye seid maner, but all only ye mynystours of ye seid Prior and Convent." Cnut died in 1036 and Emma in 1052. Both were buried in the Old Minster and their bones are mingled together in one of the mortuary chests in the Cathedral. But I wonder how many of the tourists, English and American (and the Americans are the most thorough of all tourists) as they pass up the narrow High Street by the Old House of God Begot—now, may the shades of departed monarchs forgive the Corporation! a jeweller's shop—know anything of the Old Lady, Queen Emma, who for half a century controlled this city and much more besides? The ancient House of God Begot is not, of course, a Saxon building. But it is early Tudor and was worthy the most careful preservation. For many years it was a hotel—and a very good one—and when it was offered to let by the Corporation there were many who thought that it should have been scheduled as an ancient monument and put to some worthy use in the interests of the city as a whole. It is too late now. Not that the firm of jewellers have ruined it; they appear to have taken as great care as possible not to spoil it, but it is no good pretending that it is what it was when I was a small boy. It is not.

Of the Saxon city there is very, very little left. Just a bit here and there, indistinct, a background. The Normans were thorough conquerors. They swept it all away. Buildings, laws, language, everything disappeared. But the Normans were not content with a vacuum. If they were great destroyers, they were even greater builders. And Norman Winchester remains, and Norman Winchester, in the great Cathedral, dominates the city even in this twentieth century. To the Saxon no doubt Athelwold's building was the last word. To the Norman it was altogether small and crude. Of Athelwold's Cathedral the crypt remains. Walkelyn, the first Norman bishop, set to work immediately pulling down the old and setting up a new Cathedral, which in its general conception is the Cathedral of to-day, though the limits of the building were enlarged after Walkelyn's death.

The new building was consecrated in 1093 in the presence

of almost every bishop and abbot in England. It was, even for those early Norman builders, very massively built, and its core and part of its actual fabric stand to this day. Of the building of the roof there is an interesting story. Walkelyn applied to the Conqueror for a grant of timber, and was told that he might take from one of his woods—Hempage Wood—as much timber as he could fell and cart away within three days. The Conqueror sadly under-estimated the Bishop. Walkelyn collected together every woodcutter and every carter and every horse that he could lay hands on, and in three days removed every tree in the wood except one. The Conqueror was very annoyed, but the roof was built.

Apart from the reconstruction of the central tower, which, so legend says, collapsed when the body of William Rufus was brought into the Cathedral, no further building was done until Bishop de Lucy succeeded in 1189. He extended the church eastward by adding the retro-choir, and to do so was compelled to build on a water-logged marsh. He made an artificial foundation of beech trunks, embedded them in the peat, laying them horizontally one over the other, and upon this he built. He did his work well, astonishingly well, for those timbers bore their enor-mous burden for 800 years. Towards the end of that time, however, a slow but progressive subsidence made itself apparent at the east end, causing the walls to bulge and fissures to appear. The great Cathedral was sinking into the bog. At the beginning of this century the situation had become really dangerous. There was much consultation in Winchester, and finally a famous engineer, Sir Francis Fox, was called down to meet a very worried Dean and Chapter. He found that in some places the Cathedral had already sunk by more than two feet and that walls and buttresses were leaning, that arches were distorted and great cracks were showing everywhere, even that stones were falling from the roof. Winchester was, in fact, in danger of losing its Cathedral which for 800 years had stood on New Forest beech trunks in a bog. Fox had a pit sunk by the south wall. Eight feet below the turf he found that the masonry stopped and that the beech trunks began. But he found, too, that the walls were in no condition to stand the vibration which would be caused by hammering, and he knew that the marshy foundations would not stand pumping dry. He decided to underpin the Cathedral.

William Walker did the job for him. William Walker was a diver. He worked for more than five years under Winchester Cathedral. The fabric was first strengthened by scaffolding and grouting, a mechanical operation which, reversing the action of a vacuum cleaner, exerts any pressure up to one hundred pounds an inch. This grouting removed dust, 800 years of dust, from the walls, and blew from cracks and crannies bats and rats and mice and house martins and jackdaws and a great many bees. Then water was forced in to clean the walls, and finally a stream of cement was poured into the cracks. That done, the work of underpinning began. Walker went down into the bog. The water was so dark with peat that artificial light was useless. He worked in the darkness, guided by touch alone. He removed the peat handful by handful, and laid down bags of concrete in its place on the gravel bottom. He laid four layers of concrete bags to cut off the water which was then pumped from the pit in which he was working. Then concrete blocks were built on the bags and pinned securely to the underside of the Cathedral. Walker went from pit to pit for more than five years, working always in darkness, until at last, working quite unaided, he had relaid the foundations of Winchester Cathedral, and made them secure. Let me repeat: William Walker relaid the foundations of Winchester Cathedral with his own hands.

On St. Swithun's Day 1093 the Norman Cathedral was consecrated. On St. Swithun's Day 1912 a huge congregation, headed by King George V and his Queen, gathered in the Cathedral to give thanks that this great shrine of England was safe. The Archbishop of Canterbury preached, and his text was "Prosper Thou the work of our hands, O prosper Thou our handiwork." In the congregation was almost every bishop in England, peers and peeresses, scholars, soldiers and sailors, the Prime Minister and many members of his Government. Looking down, yes surely looking down, must have been the great of the past—

kings and princesses and prelates—and those first builders. And in the congregation, sitting there with the King and Queen, was William Walker, diver—and the greatest builder of them all.

You will find his name on the west wall. There should be, I think, some greater memorial to him than that. For though every schoolboy knows the name of Walkelyn, there is scarcely an adult—yes, even in Winchester—who knows the name of William Walker.

The retro-choir that caused all the trouble was built by de Lucy to provide extra accommodation for the pilgrims who were coming in ever-increasing numbers. The pilgrims, if not encouraged, could not be prevented, but they were not welcomed at close quarters, so they had to enter by a door in the north transept, and then had access to the retro-choir, the ambulatory, and the north transept, but the nave and the choir were barred to them by iron gates. If the monks had a low standard of personal cleanliness, personal cleanliness was quite unknown to the pilgrims.

The greatest period of building, the period that saw the transformation of the Cathedral into its present mould, the building of a Cathedral within a Cathedral as it were, was planned and commenced by Bishop Edington in 1346, and completed on a more generous scale by William of Wykeham. This was a colossal task, almost equal in magnitude to the building of the fabric itself. The columns near the choir steps, where the transformation is not complete, show us in some measure how the change was effected, partly by cutting away from the face of the columns and partly by pulling down and rebuilding. The result of the whole was to impart grace and light and to give an added sense of height. The triforium was removed bodily, and the triple series of Norman arches in the elevation were thrown together into a single range of lofty perpendicular arches, surmounted by smaller perpendicular windows, serving as a clerestory. Truly a gigantic task, magnificently accomplished. Willis describes it in his Winchester monograph very succinctly:

The old Norman cathedral was cast nearly throughout

its length and breadth into a new form; the double tier of arches in its peristyle were turned into one, by the removal of the lower arch, and clothed with Caen casings in the Perpendicular style. The old wooden ceilings were replaced with stone vaultings, enriched with elegant carvings and cognisances. Scarcely less than the total rebuilding is involved in this hazardous and expensive operation, carried on during the ten years with a systematic order worthy of remark and imitation.

The impressiveness and beauty of the effect produced by the transformation is quite beyond description. As you enter the west end the majesty of the whole thing is such that it induces in me at least—yes, and even in American tourists—awe-struck silence. There confronting you are massive pillars, and rising above them a forest of lofty pillars and shafts towering up, and then branching out and interlacing in the lovely intricacy of the fan tracery of the roof. William of Wykeham has many memorials to his name up and down the country, but none more splendid than the nave—the longest, by the way, in Europe—of this Cathedral. It is fitting, indeed, that both he and Edingdon should be buried here in the beautiful chantry chapels that they respectively built.

The bishops who succeeded Wykeham continued his tradition. Beaufort, Waynflete, Courtenay, Langton, Fox and Gardiner all added their bit to its splendours, not least among them the magnificence of their own tombs, beautifully painted and beautifully carved, which make an unrivalled array east of the High Altar. The fabric suffered but little at the Reformation, though Cromwell—Thomas, not Oliver—destroyed St. Swithun's shrine. But with the Civil War the troops of that other Cromwell violated the interior, smashing all, or nearly all, the old glass, tearing down the statues and stripping the shrines. The Roundheads were the Nazis of their day. For all that, Winchester remains magnificent—to my mind without peer among the cathedrals of England.

I have heard it said that Winchester is not so impressive

exteriorally as some of our other cathedrals. I should have said myself that it was the most impressive of the lot. It has not so graceful an exterior as some, it is true. But it is certainly impressive, altogether grand. The west front is flat and, perhaps, rather lacking in interest. The long straight roof of the nave is, perhaps, rather monotonous. But the whole with the massive tower gives an impression of stately dignity, of tremendous power that cannot be gainsaid. The lime avenue, the close green turf of the churchyard, the Deanery, the houses in the Close are all beautiful in their quiet serene dignity. The cloisters and the convent buildings lay on the south side, and of them there remains but the Pilgrim's Hall, the Close Wall, the great gate and the church for the lay servitors—the tiny church of St. Swithun perched above the King's Gate just outside the Close.

Of the interior books could be—and have been—written. But no book on Hampshire would be worthy the name that did not deal in some measure with the building that for six hundred years at least was the hub round which the whole country revolved. It is a veritable museum of medieval craftsmanship, a museum of national history, too. A museum—yes; yet a museum at once beautiful and impressive and friendly, a museum not of dead things, but a museum of the living.

First, two facts. It is the longest Cathedral in England: and it covers, *within* its walls, a little over an acre and a half. It is the spaciousness of Winchester that first impresses, and then you are held spellbound by the height and the vastness of the nave. And the more you walk about this great place the more you are held in wonder. The view up the nave is the most beautiful of any in any cathedral in England, or for that matter in Europe. There is nowhere a finer example of English Gothic—and the work is so shapely that it gives no hint of the massive Norman masonry that lies beneath. So wonderful is the moulding that the piers seem fragile, whereas they are actually of a tremendous solidity. The sense of height is ever present, ever insistent, and is due to the tall vaulting shafts which are definitely slender into the clerestory. The panelled spandrels of the main arches are characteristic of Tudor work, and above them is the triforium, which is no more than a section of pierced parapet to each bay, carried on a simple cornice with carved heads and floral bosses. You should sit and look, as well as walk and look. You can sit on an old settle in the south transept. It is an oak settle and it was here in Norman times and on it, no doubt, Norman monks sat and looked at the great building in which they served God. There is much that is Norman still in this Cathedral but there is nothing so intimate as this old oak settle.

In the south transept, too, there is a superb piece of Norman carving on the wall. This is a double arch that once formed a noble entrance to the de Blois treasury. It is built up now and there is a plain doorway, but the two arches with their lace-like carving are just where the Normans put them and they are outstanding as examples of the delicacy with which the Norman mason could work. On the south side the fifth bay is filled with the Perpendicular screenwork of William of Wykeham's chantry. Here is the effigy of the great scholar and builder, supported at the head by angels and at the feet by the three curious little figures of monks, which are supposed to represent his master-mason, master-carpenter and clerk-of-works. In the tenth bay is Bishop Edingdon, whose plan originally it was. On the north side in the sixth bay is the square black font of Tournai marble, on which are carved scenes from the life of St. Nicholas; and in the eleventh is an original Norman pier uncased and untouched from which one may gather a good idea of the skill of the masons employed by William of Wykeham and of the magnitude of the task they undertook and completed so faultlessly.

There are two features in the nave that should not be missed; the medieval minstrels' gallery with its flowered cusps and bosses, resting in arches springing from the piers; and the oldest iron grille in Britain. Flights of steps lead from the transepts to the presbytery aisles. Those on the south side are shut off by this iron grille, which is one of those made to shut off the pilgrims from St. Swithun's shrine. It is remarkable in that it is pure Norman work,

324

dating probably from the eleventh century (at the very latest the early twelfth) and it was probably the earliest metal work to be used in Britain. It is worthy of more than the passing glance that it usually receives. This grille is made up of four pieces of iron work, scrolls branching out from a central stem, forming a mass of quatrefoils. There are 278 rings (I have counted them more than once, and the guide-book statement that there are 264 is wrong) and the general effect is that of ostrich feathers.

The east end of the Cathedral rises nineteen steps above the nave. There is (and I think it unfortunate) an oak screen. The screen itself is a noble piece of work by Sir Gilbert Scott, and taken by itself it would be magnificent, but it breaks the incomparable line of the interior. Were it not there you would have a view of at least 175 yards from east to west. But the screen will not be moved and we must put up with it. Beyond the screen you will find some of the finest medieval stalls in England. They date back to the early fourteenth century—probably to 1300—and they have a large number of carvings of animals and humans, and a lovely series of misericords. Behind each stall is a wide arch with two trefoiled arches below a circle, and the spandrels are enriched with many birds and animals and a mass of foliage. The misereres are older than the canopies, and on them you will find all the things that you expect to find. But you will have some surprises also. There is a bishop in a fool's cap, a monk grinning at an owl, an old woman with a cat and a distaff, a man fighting a wolf, and a simply delightful group of a sow piping away the while her little pigs are munching away apparently enthralled with the music. There are, too, by the way, some excellent carvings in stone in this Cathedral and some of them are amusing, particularly one in the Lady Chapel depicting a choir boy in the act of taking off his surplice, dragging it over his head in the most life-like manner.

The stone screens which border the aisles were added by Bishop Fox early in the sixteenth century, and they are really beautiful with their delicate Perpendicular tracery and Renaissance cornices, which bear the six carved chests that contain the bones of Saxon kings and queens and

Chilcomb Church

bishops which were collected from the crypt. I think that these six chests are the most significant things in England. They have been cleaned and painted in our own time, restored as they were in medieval days. But think what is in them. Here are the bones of the kings who founded this great Cathedral, here are the bones of the first Saxon bishop, here are the bones of a Norman King and the bones of a Danish King. We do not know now which chest contains which king or queen or bishop, for they were opened in the Civil War and the bones got mixed up. There are the remains of twelve people in the six chests, and they are:

Cynegils, King of the West Saxons and the first founder of the Cathedral.

Ethelwulf, King of Wessex and father of Alfred the Great.

Egbert and Kenulph, builders of the first cathedral.

William Rufus, Bishop Stigand, Bishop Wina, and Bishop Alywn.

Eldred, buried by his friend Dunstan, with this inscription: "The pious Eldred rests in this tomb, who admirably well governed this country of the Britons."

Edmund, the eldest son of Alfred, who was crowned in his father's lifetime, and whose chest was inscribed: "Him whom this chest contains, and who swayed the royal sceptre while his father was still living, do Thou, O Christ, receive."

Cnut and Emma, the fair maid of Normandy, on whose original chest were these words: "Here in this chest rests Queen Emma. She was first married to King Ethelred, and afterwards to King Canute: To the former she bare Edward to the latter Hardicanute. She saw all these four kings wielding the sceptre, and thus was the wife and mother of English Kings."

It was Henry de Blois who first gathered together these remains and placed them in chests, but it was Bishop Fox who made the chests that we see now.

Between the stone screens which bear these chests is the great glory of the choir, the original altar screen. It is fifteenth-century work and Beaufort's contribution to the Cathedral, and is pretty well identical in treatment with those at St. Albans and All Souls College, Oxford. But if almost identical in treatment, that is all. It cannot be matched anywhere else. It fills the whole space—1,700 square feet between the pillars—and is awe-inspiring because of its immensity. It is of white stone and arranged in three tiers of canopied niches filled with big and little statues of angels and saints and kings. The canopies have remained more or less intact, but the figures are modern substitutes for those smashed by Cromwell's fanatics. Modern they may be, but unlike so much that is modern they are beautiful, beautifully executed and in perfect keeping with the original work. It would be difficult, indeed, to find anywhere else so remarkable a series of Christian saints as those grouped in effigy around the Saviour here. Here are the four archangels, the Virgin, and St. John, St. Paul and St. Peter. Here are missionaries like Birinus, and bishops like Swithun, Wykeham and Wolsey; teachers like Ambrose, doctors like Jerome; sovereigns like Egbert, Alfred, Athelwold, Cnut and Victoria. Here are Earl Godwine, Izaak Walton, Ken and Keble. Many lie buried within the Cathedral walls, many have left their mark stamped indelibly, and for the most part honourably, upon the city's history as upon the country's history. And of what other building in the country, except Westminster Abbey, could you say the same?

Bishop de Lucy's retro-choir forms a modest and unassuming background for the series of tombs and chantries that are one of the features of the Cathedral. Facing one another across the floor are the chantries of Waynflete and Beaufort. Neither is as beautiful as that of William of Wykeham, and they are very similar in design to one another, Beaufort the prince who so earnestly desired power and Waynflete the pietist, headmaster of Winchester, first headmaster of Eton, and bishop of Winchester. Beaufort, the strong man who schemed, has for company a beautiful

figure of Joan of Arc set up in historical expiation. Waynflete rests alone. Fox's chantry on the south side is most
elaborate in its wealth of carved detail. Bishop Gardiner's
tomb has tracery somewhat after the design of Fox's
screen but is Renaissance in general treatment. And on
the south is Bishop Langton's chantry filled with richly
carved woodwork of the late fifteenth or early sixteenth
century. The majority of the bishops of Winchester have
been buried within the Cathedral walls, but many without
a memorial to mark their tombs. No less than three were
founders of Oxford Colleges, and to the example of one
Eton is due. Winchester can in fact claim to be father of
both Oxford and Eton, for Wykeham, the founder of
Winchester College which itself gave birth to Eton, founded
New College; Waynflete founded Magdalen and Fox Corpus.
Much indeed has sprung from these walls.

And what rare scenes they have witnessed! The corona-
tions of kings, the marriages of kings and queens, the burials
of monarchs and monks, the consecrations of bishops and
the building of their tombs. Here, within these walls, is
the ancient history of England—and the most modern too.
Every yard of wall and pavement bears a legend, drives
home the lesson of Empire and its responsibilities. Side by
side almost without a break are brasses and little statues
and brief announcements—the blood of the history of
England. There is the beautiful memorial to the Portal
brothers of Uganda fame. And there are others: memorials
to colonels and majors and captains and lieutenants who
died at Sebastopol, in Afghanistan, in Africa, at Alma and
Kandahar, at Mons and Gallipoli and Arras. And soon
there will be a lot more. Young men whose names were
the history of England in Norman times, who died for
England at Inkerman and Lucknow, Cawnpore and Mafeking, Mons and Kut. Soon there will be the names of young
men who died at Teruba and Alamein, at Tobruk and
Falaise. There are the names of old men who "having by
God's will been preserved at Alma and Inkerman died of
wounds at Sebastopol"; of young men in a new regiment
called the Artists' Rifles who were only twenty-four years
old when they spewed out their blood at a place they called

Plug Street in order that England might live . . . for what? Soon there will be the names of other young men who died in just the same way for just the same purpose. And there will be no more than twenty years between them. For what? There are the names of men here who died for England on the Nile, in the desert, on the Irrawaddy, in the snows of Russia, in the mud of France, in the deep waters of the Atlantic and Pacific, in the Indian Ocean and in the North Sea and in the English Channel. Soon there will be the names of other young men who will have died in just the same places. There is here more than a history in blood of the British Empire; there is here a history in blood of the folly of men. If this place is a museum to the glory of English youth, it is no less a memorial, everlasting and stupendous, to the folly and greed and conceit of politicians. But what a museum! Here is a window to Jane Austen and next to it a window to the Artists' Rifles. Here is a window to Izaak Walton, here a model of the *Mauretania*, here a window to King George V. Here is the tomb of William of Wykeham and hard by a small brass plate to a subaltern "contributed by officers and men." Here are memorials to scholars and saints, poets and philosophers, soldiers and sailors. Here for all to see is the history of England—in stone and brass, in blood and fire and water, in dysentery and muck and mud—here in this great temple that was built nearly a thousand years ago to the Glory of God, who died upon a Cross that Man might Live.

And now high overhead as you stand outside this temple and look upward you will see machines droning through the sky. They have, too, the shape of the Cross. The cross that will one day see crucified this civilization that so many laboured for so long to build, so many died to preserve.

A mile or so lower down the river is St. Cross—the Hospital of St. Cross. There are some very early records of Hospitals in Winchester—St. Brinstan's was in existence long before the Norman Conquest—but St. Cross is the earliest of those still in existence. It owes its existence to Henry de Blois. De Blois was a most extraordinary character. He was a very great bishop, but he was also an able and scheming politician and an extremely masterful man. He was quarrelsome and ambitious, virtuous and beneficent. As a bishop he is among the greatest that have held the see of Winchester. As a builder of castles he was at least as good a soldier as any of his time. He would help churches and rob them. To further his own ends he would have changed the English Church beyond recognition. He was quite as clever at sitting on the fence as any twentieth-century politician. He was, in fact, a mixture of good and bad. But in his case he proves the old adage wrong. He did much evil, but it is not the evil that has lived after him, it is the good. His memorial is St. Cross.

He founded the hospital to make provision for "thirteen poor men" who were to be housed, boarded and clothed. But he did more than that, for he also arranged for no less than a hundred men to have a good meal given them every day. After his death it did not run on quite the lines that he had intended. There were times when the authorities were far too busy pocketing the income to bother about the poor within the walls. Some of the masters, like Geoffrey de Welleford and Bertrand de Asserio, never came near the place though they lost no opportunity of pocketing the money. St. Cross in fact became a racket. Bishop Edingdon (to whom we owe the proverb, now too little known—Canterbury is the highest rack, but Winchester has the deepest manger) was Master of St. Cross, and he did some rebuilding, but the pensions gradually disappeared. It was William of Wykeham who saved it from falling into complete decay, but he was too busy elsewhere to do much more, and it was left for Cardinal Beaufort to restore de Blois' foundation and to endow a new one—the Brotherhood of Noble Poverty, mainly, it would seem, for his own retainers. During the Wars of the Roses only Bishop Waynflete saved the place from destruction by pleading with the Yorkist leaders, but thereafter, though there was a good deal of trouble and many passing storms which no doubt at the time seemed deadly enough, the place was in no real danger. Mismanagement and the misappropriation of funds did not cease, however, with Beaufort's reforms. There was, in fact, the more to pocket.

And finally, in 1857, after a number of abuses had been brought to light, the whole scheme was revised and placed on its present footing under trustees.

But to return to the original foundation. That was in the year 1136. There is a contemporary record in the *English Chronicle* for the year 1137, which makes interesting reading:

> Then was corn dear, and flesh, and cheese, and butter, for there was none in the land; wretched men starved with hunger . . . some lived on alms which had been erstwhile rich. . . . The earth bare no corn; one might as well have tilled the sea . . . it was said openly that Christ and His saints slept.

It was under such conditions that de Blois endowed the hospital. And it has survived because he did not make it a monastic foundation, and it therefore escaped the attentions of Henry VIII's commissioners. Or rather it did not escape attention, for we find Thomas Cromwell, after the visitation of 1535, advising that "The Master shall in no wise diminish the number of priests, presbyters, sacrists, and others within this House that have been used to minister here on the Foundation or by custom." Thomas Cromwell did not as a rule show such tenderness towards priests or presbyters or sacrists and he showed no tenderness whatsoever towards ancient foundations. I cannot help but wonder what bargain was struck. The purse was deep. Be that as it may, St. Cross survived.

The foundation of St. Cross was due to the early training of de Blois. The relief of the poor was a feature of all Cluniac houses. It was achieved not only by the giving of alms but also by the giving of employment under the supervision of the monks, and by this means the teaching of useful crafts was spread over a wide neighbourhood. As in all religious houses hospitality was also provided for travellers, but the Cluniac houses were much more liberal in this respect than any of the other orders. Every foot-traveller was given a piece of bread (in size about the equal of a modern small loaf) and a generous measure of wine.

And on the death of a monk his portion was for thirty days given to the first poor man that presented himself. All this had been well learned by de Blois, and at Winchester he put it into practice again. Even to-day there is a "Wayfarer's Dole": the tradition remains. If you ask at the buttery hatch in Beaufort's Tower you may still have for the asking ale in a horn and bread upon a wooden platter. The ale is no longer home-brewed and the bread is no longer home-baked. There is not enough ale to quench thirst, barely enough to wet the lips of a grown man; there is not enough bread to banish hunger, certainly nothing like enough to sustain a man from breakfast to supper. You will not find that any tramps or other wayfarers visit the buttery in these days, unless they do so for fun. The visitors nowadays are sleek and well-breeched tourists who think it "quaint" to get something for nothing. And that being so there is no need to provide as de Blois intended provision. The tradition remains and that is the great thing.

St. Cross was once a small village well beyond the city walls. Now it is well within the city, and you turn off the main Southampton road by the Bell Inn and run down a gentle slope to the hospital itself. Or you can go—and it is much the better way—by the river all the way from the old town mill at the foot of the High Street. The entrance gate is magnificent and all the buildings combine to form a really restful picture. Through a gabled archway is a small courtyard across which rises the noble Beaufort Tower, and a lovely green quadrangle. In front is the church, one of the finest specimens—probably the finest—of transitional Norman to be seen in England; on your right is the great Hall and the kitchens, across the lawn the ancient cottages of the brethren with their tall chimneys and mullioned windows, and facing them the long sixteenth-century timbered ambulatory and above it the infirmary, the east window of which opens into the church so that a sick brother might sit there and receive comfort. A doorway in the wall here opens on to a lawn and it was here that Dendy Sadler found the inspiration for his famous pictures of Thursday and Friday.

The church is worth close inspection (preferably without a guide; the St. Cross guides, in my experience, are well-meaning but even more parrot-like than the normal run of their kind) for it is an outstanding example of the transition from the Romanesque Norman to the Early English. I think that there can be no doubt that only the eastern portions of the church, but including the transepts, were the work of de Blois. But even here alterations have been made more than once. For all that there is here the best preserved specimen of the transitional period, and there are some good examples of later styles. The nave and the north porch are Early English, and the west front has much Decorated work. The west window is usually attributed to Bishop Edingdon, who was Master here from 1334–45. I personally find this very difficult to believe, comparing it with the work attributed to him in the Cathedral during his episcopate. And I think that if you go and compare the two you too will find it very hard to believe. There used to be a story that the west window was the work of Sancto Mario, who was Master from 1289–96, and though this is, I understand, discredited by the experts, it seems to me to fit in with the architectural details much better. The Brethren's Houses and the Master's House are the work of Cardinal Beaufort. This Beaufort foundation was evidently intended to provide for members of his own family and their retainers in case they came to grief in the Wars of the Roses. They were Lancastrians, of course. These rooms were not always full, of course (there was money to be made from empty rooms) and sometimes empty rooms were let to strangers at a good rent. The Speaker of the House of Commons at one time in the eighteenth century rented rooms here. The present Master's House, which is outside the hospital proper, is modern.

The Master's garden, which is behind the ambulatory and has a fish stew, must be one of the most beautiful gardens in England. The Brethren also have little gardens divided by a stream which runs beneath little stone bridges and sometimes holds really big trout. The beauty of the Brethren's garden plots depends entirely upon their owner;

some are cared for most lovingly and are as beautiful in their simplicity as any cottage garden anywhere.

Henry de Blois placed St. Cross under the protection of the Knights of St. John of Jerusalem, an order whose special care was the welfare of pilgrims and wayfarers, and the Brethren of St. Cross still wear to this day the eight-pointed cross of the order and the black gown that distinguishes the Knights Hospitallers. The Brethren of the Beaufort extension of Noble Poverty wear the dark red cloak of Beaufort. Modern Winchester knows them as Black Brothers and Red Brothers, and if ever there was a misnomer it is the latter. Die-hard Toryism could not flourish more strongly than among these "Red" brothers.

St. Cross, so near the ceaseless traffic of the Southampton road, has remained peaceful and quiet. Set by the water-meadows of Itchen, it is indeed a haven for the poor and the aged, for those that have found the bitter struggle of life too much for them. One could not but end life serenely here in de Blois' Hospital. And the faces of the inmates are serene.

One cannot leave St. Cross without mention of Anthony Trollope. *The Warden* is, of course, based upon the history of St. Cross. Trollope wrote the novel just when public attention had been drawn to the irregularities in the administration. And there can be no doubt at all that Trollope had studied the early history of the hospital very closely. Hiram's Patch, for example, may well be identified with Oram's Arbour; and so on. How much closer he got to actual characters is a matter of opinion.

St. Cross, although enthusiastic guides will sometimes show you "a leper's window," was never a leper's hospital. There were lepers' hospitals in Winchester, of course. Towards the end of the twelfth century Bishop Toclive founded the Hospital of St. Mary Magdalen on Morn Hill for eighteen lepers. After the Dutch War Charles II used the building to house prisoners, and put the pensioners out in the city. Later this building was pulled down. In the thirteenth century, actually 1289, Alderman John Devonshire founded the Hospital of St. John Baptist. This is one of the oldest charities in the country. There is a lovely old tower at the bottom of the High Street with a charming niche over an archway, and inside the almshouses are set round a smooth lawn. The chapel has been restored (better than most restorations of the period) and the hall is fine but modern. It is, however, altogether a charming place, if without history. And that can only mean that it is unique among old-established charities in having escaped the breath of scandal.

Between St. Cross and the Cathedral is the College. The College of St. Mary was not the first school in England by any means. But it was the first school to be modelled on college lines. The earlier schools had been mere appendages of church or cathedral: Wykeham made his an independent foundation where the boys and their education formed the sole reason for the school's existence. And so he provided the pattern for the public school of to-day—an independent and largely self-governing foundation. And it is, too, to Wykeham that we owe the idea of internal discipline being conducted largely by the boys themselves. No matter what other, and lesser, schools may say, Winchester is the oldest public school in the country. And Winchester is also the Father of Eton. Before Henry VI arranged the statutes of Eton he spent many days in the College of St. Mary at Winchester studying the statutes and learning the methods by which it was run. And the first Headmaster of Eton was Waynflete, Headmaster of Winchester, and afterwards Bishop of Winchester.

The foundation stone was laid on 26 March 1387, nearly nine years after Wykeham had obtained a Bull from Pope Urban VI for "a college of seventy poor scholars, clerks, to live college-wise and study grammar, near the city of Winchester." In the interim the school was started in temporary buildings on St. Giles' Hill. On the morning of 28 March 1393 "at the third hour before noon" it was opened publicly. There was a procession through the meadows on the south side of the town of the newly-appointed Warden, Fellows and Scholars "preceeded by the Cross erect." The buildings were as yet unfinished, but the school was open. Five hundred years later, in 1893, from the same court that had received that first procession there issued forth another, and far larger one, to do honour to the five hundredth anniversary of the founding of the College. There were too many people to worship within the walls of the Founder's Chapel and this time they had to go to the Cathedral. It was fitting that they should do so. Five hundred years of success should be so marked.

Now why did Wykeham found his school? There were plenty of schools in England. There were even schools that might lay some claim to being public schools (whatever that term really means), schools that drew their scholars not only from the city in which they were situated but from the country as a whole, from all parts of the kingdom. There was, for example, St. Peter's School at York, which was in existence long before the birth of Winchester. There was even a school in Winchester, "the High School of the City of Winchester," which was in existence before Wykeham's College and was not killed by it. Why then did Wykeham found a new school? I think that the objects he had in mind when he founded his two great educational establishments at Winchester and Oxford are clear enough. He wanted an educated clergy. The Black Death had left its mark on England in many ways. But it may be said to have left a permanent memorial in the presence at Winchester of St. Mary's College. There were grievous casualties in the clerical army. There was a great "want of clergy." Wykeham designed his two colleges, the one to be the feeder of the other, so that there might pass out into England a steady stream of educated clergy to the greater glory of God. And there can be no doubt at all that he found his model partly in schools already in existence, taking the best points from many, but particularly in Merton College at Oxford. There was some decline in the monastic system at the time, a considerable movement in favour of secularism, and Wykeham was too much a man of the world to ignore such symptoms. He borrowed liberally from Merton. But he was too great a man to be a mere copyist. Merton had a school attached to it as a feeder. Wykeham placed his feeder at Winchester and so gave it a life and an individuality of its own. And yet even this was not quite original, for Bishop Stapledon had already founded a school at Exeter to be a feeder for his college at Oxford.

You might think that we had now destroyed any claim that Wykeham may have had to originality (it used to be thought that Winchester College sprang complete from his brain one night over supper) and any claim that Winchester College may have had to being the first public school. But both claims hold good. For Wykeham made his foundation at Winchester quite independent of his foundation at Oxford, giving it its own government, making it in fact a sister to the Oxford College and not a daughter. And as for the College itself. By selecting the best features from the schools already in existence he made of his own something quite new, something that was destined to be a model; and particularly a model for Eton fifty years later.

And Wykeham was determined that his school should be on a scale much greater than anything yet contemplated. The Warden and thirteen scholars which formed the school at Merton College expanded into a school of one hundred and five. There was a warden, schoolmaster, usher, seventy scholars, ten fellows, three chaplains, three lay clerks, sixteen choristers, and an indefinite number of servants. (The Government of the College was vested in the Warden and Fellows, and this remained unaltered until 1871, when a Governing Body of eleven members was set up. The Warden was appointed for life, and this continued until 1904 when life appointment was abolished.) Wykeham's scholars were chosen in the first place from among his own kin, and after them priority was given to "poor and needy scholars, of good character and well conditioned." There has been a good deal of argument about the meaning of the words *pauperes et indigentes* but it is clear enough that it cannot mean absolute poverty. It must mean something like the *paupertas* of Horace, which indicated a state midway between poverty and affluence. Wykeham in fact intended his school for the middle-class. (*Pauperes et indigentes* would be a good description of the middle-class of the nineteen-forties.) And that this is the right interpretation of the term is shown, I think, by the fact that

337

some of the commoners at the College, though "sons of noble and powerful persons," who were allowed to be educated at the College (though not without payment), occasionally passed into the ranks of scholars. Though they were able to pay their boarding fees they were not barred from classification as "poor and needy." I think that there can be no doubt that Wykeham was catering for the middle class.

In addition to the educating of a specially qualified class of clergy, Wykeham was determined to produce men. Everyone knows the Winchester motto, *Manners makyth Man*. If you take manners in its modern meaning you may well get a shock, particularly from Wykehamists now in their early thirties. Their manners are no better than those of boys from any other public school and as a rule cannot compare with the manners of Etonians. But Wykeham's word was *mores*, and that does not mean manners in the modern sense at all. It means character. And Wykeham interpreted his motto in its widest sense. *Ant disce, ant discede, manet sors, tertia, caedi*—Learn or Leave, or Linger and be Licked. Wykeham was thorough. He knew that what a man depended upon was his character. And Winchester has always given to her sons character in good measure. Men who have left their mark on every generation of England's history since that far-off day when the College was opened are to be found in the roll of pupils. And so may it always be.

The buildings are solid and have little that is ornate about them. If you come straight from the Cathedral Close the first impression is one of austerity. The street is usually sunless, and the fronting wall is high and built of flint and stone and is almost windowless. The oak door is massive. There is the grime of centuries everywhere. It's all pretty gloomy. But the place is not without structural beauty. And once you are through the gateway the beauty of the inside is all the greater because of the reticence of the exterior. Even so it is more a matter of the subtle charm that comes from well-considered proportion than of any outstanding grace of architecture.

The College itself has had a comparatively uneventful

338

history. Cromwell's troops played havoc with the Cathedral and with the Castle and with the Palace, but the College was guarded by Puritan Wykehamists, and two stood on guard with drawn swords beside the founder's tomb in the Cathedral. So the College was saved from the zeal of the Roundhead troopers. Indeed the only serious loss occurred during the latter half of the nineteenth century, when during restorations lists were taken out of the chapel and stored—and disappeared. They have been replaced by facsimiles copied from old rubbings. (Incidentally the interior of the chapel is not so fascinating as the exterior; it has been greatly altered and has not the charm of the outer walls.) If you look upon these rubbings you will see the names of famous men who were once small boys in this great school. I like to think of them as small boys rather than as great men. Especially do I like to think of Bishop Ken, the brother-in-law of Izaak Walton. Here on a stone on a buttress in the cloisters you can see cut "Tho. Ken 1646." A small boy following the immemorial custom of the English, carving his name where no name-carving should be. "Tho. Ken" . . . that Bishop Ken "who would not give poor Nelly a lodging" when Charles II brought her to Winchester.

There are all sorts of pleasing memories like that. You go through the Outer Gateway and then under Middle Gate and into Chamber Court, and you are immediately in the Middle Ages. There over Middle Gate is the figure of "Sainte Mary." Scholars used to doff their hats to the Virgin as they crossed the quad. I believe that they still do—when they remember. Indeed wherever you go, chapel, Fromond's chantry, Hall, the place is as crowded with history as it well could be, almost as crowded as the Cathedral. And especially the cloister in memory of the 500 Wykehamists who gave their lives in the first German War.

This memorial is one of the most noble and inspiring of all the many war memorials in the country, equal, I think, to that miracle at Edinburgh. It is the work of Sir Herbert Baker and almost every one of the men who worked under him was a Winchester man. There is real craftsmanship here, work done in a humble spirit to the Glory of God, work that is fit to take its place beside the work of the great masters of the fourteenth and fifteenth centuries.

It stands, this memorial, between Kingsgate Street and the Meads. You come to it through the Boer War Gate into a small forecourt where a stone tablet is set in the old wall inscribed with the immortal words of John Bunyan, tinker:

Then, said he, My sword I give to him that shall succeed me in my pilgrimage, and my courage and skill to him that can get it; my marks and scars I carry with me, to be a witness for me that I have fought His battles; who will now be my rewarder. So he passed over, and all the trumpets sounded for him on the other side.

There are four lion heads in the old wall of this court. In the cloister the four paved ways meet between the grass squares at a stone column crowned with a cross, and guarded by two crusaders facing east and west. Round the outer walls, set in the background of flints, are these words:

Thanks be to God for the service of these five hundred Wykehamists, who were found faithful unto death amid the manifold chances of the Great War. In the day of battle they forgat not God, who created them to do His will, nor their country, the stronghold of freedom, nor their school, the mother of godliness and discipline. Strong in this threefold faith, they went forth from home and kindred to the battlefields of the world, and treading the path of duty and sacrifice laid down their lives for mankind. Thou, therefore, for whom they died, seek not thine own, but serve as they served, and in peace or in war bear thyself ever as Christ's soldier, gentle in all things, valiant in action, steadfast in adversity.

In the spaces between the arches of the four walls there

340

Corhampton Church, a Saxon
Church on a prehistoric mound

are the arms of the Navy and the various National forces, and the symbols of the various aspects of life and government. The four corners are covered with domes dedicated to the Dominions and India, and in the pavements below the domes are round stones quarried in the dominions and inlaid with brass symbols. The badges of the 120 regiments in which the 500 served are blazoned on the corbels and beams of the roof, and there are four badges, belonging to those regiments that are closely associated with Winchester, carried by angels on the oak struts of the roof. Looking across the cloister from the north wall is the angel of Victory, and looking from the south wall is the angel of Peace and Plenty. In the floor at the gateway into the Meads there are four stones from the ruins of Ypres. In other pavements there are: an anchor of granite brought from Table Mountain, crosses in stone from Australia and New Zealand, the Great Bear carved in marble from British Columbia, the Star of India carved in marble from New Delhi. On the walls there are engraved camels for Arabia, the Zimbabwe Bird, a Pacific canoe, a fully rigged ship (an East Indiaman), St. George and the Dragon, a rhinoceros and a snake, a peacock with tail spread, palm trees, the sacred rivers of the East, and other symbols for all those other parts of the world in which Wykehamists fell for Britain. And on the inside walls are the names on great tablets of the five hundred.

There is one thing in the College that should not be missed. That is the Library, one of two great libraries in the city. The library of the College is a store-house of book craftsmanship through the ages, but I think that the most wonderful thing in it really is a clock, for here is craftsmanship that the ancients could not have attempted. The style of the clock is by Sir Herbert Baker, and the works are by Mr. Henry Baker and Mr. Robert Stewart. It is an Empire Clock. There are two dials; the inner one is a twelve-hour clock, the outer a twenty-four-hour clock, and the time is shown at Greenwich and throughout the Empire. Above the great face is Phœbus Apollo with the horses of the sun, riding in splendour at the hour of noon. Below is Selene sleeping in her crescent moon at midnight.

View of Alton High Street
from near the library

But quite apart from beauty the clock is a marvel of mechanical ingenuity. The various time zones are marked by symbols—the lion represents Greenwich time, the Springbok and the protea flower South Africa, the Great Star of India for India and a peacock's feather for Burma, the stars of the Southern Cross for Australia and New Zealand, for Singapore an anchor, for Canada a maple leaf, and a three-master for the Pacific Ocean, for the United Kingdom the leek and the shamrock and the rose and the thistle, a fish for Newfoundland, and a two-master for the Atlantic Ocean. The movement of the clock is controlled by an electric engine running at a constant speed of 120 revolutions a minute. I have been told that there are 13,000 ball bearings in the machine. I can well believe it.

The Cathedral library was built just after the Great Fire of London and is reached by a wooden stairway from the south transept. Here there are treasures covering a thousand years. There is a charter signed by King Ethelwulf and his young son Alfred, who was to become Alfred the Great. There is an eleventh-century copy of Bede and a twelfth-century copy of the life of Edward the Confessor. But the greatest and rarest of all the many treasures in this library is a Bible of the twelfth century written in three volumes on vellum. Superbly illuminated, this Bible is the finest known work of the Winchester school of craftsmen. It was considered a masterpiece even in its own day, and now it is a masterpiece such as you will see nowhere else in the world. Of Anglo-Saxon art there is a Benedictional produced for Bishop Ethelwold in the tenth century, which has twenty-eight miniatures every one of which is the earliest known treatment of its subject in English art. Of later treasures there is the original Cathedral Charter of Henry V and some early books with their chains. And of what should properly be called museum treasures there are the episcopal staff and ring of Bishop Fox, the ring of Bishop Gardiner, and a ring set with a sapphire, which was found in the tomb that was supposed to be that of William Rufus, and which shows pretty clearly that the tomb was that of Bishop Henry de Blois. Very few people go to the Cathedral Library, which is probably quite a good thing.

On the high ground at the south-west of the city is the Castle Hall, which you may visit free of charge on week-days and which seems to be visited mainly by Americans. Only the Hall is left; the rest of the Norman stronghold was destroyed by Cromwell's soldiers. The interior is magnificent, and again full of history and crowded with memories. Here Parliament met, one as early as 1265, within a year of the death of De Montfort, the inventor of the representative assembly (and little did he think that he was giving to the English people a never-ending subject for gossip and grumble and bitterness and amusement and thankfulness). Here weighty statutes have been framed, and here justice has been dispensed, and hard by still is. Two famous trials were staged in this hall—those of Sir Walter Raleigh and Dame Alicia Lisle. Raleigh's was but a travesty of justice, a mere bag of tricks and lies. As he wrote to his wife:

All my good turns forgotten, all my errors revived and expounded to an extremity of ill. All my services, hazards and expenses for my country . . . plantings, fights, councils, and whatsoever else . . . malice hath now covered over. I am made an enemy and traitor by the word of an unworthy man. He hath proclaimed me to be a partaker of his vain imaginings, notwith-standing the whole course of my life hath proved to the contrary, as my death shall approve it.

But eighty-two years later, even that travesty of justice was excelled when Judge Jeffries, foul-mouthed and cruel, condemned the aged wife of John Lisle to a shameful death.

And here hangs King Arthur's Round Table. Be it what it may—and it is certainly not King Arthur's Round Table —it is a treasure of unique interest, and is possibly eight hundred years old. When Caxton published *Morte d'Arthur* and quoted this table in proof of the story, there were even in the uncritical fifteenth century those who were doubtful.

But it was sufficiently a curiosity in 1522 for Henry VIII to show it to his guest the Emperor Charles V. We are told that the paintings which were then much worn were refurbished for the occasion. Now there are bullet holes in it caused by the soldiers of Cromwell.

Adjoining the Castle Hall is the West Gate, one of the two gates still standing. This was formerly a blockhouse as well as a gate and later was used as a prison. It is now a museum and admission is free. Perhaps because of that very few people seem to enter. I have been going there pretty regularly for more than thirty years and I have always been the only visitor, except once in the last war when I was joined by two American negro soldiers. (These later, finding that I knew something about the city, managed by some means strange to me to collect some more of their countrymen, and the afternoon ended with myself conducting a party of forty-three negroes round Winchester, and having an amazingly good supper with them too.) As a prison the West Gate was used for debtors and other "small-time" criminals, and vagrants were stowed away in the Black Hole by the stairway that leads to the room above the Gate. The prisoners did not have a pleasant time. Men and women were herded together, and no one minded in the least what happened to them as long as they did not escape. The room over the Gate was turned into a museum in 1898. Before that it had been an annexe to a public house, the Plume of Feathers, and this alone had saved it from destruction at the hands of the city council. It is a low room—"a valuable specimen of the military architecture of Henry III"—and in the west wall there are two loop-holes. The walls are rough and on them hang curios in the shape of fetters and weapons. Personally I find it a remarkably dull museum with only two things of more than passing interest—a set of standard weights, which includes the famous bushel and which must surely be unique, and the Moot Horn, the largest and oldest in England—and I go to the museum not to look at the things in it but to look out of it, for it has the finest view of Winchester and the narrow High Street and St. Giles' Hill.

St. Giles' Hill is on the eastern outskirts of the city and from the top of it you can get quite a pleasing view of the whole. It was here that the Conqueror caused to be executed Waltheof, the last hope of the old Saxon regime. Legend has it that he was betrayed by his treacherous Norman wife. He certainly plotted against the Conqueror and William was not the man to plot against and be found out. Anyway it was very foolish of him, having married a Norman wife, to plot against the Normans. Legend also says that he was saying the Lord's Prayer as the headsman struck, and that as the severed head bounced from the trunk the lips were still moving and the words "But deliver us from evil" were distinctly heard by those who had gathered round to see the fun. Waltheof may have been a fool, but he must also have been a hero to have given rise to such a legend. But St. Giles' Hill is better known for St. Giles' Fair. I do not know when the fair started, but it was certainly well-established long before the Conqueror came, for William gave it to Walkelyn, who was then engaged on the building of the Cathedral. In later years it became famous not only throughout England but throughout Europe, and when Piers Plowman "went to the fair" at the end of the fourteenth century it was one of the great events of the English year.

It was then a great city in wood, a very much busier city than the stone one in the valley below. Here were streets —the Pottery, the Drapery, Bristol Street, Flemings' Street—and here were the men and women of all nations and all tongues, English, French, Irish, Scots, Venetians, Genoese, Poles, Saxons, Prussians, Danes, Muscovites, perhaps even Turks and Chinese and Moors and negroes, certainly many Jews. There was then much babble, huckstering and gesticulating. Men traded honestly with hard-bargaining with the local countrymen, with the merchants from far distant towns; and there were ballad-singers and contortionists and jugglers; and mountebanks and thieves and murderers. The world came to St. Giles' Hill six hundred years ago. And in control of the world were the bishop's bailiffs on the watch for cut-purses and deficient weights. For on the eve of St. Giles' Fair the keys of the city of Winchester were handed to the bishop's deputy and for the sixteen days of the fair (originally it was but three) the bishop's officers held the city gates and controlled the city life and the life of the country for miles around. They prohibited all trade in Winchester and for seven leagues in every direction from Winchester (which was the cause of much complaining in Southampton) for the bishop was a strong believer in making hay while the sun shone. Not altogether surprisingly this was the root of a good many quarrels between the episcopal authorities and the civil authorities. Of this there is ample evidence, among other things a parchment bearing the red seal of Bishop Waynflete, with details of a dispute between the bishop and the mayor over the customs and franchises of St. Giles' Fair in 1451. But at this date the fair was already in decline. For a few years a fair on St. Mary Magdalen Hill, about a mile to the east, was a popular and successful rival, but the greatness of Winchester as a trading centre was drawing rapidly to a close. To-day the object for which fairs came into existence no longer exists. St. Giles' Fair has joined other Winchester memories. There is still a St. Giles' Fair—a poor emasculated thing of roundabouts and pin-tables—but it is no different from any other so-called fair anywhere else in the country.

There is in fact nothing about the view from the West Gate to suggest the ancient Winchester unless you have some imagination. There is nothing to bring to mind Waltheof being led out to execution; or the Empress Matilda escaping to Ludgershall, carried in a coffin from the Castle where she had been held for seven long weeks; or the great Emperor Charles V coming on his state visit to Henry VIII; or Philip of Spain arriving for his marriage to Mary in the Cathedral; nothing of pageantry and romance and gallantry and history and tragedy. In the room you can sense all these things; in the Cathedral and the College, in St. Cross and by Wolvesey ruins; even here and there in the streets—in Jewry Street that recalls the ghetto, in Staple Garden where the Tron of the Wool Staple was kept in the days when Winchester was the town where the wool trade of the south of England centred; but there is none of them in view, Cromwell's fanatics saw to that, and what they left the City Council got rid of. The East Gate, because it interfered with traffic; the tomb of Alfred the Great, because—well, presumably because it was useless; many valuable records because nobody bothered. The City Cross itself was condemned, but this did arouse popular indignation and the Cross still stands. The record of the City Council in Georgian times was little short of criminal and has left the oldest city in England with but a fragmentary record of its history. There are many old records and many scraps of old buildings, but Winchester is in the main a city of associations.

And you do not see associations as you look down from the West Gate. You see traffic lights, and pedestrian crossings. You see an endless and very congested stream of traffic, which is, I think, as it should be, despite the delay and discomfort it not infrequently causes me, for Winchester has from the earliest times been a great junction, receiving and distributing traffic.

The City Council does not agree. A by-pass has been built. It is, I believe, a good by-pass as by-passes go. It scars the country-side horribly and it has been made on the wrong side of the town, but it does take the traffic away from the town and relieve the narrow streets. It takes a lot of money away from the town also. And by-passes are dangerous. They attract a peculiarly horrible type of house, and they attract them, as manure attracts flies, in large numbers. Think—if you can bear to do so—of the Kingston and Barnet by-passes for a moment. They should be sufficient warning. But such is the greed of man that I fear for the Winchester by-pass and the lovely country through which it travels. Building around Winchester proceeds apace. To all intents and purposes Otterbourne, once an attractive little hill-top village (yes; I well remember it so) is now attached to Winchester on the one side and to Chandler's Ford on the other, and Chandler's Ford is to all intents and purposes attached to Southampton. And on the other side Eastleigh (and I can remember almost all the modern Eastleigh being built) has stretched out its tentacles to embrace Allbrook, and Allbrook is now

347

joined on to Otterbourne. It was grand country once. I used to catch butterflies where now is a large printing works. I used to get the Purple Emperor where now are many mean houses. But why go on? This is progress.

All the same I view that by-pass with misgiving.

CHAPTER XII

THE MEON VALLEY

NEAR the mouth of the Meon River lies the old town of Titchfield. Once it was a much more important place than near-by Fareham (where once playing cricket I caught some of the largest and hungriest fleas it has ever been my misfortune to encounter), but now it is really no more than a large and attractive village. Hampshire has a number such, Georgian or Stuart, that seem to have escaped the bustle and urge of modern life and linger on peaceful and quiet. But Titchfield had a market in *Domesday*, and once the parish reached as far as Wickham and Warsash, where the Crab and Lobster Inn tells every visitor what the sole industry is. The parish is smaller now, but it still reaches to the mouth of the Meon and includes Titchfield Haven.

The streets are wide and the houses charming, and the beamed gateway at the end of East Street is worth going miles to see. Part of the Norman church stands to this day, and, indeed, parts of it are older even than the Normans. The base of the tower has at the corners exceptionally fine long and short work, and that indicates the work of the Saxons; and if you go up the outer stairway leading to the upper tower, you will notice (if you keep your eyes open) at the head of the first stage a course of Roman bricks, three deep and laid round the four sides. These bricks have been used three times by builders, by Romans and Saxons and Normans, and it is quite possible that they were here before there was a Christian church at all. The Norman doorway is one of the best in the county. It is built of huge blocks of stone, and they bear the consecration crosses of five abbots. Inside the doorway, leading into the porch, there are two finely wrought iron gates bearing the date 1651, and they were probably made at the old iron mills on the river near by. The curved shingle spire was added in the fifteenth century.

The memorial chapel of the Southampton family was built in accordance with the will of the second Earl, who left £1,000 for the purpose. (At 1946 values that £1,000 would be worth about £24,000!!) The tomb is one of the finest in all England. It rises magnificent from the middle of the floor, gleaming alabaster and many-coloured marble. On the raised central part lies Jane, the first Countess, and below are her husband and their son, the second Earl, who put up the memorial. There are also his two sisters, his daughter and his son, a sculptured group in striking contrast to the simplicity of a little figure close by. This is the Lady Mary, the daughter of Shakespeare's friend and patron, who died at the age of four.

There is always some argument as to whether Shakespeare visited his patron here. That the third Earl was his patron is beyond question—*Venus and Adonis* and *The Rape of Lucrece* are dedicated to him—but were they on such terms that the playwright would come to stay with the Earl? There is a local tradition connecting Shakespeare with the place—that here in the wooing of Elizabeth Vernon by the third Earl, Shakespeare found the plot of *Romeo and Juliet*. He may have done so, but there were plenty of other wooings that would have suited his purpose just as well. That must remain tradition, a pretty tradition, but no more. Yet I think that there can be no doubt that Shakespeare came here to stay, and the proof is to be found in the Parish Registers. You will remember, in *The Merchant of Venice*, old and young Gobbo. It is a curious name. Get the Vicar to show you the Parish Registers. There in the year 1593 you will find that there was buried here one Augustine Gobbo. And *The Merchant of Venice* was not written until 1596. Oh yes, I think that there can be no doubt that Shakespeare came to Titchfield. (Incidentally the name Gobbo occurs in the register later on: William Gobbo was married here in 1637. And the name is not dead in Hampshire yet—not long before the war I played cricket against a village side that contained two men of the name. It is a relic, of course, of the days when the Venetian galleys came to Southampton.)

There is one other piece of history here in the church that

is not usual for a church. Hanging on the wall of the Southampton Chapel is an old flag. It is the first Union Jack that flew over Government House in Pretoria, and it was set there by Lord Roberts at the end of the Boer War. The then Vicar of Titchfield was chaplain to Lord Roberts and he rescued (is that the right word, I wonder?) the flag for his village.

But the real history here is, as one might expect, a ruin —the ruins of the home of the Earls of Southampton standing on the ruins of the Abbey of Titchfield. At the Dissolution Henry VIII gave the Abbey to Thomas Wriothesley, Earl of Southampton, as a reward for his help in the King's "Great Business" (which was how he termed the getting rid of Catherine). Wriothesley was one of the cruel men of Tudor or any other times, and one of the worst men to rise to power in England in all her history. He "converted" the Abbey into his home—"a right stately home embattled" as Leland says—in other words he pulled it down and built Place House with its stones. Titchfield Abbey was the last house of the White Canons to be established in England. By the Premonasterian rule a great deal of time was devoted to reading, and the library was an important feature of the house. Here at Titchfield was one of the finest monastic libraries in England, containing some 224 volumes. At the Dissolution these volumes were conspicuous by their absence!

Place House, too, is now a ruin—a ruin that is the care of the Government. On the death of the fourth Earl of Southampton his estate was divided up between his co-heiresses and ultimately the property came into the hands of the Delme family. The Delmes preferred the Cams Hall to the old Place House, and they used the latter as a quarry when they rebuilt the Fareham House, so that now there is but a shell standing.

To Place House came Edward VI on his way to Portsmouth. To Place House came Mary and Elizabeth. To Place House came Charles I, on his way to Carisbrooke and the final tragedy. He came as 12 November 1647 was drawing to a close. He came with one faithful friend, Colonel Legge, and he came tired, for he had ridden fast and far. On the previous night, which had been dark and windy, the King had left his cloak in the gallery and stolen down the back stairs at Hampton Court with Colonel Legge to join at the gate two other loyal and trustworthy men, John Ashburnham and Sir John Berkeley. They passed through the garden and crossed the river at Thames Ditton. A relay of horses had been sent on the day before to Bishop's Sutton near Alresford. The little party rode south-west through Windsor Forest and "in the dark, cloudy, rainy night" lost their way for more than ten miles, according to Sir Richard Bulstrode, who says that the next morning they found themselves at Farnham. When they reached the inn at Bishop's Sutton—probably the present Ship Inn —they found that the Hampshire Parliamentary Committee was holding a meeting there. That meant that "Idle Dick Norton" was there, and he was the intimate friend of Cromwell, and the very last thing to do would be to fall into the hands of such a man. And so they pushed on, wearied as they were. And then came the memorable and fatal council. "Walking down the next hill, and holding our horses in our hands," they decided that Berkeley and Ashburnham should make their way to Carisbrooke via Lymington to sound Colonel Robert Hammond as to what treatment the King might expect at his hands. Ashburn-ham had spoken to Hammond some while before and the Colonel had said that he was going to the Isle of Wight "because he found that the army was resolved to break all promises with the King, and that he would have nothing to do with such perfidious actions." Apparently this had made Ashburnham think that Hammond might be disposed to treat the King well, perhaps even more than that. It was, as we have seen, a sad misjudgment of character. The original idea on leaving Hampton Court had been to go to the Isle of Wight and to hide in the house of Sir John Oglander until arrangements could be made. Oglander was a gentleman and a loyal Englishman, and that plan, if followed, might have turned out very differently for the King. However, Ashburnham and Berkeley went to Lymington and thence to Carisbrooke, and from there to Newport where finally they caught up with Hammond.

In the meanwhile the King and Colonel Legge went to Titchfield to the home of the Earl of Southampton. They were received with great joy by the old Countess. Clarendon says of her son: "The Earl of Southampton was indeed a great man in all respects, and brought much reputation to the royal cause." And that though he "was small in stature, his courage and all his other faculties very great." It was he who watched the King's body after execution, and saw the entry of a muffled figure, whom he believed to be Cromwell, and who said "Stern necessity." So said Hitler at the time of the Blood Bath and the murder of his friends. This too was murder, for the trial was a farce (as big a farce as the trial of Mihailovitch by Tito) and the King was to be done to death, trial or no trial.

Ashburnham and Berkeley, no match for Hammond in the battle of wits, returned with him to Place House. When Ashburnham went upstairs to tell the King that Hammond was below, the King, striking himself on the breast, exclaimed: "What! have you brought Hammond with you? Oh, Jack, you have undone me; for I am by this means made fast from stirring!" Ashburnham offered to go down and "get rid" of Hammond, but the King would be no party to murder, and surrendered himself to Hammond. He had spent his last night in freedom. Had the whole affair not been so hopelessly bungled he might easily have got over to France.

It is a good thing, I think, that Place House is a ruin. For more was lost that night than the head of a King.

But we must leave Titchfield and go up the Meon Valley. I am not a Meon man myself, though for a while I lived in the valley, but I must admit that this part of Hampshire, the valley and the highlands to the east of it and the hills to the west, this south-eastern division of Hampshire contains some of the finest country in the county, or for the matter of that in the south of England.

Inland from Titchfield lies Wickham, a most picturesque village with its large broad Place, where tourneys were held of old. It is a village without architectural order. There are houses round the Place of every known style and period, but the whole effect is just as it ought to be, nothing jars at all. And Wickham has no history at all, yet has a place in English History held by no other village in the country. For it was here that the great William was born and it was from this little quiet village that he took his name. I have called it a village and quiet; and so it is. But what is a village, when does a village cease to be a village and become a town? In Hampshire, at any rate, it is very difficult to distinguish between the two. Take Odiham: Odiham has a population of about two thousand five hundred, and it is quite definitely a town, and so is Bishop's Waltham, which is close to Wickham, and so is Whitchurch. All three are towns. But Overton and Wickham, which have very much the same population as Odiham, are villages. Large villages perhaps, but still villages.

Bishop's Waltham, which, if not quite in the Meon Valley, belongs to this part of Hampshire, is old and has nice narrow streets and an imposing ruin in the form of Henry de Blois' Palace. But it is quite the most moribund place in the whole county. It has a railway which no longer functions, and it has no more life in it than a small Wiltshire hamlet. But it is a town. Wickham, though quiet, is a centre for many buses, and has a railway which still functions though not very frequently, but it is a village. And that is in keeping with the area. The Meon Valley is a valley of villages, all of them lovely and all of them small. Droxford, Soberton, Meonstoke, Warnford, Corhampton, West Meon, East Meon, Privet, Tisted, Faringdon, and so to Alton. Through them runs the little Meon, which is quite the prettiest stream in the county and provides the most difficult fishing of any chalk stream that I know. Happily the fish do not run large and so there is not the insistent demand for water that has put the Test and the Itchen out of reach of all but wealthy men. It is indeed a stream to linger by for it runs through a narrow valley between steep hills and it is well wooded all the way. There is Beacon Hill, with woods hanging from one side, and opposite there is Old Winchester Hill with the dark lines of an ancient camp searing the turf at the crest. These two hills guard as it were the entrance to the highlands beyond. Pass them and you are again in chalk country. Just before you come to them as you travel north are the three villages of Droxford, Meonstoke and Corhampton, with which one might well join Exton. Izaak Walton was the father-in-law of the Rector of Droxford, and it was in Droxford that he spent much of his last years, and fished the clear waters of Meon. Meonstoke on slightly higher ground has a pleasant church with a black marble font, but its chief record in fame must be its casualty list in the First German War. It is a tiny place but twenty-two of its young men died in that war, and five others were seriously wounded. There is a village in the Cotswolds which sent eighteen men and one woman to that war and they all came back safely. Meonstoke sent thirty young men and two women. One man came back unharmed only, for in addition to the twenty-two killed and five seriously wounded, two were slightly wounded and both the young women were drowned when a hospital ship was torpedoed. I wonder if there is another village in all Britain with such a tragic record?

Just over the river is Corhampton. Corhampton must be visited for its church. In our own times a stockaded village has been found here, and its church is said to be the oldest in Hampshire. Yet it does not appear in *Domesday*! For all that there can be no doubt that it is a Saxon church, more than that it is pure Saxon with the exception of the chancel wall. Who founded it and when is anybody's guess, but the most popular theory is that it was built by Wilfrid when he came here to convert the Jutes. It has too a sundial which is at least 950 years old, and may be a good deal more. At any rate people were telling the time by this sundial before the Conqueror came, and perhaps before he was born. Now you cannot tell the time by it because it has lost its hand. One stone within the church, the priest's seat by the altar, which was later used as a sanctuary seat, is Saxon, and so is the altar, which is the original stone that was there when the church was first built. Of the font there is some doubt. It may be Saxon, but the single band of cable moulding round it suggests that it was the work of some very early Norman craftsman. In the churchyard is an old yew—a thousand years old, like all churchyard yews—which is 36 feet round the trunk and which is probably a good deal more than a thousand years old in fact. Near by, if they have not moved it, is a huge stone coffin. And this is pre-Saxon. It was dug up in a field in Meonstoke in 1917 and is the coffin of a Roman—the villagers will tell you that it is the coffin of a Roman centurion—and there was within it the skeleton of a very tall man. The coffin, empty now, still retains its lead lining.

Further up the valley is Warnford. Warnford Park is an ugly house—a stronger adjective might well be used—but here the river widens to a biggish pool, and is exceptionally pretty. I have fond memories of Warnford. Here I have collected different kinds of dragon-flies—you get both the big black and yellow ones here (the only place outside the New Forest that I know) and here also you may find the very rare orange and green one—and it was here that I found Leisler's Bat for the first time, and watched a colony of Noctules through four seasons. And here in the migration season you may come across strange waterfowl resting on their way southwards in the autumn. For some reason they never seem to come during the spring. The small church by the ruins of a Norman manor-house of the de Ports in the Park grounds was founded by Wilfrid, and though most of the present building is Norman there are some Saxon stones and a sundial like the one at Corhampton. There are Latin inscriptions in the south porch and on the north wall:

> Adam hic de Portu, solis benedicat ab ortu
> Gens cruce signata, per quem sum sic renovata
>
> Frates orate, prece vestra sanctificate
> Templi factores, seniores et juniores
> Wilfrid fundavit, bonus Adam sic renovavit.

which Gatehouse translated (somewhat freely):

> Good folks, in yr devotions ev'ry day
> For Adam Port, who thus repaired me pray.

View between Selborne and Petersfield

All you that come here
Bestow a kind pray'r
On the churches builders,
Both youngers and elders;
What pious Wilfrid raised
Good Adam increased.

Inside the church there is a Norman font, and some lovely
fifteenth-century benches and the magnificent tomb of Sir
Thomas Neale, who died in 1621, and who lies by his two
wives. He is in armour and his beard flows over his ruff,
and his wives are in their best clothes. There are nine
children. His knight's coat-of-arms is flanked by Faith and
Charity, but there seems to have been little charity about
the gentleman, judging by his epitaph.

The marbles that adorn this mournful tombe
Doe sweat their vocal teares tho they be dombe
And every change of weather do portend
What pious mind should doe at such an ende
Then let each one that seeth this with an eye
Quite void of moisture be turned stone and dry.

Warnford is still an exceptionally damp place, though not
quite so bad as the rhyme by Lord Clanricarde would
suggest

Oh what a blundering Irish dog
Who calls this a mount, when 'tis but a bog.

It is not a bog now, for the marshes have been drained, but
you have only got to be here after heavy rain to understand
what it was like before the draining. Indeed, I have sometimes wondered about that draining.

West Meon has some nice gables and thatch and tile and a
quantity of lovely old timber, and little else. But here lies
the body of Thomas Lord, and it is appropriate that he
should be buried in Hampshire. Lord was a Scotsman born
in Yorkshire. His parents had had to leave Scotland in
rather a hurry to avoid the attentions of Cumberland after

357   z

the '45. He was born in 1757, but it is not until 1790 that we hear of him, and then he was acting as groundsman to the White Conduit Club where the M.C.C. played their matches. Seven years later he opened his own ground on what is now Dorset Square, and such was his reputation as a groundsman that the M.C.C. transferred their matches to his turf. The growth of London forced him to move, and he took up his turf and moved to a ground close to where the Regent's Park Canal now is. The making of the canal forced him to move again, and he went to the present Lord's Ground and again the M.C.C. followed him, and again he took his original turf with him. It was not until he was seventy-three that he could bear to give up the turf that he had carried round with him for so long, and then he retired to West Meon and set up as a farmer. Two years later he was dead. He had nothing whatever to do with Hampshire cricket, but it is appropriate that he should have come to die in the county that first raised the game to the level of a national sport, and that he should have come to the immediate neighbourhood of Hambledon and Broadhalfpenny Down.

From West Meon you can do one of two things. You can go straight on up the main road past the Hut to Alton, a pretty undulating road all the way; or you can turn sharp right and take the secondary road which follows the river to East Meon. Almost every one takes the first road. We will take the second because it is much the prettier and because it goes through country that is so little frequented that it is still really wild.

East Meon is three miles from West Meon. It is that distance from a railway and that distance from a bus service. As a result it has escaped progress, and remains wholly delightful. In fact it is I think the most unspoilt of all Hampshire villages and the nicest. The scenery is superb; a lush and fertile valley and all around the high downs, many of them tree-crowned. And here you will find the finest village church in all Hampshire—I think the finest village church that I know in all the south of England. Along the road by the churchyard there is a fine row of limes and they are backed by a steep hill down which the

trees tumble. It is not called a "hanger," this hill, but we
are now in the "hanger" country, and it is as true a hanger
as that famous one at Selborne. And as for the church
itself. There is argument as to its exact age. The walls
are at least four feet thick, which makes it a very old
church and it is said to have been built by Bishop Walkelyn,
the builder of the first Winchester Cathedral. There is no
proof of this, but I should say that it is not at all unlikely.
The central tower is twelfth century. The arches, too, are
twelfth century, and there are still traces of paintings on
them. The south aisle and the chancel are Early English.
Here is one of the four famous black fonts, with carvings
of the creation and the fall of Adam and Eve. Of all the
Tournai fonts this is by far the most magnificent. In the
floor of the transept there is a stone with the curious inscription "Amens Plenty." This is said to mark the
hurried burial-place of four of Cromwell's soldiers, who
were killed in a skirmish here just before the battle of
Cheriton. Better I like a tablet of 1633, which says:

Here lieth the body of Richard Smytter
Who departed this life in hope of a better.

But no mere description can do justice to East Meon
Church. It must be visited. It has something of the airi-
ness and grace of Romsey Abbey, something of the solidity
of Winchester, and an atmosphere all its own. And it is
beautifully cared for. And when you have gazed your fill
on this church, you can go and see the old Court House.
This is the lovely medieval manor in which the Bishops of
Winchester held their courts for many generations. Here,
too, the stonework in the walls is four feet thick; there is
a mass of old timber, the corbels of bishops and kings,
some beautiful windows, and from a distance, looking
down from one of the surrounding heights, red-brown roofs
that seem to welcome one as the same roofs do on the old
farm-houses of Sussex.

East Meon nestles in a deep valley, with the Meon here
no more than a tiny rivulet splashing down from the springs
in the chalk of the hills that rise to the south. This is

country that must be explored on foot and you need to be a good walker to enjoy the exploration. There is Salt Hill and Hyden Hill and Tegdown Hill, all of them just below the 800-foot contour, and away to the south-east is Old Butser, which is just below the 900 feet. On the other side of the valley is the wooded crest of Henwood Down and the rounded sweep of Park Hill, and east to Petersfield the road runs by Barrow Hill, from the top of which you can get tremendous views of the downland for miles and miles. I have walked most of this country. From East Meon to Meonstoke, all along the tops: from Winchester all along the tops to Beachy Head; from East Meon to Alton; from East Meon to Hindhead; from East Meon to Alresford and on to Basingstoke. Once even from Beachy Head to Salisbury, the most of the way on the downs. And all around here you can walk for a day and scarcely see a soul, see never a motor-car nor the smoke of a train. There are not many places where you can do that in England, and this area is not more than fifty miles from London! And fortunately it is so isolated that it is likely to remain so. Places only get "opened up" these days when some Big Business man sees a chance of making an easy and quick profit. And there is not one to be made in East Meon or anywhere round here.

A Jutish tribe settled in this neighbourhood after the Roman evacuation. They were, incidentally, the last of the pagan conquerors to accept Christianity. But I do not think that it is quite true to say that they were conquerors. I think that it would be more true of the Jutes here that they settled and assumed an overlordship. They certainly did not drive out the Britons. The name, Meon (from the tribal name Meonwara), is Celtic. In fact this whole area—the country lying between Alton, Alresford, Meonstoke and Petersfield, the area of hilly downs and narrow deep valleys, the country in which the Itchen, the Meon, the Rother and the Wey rise—must have retained a large population of the Britons all the while. We know from the Normans how wild it was. You have only got to walk over the hills south and south-east of East Meon, over the hills by Hawkley, from Hawkley to Alton, anywhere, to see that it is still wild. It is, indeed, astonishing country. The more you know it, the more astonishing.

Take the people, for example. You will get throughout this area two quite distinct types. There is a dark type and a fair type. The dark men are almost always tall and strong and active, their voices are higher pitched (especially when they are excited), and they are more vivacious and much more talkative. They are altogether quicker in the uptake than their neighbours. The fair men are stockier and slower of speech and thought. You would have thought that in a thousand years the types would have been merged. It is not so. You can still easily pick out the Jute and the Celt. And more than that: marriages between the two are rare. They get on perfectly well. There is no animosity whatever. The two work side by side in the fields, play side by side in cricket teams, live side by side, drink together. Both regard themselves as Englishmen. Neither, for the most part, has ever heard of the Jutes or the Celts. And yet it is rare to find a fair man marrying a dark girl, rare to find a fair girl marrying a dark man, hereabouts. Yet there is nothing conscious about it at all. And there is another strange thing, and that is that if a "mixed marriage" should take place—and, of course, they do—then the dark is almost always the predominant factor in the children. I am not geneticist enough to tell you why. I only know that it happens.

But it goes far back, this dark strain. You may notice it in the names. One of the common names round Alton is Cæsar. I do not mean that it is common in the sense that Smith is common in London, for it is not. But it is common enough not to be noticed. Yes, and one of the common Christian names in the Cæsar clan is Julius. It is a funny name, you may think, to find in a small Hampshire market town. But it is a very old name around these parts. I do not suggest that the great Roman had anything to do with it—for so far as we know he was not in Hampshire at all—but I think that it must go back to the Roman times. One of the hairdressing shops in Alton is owned by a Julius Cæsar at the moment, and there is another Cæsar owns a stationer's. The hairdresser has cut my hair a few times, and I suspect that quite a lot of people stop in Alton to have their hair cut just to be able to say that they have had their hair cut by Julius Cæsar. Well, his father and his grandfather were named Julius and his son is so named. Now, you might think that this is a name that might stick, starting as a nickname or something like that. But another common name in the Cæsar family is Cassius. There is a Cassius Cæsar at this very time. No, it must go back a long way, a very long way indeed. We know that it does go back for some centuries. In Henry VIII's reign there was born at Anstey, which is part of Alton but was then a village on the outskirts, to Julius Cæsar a son Julius, and this man had a son who was also christened Julius. He became Doctor Julius Cæsar and the Judge of Admiralty in Queen Elizabeth's reign. He was the man who dealt with the prizes captured by Drake and Hawkins and Raleigh. And then there was a Julius Cæsar from Alton who sailed with Cook to the Antipodes. And there was another Julius Cæsar from Alton who was a very famous cricketer. He played for England against Australia in 1863. Actually he played for Surrey and not for Hampshire because at the time Hampshire was not playing first-class cricket. He went to live in Godalming, sixteen miles away as the crow flies, but he kept a house and a wife in Alton all the time! It must have been something to do with qualifications. He had two brothers who were also very good—almost good enough to go to Australia—and between the lot they turned a full eleven of Cæsars out, and played a lot of matches in this eastern corner of Hampshire. And in this eleven there were two Juliuses and a Cassius.

But we can go further into this name business around here. There are a lot of the old English names that are Norman in origin—Diggory, Fulke, Robert. There are quite a lot of Saxon names—Aelfric, Ethelred, Egbert. You will find that the Norman names are used by fair and dark alike, as you will find the Biblical names. There are a lot of these—Joshua, Job, Izaak, Joseph, Aaron, Obadiah, Luke, Jeremiah, Mark, Matthew, and so on. (Incidentally it is an astonishing thing, but true, that most shepherds have Biblical names. I've known four pretty well in my time, and they have all had Biblical names—Luke, Matthew, Aaron, Joshua. Shepherding, of course, is more than a profession, much more than a job; it is a vocation, a calling, almost a religious calling, even as it was in Biblical times. All the same it would be interesting to know how their mothers know that they are going to be shepherds when they have them christened.) Yes, the Norman names and the Biblical names you will find used by fair and dark alike. But it is rare to find a dark man with a Saxon name. It is rare to find a dark Egbert or a dark Aelfric. You may have dark Smiths and fair Smiths in the same village, but you will not find that the dark Smith has a Saxon Christian name ninety-nine times out of a hundred. And in just the same way you will not find that a fair man has a Celtic name ninety-nine times out of a hundred. There are still Celtic names in this part of the world. I know Ivors (and the name will be pronounced in the Celtic way invariably Ifor) and I know Iowerths. Arthur is as common among the dark race as Alfred is among the fair. And for girls I know Eiluned, Brigid, and Olwen. Those are Welsh names you may say. And so they are. And who lived around here before the Teutons came? But all that pales before this. In 1943 there was christened in a little village here a boy, and he was christened Cynric. Ask the average English-man how to pronounce that name, and he will say Sinrik. The correct Celtic pronunciation is Kunrik. And that was how the parents of this boy pronounced the name. Now Cynric was King of this area, he was King of Wessex, in A.D. 500. You could not trace the descent, but who knows what blood flows in those veins that prompts a family to cling so passionately to a name that is unfashionable, to spell it correctly and to pronounce it correctly; to know that once there was a great man in their family who bore that name? This family is but a labouring family. The man is dark and the woman is dark. They are both lively and quick-witted, but neither has had more than the so-called education handed out by the elementary school. Neither read history and neither had ever heard of Wessex and cared less. But Cynric was a name that had been handed down in the woman's family—her grandfather was named so—and they knew that there had once been a great man of that name in the family. A conservative race. And one that goes back a long way in these hills. Can you wonder that they look with contempt on some of the new rich with titles that come to live in this land?

But enough names. From East Meon you should walk to Petersfield, for it is a pretty walk and all the time you have Old Butser to keep you company on your right hand. That is the easy walk, for the road keeps to the valley all the way. But the best walk is from East Meon direct to Old Butser, and you should climb to the top, for Old Butser, rearing his head above the Portsmouth road, is the highest point on the South Downs, and from the top, with its early British camp, the view is magnificent. Right over the back of the Downs runs A3, the famous Portsmouth Road, and it runs even to this day through lonely country from Horndean to Petersfield. From great Butser you can look over hill and hollow from the North Downs to the north-west (they say you can see Inkpen, but I am pretty sure that you cannot) to the distant blue that is the woodland of the Sussex Weald. To the north-east is as good and typical a view of South Downs scenery as anyone could want—close turf dropping to wooded valley and here a chalk pit brazenly white and there the dark, almost ominous, green of the junipers. To the south is the Channel and the Isle of Wight, on a clear day so close that it seems you could walk there in half an hour; and when you see it so you may know that rain is not far distant. And to the west downland and more downland for miles and miles and miles (and they say that on a clear day you can see the spire of Salisbury Cathedral, a slim needle above the skyline, but again I am pretty sure that you cannot). You can walk up here and all the way to Winchester in the one direction and Cocking in the other through the sweet scents of thyme and gorse and free grass to the accompaniment of song of lark and pipit and the cry of curlew and peewit and crow; and in the hollows there are the pigeons and the jays and the magpies and the blackbirds. Sheep are not so common as they used to be and as they ought to be. The downs, the best grazing in all England, are for the most part idle, given

over to rabbits. (In the war they grew good corn crops on
some of these downs, which only serves to show that the
land is as good as ever it was, and that British farming is
not so good as it might be if we had a House of Commons
that would allow it to do as it knows best.) Sheep are the
crop of the downs. But nowadays it is infrequently indeed
that you may hear a sheep bell. Sometimes you may dis-
turb roe-deer, and in most of the hangers there are fallow-
deer. And here grows the Viper's Bugloss. Few people
connect that flower, I find, with the South Downs. But for
me it is *the* flower of the South Downs, for here I have
found it growing in all its glory, in all the full power of
great strength, tall and bold and prickly. And I like the
Viper's Bugloss, blue against the green of the downs.

Below in the green valley between the wooded hills lies
Petersfield, and behind in the blue distance is the long line
of Hindhead. It is from Old Butser that you should first
see Petersfield. Few towns can be viewed so advantageously
—and when you have climbed to the top of Old Butser you
will realize fully what I mean.

Petersfield was originally no more than a chapelry of
Buriton, an old village hidden away in the downs. In 1108
William, Earl of Gloucester, and lord of the manor, granted
to the guild merchants of Petersfield the same rights and
privileges as those enjoyed by the citizens of Winchester.
And for a while the town was a busy woollen centre. The
church was built in the twelfth century, but has undergone
at one time and another much alteration and restoration.
The fine Norman chancel arch remains—but the rest of the
church might be anything. But the church has done something that might well be copied by others. The beautiful
old headstones of the old graves have been removed and
set up as a wall round the churchyard. And here lies John
Small, an original member of the Hambledon Cricket Club,
and on his stone you may read:

> Praises on tombs are trifles vainly spent
> A man's good name is his best monument.

Petersfield itself is a mixture of the old and the new, but

the new has mellowed and the whole town, except for the very new, is good to look upon. Some of the old houses with tiny latticed windows are really good, and so are some of the buildings round the dignified market square. In the market square stands Petersfield's "Golden Horse," given to the town by one William Joliffe. The statue—just in case you should not recognize the gentleman—is of William of Orange, William III. It is quite the most ridiculous statue in England (and we are a country with a habit of putting up ridiculous statues) and I can only imagine that Petersfield keeps it because they know in the town that they have something that you would see equalled nowhere else in the world. The horse is very fat and prances upon its pedestal self-consciously and ponderously. Its tail, a touching thought upon the part of the sculptor, is tied with a bow. And William III—poor Dutch William! I do not know what dress he is supposed to be wearing; certainly no dress of which he had ever had knowledge. I think it most nearly approaches the sort of garment one might have expected a Roman cavalryman to wear. Poor Dutch William! He was altogether too dignified to deserve such a guying, unconscious guying though it undoubtedly was. But Petersfield also had its famous man. There is a plaque on The Spain, one of the oldest houses in the town, saying that John Goodyer lived there. Few people in Petersfield know who John Goodyer was, few even know of the existence of the plaque. John Goodyer was an Alton man. He became one of the most famous botanists in the world, and when he came to live in Petersfield after marrying a local girl named Patience Crump, all the great botanists of the time used to come and visit him.

In the days when Pepys journeyed to Portsmouth, he used to stop at Petersfield. In those days there was no A3 with white lines and signposts and A.A. men and telephone-boxes. Then there was forest, miles and miles of forest, and the way was not easy to find and the journey was something of an adventure and a dangerous adventure at that. Pepys mentions the need of a guide from "Gilford" to Petersfield; and on another occasion he had to get a countryman to guide him to Havant to "avoid going through the Forest."

We hear, too, of Mr. Pepys and his friends making merry in Petersfield playing "at bowles" with their wives. Truly manners change! And we learn, too, that he stayed in the room "which the King lay in lately at his visiting there." Later the country round Petersfield was much fancied by highwaymen. The Anchor Inn at Liphook has entertained many notables from Stuart times to the present day. Queen Anne was there and Blucher, the Prussian General at Waterloo, and Victoria before she was Queen. (During the war the Anchor was a great resort for the military, and the ordinary civilian had a poor time as a rule.) You hear of these, but not of the highwaymen who frequented the neighbourhood and picked up many a useful piece of information at the Anchor. Close by on Rake Common occurred at least one grim tragedy, the history of which has come down to us, but not the inevitable gibbet which it ultimately called forth. In 1748 a custom's officer and his companion were trapped in an inn at Rowland's Castle and carried off. He must have been a highly efficient officer and in his time he had probably accounted for a number of smugglers, and perhaps not too nicely, for his captors whipped him along the road until he fell dead. His companion was chained in a turf cutter's shed for three days, and then thrown into a well. The murderers would never have been found had not the matter preyed upon the conscience of one of them, who, months afterwards, turned King's evidence. And so in due course a gibbet was erected on Rake Common and the debt paid in full.

To-day Petersfield is an agricultural town and has a market. In other words, any glory it might once have had —and in the days of the woollen industry it certainly had some—has departed. Agriculture, England's greatest industry, does not really prosper except in war-time (politicians' funk is now the best manure), and in war-time markets are at a discount. But actually, though Petersfield is not what it was, it never really arrived. It is a pleasant rather sleepy town, which gives me the impression that it missed success centuries ago and has been waiting ever since for another chance to turn up. It is on A3 and it makes rather pathetic efforts to catch the people who rush along A3, and particularly those who rush along in motor-cars. At the same time it treats the bicyclist and the walker with ill-concealed contempt, takes his money, and then hustles him out just in case a motorist should happen to stop and might be offended at feeding in such low company. This rule is broken by one inn (I mean hotel) which does give the traveller, no matter what his means of conveyance, a real welcome. In fact, though Petersfield's air of waiting is very attractive, it is really only waiting for rich motorists, and the manners in its tea-shops and cafés leave much to be desired.

Nowadays Petersfield has a first-class train service to London. As a result a number of business men have come to live in the town and the neighbourhood, and the local shops benefit a little. But I do not think that Petersfield will ever become a "first-class season" town. I think that it is going to miss that opportunity too.

From Petersfield you should walk to Selborne—you can go by bus—and you should walk by way of Hawkley. It is wild country and high, and it is by no means an easy walk, but the views over to the long ridge of Hindhead and the Hog's Back make it very worthwhile, and the whole of this range of hanger-clad hills is very attractive.

The best description of the surroundings of Selborne that I know is that of the man most fitted to give it:

> The high part to the south-west consists of a vast hill of chalk, rising three hundred feet above the village; and is divided into a sheep-down, the high wood, and a long hanging wood called the hanger. The cover of this eminence is altogether beech, the most lovely of all forest trees, whether we consider its smooth rind or bark, its glossy foliage, or graceful pendulous boughs. The down, or sheep-walk, is a pleasing park-like spot, of about one mile by half that space, jutting out on the verge of the hill-country, where it begins to break down into the plains, and commanding a very engaging view, being an assemblage of hill, dale, wood-lands, heath and water. The prospect is bounded to the south-east and east by the vast range of mountains

called the Sussex Downs; by Guild Down, near Guildford, and by the downs round Dorking and Ryegate
in Surrey, to the north-east, which altogether, with the
country round Farnham and Alton, form a noble and
extensive outline.

Well, I have read a good many descriptions of the
country about Selborne, but never a better one. You may
smile at the description of the South Downs as "a vast
range of mountains," thinking of the Alps, or (if you are a
globe-trotter or an empire-builder) of the Andes or the
Himalayas or the Caucasus. But you are wrong to smile.
White was right. The South Downs are vast, and if you
stand in the valley and look upon them in the evening of
a stormy day, or in rain, or with the sun dropping below
the horizon, you will realize just how right White was. The
South Downs have then truly the aspect of mountains—
and I have seen and climbed real mountains, judging by
height alone. White may have made mistakes—in the
light of our present knowledge we know that he did—but
he *never* exaggerated.

So much has been written about Gilbert White already,
so many editions of his works have been published, each
with its introduction fulsome or critical, that it would be
foolish to try to find anything new to say. I do not think
that there is anything new that can be said. But I am
quite sure that there will be many more editions and many
more introductions, fulsome and critical, by many more
editors. And, in passing, for those who have not read
Gilbert White (and an astonishing number of people have
not) may I, for those who feel that they would like to do
so, recommend two editions from my not inconsiderable (I
think that I have read them all and own them all) experience? For those with money the really beautiful Non-
such Edition edited by H. J. Massingham; for those with
a little less the excellent volume edited by E. M. Nicholson.
In my own opinion those two stand head and shoulders
above the rest.

Gilbert White was a real Hampshire man. He was born
at The Wakes in the village of Selborne in 1720. He came

of a Hampshire family. He lived almost all his life in Hampshire. He died in the house in which he was born. And furthermore he wrote only about Hampshire and the things he saw in Hampshire.

He was educated at Basingstoke Grammar School and at Oriel College, Oxford, of which College he later became a Fellow. He was clever enough and might have made for himself a good career at the University. In due course he became ordained, and in the Church, too, he could easily have secured preferment. He preferred quiet and seclusion. For twenty-four years he acted as curate of Faringdon and for more than fifty years he was curate (but *never* vicar) of his own village of Selborne.

This eastern corner of Hampshire is Gilbert White, and Selborne will be for ever associated with his name. The circle of those who have never put foot in the village but to whom the Hanger and the Plestor are as real and as living and as familiar as their own home is enormous—not so large as that connected with Stratford-on-Avon, but larger beyond doubt than that associated with any other English town or village. White of Selborne: it is a title, a title as meritoriously earned as any for deeds of valour, a title far more meritorious than any given "for public services," a title that will outlast them all. White of Selborne, a quiet, humble, retiring country parson: White of Selborne, whose fame rings the world: White of Selborne, who started, albeit unconsciously, a work that will never end, a work that year by year collects more devotees.

"Unconsciously." That is the secret of Gilbert White's success. He never imagined that he would become an immortal, never for one moment. He never thought that he would make Selborne, quiet and secluded Selborne, historic ground. He never dreamed that a hundred and fifty years after his death his writings would still be read. He would have been most upset had anyone even hinted at the possibility. The desire for fame, the desire for wealth, was not in his make-up. He had in him something far transcending that—genius: a genius for observation, a genius for methodical notation, a genius for trivialities—and a genius for description. The whole of his success was due to his unique knack of noticing small things. Nothing was too minute or too trivial. And he had perseverance, for he managed to keep his diary, a thing even Mr. Pepys could not do consistently. White used his eyes and recorded what he actually saw with them—the first appearance of the leaves in spring, the arrival and departure of the summer and winter migrant birds, the weather, the variations in the sky and the variations in the earth. To the men of his generation Nature meant little or nothing; it was a background, a pleasing background, to the business of life, of drinking, of loving, of dying: it was of no importance. He lived at a time when men thought, and could actually write, that cows changed their horns every year. (Yes, Goldsmith wrote that and Doctor Johnson praised his observation.) He lived at a time when conversation meant much, accuracy little or nothing. Accuracy meant a great deal to Gilbert White. He noted what he saw, not what he thought he saw, or wished that he had seen. And so, unconsciously, he became the father of that school of careful observation to which we owe our knowledge of wild life and its ways. He was a pioneer in field natural history, and indirectly of many "ologies"—ornithology, zoology, entomology, ecology, oology, biology, all (as we know them to-day) sprang from Gilbert White. No man in history has fathered a bigger family than Gilbert White of Selborne. It was fitting that he should live in Hampshire, the county that fathered England.

Gilbert White is buried in Selborne Churchyard. On the walls of the church (a pleasant but not remarkable church) are memorials to the White family (and on the wall opposite a memorial to another famous naturalist who also lived at The Wakes: Thomas Bell, F.L.S.) and an inscription records the burial "in the fifth grave from this wall" of "the Rev. Gilbert White, M.A., fifty years Fellow of Oriel College, in Oxford, and Historian of his native parish." A stone marks the grave. Upon it is inscribed:

G. W.
26 June
1793

Nothing more. No more is needed. And White of Selborne would not have had it otherwise.

The Wakes, the home of the Whites, remains. It is, naturally, somewhat altered. It may be visited by arrangement with the owner, and on payment of sixpence per person. The sixpence goes to charity. There is also a Selborne Society. It has apparently nothing to do with Selborne. And, of course, there is no museum. So the sixpence goes to charity. I am glad. It is what White, had he known, would have wanted.

Gilbert White is immortal. No less immortal is Jane Austen. Until the outbreak of the war she was comparatively little read. You could then buy her books in any number of good cheap editions. But until 1939 few young people of good education—taking young to mean educated during or after the First German War—had read any of her books, few could name the titles of even two of them. Now, you cannot buy a Jane Austen for love or money. Now she is as widely read as Anthony Trollope. She is, of course, a much greater writer than Trollope. Jane Austen occupies as prominent a place in English literature as Gilbert White. If White gave form and meaning and impetus to the study of natural history, Jane Austen may surely lay claim to doing much the same for the English novel.

Jane is as truly Hampshire as Gilbert White. She was born in the Parsonage House at Steventon, a village about seven miles from Basingstoke, in 1775. For twenty-five years she lived at Steventon. For four years she lived in Bath. Then she returned to Hampshire to spend four years in Southampton. Then her family moved to Chawton, a village just outside Alton and only about four miles from Selborne. And here she lived until a short while before her death at Winchester in 1817. The daughter of a country parson, she spent the first twenty-five years, the most susceptible years, of her life in a quiet country village, with no greater excitement than an occasional dance in Basingstoke and with no wider horizon than that supplied by the extremely limited social circle of any small country village and its neighbours. One would not expect to find genius in such surroundings. But genius knows no limits. It was

The Wakes, Selborne

at Steventon that Jane wrote *Pride and Prejudice*, *Sense and Sensibility*, and *Northanger Abbey*, but she was unable to find a publisher and the works remained in manuscript for some years. Each is a perfect study of life and character. Each is written with an assurance that one would associate with a keen student of manners, with someone who had moved for years in the society described, rather than with the daughter of a country parson, a girl who, moreover, had rarely, if ever, been twenty miles from her home village. At Bath and Southampton she wrote not at all. But at Chawton, in the eight years remaining of her short life, she wrote *Mansfield Park*, *Emma*, and *Persuasion*, novels that aroused great enthusiasm and drew forth high praise from such men as Lord Macaulay and Sir Walter Scott, and which, in the opinion of Lord Tennyson, placed her "next to Shakespeare." That is high praise indeed, but I do not myself think that it is too high. Jane Austen, from the literary point of view, is a puzzle. Other authors of her time moved in a more or less literary environment, had their particular circle of cultured and literary friends and acquaintances. Authors always have done so. They do so to-day. Jane Austen had not one single literary acquaintance. In the literary sense she lived absolutely alone. She had, in fact, a very small circle of friends, and that circle was composed entirely of relatives and "Old friends of the family." She had, it would seem, but little foundation upon which to build her books. But she had eyes and she had ears, and she used them both. She was not unlike Gilbert White. She had the same uncanny gift for observation, the same meticulous regard for detail, the same love of accuracy, the same perseverance: yes, but she had something more—something altogether lacking in Gilbert White—a fertile imagination. We may be quite sure that her Mr. Elton, her Mr. Collins, her Mr. and Mrs. Bennetty (a good Hampshire name, by the way), her Miss Bates, her Mrs. Norris, her Sir Thomas and Lady Bertram, we may be quite sure that they were, all of them, drawn from Life, that she had met them all in her limited social circle. She had met them all: they were real and living people. It is with no surprise that we read in Austen Leigh's

*Jane Austen's House and
old cottages, Chawton*

memoir of her that her characters were like children to her, that she would talk confidentially to her friends about the future of her heroes and her heroines, and reveal small details about them which were not to be found in her books. It is not in the least surprising. But she would only talk thus to her intimate friends—and they were few. She wrote secretly on odd bits of paper, and these she would hide as soon as a maid or visitor came into the room.

What was she like? Mrs. Mitford, the mother of Mary Russell Mitford, described her as "the prettiest, silliest, most affected, husband-hunting butterfly." Well, well, well. Her books and her life plainly give the lie to that description. And anyway, Mary Russell Mitford, to put it baldly, was fat and ugly. Mrs. Mitford, I feel, was biased and ungenerous. In place of Mrs. Mitford's description let us take that of Sir Walter Scott:

> That young lady had a talent for describing the involvement, and feelings, and character of ordinary life, which is to me the most wonderful I have ever met with. The Big Bow-wow strain I can do myself like any now going; but this exquisite touch, which renders ordinary common-place things and characters interesting, from the truth of the description and the sentiment, is denied to me. What a pity such a gifted creature died so early.

Jane Austen was a very pretty girl. We have Mrs. Mitford's word for that, and to get any praise from Mrs. Mitford she must have been pretty indeed. She was gay and vivacious when with people she knew well. She was also very shy and retiring when in the company of those she did not know well. But in any company she kept her eyes and ears open.

There is curiously very little of Hampshire in her books. Meryton, where the young ladies of *Pride and Prejudice* went to their balls, is obviously Basingstoke. Fanny Price's family lived in Portsmouth, and Fanny shocked her Mansfield cousins by calling the Isle of Wight "the Island, as if there was no other island in the world." (That, by the way, is a very sound piece of observation: the people of the Isle of Wight and the people of Portsmouth still speak of the Isle of Wight as the Island.) But though there is so little mention of Hampshire in her books there can be no doubt that the background of all of them is her own county. It is worthy of note that she did not write a word when she was outside Hampshire.

It was while she was writing *Persuasion* that her health, which had never been really good, began to give way. It was with the greatest difficulty that she managed to finish the last chapter. In order to obtain better medical treatment she moved to Winchester with her sister Cassandra, and took rooms in College Street, and it was here that she died on 18 July 1817. Cassandra wrote some very sad letters about the event, but was consoled to some extent by the fact that her sister's "dear remains were to be deposited in the Cathedral . . . in a building she admired so much." The funeral was carried out without fuss, which was as Jane would have wished; but which was done, I suspect, not because of any expressed wish but because the Cathedral authorities had no interest in Jane. The service was taken by a petty-canon! A stained-glass window to her memory has a brass tablet beneath it with these words:

Jane Austen, known to many by her writings, endeared to her family by the varied charms of her character, and ennobled by Christian faith and piety.
She opened her mouth with wisdom, and in her tongue is the law of kindness.

The grave is in the north aisle, a little west of the font, and is marked by a flat black marble slab. Few Americans who visit the Cathedral—and most Americans who visit England seem to visit the Cathedral—fail to pay homage at the grave. This was most noticeable during the war, when literally thousands of Americans, soldiers and sailors and airmen and women auxiliaries, must have stood for a moment looking down on that marble slab. I was almost daily astonished to find how well known Jane Austen was in the United States. Few Englishmen even know that she is buried in the Cathedral.

We have mentioned Mary Russell Mitford. She, too, was Hampshire, and she came from close by Jane Austen and Gilbert White. She was born at Alresford on 16 December 1787, and Alresford is but a little way down the valley from Chawton. Alresford was once a prosperous country town with an ancient Grammar School and a flourishing trade; it is now a large village depending on Winchester and Alton. It was a Bishop of Winchester, de Lucy, who founded the place at the head of what he hoped would be a great trade waterway through Winchester to Southampton. He built a great dam across the river and dug a reservoir of 200 acres to make the Itchen, into which the Alre flows, navigable at all seasons. And modern traffic going from New Alresford to Old Alresford still crosses over Bishop de Lucy's dam. The reservoir—now called Alresford Great Pond—has shrunk to a mere 60 acres, but it is still beautiful and it is large enough to attract a great many water birds. The great house by the church was built by Admiral Rodney, and he is also credited with the building of most of the pubs in the village of which there are a great many neatly spaced out on opposite sides of the straight road, spaced, so rumour has it, in this way, in order that the admiral might "tack" from one to the other and home again. And beside the connexion with Mary Russell Mitford, Alresford has another claim to fame. It was an Alresford woman, the wife of a rector of Old Alresford, who founded the Mothers' Union. From small beginnings in a little hall here the Union has grown to almost a million members spread all over the world. There is a memorial to Mary Sumner in Westminster and there is also a Mary Sumner House in Westminster. So far as I know there is no memorial to Mary Sumner in Alresford.

But we were dealing with Mary Russell Mitford. Her mother was the daughter of a Doctor Russell, Rector of Ash in the north of the county and later Vicar of Overton. He was a member of the Bedford family. Her father was a Doctor George Mitford, a man with an Edinburgh medical degree of which he made no use. That he was a most attractive man there can be no doubt. He was also a wastrel. He ran through his own fortune and the fortune of his wife, who was an heiress, and then he managed to rush through the £20,000 that his daughter won in a lottery. Mary Russell Mitford knew all the extremes of fortune. She lived in large houses that cost thousands a year to keep going, and she lived in the humblest labourer's cottages with the roof falling in because there was not money enough for repairs. Her two most famous books (she wrote a great many books, almost all of them forgotten now) are *Our Village* and *Sketches of Rural Life and Character*. It is sometimes said that she is no whit behind White and Jane Austen as an observer. Be that as it may, she was certainly not nearly so exact. She had a much wider range of country experience than either of the other two, but she was not above colouring when she was not writing fiction, and she could not write nearly as well as the other two. In comparison with either of them she is quite superficial. But one must not be too hard on her. She wrote for money, and such was her father that she wrote for the most part against time. She worried about cash, not about accuracy. Her descriptions are frequently far from accurate, and her judgment is often far from just. She found that Jane Austen's work was deficient in taste and lacking in a "perception of the graceful as well as of the humorous." I think that Miss Mitford was a wee bit jealous, and more than a wee bit biased, just as her mother was obviously a nasty old cat.

I have some fondness for this part of the county. It was around here—actually between Alresford and Alton—that the FitzGeralds first settled. Robert, the son of Gerald of Windsor, was granted land here and in many other places in Hampshire, but the first grant was made here, and appears (as do all the others) in *Domesday Book*. And though the family has been Irish for centuries it is worth remembering, I think, that they were Hampshire before they were Irish, and Welsh before they were Irish, though after they were Hampshire. And it is perhaps worthy of note, in these days, that they have always been in Hampshire. One of the other grants made to Robert was that of

Oakley in the New Forest. It was on the outskirts of Oakley that I spent quite a time in my boyhood, and there are still members of the family living just on the outskirts. The last bailiff of Alresford, the office was done away with in 1928, was an uncle of mine—the first bailiff, the grant having been made by Walkelyn, was one Odo FitzGerald. The manor of Herriard, now held by a Jervoise, and in which are kept papers and charters going back to the time of Edward II, passed to that family on the marriage of Elizabeth FitzGerald. And so it would be possible to go on. Even the public houses in these parts often bear the Christian names of the family—the Purefoy Arms, the Seymour Arms, and several more. I may, I hope, be excused my unashamed affection for this part of the county and for the New Forest.

Alton is very old—the name means Old Town—and stands at the head of the Wey Valley. Close by there are still a few remains of the great forest that once stretched all around, the forest of Alice Holt. Even in prehistoric times there was, it would seem, a clearing through the great Anderida Forest by the pass of Alton; there was certainly one in Roman times, as the great number of Roman remains found in the neighbourhood bear witness. The main road runs through Alton to Farnham and has always run so. Part of it in Alton is still called Normandy Hill, a reminder of the days in 1101 when Henry I and Robert of Normandy met here and signed the Treaty of Alton. It was a very dangerous road until the area was disafforested in medieval times. Gangs of robbers made good use of the covering woodlands and played havoc at festival times. During the period of St. Giles' Fair the Bishops of Winchester employed five mounted sergeants-at-arms to keep the road secure, and the spot they patrolled particularly was the pass of Alton near Bentley where the forest encroached closely on each side of the road. Henry III commenced disafforestation, though not actually at Bentley but on the Chawton side of Alton. He did this because some Brabant merchants who were bringing goods to him at Winchester were held up and robbed. When the merchants arrived without the goods Henry was very annoyed. He called the citizens of Winchester together and told them in no uncertain terms what he thought about it all. He then ordered the gates to be shut and said that no one was to be allowed out until the matter of his goods had been cleared up. Twelve leading citizens of the capital were formed into a jury and an inquiry commenced. No light was thrown on the matter. Henry had them all thrown into prison. Another jury was formed, and this one took the hint. After due consideration a vast conspiracy was revealed, the "guilty" were hanged, and the roads were, for the King's goods anyway, rendered safe. The most famous robber of this time was Adam de Gurdon (Sir Adam of Selborne), a member of an old Norman family in the district. His exploits became so notorious that they gained the attention of Prince Edward who challenged and fought him in single combat near Long Sutton. Edward won, and pardoned his enemy, thus making him a loyal subject. But this and the broad hint of Henry III and the disafforestation did not put an end to the robbery. Indeed the road was dangerous until well into the last century. Gangs of robbers and highwaymen, playing a lone hand, used the cover of the woods around Chawton and Bentley until the early years of the Victorian era.

Alton has seen other history too. Alton fight did not mean much in the history of the Civil War as a whole, was no more than a stray skirmish, but it produced the one great hero of that dreadful and sordid struggle. A tablet on one of the pillars of the church tells the story of Colonel Richard Boles:

A Memoriall

For this renowned Martialist Richard Boles of ye Right Worshipful Family of the Boles in Linck horne sheire, Colonell of a Ridgment of foot of 1300, Who, for his Gratious King Charles ye First, did Woanders att the Battell of Edge Hill: his last Action, to omitt all Others, was at Alton in this County of Southampton, was Sirprised by five or Six Thousand of the Rebells, which Caused him there Quartered, to fly to the Church with neare Foarscore of his men, who there Fought with them six or seven Houers, and then the Rebell Breaking in upon him he slew with his Sword six or seven of them and then was Slayne himself, with fifty of his men about him

1641

His Gratious Soveraigne hearing of his death gave him his high Commendation in ye pationate exprefsion
Bring me a Moorning Scarffe, i have lost one of the best Comanders in this kingdome.

Alton will tell you of that famous Fight
Which ye Man made and bade this World good-night
His Vertuous Life fear'd not Mortalyty
His Body Must, his Vertues cannot Die
Because his Bloud was there so Nobly spent
This is his Tombe that Church his Monument.

Ricardus Boles, Wiltoniensis in Art. Mag.
Composuit Posuitque Dolens
An Dom 1689

"That Church" is Alton Church, for Colonel Richard Boles is actually buried in Winchester Cathedral. The brass in Alton Church is a facsimile of that in Winchester Cathedral.

But Alton will not tell you of this famous fight. Colonel Boles is forgotten except by the guide books.

At the time of Alton fight Sir William Waller was at Farnham preparing to deal a shattering blow at the Royalist forces, not by attacking General Hopton at Winchester, but by sweeping with overwhelming forces upon the small Royalist garrisons at Alresford and Alton. Lord Crawford was in command of the garrison at Alton, and though he kept a constant patrol of the Farnham road by means of mounted scouting parties he also spent a good deal of time exchanging ironically friendly messages with Waller at Farnham. One such message offered to exchange a fat ox for a cask of wine—the Royalists being a bit short of liquor. The wine was duly sent, but Crawford failed to send the ox. Accordingly Waller sent a message to the effect that his Lordship was not to worry, he (Waller) would come and fetch it in person. The message was received as a jest, but it would not appear that it was sent as a jest. The night of December 12th was cold and frosty. Waller gathered his troops in Farnham Park. About two hours after sunset he marched out along the road to Odiham, and at nine o'clock he halted at Crondall. Having by then mustered about four thousand infantry and one thousand cavalry, he marched towards Basing, but at midnight wheeled round between the woods and hills towards Alton. And in the grey cold of December 13th he was on the hills to the west of Alton. He had evaded the Royalist patrols and taken Crawford absolutely by surprise. His Lordship could not retreat to the east, for that direction was barred by Hazelrig and his "Lobsters." Only the road to Winchester was open. Crawford was a good deal better at drinking than fighting. He did not hesitate. He retired to Winchester just as fast as horses could move, leaving Colonel Boles and a handful of men to hold Alton until he should return with help from Hopton at Winchester.

Boles had about five hundred men—the brass is mistaken in more than the date—and he must hold Alton for a good many hours before help could arrive. Waller, in the meanwhile, had cut the Winchester road and so delayed the arrival of yet more. Five hundred against five thousand, odds of ten to one. And Boles had not got veteran troops. He had only undisciplined recruits from Ireland and Wales. Magnificent material, but more than that was needed if Alton was to be held. Boles, however, was made of sterner stuff than Crawford, and was not daunted. (It is an interesting thought, what would have happened in the Civil War had Charles entrusted his commands to good fighting men of the type of Boles and not to the loyal but ineffective members of the nobility that thronged round him.) He defended the outskirts as long as he could, and then retired to the market-place. The market-place, it seems, fell about midday, and Boles then retired to an entrenched position near the church. He held up the advance for a while by firing a house or two, but numbers told and the south-eastern wall of the churchyard was stormed. There was a tremendous fight in the churchyard and numbers of the Royalists were killed, but ultimately Boles and about forty men gained the church, piled dead horses in the aisles and barricaded the door. The door gave to severe musket fire and a hammering; and there in the church the final struggle came. Some few Royalists surrendered, the majority were killed. And Colonel Boles died last of all, fighting in the pulpit, blood-stained sword in hand. He was a man who saw his duty clearly and did not flinch. He was a stranger to fear, a stranger to divided loyalties. There have been many worse sermons preached in Alton pulpit than this one by Colonel Boles.

Alton Church is impressive, the most impressive church —in one way at least—in Hampshire. The great door still shows the scars of Alton fight; deeply embedded in the pillars are the bullets of the Roundheads. Over all the church breathes the spirit of a very gallant gentleman. And Alton Church is one of the very rare churches with two naves and two chancels, one nave and chancel fifteenth century, the others having grown up around the church that the Normans built.

Hidden away in a small crowded street leading from the market-place—Amery Street—there is a small brick house, now two cottages, bearing a plaque which states that Edmund Spenser, the great Elizabethan poet, lived there. John Aubrey says, "Mr. Spenser lived some time in these parts, in this delicate sweet air, where he enjoyed his muse and writ a good part of his verse." The tablet says that he lived here in 1590. We know that he was in England at this time, but we have only Aubrey's statement about his living here. However, Aubrey was writing only fifty years after Spenser's death, and it may be taken that he would know. The date indicates that it was probably in this house that the *Ruines of Time* was written. Spenser cannot be claimed as an Alton man. But Alton has produced two very famous men, both of them strangely enough botanists: John Goodyer, whom we have already met in Petersfield, who was an Elizabethan, and William Curtis, who lived through the latter half of the eighteenth century.

It is said that Curtis was first interested in botany by an ostler at the Crown Hotel. It is a pleasant story and it may well be true. But Curtis was a doctor and I think that it is more likely that his fondness for botany arose from his scientific leanings. He became the most famous botanist in the world. He was born on 11 January 1746 in a house in Lenten Street, which may still be seen. His father was a tanner in comfortable circumstances and William received a good education. On leaving school he was appointed apprentice to his grandfather, who was a surgeon-apothecary, whose house adjoined the Crown Inn. The ostler at the inn was named Thomas Legg, and it is to him that Curtis is supposed to owe his initiation into botany. It is possible also that he received help from Gilbert White, who lived within walking distance, but on the whole I think that this is unlikely, for the Curtis family were Quakers. All the same there is no doubt that later in life Curtis was on the best of terms with Gilbert White's brothers Benjamin, the publisher, and Thomas. Curtis is best known to-day for his *Flora Londinensis* and as the founder of the *Botanical Magazine*. The *Flora* was a financial failure, but it benefited botanical study enormously at the time. The *Botanical Magazine*, however, has benefited the science to a far greater extent. As was clearly indicated by the sub-title, "the Flower-Garden Displayed," it "was to be a serial of plant pictures drawn and coloured from life. It excluded native plants but was open to any other plant as long as it was amongst the most ornamental and in actual cultivation either in the open ground or in the greenhouse or the stove." Each part consisted of three hand-coloured plates with explanatory text and each part cost one shilling. Monthly publication continued regularly, and the magazine was a most definite success for the circulation reached the figure of 3,000. That seems low in these days of mammoth sales, but it was a high figure in those days, and no mean figure for a specialist magazine even in these. Actually during Curtis' lifetime the magazine contained little of scientific value and the plates were not nearly so good as those of the *Flora*, but Curtis was not aiming at botanists, but rather at gardeners. After his death the magazine was changed a great deal, though only gradually. It became associated with the Royal Botanic Garden at Kew, and publication has continued right down to the present day, though the price per part has increased to 17s. 6d. Curtis was also an entomologist of note, and a most knowledgeable man on birds. But it is, of course, as a botanist that he attained world fame, and it is as a botanist that he will always be remembered.

The manuscript and lecture notes of William Curtis may be seen in the Curtis Museum at Alton together with the fine drawings by Sydenham Edwards and Moses Harris, and here, too, is a brown ware jug beautifully moulded with hops and barley which was specially made for Curtis in 1781. This museum should be visited by everyone who has the chance. It is quite the best small museum in the country, and one of the best museums of its type outside London.

It was founded in 1855 by William Curtis, who was born at Alton in 1803, a member of the Quaker family that had lived here since 1720. His father, also a William Curtis, was also a doctor and had attended Jane Austen when she lived at Chawton. William Curtis, the founder, became apprenticed to his father in 1819, and in due course became a doctor himself. But great as his interest in medicine was, his interest in geology was at least as great, and a geological hammer was his constant companion throughout life. But he had the widest interest in natural history generally, and both he and his elder brother became experts at skinning and stuffing. They imparted their skill to John Cooper, their father's stable and errand boy, and in later years their groom, and eventually Cooper mounted most of the birds in the museum, and after retirement set up as a taxidermist. William Curtis became his father's partner in 1827. John Gould, the famous bird artist and ornithologist, came frequently to Alton and his visits must have influenced William, whom he knew well, greatly. But the whole family were interested in natural history. The younger brother, John Wright Curtis, was an accomplished naturalist, whose name appears often in the footnotes to Bell's edition of Gilbert White, and so was his son William and his nephew Philip Crowley, F.L.S. The idea of a museum must have been in the minds of such a family for a long time. What appears to have decided them was the sale at Hackwood Park of Keeper Bond's effects. They bought an osprey, a pair of honey buzzards, a pair of ravens and "a marten cat, this being very rare and valuable as it is now extinct in this county." The museum was founded. In order to attract interest in it a formal opening was arranged for 1 January 1856. The first catalogue was published in 1875. A second was issued in 1889. By them the number of cases had increased to sixty-three, and the collections were then housed in their present building. William Curtis died in 1881, and was succeeded by his son William as curator. This William continued to hold the office until the outbreak of the First German War, when the building seems to have been closed and part at least of it used as a Red Cross store. In 1919 the buildings were made over to the town as part of a War Memorial. Interest in the museum appears to have been at a very low ebb at this time and for some years afterwards. Fortunately in 1925 W. Hugh Curtis, the grandson of the founder, was appointed Curator, and from that moment the museum has progressed at a most astonishing rate. Now there is a society, which was prompted by the late Sir Harry Wilson, called The Friends of the Curtis Museum, and the place is in the most flourishing condition. In 1944 a further extension was added of agricultural implements, which I had the great honour of opening in the presence of a large audience from all over the county.

This museum is so outstanding that it is a pity that it is so cramped. It deserves the best possible lay-out, and such a lay-out would do the town a great deal of good. It is to be hoped that as soon as conditions are better the town authorities will do something towards giving the collections the sort of background that they deserve.

In the eighteenth century the manufacture of drugget and shalloon was carried on in the town, and there was also a considerable industry in silks and serges, bombazine and barragon. Gilbert White records that the poor of Selborne assisted the Quakers of Alton in the making of barragon, "a genteel corded stuff" as he called it. In those days the trade was mainly in the hands of the Quakers. There are still Quakers in Alton, indeed the Society of Friends is very strong in the town and district, but the silks and serge and bombazine and barragon have disappeared from local industry. Brewing to-day is Alton's business. They have brewed fine ales here for close upon two hundred years, and they brew ale here to-day that has no superior in England and, I think, no equal. When you are in Alton you are in the heart of the Courage country, and you should sample Courage ale. And it was in Alton that I once saw a magnificent, if unconscious, advertisement for the brewery: a Wayside Pulpit imploring passers-by to TAKE COURAGE.

Alton is a town that grows on you. I have said some rather blunt things about Alton in the past (and I have said them to the town as well) but as I say, the place grows on you. There are some blunt things that need saying still, but, for all that, Alton is a most attractive town. It is quiet and humble, and genuine. The wide main street that seems at first to be a rather untidy jumble of styles and no style at all becomes with acquaintance one of the most attractive streets in the country. And I think now—indeed I am sure now—that I would rather live in Alton than in any other small town in the county. It is a busy place and prosperous. It does not pretend to be anything other than it is, a market town and the centre of an agricultural and rather thinly populated district. It has hop-fields, which, if they are not as famous as those of Kent, at least seem to escape depressions. It has the famous Treloar Hospital, which means that it is particularly healthy. It is altogether a very pleasant little town . . . and friendly.

And now it is at the end of an electric line from London. There is a half-hourly service in each direction. Fortunately for Alton the trains stop at almost every station, and the journey is not one that is likely to attract the stockbrokers and the rich business men who have to go up to Town every day. The railway is, therefore, a blessing and not an evil in disguise for Alton.

And here, if you get on a train, you may be out of Hampshire through Bentley and over the Surrey border to Farnham in a matter of seven minutes or so. In a matter of another three you will be back in the county at Aldershot, for the boundary here does some ridiculous things. And it was at Aldershot that we entered the County of Southampton.

CHAPTER XIII

HAMPSHIRE CRICKET

Assist all ye muses and join to rehearse
An old English sport never praised yet in verse;
'Tis cricket I sing, of illustrious fame,
No nation e'er boasted so noble a game.

Great Pindar has bragged of his heroes of old,
Some were swift in the race, some in battle were bold;
The brows of the victor with olive were crowned,
Hark! they shout, and Olympia returns the glad sound.

What boasting of Pollux and Castor his brother,
The one famed for riding, for bruising the other,
But compared with our heroes, they'll not shine at all,
What are Castor and Pollux to Nyren and Small?

There's guarding and catching and throwing and tossing
And bowling and striking and running and crossing,
Each mate must excel in some principal part,
The Penthalon of Greece could not show so much art.

The parties are met and arrayed all in white,
Famed Ellis ne'er boasted so pleasing a sight,
Each nymph looks askew at her favourite swain,
And views him half stript both with pleasure and pain.

The wickets are pitched now and measured the ground,
Then they form a large ring and stand gazing around;
Since Ajax fought Hector in sight of all Troy,
No contest was seen with such fears and such joy.

Ye bowlers take heed, to my precepts attend,
On you the whole fate of the game must depend,

Spare your vigour at first, nor exert your full strength,
Then measure each step and be sure pitch a length.

Ye strikers observe when the foe shall draw nigh,
Mark the bowler advancing with vigilant eye,
Your skill all depends upon distance and sight,
Stand firm in your scratch, let your bat be upright.

Ye fieldsmen look sharp lest your pains ye beguile,
Move close like an army in rank and in file,
When the ball is returned, back it sure, for I trow
Whole states have been ruined by one overthrow.

The sport is now o'er and victory rings,
Echo doubles the chorus and fame spreads her wings,
Let us then hail our champions all sturdy and true,
Such as Homer ne'er sung of, nor Pindar e'er knew.

Buck, Curry, and Hogsflesh, and Barber and Brett,
Whose swiftness in bowling was ne'er equalled yet,
I had almost forgot, they deserve a large bumper,
Little George the longstop and Tom Sutor the stumper.

Then why should we fear either Sackville or Man,
Or repine at the loss both of Boynton and Lann?
With such troops as these we'll be lords of the game,
Spite of Minshul, and Millar, and Lumpy, and Frame.

Then fill up your glass, he's the best who drinks most:
Here's the Hambledon Club! Who refuses the toast?
Let us join in the praise of the bat and the wicket,
And sing in full chorus the patrons of cricket.

So sang the Reverend Reynell Cotton of Winchester in
1767. But his second line is not quite accurate. Cricket
had been honoured in verse already by J. Dance, who
wrote as J. Love, in 1744:

Hail Cricket! glorious, manly, British game!
First of all Sports! be first alike in Fame!

But there are many things like that about cricket. No one knows where the game first started. The first mention of the word seems to have been in 1598 when we hear of a game at Guildford, but there can be no doubt that it was played long before that. I do not think it matters in the least where it first started nor who wrote the first verse about it. The great thing is that it did start, and that many people have written about it.

But there can be no doubt that it has been played in Hampshire for a very long while—there is a record of Bishop Ken playing cricket at Winchester in 1650, and nothing about the record to suggest that this was anything but a normal pastime for Winchester boys at that time— and there can be no doubt at all that the modern game was born in Hampshire and on Broadhalfpenny Down near Hambledon. There is, in fact, no place in the whole world of cricket equal in glory to this little Hampshire village.

I think that we must discount the legend that the game was first played here—there is nothing at all improbable about that legend, for cricket is beyond doubt a downland and south country game in origin, and if it was not very old in Hambledon there seems to be little reason why the village club should suddenly have risen to such great heights and attracted such huge crowds—but I think that we may properly claim that it was here that the first club proper came into being, and with it the birth of the modern game.

The club was founded about 1750. By 1756 it was a very strong club indeed. The late F. S. Ashley-Cooper, the greatest of cricket historians, once wrote: "The story of the Hambledon Club is one of the most remarkable in the whole history of cricket. How a village organization should have developed into such prominence unchallenged and un-changeable, and have been supported in its almost in-accessible quarters at Broadhalfpenny by most of the chief contemporary patrons will probably always remain a mystery." But that is what happened. This little Hampshire village, remote in itself, and playing the game on a still more remote down on its outskirts, rose to the foremost place in the national game, and even in 1777, defeated the might of All England by an innings and 168 runs. "Little Hambledon, pitted against All England, was a proud thought for the Hampshire men. Defeat was glory in such a struggle . . . victory indeed made us only 'a little lower than the angels'," so wrote the author of *The Young Cricketer's Tutor*. Yes, Hambledon also produced the greatest literature in the annals of the game.

The historian—but, no, he was more than that—the bard was Nyren. He had a wondrous tale to tell, of course, but he was a born writer too and he was in love with his subject. He was a member of the club, and he writes with a natural sentiment in its favour, but he is supported by the score-sheets and the minutes; there is no exaggeration in Nyren. His father was the landlord of the Bat and Ball Inn on Broadhalfpenny, and a farmer as well (it is a combination that still survives in some parts of the county) and it was he who became the mainspring of the Hambledon Club. The years of its greatest glory were from 1772 to 1787, when the M.C.C. was founded, largely through the initiative of the Hambledon president for the year. Up to that time the Hambledon Club had occupied much the position in the world of cricket that is to-day occupied by the M.C.C. They passed the rules and the rules they passed were observed throughout the cricket world. For example, one of the Hambledon men, Tom Walker, attempted overhand bowling, and the Hambledon Club ruled that it was illegal, and the ruling was accepted wherever cricket was played. And again one White of Reigate arrived to play in a match at Hambledon with a bat so broad that it completely covered the wicket. A rule was forthwith passed limiting the width of the bat, and an iron frame was made to measure bats, and kept in the Bat and Ball, just as the M.C.C. would keep it now.

And now for some of the achievements of this little village. In a challenge match in 1777 Hambledon played All England at Sevenoaks in Kent. Here is the score:

HAMBLEDON

Lord Tankerville, b Wood	3
T. Brett	9
Small, c White	33
Francis, c Wood	26
R. Nyren, b Lumpy	37
Sueter, b Wood	46
Leer, b Wood	7
Aylward, not out	167
R. A. Veck, b Lumpy	16
T. Taylor, c Bullen	32
E. Aburrow, c Minshull	22
Byes	5
	403

ALL ENGLAND

Duke of Dorset, b Brett	0	c Tankerville	5
Lumpy, b Brett	1	not out	2
Wood, b Brett	1	b Nyren	1
White, c Veck	8	run out	10
Miller, c Small	27	b Brett	23
Minshull, not out	60	c Taylor	12
Bowra, b Brett	2	b Taylor	4
Bullen, c Tankerville	13	b Nyren	2
Booker, b Brett	8	b Brett	2
Yalden, b Small	6	c Nyren	8
Pattenden, b Brett	38	c Sueter	0
Byes	2		
	166		69

This is the match in which Aylward (who is buried in Corhampton churchyard) batted from five o'clock on Wednesday to three o'clock on Friday.

Later in the year the Hambledon men played again against a side called "Any Eleven of England." This match was also won by 30 runs, the top scorer for Hambledon being Leer with 69.

Men were not the only sex that played cricket in those early days. I remember that when women took up cricket after the end of the First German War, there was a good deal of amusement in some quarters. There would be none now, for the standard of women's cricket is remarkably high. But there is nothing new about women playing cricket. In 1811 Hampshire played Surrey and won by fourteen runs. This was a three days match and was extensively advertised at the time. The Surrey colours, by the way, were Orange and Blue, and those of Hampshire were True Blue.

The Hambledon Club did not always play on Broadhalfpenny. Because of the bleakness of that down they transferred to Windmill Down. But it is Broadhalfpenny that the cricketer remembers, and it is Broadhalfpenny that is left. Windmill Down is just a part of the countryside, another down among many downs. Broadhalfpenny would have shared the same fate had it not been for the initiative of the Winchester College authorities. And here is the historic inn, the Bat and Ball—a place of pilgrimage for cricketers; or, if it is not, it ought to be. The Bat and Ball is inseparable from Hambledon in the minds of all those who know their cricket literature, but actually the inn is not in Hambledon at all. I believe that the front door is in the village of Hambledon, but the rest of the inn is in the village of Catherington, and the correct postal address is Catherington. But what matter? The men of Hambledon did not all come from the village of Hambledon itself. (Some, like Silver Billy Beldham, came from over the Surrey border. Two or three in fact came from Farnham, which is just in Surrey. But though it is just in Surrey, that does not detract from Hambledon as an All-Hampshire Club. The town is right on the border—as a matter of fact a good deal of the Rural District Council area is in Hampshire even to-day—and to this day you will meet old Farnham residents who, though they were born in Farnham and have lived in Farnham all their lives, will tell you that they are Hampshire men.) The Bat and Ball stands on the crest of the down and at the juncture of four roads. It was a focal point, and the men came in from the neighbouring villages to play the English game. Was not Thomas Brett, "the fastest as well as the straightest bowler that ever was known," born in Catherington?

The Bat and Ball is not the inn that once it was. A few years before the war the proprietors laid hands upon it in the name of Progress. They announced their intention of pulling it down and rebuilding it on more generous lines. And again Hampshire, and cricket lovers all over the world, have to thank the Winchester College authorities. They managed to prevent the full execution of this fell plan, but they could not save the old inn entirely. The frontage and the front door remain as they were in the days of Beldham and the Walkers: the original long and narrow bar remains; the oak beams are there still. But one of the walls has disappeared and given place to a long counter, green-topped and as out of place as a dandelion on the pitch at Lord's. And now there is an annexe and a car park and a saloon bar. One can shut one's eyes. But one cannot altogether recapture the old atmosphere.

The Bat and Ball should, of course, have been kept as an old inn and as a museum. That is impossible now; perhaps it was never possible. Now there are a few old prints, including a facsimile of the score sheet of the famous 1777 match, but you might see them anywhere and they do nothing to restore atmosphere. But there is one modern addition that deserves the highest praise. That is the sign. The old sign was used to light the oven! The new sign is a most worthy successor. It depicts four tight-breeched cricketers of the very early days—the days when there were but two stumps—facing the down, and on the other side there is a very pleasing portrait of Richard Nyren. There never was, you will remember, "a finer specimen of the thoroughbred old English yeoman."

Across the road is the ground. It may be the oldest ground in England; it is certainly one of the two oldest. There are records of cricket being played on the Vine ground at Sevenoaks some two hundred years ago, and it would be interesting to know which was the older ground of the two. Considering how very isolated Broadhalfpenny was in those days—and it is still well off the beaten track—it may well be that the game was played here for many years before it was widely known to the outside world. There is a thatched shed just as there used to be a booth "for the convenience of members" and there are two rollers (I wonder what Nyren would think of them?) and the boundary slopes away to give a huge view of the Hampshire landscape, almost as unspoilt now as it was then. Sit here of an evening, and you a cricket devotee, and you will soon believe in ghosts. It does not need much imagination to repeople this ground with the great, almost legendary figures of the past—Lumpy Stevens and John Small and Noah Mann and Thomas Brett and Richard Nyren and Silver Billy Beldham.

It is fitting that Hampshire, which is the birthplace of modern England, should have such an early connexion with the most English of games. It is fitting that England, which made her first groping steps towards an organized society on these downs, should have chosen these downs also for her first steps towards the present game of cricket, with its Test Matches, and its huge score boards, and its record crowds. There would be no Oval, no Lord's, no Wanderers at Johannesburg, no Adelaide, were it not for Broadhalfpenny Down.

Cricket is in essence a village game. More even than that: it is in essence a downland village game. It should be played on the heights with far horizons, in keen air to raise a thirst and near an inn to quench that thirst. Broadhalfpenny is the ideal cricket ground.

But there are many grounds like it in Hampshire. I have walked almost all over the county, and there can be few hamlets that I have not visited at least once. I cannot say that I have played cricket all over the county, but I have played on a great many village grounds in different parts of it. I should doubt very much if there are as many as ten hamlets in the county without their cricket ground. The game is played with a passionate devotion in Hampshire, as passionate devotion as it was in the days of Nyren and the Hambledon men. And it is played with no little skill also.

And yet Hampshire's record in the County Championship is undistinguished. The county first played in the County Championship in 1895. The highest position that it has occupied has been sixth—in 1910, 1912, 1921, 1922.

It has occupied very lowly positions frequently. Why is difficult to understand. It is not that there are not many good players in the county, for there are. Hampshire has produced a number of Test Match players, and two captains of England in C. B. Fry and Lord Tennyson. Many Hampshire players have achieved distinction in the highest company. Yet the county eleven has rarely proved consistent and has never done really well.

For example, in 1912 Hampshire defeated the Australian Touring Team by eight wickets and in that year the three leading batsmen in England were Hampshire players—Mr. C. B. Fry with an average of 56.85 for 1,592 runs, Mr. A. C. Johnston with an average of 54.94 for 1,044 runs, and C. P. Mead with an average of 50.86 for 1,933 runs. They had a good bowler, too, in A. S. Kennedy, who took 139 wickets for an average of 17.60. Yet they could only finish sixth.

Again in 1927 Mead was second in the batting averages with 74.53 for 2,385 runs, and in the Gentlemen v. Players match Hampshire was represented on the Gentlemen XI by the Hon. L. H. Tennyson, C. P. Brutton, R. P. H. Utley and J. P. Parker, and on the Players XI by Mead, Kennedy, Newman and Livsey. Yet in 1927 they could only finish thirteenth.

Time and again they have as a county brought off the most astonishing feats. They have defeated the Australians, they have dismissed New Zealand for 79 and India for 51. But quite the most astonishing performance they have ever accomplished was at Edgbaston against Warwickshire on 14, 15 and 16 June, 1922. Indeed this is one of the most astonishing performances in the history of cricket. In their first innings Hampshire were dismissed for a mere fifteen runs and no fewer than eight of their batsmen failed to score. They had to follow on against a Warwickshire total of 223, and few people on the ground thought that the match would last into the third day. Hampshire made 521. Newman and Kennedy bowled very well and Warwickshire were dismissed for 158, and Hampshire won by 155 runs. I think that that match may be taken as typical of Hampshire cricket. They are frequently beaten, much more frequently than they should be, but not more frequently than they deserve to be. But they are never beaten until the last ball is bowled. I give the scores in this match. No account of Hampshire cricket, however brief, would be complete without them.

WARWICKSHIRE

Bates, c Shirley b Newman	3	c Mead b Kennedy ...	1
Smith, c Mead b Newman	24	c Shirley b Kennedy...	41
F. R. Santall, c McIntyre b Boyes	84	b Newman	0
W. G. Quaife, b Newman.........	1	not out	40
F. S. G. Calthorpe, c Boyes b Kennedy	70	b Newman	30
E. F. Waddy, c Mead b Boyes...	0	b Newman	0
B. W. Quaife, b Boyes............	0	c and b Kennedy	7
Fox, b Kennedy	4	b Kennedy	0
Smart (J.), b Newman	20	b Newman	3
Smart (C.), c Mead b Boyes ...	14	c and b Boyes	15
H. Howell, not out	1	c Kennedy b Newman	11
Extras	2	Extras	10
	223		158

HAMPSHIRE

Bowell, b Howell	0	c Howell b W. G. Quaife	45
Kennedy, c Smith b Calthorpe	0	b Calthorpe	7
H. L. V. Day, b Calthorpe	0	c Bates b W. G. Quaife	15
Mead, not out	6	b Howell	24
L. H. Tennyson, c Calthorpe b Howell..............................	4	c C. Smart b Calthorpe	45
Brown, b Howell	0	b Smart	172
Newman, c C. Smart b Howell...	0	c and b W. G. Quaife...	12
W. R. Shirley, c J. Smart b Calthorpe	1	lbw b Fox	30
A. S. McIntyre, lbw b Calthorpe	0	lbw b Howell	5
Livsey, b Howell	0	not out	110
Boyes, b Howell	0	b Howell	29
Extras	4	Extras	27
	15		521

Hampshire Bowling

	O.	M.	R.	W.		O.	M.	R.	W.
Kennedy	24	7	74	2		26	12	47	4
Newman	12.3	0	70	4		26.3	12	53	5
Boyes	16	5	56	4		11	4	34	1
Shirley	3	0	21	0	Brown	5	0	14	0

Warwickshire Bowling

	O.	M.	R.	W.		O.	M.	R.	W.
Howell	4.5	2	7	6		63	10	156	3
Calthorpe	4	3	4	4		33	7	97	2
					W. G. Quaife	49	8	154	3
					Fox	7	0	30	1
					Smart (J.)	13	2	37	0
					Santall	5	0	15	0
					Smart (C.)	1	0	5	1

This season, 1922, was the first complete season without C. B. Fry, though the Commander had not played much in 1921. Fry was an inspiration to any side. In all he played 65 innings for Hampshire, scored 3,445 runs with a highest score of 258 not out, for an average of 57.41. He headed the all England batting averages in 1911 and again in 1912. In 1911 the second place was occupied by Mead, and in 1912 the first three places were occupied by Hampshire batsmen.

And this brings me to Mead. Mead first played for Hampshire in 1906 and he continued to play until 1936. In that time he scored for the county in 1,115 innings 46,298 runs, with a highest score of 280 not out and an average of 48.32. In 1909 he was tenth in the all England batting averages, in 1911 he was second, in 1912 he was third, in 1913 he was first, in 1914 he was third, in 1919 fourth, in 1920 fifth, in 1921 first, in 1922 third, in 1923 second, in 1924 eighth, in 1925 eleventh, in 1926 fifth, in 1927 second, in 1928 fourth, in 1929 fourth, in 1931 eleventh, in 1933 second, in 1934 eleventh. He was, it can be seen clearly, right in the very front of batsmen for almost the whole of his career. As a matter of fact, if you take the whole of English cricket up to 1939, from the run scoring point of view, Mead comes out right at the top.

Of the men who have scored a thousand runs or more in a season the first is W. G. Grace, tied with F. E. Woolley. They both scored a thousand or more in a season twenty-eight times. Next comes Mead. He did it twenty-seven times. (Hobbs did it twenty-four times.) Nor is that all. In all first-class cricket Mead scored over 55,000 runs. He played in 17 Test Matches, and in Test Cricket his average was just on 50 per innings—an average that not very many players even hope to approach!

Yet Mead was never throughout his career a first choice for England. It is an extraordinary thing. One may well wonder why. And one may well wonder if our record in Test Matches—especially just after the war—would not have been a great deal better if the selectors had not been quite so blind.

It is often said that Mead was a bat only—and an ugly and ungainly one at that. But that is not true. He was a magnificent fielder as well. He made an average of 22 catches a season, and that is an average that only seven men have exceeded. In all, Mead made 595 catches in first-class cricket, and that, according to E. L. Roberts, puts him among the first twelve English fielders. Mead could bowl also. How many people remember his 7 for 18 against Northamptonshire in 1918? Naturally he was not used as a bowler very much—a county that had Kennedy and Newman and Boyes had no need to use him much—but all the same for Hampshire he took 253 wickets at an average of 34.23, which for a change bowler invariably put on when opposing batsmen were well set and seeing the ball as large as life is not bad at all.

No. Mead's career is an outstanding example of a great player consistently missing the eye of the selectors to the detriment of the country's chances of success.

He was always regarded as a slow bat. He was not at all slow. His 182 not out against the Australians at the Oval in the fifth Test of 1921 was made very quickly considering the conditions, and at a gallop compared with Hutton's innings seventeen years later. Mead, it must be remembered, had all through his career to give backing to a side that was always prone to tumble out, even on the best of

399

wickets. Put him in a side that had already ballast and the change was remarkable. Consider, for example, his scoring in the West Indies with Tennyson's team. That he looked ungainly is true. He was a big man crouched over a little bat, and he had a habit of shuffling a few paces and pulling at his cap before every ball that used to annoy the spectators. But nothing can detract from his record. He was one of the best batsmen that this country has produced. If he had lived in Australia, England would have realized his worth.

And then George Brown. Vast George Brown with the hands of a giant and the kindliness of a saint. Rough of appearance and gentle as a woman. Sometimes harsh of tongue, but generous to a fault. George Brown, who was the hero of the Hampshire crowds, and the idol of small boys, and one of the best all-round cricketers that ever lived. And who remembers George Brown now? What does his name mean to those who only know Bradman and Hutton and Oldfield and Larwood?

Yet consider George Brown. For Hampshire he played 859 innings and scored 22,113 runs with a highest score of 232 not out for an average of 27.13. As a bowler for Hampshire he took 584 wickets for an average of 29.11. I do not know how many catches he made, but he was beyond doubt one of the finest fielders that the game has ever seen, and quite the finest mid-off in the history of cricket. He saved more runs for Hampshire than he scored, and he made some miraculous catches very close to the bat. I remember one in particular. It was at the Oval and he was fielding at silly mid-off to Kennedy's bowling and Hobbs was batting. Hobbs got tired of seeing him there close to the bat, and suddenly off a half volley had a full-blooded wang. Brown spun round like a top and the crowd gasped, and looked to the boundary for the ball. Hobbs stood amazed. And then Brown pulled the ball from his trouser pocket, and Hobbs walked to the pavilion—out to the finest catch I shall ever see. But that was not all that was to Brown. He played in seven Test Matches. He played against Australia at Leeds, Manchester and the Oval in 1921—and he played as a *wicket-keeper*! He was not the County wicket-keeper.

That was the year of the doldrums for English Cricket. But George Brown was never so good as when his back was to the wall. It was after Hampshire had been put out for 15 that he made 172 and flogged the Warwickshire bowling all over the field. And so at Leeds he made 57 in the first innings and in the second 46 (which was the highest score). At Manchester he opened the innings and made 31, and at the Oval he opened the innings again, made 32 in the first innings and 84 in the second. And he caught two and stumped two as well. Gallant George Brown! You do not find his like in cricket nowadays.

Two other Hampshire players of the years between the wars deserve special mention: Newman and Kennedy. Newman must go down to history as one of the best players who never played for England, perhaps as the best player ever to be completely ignored by the selectors. For Hampshire he scored 13,099 runs with a highest score of 166 not out and an average of 20.72. As a bowler he took 1,861 wickets for an average of 24.77. As a bowler he did the "hat-trick" against the Australians in 1909. He was the first man to reach the "double"—100 wickets and 1,000 runs—in 1926. He did the double in 1921, 1923, 1926, 1927, and 1928. He scored a century in each innings of the match against Surrey in 1927. He took 100 wickets in a season nine times. He took sixteen wickets in the match against Somerset in 1927.

Alec Kennedy did even better with the ball. He took 100 wickets in a season fifteen times. He accomplished the "double" in 1921, 1922, 1923, 1928, and 1930. For Hampshire he scored 14,357 runs with a highest score of 163 not out for an average of 18.67. As a bowler he took 2,424 wickets at an average of 21.20. Kennedy did play for England against South Africa. He was a better bowler than Newman, but not so good a bat. Together, however, they were for some years the best pair of all-rounders possessed by any county in England. Sharply contrasted—Kennedy thick-set, dark, with a Celtic temperament, and Newman an unruffled Saxon—they, with Mead and Brown, carried Hampshire on their shoulders between 1921 and 1935.

Yet, though there has been plenty of talent in the side,

it has rarely done well. Always it has seemed as if it could not keep it up. There has been a sharp falling off in performance as a team as the season has progressed. And no one, even one as enthusiastic for my county as I am, can pretend that Hampshire has been an entertaining side to watch in the years between the wars. There have been the high lights, of course. But, oh, there have been the shadows too. There is just as much talent in Hampshire as there is in Kent or Sussex. But no one could pretend that Hampshire is as attractive a side to watch as Sussex, even, as has not been infrequent, Sussex has not occupied a high position in the championship. There has never been the same snap in the field, never the same obvious enjoyment in the game. And yet Hampshire is a county in which cricket is played regularly in every village and town, and with the greatest devotion and enthusiasm. The fault, it seems to me, lies with the Committee. Little is done to arouse enthusiasm in the county side. They do not tour the county. The captains—and there have been far too many captains lately—do not visit the villages and the small towns as the Gilligans visited the villages of Sussex. And this reacts on the players as much as on anyone else. In Sussex it seems to me that every goodish village player or small town player—I am writing as one who has played a lot of village cricket in both Hampshire and Sussex—has the ambition to get into his county eleven, and believes that he may catch the eye of the selectors or of the county captain and be given a chance with the club and ground team. And indeed there is more than one Sussex lad from the country who has been found in just this way—a visit from the county captain to his village. I have never seen a Hampshire village player who thought he had the slightest chance of getting a trial of any sort, and that is particularly true of players in the north of the county. It is a pity. It is a bad thing to hear, as I have heard more than once, "Oh, you've got to live in Southampton if you want a chance." Yes, and I have heard ruder things than that said about the Committee.

Village cricket happily is not affected. The spirit of Broadhalfpenny has not been lost.

CHAPTER XIV

EPILOGUE

THERE is not, I can hear someone saying, very much about modern Hampshire in this book. Well, what is modern Hampshire?

At the end of the eighteenth century the population of England and Wales was between eight and nine millions. About 78 per cent of that population lived in the country and about one-third was employed in agriculture. Now in a country that is designed by nature to support a population of about nine millions (at the outside) there are living nearly fifty million people. About thirty-three millions live in towns, less than a million are employed in agriculture. We are a grossly over-populated country.

Because we are a grossly over-populated country, because almost all of us are townsmen, because all our laws are designed by townsmen for townsmen, we have come to think that there is very little country left in England, and that what there is is inaccessible (if it was not it would be built over; that is obviously the chain of thought), Dartmoor and Cornwall and places like that. Curiously enough it just is not true.

Take Hampshire, for example: mainland Hampshire is 933,696 acres in extent. The population is 1,014,316 at the latest figures. But the population of the administrative county is only 469,085. In other words more than half of the population of Hampshire lives in towns—in three towns at that, Bournemouth, Portsmouth (with Gosport) and Southampton. The area of the Isle of Wight is 94,146 acres and the population is 88,454, and by far the greater proportion of these live in three towns. You can work it out for yourself. Exclude the big towns on the mainland and you will find that Hampshire is not heavily populated in persons per acre. Far from it. And you can include the towns in the Isle of Wight, and you will find that the same is true.

Well, what is modern Hampshire then? The towns? They are the most important part of the county under our present system, I grant you. But they are in essentials no different from towns anywhere else in the south of England. They are in Hampshire, but they are not Hampshire. (Unlike the towns of the north and of Wales which are both in and of their country.) No, Hampshire is still rural Hampshire, and that is why I have written mainly of rural Hampshire. And if you think that I have written too much of the past, too little of the present, I must disagree. I can find little in the present to enthuse about. And I would point out that whenever any modern Englishman finds himself moved by a building, nine hundred and ninety-nine times out of a thousand it is an old building, a building several hundred years old. I will go even further than that. What is the highest praise that we can give to a town, or a village, or an inn? It is that it is "unspoilt." And that can only mean that it is old and has not been built by moderns; that it is old and has escaped as yet the attentions of the moderns.

Which is why I have written more of the old Hampshire than of the modern.

But Hampshire is changing, and changing rapidly. Between the wars the county altered enormously, and the change is still going on. It is most noticeable in the country districts, particularly in the villages, and it is due chiefly to the roads.

The main roads of the county connect the larger towns. At one time there were only these roads, and some (judged by modern standards) very tenth-rate roads, and some roads that were really little more than tracks. And that, though it is impossible to believe it now, was the position as recently as 1920. But during the last twenty years there has been an enormous development in the road system. The main roads have been improved beyond recognition; and from the towns a secondary network, almost as good and in some cases quite as good as the main system, has sprung up connecting the various villages to the towns.

And this has meant that the rural districts have been "developed." Nobody thought about rural development. They were only concerned with the urban development.

Almost all Englishmen looked with indifference upon the decline of the country-side. Many of them actually welcomed it. The towns were growing, and the interests of the town were in cheap foods and cheap amusements. Cheap foods meant imported foods, foods that were sold against the exported products of the towns. Farming could go to the wall (until the next war!). Urban development was all that mattered.

The greatly improved road system helped the town. It meant that the town could now serve a bigger rural area. The town trader was not slow to seize the opportunity. The travelling salesman, of course, has always been a feature of village life, and it might well be thought that the town trader's van is not so very different from the travelling salesman, if indeed it is different at all. But the travelling salesman (he has pretty well disappeared from Hampshire, indeed he exists now only in very isolated districts of Britain) was a person of character. He had to be. He was almost invariably much more than a salesman; he was also a counsellor, a friend, and a newspaper. He was the village link with the Big World. There is no personality about the trader's van. The trader's van is not a counsellor nor a friend nor a newspaper. The driver does not know a single one of his customers except by name. He has not the time. He works to a time-sheet, and he has to bustle to keep to the time. He brings, it is true, a much wider range of goods than the travelling salesman used to do, and he provides a better service. But his effect on the village is by no means all to the good. He is slowly but surely killing the village shopkeeper. The village store was also the village club, as important in the life of the village as the village pub. It stocked everything, including gossip and news. The urban trader is too strong an invader, and though the village shopkeeper puts up a sturdy fight, he is quite surely doomed. In my own home village the shop that has been in the same family for upwards of one hundred and fifty years has just been bought by the big grocer in a town some sixteen miles away, and that grocer is a branch of a big London store. The only way in which the village shop can fight is by stocking a greater variety of goods, by giving more credit, and by the shopkeeper reducing his own standard of living. That is not good. The urban trader's van is something of a mixed blessing. So much that is not easily seen follows in its train.

The urban trader, however, both the privately owned and the multiple store, has recently found a powerful competitor in the Co-operative Society. The Co-op. has gained a footing in many Hampshire villages, and is gaining ground in many more, and its success is most significant. Countrymen generally have always resisted anything in the form of co-operation. They have always had a strong bias to the personal. But modern roads have brought the Co-op. van along with the others, and the Co-op. is proving a most formidable competitor. I do not say that the Co-op has yet swallowed the village; I do not say that the Co-operative ideal has yet been swallowed by the village. But the ideal will quite certainly follow the service (has already done so in many villages), and when that does happen, many things are going to happen.

Perhaps none of this is bad. I am personally sorry to see the village shopkeeper go. But I realize that he may well have outlived his time. I am glad to see the Co-op. come. In my experience they have done nothing but good, and I have a fairly considerable experience. The world is changing and we must change too.

But other things have been brought by the roads as well as the town trader's van and the Co-op. The roads have brought the daily paper. That is very good. The countryman is no fool. He has long ago come to the conclusion that there is very little in the penny paper that you can believe so far as events are concerned in world history; he reads it for amusement and forms his own opinions. (The townsman, too, has ceased to be influenced by the penny paper.) And the roads have brought the wireless; and that too is very good. It has brought such things as silk stockings (in peace-time) and it has brought new ideas and new trends in thought. And with these new ideas and new trends of thought have come, naturally, new customs.

The most important of these new customs is the "club." There were "clubs" of course long before there were improved roads. They were generally speaking insurance clubs and savings clubs. The roads brought the club agent. The modern club is different. They are of many different types, and the club agent is extraordinarily ingenious in suggesting convenient methods of payment. One of the most popular works like this: twenty people (or ten or thirty or any number in excess of five) agree to pay one shilling a week for twenty weeks. Each week one person, chosen by lot, receives the goods ordered. That is, one person a week gets the goods; one person gets the goods in the first week and goes on paying for another nineteen weeks; the second week another person gets the goods and goes on paying for eighteen weeks; and so on. The "club" system is spreading extraordinarily rapidly. It encourages spending and not saving. The village people, though they will join willingly enough (over-persuaded by cunning advertising and loquacious agents) seem vaguely disturbed by it, for it is very difficult to get them to talk about it freely. There is, in fact, nothing to say in favour of these clubs. If the goods supplied are of good quality, the price charged is very high indeed; if the price is reasonable, then the goods are certain to be of poor quality. Moreover, a shilling a week is a lot out of an agricultural labourer's wages, even out of the increased wage of to-day. I wish that the clubs could be stopped. The urban trader does not do anything to stop them. But the growth of the Co-op. will have a disastrous effect on them (*all* club agents are strong Tories!) for the dividend is a great thing in the eyes of the villager.

These are but a few of the things that the roads have brought. But the roads have not only brought, they have also taken away. And what they have taken away is much more important than anything it has brought.

The towns, even the gloomiest of them, are attractive compared to the village, at least to the younger generation.

They have cinemas and a variety of pubs and a variety, a much wider variety than can be found in any village, of young men and maidens. The younger generation makes for the town. It is assisted to do so by the excessive nobility of the age. The effect, throughout the years between the wars, was to hasten the movement from the village to the town. I can see no sign myself that there has been any slackening in that movement—the Return to the Land that we read so much about seems to me to be purely a week-end movement.

All this has changed the village. Villages are now being organized. (And there seems to be a movement on foot in the Ministry of Town and Country Planning, which is controlled entirely by townsmen, to get rid of the small village altogether as being "uneconomic.") The old pattern of life has been destroyed, a new is in the process of being set up. We should examine it.

The old system of personal government has gone. That was the government of the squire and the parson. It lingers on in a few villages in Hampshire to this day, but over the vast majority of the county, as over the vast majority of the country, it has gone, and, it has gone for good. In the few villages in which it lingers on, government is simple and efficient and is respected by the villagers. Squire and parson have tradition, many generations of family tradition, behind them. There are yet one or two districts in Hampshire controlled by the tradition of the big landowner, men who have lived all their lives on the land of their family, men gifted with imagination and foresight, men above party politics, rural aristocrats. It is instructive to compare these villages and these districts with those from which the tradition has disappeared.

The traditional landowner has gone, taxed out of existence, and his place has been taken by the successful business man, the magnate, the man who has made a fortune out of cotton or coal or stocks and shares or newspapers. He made the fortune in the town. He sets up as a "country gent." If he made his fortune in the north of England he does not settle in the north, he comes south of the Thames, a foreigner in a strange land, a man who thinks all

408

"southerners" soft. But wherever he comes from, he is still a foreigner in a strange land. He thinks only of money: it was brass that made him. He tightens things up. The new generation of landowners has closed more footpaths than all the previous generations put together. He has tightened up the game laws. He has to do so. The old type could admit that they were in the wrong, the new type dare not. The old type understood the needs of the people, the new type is not interested in the people. He bought his land, not because he was interested in the land, but because it was a step up the social ladder. But the worst thing about this new landowning class is not their ignorance, not their lack of common courtesy to their inferiors (few of them do anything for their villagers) but the fact that they are almost all of them "absentee" landlords. They just come down for the shooting. It is no wonder that the average countryman, though perfectly polite, regards them with a quiet contempt. It is a great pity, for this new class could have been the saving of the country. Perhaps their sons will do better.

But the fact that the landlord—pronounce that as two separate words and you will see what the old landowner was—has gone has meant that all sorts of things have come in to take his place and the place of the things that went with him.

Villages are being organized. I have no particular brief for the old-time village. If picturesque, it was generally insanitary. I do not believe that educational facilities have worsened in country districts, though I deplore the disappearance of the old country schoolmaster. I know that there is yet much social tyranny in villages: I know that school managers resist all attempts to alter and improve black-listed schools (that will now improve rapidly); I know that there is still much child labour in some districts, but none, I think, in Hampshire. I know that there is much decadence and a good deal of dirt; I know that there is a good deal of social pressure to influence votes (but the new landowners are breeding socialism as fast as they can go; and should be encouraged, therefore, by the Labour Government!); I know that there is a good deal of petty corruption; I know that farmers have been known to block parish meetings to prevent improvements that would increase the rates, particularly if their farms do not benefit directly; I know that the Church has ceased to be effective, or indeed to have any meaning at all over large parts of the country; I know that many country parsons are little tyrants (ask the village school-teachers!); I know that there is much ignorance, some bestiality. I know all this. I know that the extent of it has been much exaggerated. I want it all, all that does exist, changed.

But the method by which it is changed matters a good deal. County Councils vary enormously. A few are good—Hampshire is definitely one that is very good—the majority are very mediocre. But all appear to me to be assisting in the depopulation of the country-side of countrymen. And centralized government—government from Whitehall by theorists—will hasten the process still more. Do you remember this sentence from G. M. Trevelyan's *English Social History*? "The men of theory failed to perceive that agriculture is not merely one industry among many, but a way of life, unique and irreplaceable in its human and spiritual values." They still do.

Too many missionaries visit the villages. And they are all townsmen or women. They are of all sorts—social workers, arts and crafters, administrators, even Oxford Groupers. They have all good intentions. They all want to preserve something or promote something or revive something. They are all quite unimaginative, all completely standardized and departmentalized. They are all fired with immense quantities of missionary zeal, and very little sense. Too often they are supported by the towns, too often by administrative grants or Treasury grants. They care little for the feelings of the village. If the village does not want to be amused or preserved or revived or promoted, they just call in urban reserves and go ahead. They care little for such physical or economical difficulties as are inseparable from every village (water-supply is a good example): they go ahead. They improve the social services. They improve. And the villager, who has a shrewd suspicion that he can get all this better done and

with less fuss in the towns, goes to the towns. The village
has ceased to be a village anyhow.

The new pattern takes shape. The depopulation of the
country-side of countrymen goes on apace.

The week-end cottage increases in number as steadily.

It is happening in Hampshire as elsewhere.

The things that kept the village together, the trades and
beliefs, are disappearing and with them the men. Take the
rural craftsman. His skill is traditional, has come down in
one family from father to son. The wheelwright, for
example, embodies the skill and the experience of innumerable ancestors. He makes (or should it be "made"?) a wheel
eminently suitable for conditions as he knows them. He
does not work to a time-sheet. He does not understand a
time-sheet. His time-sheet is the seasons of the year. His
rhythm is controlled by the weather. Craft has gone, replaced by mechanization which can conform to time-
sheets, can ignore seasons, can conform to government regulations. As the craftsmen go, the village dies. It cannot be
revived by a few missionaries from the towns. The houses
remain, the people remain (or some of them) but the village
goes. It becomes an off-shoot of the town, a suburb, a slum.

Development is needed less than work. Mechanization
has come to stay, as have all sorts of other strangers to the
country. They should be made welcome. But they should
do something for their welcome. While they stay in the
towns and come only to the country as completed things
to do a soulless job of work, they will continue to do, as
they have done so far, more harm than good.

But, so far as Hampshire is concerned, I do not think
that we need worry about things like this. Agricultural
Hampshire has gone. It revived during the war, and it will
revive temporarily during the next war. But as an agricultural county it now depends not on the normal routine of
the country-side but on the mistakes of the politicians that
lead ultimately to war. Hampshire had better be regarded
as what it really is—an estate agent's paradise.

Now this is good in one way. It means that it will remain
country to a very large extent, that it will remain largely
"unspoilt."

Hampshire is already largely populated with "retireds."
To them the village is a haven. They do not notice the
deficiencies. They have had their buffeting; they are retired. They do a little shooting, a little fishing (if the
magnates have not bought it all), play a little golf, and fight
their battles over again—oh, so gloriously! They add a
little to the economic life of the village, but they do not
add a jot to the social life of villages. That is not their fault.
The villagers, for all their hat-touching, regard them as
foreigners. But the villagers do not regard them with the
contempt that they have for the new landowning class.

I have the greatest respect for the "retireds." They have,
almost always, done things and seen things—done far more
than ever I shall do, seen far more than ever I shall see.
They deserve their quiet corner and their peaceful days.
And I am grateful for the "retireds." They preserve the
country-side for us.

But their outlook, naturally, is more in the past than in
the future. And so is Hampshire's, outside the big towns.
Which is why this book has been mainly about the past.

Hampshire's past was glorious. Hampshire's future?

The new order has yet to be designed. But the pattern
is, I think, clear enough.

BIBLIOGRAPHY

Sport and Sportsmen of the New Forest, C. R. Acton. 1936.
Sporting Reminiscences of Hampshire, "Aesop." 1864.
The Hambledon Cricket Chronicle, F. S. Ashley-Cooper.
The History of Basingstoke, F. G. Baigent and J. E. Millard.
The Domesday Inquest, A. Ballard. 1923.
It Happened in Hampshire, Winifred G. Beddington and
    Elsa B. Christy. 1938.
The Old Road, H. Belloc. 1904.
A History of England, Vol. I, H. Belloc.
Winchester, W. Benham. 1884.
The Black Book of Winchester, A. H. B. Bird. 1925.
Black's Guide to Hampshire.
Along the Roman Roads, G. M. Boumphrey. 1935.
The Family of Brocas, M. Burrows. 1886.
The New Foresters, W. Caine. 1913.
Scenes of Rural Life in Hampshire, W. W. Capes. 1901.
A History of the Vyne in Hampshire, C. W. Chute. 1888.
A School History of Hampshire, F. Clarke. 1909.
Archæology and Society, G. Clarke. 1939.
The Isle of Wight, G. Clinch. 1913.
*Notes on the Parishes of Fifield, Kimpton, Penton Mewsey,
    Weyhill and Wherwell*, R. H. Clutterbuck. 1898.
Rural Rides, William Cobbett.
The Life of William Cobbett, G. D. H. Cole.
Hampshire, J. G. Cox. 1906.
The Andover District, O. G. S. Crawford. 1923.
Wessex from the Air, O. G. S. Crawford. 1928.
A Short History of Alton, W. Curtis. 1896.
A History of Southampton, J. E. Davies. 1883.
A Tour through the Whole Island of Britain, Daniel Defoe.
The Hampshire Gate, H. G. Dent. 1924.
Nicholas Nickleby, Charles Dickens.
Sketches of Hampshire, G. Duthie. 1839.
A Walk through Southampton, H. G. Englefield. 1835.
The Story of a Short Life, Juliana Ewing. 1882.

Hampshire Registers, W. A. Fearon and J. F. William. 1907

Through England on a Side-Saddle in the Time of William and Mary, Celia Fiennes. 1888.

Winchester (English Public Schools), J. D'E. Firth. 1936.

A History of Beaulieu Abbey, Sir James K. Fowler. 1911.

The Hampshire Recusants in the Reign of Queen Elizabeth, F. A. Gasquet. 1895.

An Illustrated History of Portsmouth, William G. Gates. 1900.

Reverend Landlords and their Tenants, Florence Remington Goodman. 1930.

Winchester, Valley and Downland, Florence Remington Goodman. 1934.

The Civil War in Hampshire, G. N. Godwin. 1904.

The Mabinogion, Lady Charlotte Guest.

Early British Botanists, R. E. Gunther.

Hampshire Antiquary and Naturalist. 1891–1892.

Hampshire Field Club, Papers and Proceedings. 1885–1945.

Hampshire Notes and Queries. 1883–1898.

Hampshire Record Society, Publications.

The Old Portsmouth Road, C. G. Harper. 1923.

The Life and Work of the People of England, D. Hartley and M. Elliot. 1931.

A Short History of Southampton, J. G. Hearnshaw. 1910.

Unknown Hampshire, Clive Holland. 1926.

The Life and Letters of John Keats, Lord Houghton.

Hampshire Days, W. H. Hudson. 1903.

Afoot in England, W. H. Hudson. 1909.

The New Forest, H. G. Hutchinson. 1904.

Life in a Hampshire Village, Kathleen E. Innes. 1942.

The Isle of Wight (2 vols.), E. V. James. 1896.

Memorials of Old Hampshire, G. E. Jeans. 1906.

A History of Lymington, C. P. Jones. 1930.

The Commoners' New Forest, F. E. Kenchington. 1942.

The Hants County Book, S. C. Kendall. 1938.

Old Times Revisited in Lymington, E. King. 1879.

Yeast, Charles Kingsley. 1851.

Prose Idylls, Charles Kingsley. 1873.

Winchester, G. W. Kitchin. 1890.

Thirty-five Years in the New Forest, Gerald Lascelles. 1915.

Ancient Glass in Winchester, J. D. Le Couteur. 1929.

East of Itchen, Gordon Lee.

The Old Royal Road, Gordon Lee.

Historical Inquiries concerning Forests and Forest Laws with Topographical Remarks upon the Ancient and Modern State of the New Forest in the County of Southampton, P. Lewis. 1811.

Records of Romsey Abbey, H. E. D. Liveing. 1906.

The Hambledon Men, E. V. Lucas. 1907.

English Leaves, E. V. Lucas. 1933.

Early Wars of Wessex, A. F. Major.

Le Morte D'Arthur, Sir Thomas Malory.

Treatise and Discourse of the Laws of the Forest, Manwood. 1598.

The Children of the New Forest, Frederick Marryat.

The Little Farm, Harriet Martineau. 1857.

Downland England, H. J. Massingham. 1936.

Hampshire with the Isle of Wight, Arthur Mee. 1939.

The History of Winchester (2 vols.), J. Milner. 1798–1801.

The Hampshire Mirror of Things Past and Present, R. Moody. 1846.

The New Forest, John C. Moore. 1924.

Companion into Hampshire, L. Collinson Morley. 1940.

Hampshire; its past Condition and Future Prospects, R. Mudie. 1838.

New Forest. Register of Decisions on Claims to Rights (Commissioners acting under Act of 17–18th Vict. Cap 9) 1858.

New Forest. Deer Removal Act: Report, Proceedings and Evidence of the House of Lords, Select Committee on. 1868.

New Forest. Report, Proceedings and Evidence of Select Committee of House of Commons on. 1875.

The Smugglers of Christchurch, Bournemouth and the New Forest, E. Russell Oakley. 1944.

Nunwell Symphony, C. Aspinall Oglander. 1945.

Colonel Hawker's Shooting Diaries, Eric Parker. 1931.

Morte Arthur, Lucy A. Paton.

Arthurian Chronicles, Lucy A. Paton.

Diary, S. Pepys.

415

Highways and Byways in Hampshire, D. H. M. Read. 1908.
The History of Alresford, A. J. Robertson. 1938.
History of Hampshire, T. W. Shore. 1892.
Hampshire Papers, T. W. Shore. 1911.
Southampton Record Society, Publications. 1905 *et seq.*
The Story of Portsmouth, H. and J. Sparks. 1921.
History of Abbeys and Monasteries, J. Stevens.
History of St. Mary Bourne, J. Stevens.
The Diaries of Dummer, A. W. Stirling. 1934.
New Forest Roman Pottery Sites, H. Sumner. 1927.
Local Papers, H. Sumner. 1931.
Words and Places, Isaac Taylor.
Idylls of the King, Lord Alfred Tennyson.
General View of Agriculture in Hampshire, H. Vancouver. 1813.
Hampshire (Cambridge County Geographies), T. Varley. 1922.
Winchester Cathedral Close, J. Vaughan. 1912.
Winchester Cathedral, J. Vaughan. 1914.
Hampshire Scene, Brian Vesey-FitzGerald. 1940.
A Country Chronicle, Brian Vesey-FitzGerald. 1942.
Victoria County History of Hampshire (6 vols.). 1900-1914.
Ward Locke's Guide to the Isle of Wight.
Collections for the History of Hampshire (5 vols.), R. Warner. 1795.
The Naturalist History and Antiquities of Selborne, Gilbert White.
Journals (edited by Walter Johnson, 1931), Gilbert White.
Life and Letters of Gilbert White of Selborne, R. Holt White. 1901.
The Undercliff of the Isle of Wight, J. L. Whitehead. 1911.
An Introduction to Field Archæology as illustrated by Hampshire, J. P. Williams-Freeman. 1914.
Papers by members of the Winchester College Archæological Society, Winchester College. 1926.
The New Forest, J. R. Wise. 1867.
The Story of Winchester, W. Lloyd Woodland. 1932.
The History of Hampshire (3 vols.), L. B. Woodward. 1863-1869.

INDEX

417